KU-022-049

100 Great Stories from British History

For almost two thousand years, the mythical figure of Britannia, seated on the globe, has represented an island proud of itself and its achievements. She has waved her trident over the pages of history and turned a chaotic jumble of events into a grand pageant of heroes, adventurers, villains and comedians. She is the storyteller who rewrote the past into the kind of stories a nation wants to tell about itself.

100 Great Stories from British History

Geraldine McCaughrean
and Richard Brassey

TED SMART

for Neil and Iwona

G. McC.

for George

R.B.

Also by Geraldine McCaughrean:

Stories from Shakespeare
God's People
God's Kingdom

Myths and Legends of the World:
The Golden Hoard
The Silver Treasure
The Bronze Cauldron
The Crystal Pool

First published in Great Britain in 1999 by Orion Children's Books
a division of the Orion Publishing Group Ltd
Orion House
5 Upper St Martin's Lane
London WC2H 9EA

This edition produced for
The Book People Ltd
Hall Wood Avenue, Haydock
St Helens WA11 9UL

Designed by Louise Millar

A catalogue record for this book is available from the British Library

Printed in Italy

Contents

41

Since When Was History True?

THERE WAS A TIME WHEN PEOPLE FIRMLY BELIEVED THAT A FEW YEARS EARLIER – in, say, their great-grandfather's time – dragons and giants roamed the neighbourhood. Their past was told to them by storytellers, but they knew the stories were true, because the village down the road told a similar tale. Folklore was history.

That is why this book begins with events which no twentieth-century historian would even trouble to write down, and goes on to recount things which twentieth-century historians have long since debunked.

Over the centuries, history has been "adjusted" countless times to suit the ends of scheming statesmen. It has been "tidied up" to make for a better story. It has been "improved on" so as to paint a grand and flattering picture of Britain as "Britannia's realm", ordained and governed by God Himself.

Nowadays, thankfully, we look at ourselves more shrewdly, knowing that in every period of history our ancestors were probably just like us: good, bad and accident-prone. History has become an exact science, concentrating on known facts.

Certain stories are no longer told, because there may be only a grain of truth in them.

But wouldn't it be a terrible pity if, as a result, those stories were to wither and die? These grand adventures have forged our national identity as a race of heroes, saints and underdogs destined for greatness. In my book, that makes them history.

So watch out, as you read, for myth, propaganda, embroidery and downright lies, but remember: these stories are, in themselves, a part of British history . . . as well as our national heritage.

Geraldine McCaughrean

Gogmagog and the Exiles of Troy

about 1100 BC

As the city of Troy burned, the conquering Greeks spilled Trojan blood and laid waste to the marvels of the city. But as well as looting and destroying, they took prisoners – hundreds of prisoners – and carried them back to Greece to work as slaves.

Those hundreds became, in time, thousands – generations of slaves toiling away their days in the villas and harbours and vineyards of Greek kings. Gradually, they began to forget their Trojan heritage, the glory which had once been theirs. Not Brutus. Though born a slave and the son of slaves, Brutus felt Trojan nobility boiling in his veins, and by telling the great old stories, he stirred up his fellow slaves to remember, too, and to rebel. They fought their Greek masters, broke free and ran.

That army of freed men would have followed Brutus anywhere. All their lives they had known nothing but work and whip, whip and work. Now they were drunk on liberty and looking for a homeland to call their own.

Over mountains and plains and wintry wastes of sea, Brutus led his "Trojans", until they came to the Isle of Albion, walled with white cliffs, and they set their hearts on owning it. Sailing past the cliffs, and keeping offshore of the pebbly southern beaches, Brutus landed his fleet in an inviting river estuary, saying:

"Here I am and here I rest,
And this town shall be called Totnes"
(which perhaps sounded better in his native tongue).

So what if this place were peopled by giants with heads like haystacks and fists like club hammers? Nothing but slavery held any fear for Brutus's men. They were warriors, with warrior blood in their veins, whereas the giants were merely big, with fewer brains, for all the size of their heads.

By cunning and by military might, the Trojans drove back the giants, until, like bees trapped in a bottle, the last and fiercest were congregated all in

one narrow isthmus of the island – in Cornwall. Largest and most ferocious of them all was Gogmagog. His temper was as hot as lava, and his belch as loud as erupting volcanoes, and he stamped so hard that the Cornish rocks under him were compressed to shiny tin.

Though they had been felling giants like so many trees, even the fearless Trojans swallowed hard at the sight of Gogmagog dancing on the Cornish hills, wielding his blunt stone hammer, singing out bloodthirsty recipes for Trojan pie.

Now in those days, battles were not a scrimmaging scrum of punches and blows and the victory going to the only men left standing. Lone champions did battle on behalf of their armies. But who could wrestle Gogmagog and live?

Only Corineus was willing to try. "I am ready!" he cried, stripping off his armour and rolling up his sleeves. "I will fight him!"

Brutus's army gave a low groan at the thought of their finest general, hero of many a battle, dying in his second-best tunic, neck broken by a grinning gargoyle of a giant. But the message went out – shouted in at every cave door and down every rabbit hole: "Corineus will fight Gogmagog, if he dares to show himself!"

As the sun rose next day, high on a headland, like a lighthouse signalling danger, a dark shape loomed up against the brightness of the sky: Gogmagog. The giant picked up a cow and ate it, throwing the bones into the wind, so that they scattered among the ranks of the Trojans. "Send out your man!" he said, "or leave this island to me and mine!" He made Corineus look like a seedling beside an oak.

But Corineus was quick and nimble. By the time Gogmagog had raised his fist to crush him, Corineus was shinning up the thongs of the giant's sandals, clambering up his tunic, swinging from his beard. And Corineus was strong, too. He could twist the hairs in a giant's ear so that tears sprang from his eyes, and when he butted his head against the bridge of the giant's nose, Gogmagog's purple eyes spun.

Geoffrey of Monmouth, a cleric from Wales (or possibly Brittany) was a lecturer at Oxford between 1129 and 1151. In 1136 he produced *A History of the Kings of Britain*, merging folklore, legend and half-remembered facts into a sequence of events masquerading as history. Just when the country was trying to establish a sense of national identity, Geoffrey's book demonstrated that a kind of noble destiny was at work in the unfolding of history. It was accepted without quibble. In the Middle Ages, the story of Brutus the Trojan was firmly believed to be true (possibly even by Geoffrey), but it is actually the work of some lover of the classics who wanted to make Britain as grand as Rome and Greece. Gog and Magog are monstrous figures in the Old Testament. Every locality had its folk memories of local giants, so Geoffrey probably lent one of these a name suggestive of pagan evil and menace.

Corineus was light on his feet, and knew how to throw an opponent off balance or trip him from behind. Corineus swarmed over Gogmagog, wearying him with bruises, rattling him with laughter.All day they wrestled, while the bright sea winked and the seagulls screamed with excitement, and the grass wore thin on the headland. All Cornwall shook so that its smooth coastlines were made jagged by cliff-falls into the sunny sea.

But as the sun itself grew weary and dropped down the westerly sky. Gogmagog caught hold of Corineus and whirled him around in the air. "Fall into the sea and be lost, you bird-dropping, you pebble, you raindrop!" he bellowed, and threw Corineus towards the sea.

Only by clinging to the grass with the tips of his fingers did Corineus save himself from plunging over the cliff-edge, and as he hung there, over the deadly drop, Gogmagog put his fists on his hips and laughed. Pausing only to shout a string of curses at the watching Trojans, the giant lifted a foot to stamp on Corineus's fingers . . .

But at the last moment Corineus swung sideways, snatching hold of a thorn bush, and Gogmagog's foot broke off the cliff's edge, so that he pitched, bellowing and tumbling, heels over howling head, down into the sea below.

Thus Corineus won for himself the little dominion of Cornwall, and Brutus's Trojans the whole realm of Albion. The smaller, female giants, creeping out from their homes in caves and potholes and the mouldy boles of ancient trees, pleaded piteously for their lives. And the Trojans, lonely for wives, married them and bred a race of hard-working, deep-digging, tall-tale-telling sons.

King Leir

about 800 BC

THERE WAS ONCE A KING WITH THREE daughters. Weary of responsibility, he decided to lay aside his crown and divide his kingdom between his daughters.

"Tell me," he said, calling them before him. "How much do you love me?"

"More than emeralds or pearls or rubies," said Gonerilla.

"More than any man on earth!" said Regan.

"And you, Cordeilla?" asked Leir of his third and favourite daughter. "What have you to say?"

"Nothing," said Cordeilla.

"Nothing?"

"I love you as much as a daughter should," said the princess, declining to flatter the old man, "and I think you will find, Father, that the world respects a king because of his title. Give that up and the world may treat you more unkindly than it does now."

Leir was cut to the quick by her coldness, but he hid his hurt behind towering rage. "I had meant to give you the best and greenest part of my kingdom. But now I shall give you nothing, you unfeeling child – no, not even so much as a dowry or a place in my home!"

So the youngest princess, for speaking the truth, was banished over the sea to Gaul, and King Leir laid aside his crown, intending to spend the rest of his life enjoying himself with his friends. (He had a great many friends – 140 knights, in fact.) "I shall come to stay with each of you in turn," he told his two dutiful daughters.

But as Leir grew older and more frail, he discovered that Gonerilla and Regan did not love him quite as much as they had vowed. They turned his friends out of doors, told him they had house-room for only twenty-five, then only ten, then just one. Their husbands seized his last remaining lands, ignoring his ranting protests.

Realizing the truth of Cordeilla's words, Leir set off, through storm and hardship, for Gaul, to ask for help. He must recover his crown and depose the villains who were devouring his country. On board the ship, dishevelled and frail, he was treated no better than a common vagrant by the crew. It was true, then, what Cordeilla had said: that it was the crown people respected and not the man wearing it. What kind of welcome would he receive from the daughter he had so wronged?

If this story reads like a fairy tale, it is no surprise. Geoffrey of Monmouth, who included it in his *History of the Kings of Britain* (about 1136) probably derived it from a folk tale – maybe not even a British one at that. His King Leir supposedly came to the throne very young, owing to the sudden death of his father Bladud in a flying accident using magical wings. Raphael Holinshed, in his *Chronicles* of 1577, retold Geoffrey of Monmouth's story but altered minor details. Gonerilla became Goneril, Cordeilla Cordelia, Leir became Lear. Shakespeare used the Holinshed versions for his great tragedy. But the play's comments on old age, madness and power are all Shakespeare's own.

The place-name Leicester does not really have a connection with any King Leir.

Cordeilla, however, had found real happiness. Aganippus, King of the Franks, had taken her for his wife, despite her lack of dowry, despite her banishment. He valued her for what she was, an honest, brave and virtuous woman. As Leir found, she had always loved him more than had either of the hypocrites Gonerilla or Regan. At a word, she and Aganippus mustered an army to wreak vengeance on the heartless sisters.

Gonerilla and Regan, too intent on squabbling with each other, could not hold out against the avenging wrath of the invading army, and died, along with their husbands. Leir was reinstated King of Britain, and for three happy years he reigned, a wiser and more humane king for his one disastrous mistake. When he died, Cordeilla buried him in a vault under the bed of the River Soar, and founded a city nearby – Leicester or Leir-under-the-Soar. She ruled in his place, tempered by hardship and injustice into the most tender and just of queens.

The Three Plagues of Lud's Town

about 300 BC

DID YOU EVER HEAR IT SAID THAT TROUBLES come in threes? They did for the people of New Troy.

Several generations after the coming of Brutus, a king was crowned whose name was Lud. His one ambition in life was to make New Troy the most beautiful city in the world. He built houses and towers, wharves and storehouses, streets and council halls, and he strengthened the walls against attack by any marauding foe. But the foes who came could not be kept out by mere stones and timber. Three plagues fell on the people of New Troy.

First came the Coranieid – out of the bottomless lakes and over the shale shores, all the way from Otherworld. They were shifting, whispering shadows, picking the mud from the walls with their long fingernails, picking the nails out of ship's hulls with their sharp little teeth. They lurked in every alleyway and hollow tree, every empty ale cask and cattle trough, armed with needle-sharp swords and butterfly nets. And no matter what plans were made to drive them out, the Coranieid always knew ahead of time, always escaped.

"If only my clever little brother Llefelys were here and not living far away," Lud said, as the Coranieid whispered like starlings in the city dusk. "He would know what to do."

The next plague was of thefts – not the odd bushel of corn gone missing, but whole warehouses of wine and grain and salted beef. Lud set guards outside every storehouse, then doubled the guard, but the thieving went on, night after night, until half their winter provisions were gone. There were no more banquets, no more fairs: only hunger and worry and aggravation at never catching the thief.

"If only Llefelys were here," Lud would say. "He would know who was doing this."

Then came the shrieks. They were terrible, chilling, ear-splitting brays which pierced the ear-drum and shivered the brain to dust. Every May Day Eve, the shrieks sounded in the sky over New Troy. Men and women fell dead, and the expressions on their faces did not bear looking at. "If only Llefelys were here," Lud said. "I must speak to him before next May Day."

The two brothers met in the middle of the sea, their ships banging rail to rail. Lud clasped his brother close. "You are good to come: I need your help."

Llefelys listened to Lud describing the three plagues. "I can tell you how to defeat the Coranieid," he said. "I have met their kind in Brittany. But we must take precautions. They sieve the words from the wind, you know, and not a whisper escapes them." He took out a long copper tube which he placed against Lud's ear. Putting his mouth to the other end, he spoke in a whisper: "Kudjj eitho wihfldnn unt er sunbumflicekr wolembluch."

Lud looked at him blankly. Llefelys took the speaking tube to the edge of the ship and poured a flagon of wine down it. With spluttered curses, out of the tube slid a sodden Coranieid. It sank out of sight in the sea. Now Lud was able to hear every word his brother said down the tube, and the fairies could not eavesdrop.

"And as for the thefts of food and drink," said Llefelys, laying aside the hearing trumpet, "that's the work of a giant. I know him well: we studied under the same apothecary. He has obviously mixed himself a potion which sends your guards to

sleep, and while they sleep, he helps himself. Here's what you must do . . ."

"And as for the shriek," said Llefelys a while later, "that will cost you a pot of honey and a sail of your largest ship . . ."

Lud embraced his brother, thanked him and waved him farewell. He had the three solutions now to his three problems. "I should have liked Llefelys by my side, even so," he said to himself, and the Coranieid sieved the words out of the air and crunched them between their yellow teeth.

First Lud ordered his men to catch insects – crane-fly, mosquitoes and wasps – out of the summer air. These he crushed into a fine powder and mixed with brine. Then, when a high wind was blowing, Lud ordered the potion to be sprayed from the ramparts of New Troy, so that the air glittered with rainbow droplets. Harmless to ordinary people the infusion worked like strychnine on the Coranieid, and they could be seen shrivelling up like fallen leaves. The first plague was over.

Next Lud dismissed the guard outside the storehouses and granaries of New Troy and took their place himself. Alongside him stood a bath of cold water and his two-edged sword. At around three in the morning, a smell came to him on the breeze. At once he leapt – splash! – into the bath. The cold bit him to the bone, but it jarred him wide awake. The giant, thinking his magic perfume must have sent everyone to sleep, came whistling down the road, dragging several empty sacks. He had not even troubled to carry a weapon. At the sight of a man sitting in a bath of water, fully clothed and wide awake, the giant stopped short.

"No more of your thieving, you villainous oaf!" declared Lud, springing to his feet. The sword trembled in his chilly grasp, but the thought of his hungry people heated his temper red hot.

"All right. I shall come no more," said the giant, feeling the tip of Lud's sword against his navel, "and if you don't kill me, I'll even make good what I've taken."

"Swear it on your mother's life!" insisted Lud through chattering teeth.

"Oh, I do, I do," the giant assured him affably. "Now please let me go. It's May Day Eve tomorrow and I want to be many a mile away when that accursed shriek sounds!"

"Before you go, you can do a job of work for me," said Lud. "I want you to dig me a hole outside the city walls – a very big hole indeed."

So the giant dug a hole – at extraordinary speed, because he was so anxious to be gone – and Lud spread the largest sail of his largest ship over the hole to conceal it. A bowl of honey was placed on the centre of the sailcloth, and then Lud issued wax earplugs to his soldiers and plugged up his own ears.

At about midday on the May Day Eve, the shrieks sounded, far away to the north. Even so, several men and women fell dead and a water tower crashed to the ground. But instead of covering their heads with their arms, Lud and his soldiers were able, for the first time, to watch the sky. Winging towards them came two great dragons.

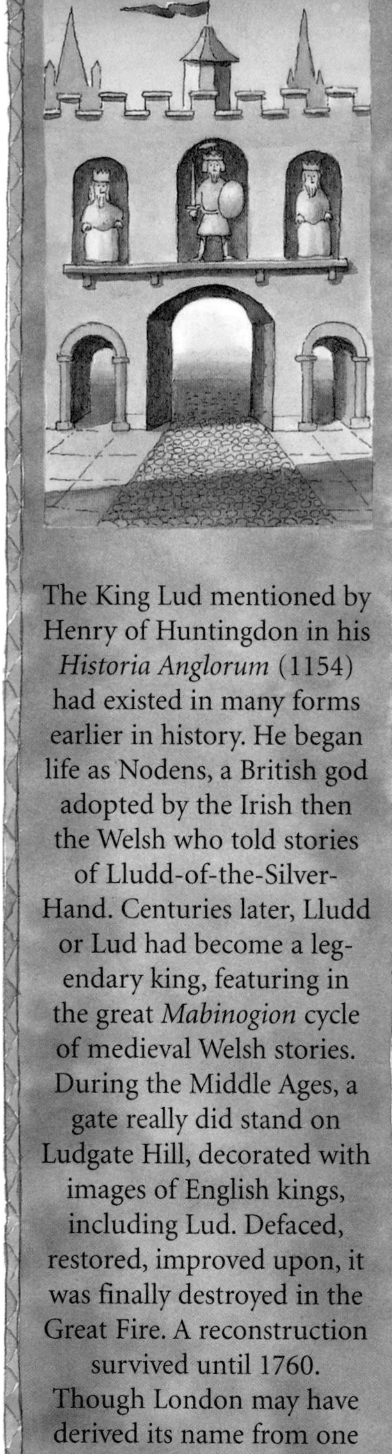

The King Lud mentioned by Henry of Huntingdon in his *Historia Anglorum* (1154) had existed in many forms earlier in history. He began life as Nodens, a British god adopted by the Irish then the Welsh who told stories of Lludd-of-the-Silver-Hand. Centuries later, Lludd or Lud had become a legendary king, featuring in the great *Mabinogion* cycle of medieval Welsh stories. During the Middle Ages, a gate really did stand on Ludgate Hill, decorated with images of English kings, including Lud. Defaced, restored, improved upon, it was finally destroyed in the Great Fire. A reconstruction survived until 1760. Though London may have derived its name from one man or a local tribe, that name was probably Londinos, or something similar. It was certainly not named after Lud.

One was red as blood, the other white as a glacier. And as they flew they lunged at one another, clashing wings, engulfing each other in gouts of fire and smoke. Above all they shrieked – that ear-splitting, brain-shattering shriek which had killed so many of Lud's subjects. Scales the size of shields rained down on the city. The fight was terrible to watch, and yet it was plain neither beast would win; they were doomed to fight every May Day Eve until the end of time.

At the sight of the honey, something astonishing happened. For the shrieking dragons broke off fighting, and hovered directly over the square of sailcloth. The smell seemed irresistible to them, for they circled lower and lower and came slowly in to land.

The sailcloth sank under their weight and spilled them into the pit, but the dragons barely noticed; they were too busy gorging on the honey. No sooner had they licked up the last dregs, than they fell deeply asleep, coiled round and about each other. Out from hiding raced Lud and his army of men. They folded the sailcloth over the dragons, and stitched it into a parcel. Then they carried the parcel as far as they could to the west, where they buried it in a stone-lined hole at the top of the highest mountain they could find, and filled it in with boulders and loose earth.

New Troy was restored to the peace of earlier, happier times, and such was the gratitude of the people that they renamed the town after their hero. City of Lud, they called it – Caer Luddein. And in time, blown on by wind and rain, that name was worn down into London. Lud was buried there, by Lud Gate. And if you walk to the top of Ludgate Hill, you may still see, spread before you, the city which Lud rescued from its three plagues.

The Tin Islands

about 100 BC

YELLOW AMBER AND PURPLE CLOTH, pottery and jewellery, spices, sponges and glass: the merchants of Phoenicia had wonders to tempt the most wary. Long before the Romans came to Britain, they knew of its existence, for Phoenician merchants were bringing tin and skins and slaves from some northern island realm they referred to as "Cassiterides": the Tin Islands.

Now tin, as a constituent of bronze, was of vital importance to the Romans. They did not want to be dependent on the Phoenicians – to have to pay Phoenician prices for this valuable commodity. So they ached to find these "Cassiterides", to tap their bottomless resource of tin.

Battening on to the wake of a Phoenician trader, one Roman captain determined to follow him to his secret source. He would not let the ship out of his sight until he had found out where the Phoenician went ashore to barter for the so-called "white lead". Day and night he matched the Phoenician's speed, though the merchant was as eager to *keep* his trade secrets as the Roman was to have them. The merchant tried altering course, veering wildly about on the open ocean to give his pursuer the slip. But the Roman clung on grimly, following every tack and gybe. It terrified him, for Roman ships were coastal vessels, not built for open sea, and the Phoenician took him into grey, heaving waters very different from the sunny Mediterranean.

"So. You dog my heels, do you?" muttered the Phoenician under his breath. "Very well, I shall lead you where you have no wish to go." And he set course for shallow water.

Inhabitants of the region now called Syria, the Phoenicians were intrepid explorers, venturing farther and farther afield in search of new markets, new commodities to sell. They were middle-men creating contact between continents and empires. Their trading visits undoubtedly enriched the lives of the Ancient Britons. But the fact that merchants found a ready market here for luxury goods dispels the picture of Ancient Britons as primitive savages.

Phoenician trading accounts for some amazing archaeological finds within the British Isles: Roman coins predating the Roman invasion, Scandinavian amber, Egyptian glass beads . . . The above story was recorded by Phoenician chroniclers in the first century BC. It is not recorded what became of the Roman ship or its crew.

Reserves of tin are largely exhausted now, but 2,000 years ago Britain was sole supplier to a Europe clamouring for bronze tools and weaponry. It was inevitable that the Roman Empire would not rest until it had found and conquered the "Islands of Tin".

Perhaps he thought he knew the coastal waters well enough to pick his way through deep-water channels. Perhaps he realized that his nation's secret had to be protected at whatever cost. With a sickening, grinding judder, his vessel ran aground. Too intent on following to put about in time, the Roman vessel too lumbered on to the hidden shoals. Within sight of one another, the two ships were quickly dismantled by pounding waves – reduced to flotsam and the cries of drowning men.

The Phoenician captain clung to a spar and kicked out for land, knees scraping on the rocks which had sunk him. The sea washed him up, limp and cold as seaweed, on a lonely beach, ship gone, cargo lost, but his life still clenched in his chattering teeth.

Months later, weary hundreds of miles away, he found his way home. Recounting his story, he was able to report to his fellow merchants, to the governors and ministers of his home town, that the whereabouts of the Tin Islands had been kept out of Roman hands. They were not slow to show their appreciation. "You shall have the value of your cargo!" they declared. "The state awards it you for the service you have done us all!"

"I Came, I Saw, I Conquered"

55 BC

FOR A LAND-LOVING MAN LIKE ME FROM A warm, sunny city, the crossing was a nightmare. The cavalry had not even managed to set sail from Gaul because of a contrary wind. Then, just as the white cliffs of Albion came into sight, a storm blew up which split the fleet and drove half of us one way, half the other. The landing site was unsuitable, the tide was against us, and the Britons were ready and waiting for us, armed to their blue-painted nostrils.

They came screaming down the beach. The keels of our big ships were so deep that Caesar could not get in close to the shore. Do you know what a Roman soldier's armour weighs? This chain mail tabard, the bronze helmet, the leather body armour? Even in August the British sea is not clear like the Mediterranean. Looking over the side, we could not see how deep the water was or where it was safe to step. If we fell over in all that weight of armour . . .

The Britons had no such problems. Their arms and legs were bare. They waded out towards us to fight us in the surf where we were at our most helpless. They were even driving their chariots in and out of the water, raising glassy fantails of spray higher than our heads: an awesome sight.

Then the standard-bearer leapt overboard, brandishing the Eagle of the Tenth Legion. To lose that to the enemy! Unthinkable! "Leap down, soldiers!" he yelled. "Unless you want to betray the Eagle to the enemy!"

There was no more hesitating then. Men from the other ships jumped in with both feet, wallowing about like seacows, staggering towards the shore, sandals slipping on the slimy seabed.

But I was one of Caesar's reserve. He was sending us in by the boatload to wherever the line looked weakest. I and four others jumped into a little boat and rowed for an outcrop of rocks about halfway to the shore. We climbed on to it and began throwing rocks and pebbles – as good a weapon as any against half-naked men. I tell you, we pelted them like shepherd boys scaring off wolves.

Unfortunately we got isolated from the main force, and to my – er – discomfort, I realized that the tide was going out. The stretch of water separating us from the beach was growing narrower and narrower; dry sand was appearing nearer and nearer to our rock. The Britons came at us with everything: rocks and chariots, spears and darts and arrows . . . The four men with me, seeing it was hopeless, jumped back into the boat and pulled away. "Come on, Scaeva!" they called. "Leave it, Scaeva!" But I had the madness of battle on me. That Eagle-bearer had inspired me, I suppose. We were within clear sight of Caesar's ship, and I did not want him to see me turn tail. So the four pushed off without me – left me standing on this pile of rocks, soaked by the waves breaking behind me, being pelted like a target at a fair. When I raised up my shield now, I could see daylight through it from the spear-holes, the axe-slashes, the tears made by their rocks and arrows.

Those chariots of theirs were terrifying: we have nothing like it. They circled me at full tilt, their wheel-hubs striking sparks from the rocks, the spray blinding me. An axe smashed my helmet, a rock hit me in the face and broke my nose: the world turned red in front of me. I used my spear first, but that was soon wrenched out of my hands. Then I used my sword. By Mars! I thought, I'll take a dozen of you down with me to the Underworld!

A sudden sharp pain in my thigh! An arrow. My sword broke like glass against a battle axe. They battered my shield out of my hand. Time to go, Scaeva, I said to myself, and I dived off the rock before the tide left me there, utterly high and dry.

Jove, that water was cold! The frigidarium at the public baths was never as cold as that sea. I could see my comrades leaning over the side of a ship, beckoning, whistling, calling my name. The sea seemed to be inside me and out, flowing through my wounds, washing the strength out of me. Arrows kept falling all round me. But at last – I hardly remember it – hands were pulling me over the rail, my blood running down into the scuppers. "My shield!" It was all I could say. "My shield!"

Once the legions were ashore, things took a different turn, of course. The men closed ranks, locked shields, formed squares, gave those barbarians a lesson in Roman warfare. Discipline. It is discipline that makes the difference, you see: discipline and years of professional training. The enemy fled. But without cavalry, how could we give chase? Hopeless. We had just to watch them run.

"My shield!" It was all I could think of. "My shield! I lost it at the rock!" It is the ultimate disgrace for a Roman soldier (except perhaps for losing his legion's Eagle) to lose his shield. When I saw Caesar coming towards me I thought it was to reprimand me. I racked my brains for an excuse, but all words seemed to have bled away down my nose.

"What is your name?" He was speaking to me. Julius Caesar, greatest of the Romans. Better I should have drowned than come back without my shield!

"Scaeva, Caesar. Forgive me, Caesar, my shield . . ."

"Scaeva, you fought today as a Roman should. You set an example for all soldiers to follow. Such courage merits promotion, *Centurion* Scaeva."

Centurion! There is no higher honour a soldier can win than to be made a centurion for his valour. One day grandchildren, as yet unborn, will talk of it as they run their little fingers over my battered nose. My wife will write it on my memorial stone: "Scaeva: he was made centurion by Julius Caesar the day Rome conquered Albion."

But Mars deliver me from actually having to *live* in this bleak, miserable country. We are going home tomorrow, thanks be to the gods.

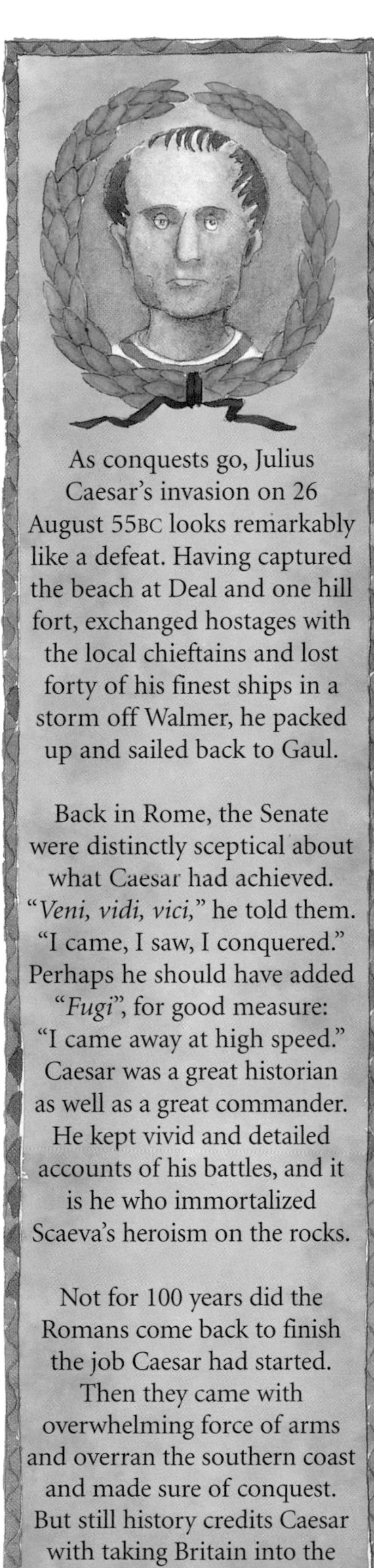

As conquests go, Julius Caesar's invasion on 26 August 55BC looks remarkably like a defeat. Having captured the beach at Deal and one hill fort, exchanged hostages with the local chieftains and lost forty of his finest ships in a storm off Walmer, he packed up and sailed back to Gaul.

Back in Rome, the Senate were distinctly sceptical about what Caesar had achieved. "*Veni, vidi, vici,*" he told them. "I came, I saw, I conquered." Perhaps he should have added "*Fugi*", for good measure: "I came away at high speed." Caesar was a great historian as well as a great commander. He kept vivid and detailed accounts of his battles, and it is he who immortalized Scaeva's heroism on the rocks.

Not for 100 years did the Romans come back to finish the job Caesar had started. Then they came with overwhelming force of arms and overran the southern coast and made sure of conquest. But still history credits Caesar with taking Britain into the Roman Empire.

The Resting Place

AD 50

THERE WAS ONCE A HILL SO CLAD IN MAGIC that it attracted legends to it like roosting birds. The Celts called it the Island of Glass and in winter it was ringed with floodwater, so that it stood rooted in its own reflection. All around it were lesser hills, like children round their mother.

But this story begins on another hill, thousands of miles away. Joseph of Arimathea, as he stood on Golgotha Hill watching Jesus die on a wooden cross, was moved to offer his own tomb to Jesus's family so that they would have somewhere to lay His body. True, Joseph was a rich man and could afford to buy another grave, but a man does not lightly give up the resting place he has chosen for his mortal remains.

Within days, Joseph's tomb was restored to him, empty, vacated. Jesus had risen from the dead. But Joseph did not choose to reclaim his resting place. He was a disciple, now, a true believer, wandering the world, passing on to people the teachings of Jesus and the news that He had risen from the dead.

With a small band of friends, Joseph sailed for Albion. His ship navigated the Severn River, from where he travelled inland to the county called Summer Land and the cluster of hills round about the Island of Glass. The friends were all weary. Climbing a small hill for a better view, Joseph leaned heavily on his thorn-wood staff and christened the place Weary-All Hill. From the crest, the Island of Glass was clearly visible. What a long way he had come from Golgotha to reach this green place. Joseph drove his staff into the soft, damp, autumn ground, curled up in his cloak and went to sleep.

He dreamed of wings and of light, of music and voices and ladders between the sky and the hill. "Rest *here*, Joseph," said the Angel Gabriel, hovering on kestrel wings. "Build *here*, Joseph."

On waking, Joseph told his followers, "Here is where we shall live and work."

They were not looking at him. They were staring at his staff. While they had slept, its smooth shaft had grown a dozen twiggy shoots, and small green nodules were starting to form. By Christmas it would be in blossom.

Weary-All Hill (though of God's making) actually belonged to a local nobleman. He was a busy man; he had no interest in stories of miracle-workers in far-off lands, who died and came back

from the dead. Frankly, he did not believe a word of it. But the hill was too steep to farm, so he gave Joseph and his friends permission to build.

Joseph built a church out of wattle and daub – a crude, draughty place, with few comforts. But the view was second only to Paradise, and the birdsong sweeter than the singing of angels. A little religious community grew up, converts to Christianity arriving one by two by three. Joseph was content. He had found his second resting place: a good place to pass eternity. He was buried somewhere on the hill: the exact spot was soon forgotten. The wattle-and-daub church fell into ruins. But one thing lasted, as fresh and new as on the day of its coming. Each Christmas time, Joseph's thorn-wood staff would erupt into blossom – a miraculous sight. Soon people were making pilgrimage just to see the Holy Thorn. Some said it reminded them of Jesus's crown of thorns. Some said it put them in mind of life springing up new out of stark, thorny death.

Some also liked to think that Joseph had brought with him a treasure far more precious than a walking stick. It was rumoured that he had owned the room where Christ and His disciples ate their Last Supper together before the crucifixion. As the owner of the room, Joseph must, of course, have owned the crockery they used. And *that* meant he must have owned the cup from which Jesus drank, saying "Take, eat. This is my blood which is shed for you and for all Mankind."

What if Joseph had brought that cup with him to Weary-All Hill? What if he had hidden it somewhere near the wattle-and-daub church? So began the greatest treasure hunt in the history of Britain – the quest for the Holy Grail: prize beyond price, wonder beyond magic, visible only to the pure of heart.

Five centuries later, in the days of King Arthur, legend claims that the Holy Grail was found by the best of Arthur's knights.

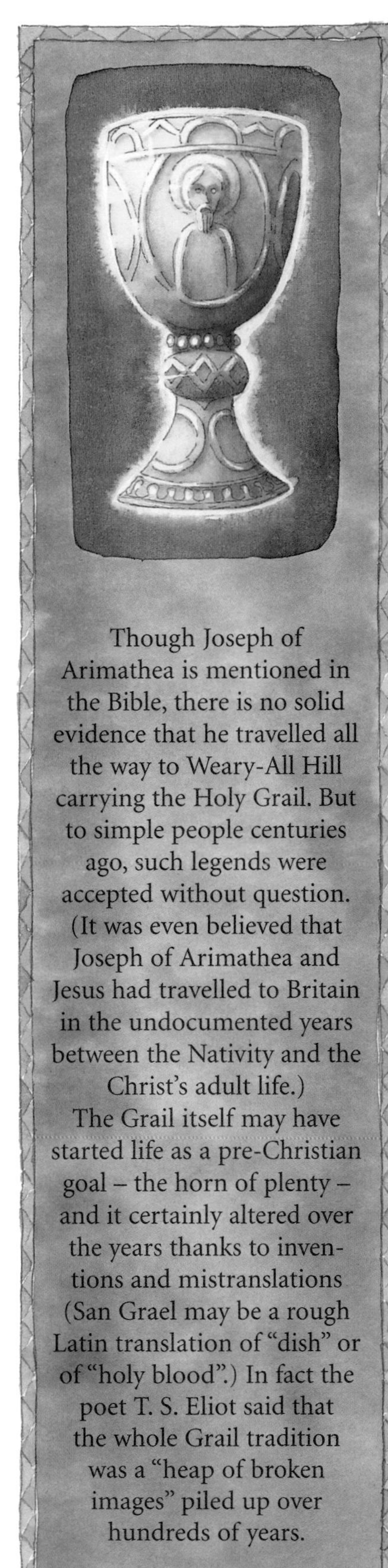

Though Joseph of Arimathea is mentioned in the Bible, there is no solid evidence that he travelled all the way to Weary-All Hill carrying the Holy Grail. But to simple people centuries ago, such legends were accepted without question. (It was even believed that Joseph of Arimathea and Jesus had travelled to Britain in the undocumented years between the Nativity and the Christ's adult life.)

The Grail itself may have started life as a pre-Christian goal – the horn of plenty – and it certainly altered over the years thanks to inventions and mistranslations (San Grael may be a rough Latin translation of "dish" or of "holy blood".) In fact the poet T. S. Eliot said that the whole Grail tradition was a "heap of broken images" piled up over hundreds of years.

Boudicca the Firebrand

60

Her name meant "victory". Even in the good days, she looked like a firebrand, that fiery red hair tumbling down past her waist. Boudicca was married to Prasutagus, chief of the Iceni tribe on the flat lands of Norfolk. Though the Romans had conquered and colonized the entire country, they allowed many of the revered local kings to keep their thrones. So Boudicca was a queen and her three daughters were princesses. Then Prasutagus, her husband, died, and his greedy and arrogant Roman landlord decided to help himself to Prasutagus's silver plate and armoury, his chariots and cattle, his lands and power. He had Boudicca lashed to a cart and flogged till her red hair was redder still with blood. And all the while, she could hear the screams of her daughters, as laughing Roman soldiers mauled them.

What were they now? A widow and three girls, dispossessed and homeless. But Boudicca was a queen, and her daughters were princesses, and the Iceni were a warrior tribe. Boudicca spoke to her people, her voice loud and harsh.

"Do you see what meekness and tolerance bought us? Will you stand by and see your gods cast down? Your priests murdered? Your old way of life swept away? *Your queen flogged?* Don't our holy Druids prophesy that the Romans will be swept out of this land of ours?" She lifted her face to the sky. "O Adraste, goddess of war! Tell us what you would have us do! Shall Boudicca run north and hide her children and weep? Or shall the Queen of the Iceni and her warriors march south *and take our revenge?*"

She pulled from under her cloak something large and live and struggling. The watching crowd thought at first it was a baby, but then they saw that she had hold of it by its long silken ears.

"The hare! The hare! Let the hare run!" cried the Iceni, knowing what powers of prophecy were in a running hare. Boudicca threw the animal down.

It froze, terrified, blinded by the sudden light. Then it saw a space where the crowd had parted, and bolted for freedom. "*To the south! To the south!*"cried the Iceni. The omen had been given. The war was under way.

All the humiliation and resentment against their Roman conquerors was focused on Boudicca now, and not only the Iceni but the Trinovantes too, and all those whipped up along the way. Rebellion kindled like a grassfire, and a great army rallied to the chariot of Queen Boudicca.

Sharp blades projected from both wheels of that chariot. It cut through a rank of foot soldiers like a scythe through ripe corn. The Romans, lulled by peaceful years of supremacy, suddenly found their villas in flames around them, their shops looted and destroyed.

Colchester was razed to the ground, and the head of Emperor Claudius' statue lopped off and thrown into the river. Hundreds died – not just Romans but anyone who had crept under their protection and begun to live in the Roman way. Murderous with hate, Boudicca was always a furlong ahead of her army, chariot blades clearing their path, her blood-curdling war cry freezing the blood.

Suetonius Paulinus, Roman governor of Britain, was far away, on the other side of the country, attempting to stamp out the subversive influence of the Druid priests. By the time news reached him of Boudicca's uprising, she had driven a wedge through the legions of Rome and rampaged south to London. He could do nothing to turn her back. The vast rambling sprawl of London could not withstand her savagery.

Over mud lanes and marble pavements Boudicca's chariot wheels rolled, and the air was so full of ash from burning buildings that her skin was spotted like a leopard's, her red hair just one more tongue of flame. Ships blazed and sank alongside the Thames wharves. And everywhere the sooty air rang with the cry:

"*Boudicca! Boudicca!* Victory! Victory!"

Suetonius Paulinus made his stand in the Midlands, his 10,000 men to Boudicca's 50,000. He chose a spot where three hills protected his army's back and rear flanks, and his cohorts formed squares, the sun snagging on their regimental eagles, on their standards, on their spear-points.

Such stillness they presented, in comparison with the torrent of men and women who teemed down on them. The cry of "*Boudicca!*" rang back off the faces of the hills. But the Roman cohorts were silent, except for the jingling of a horse's bridle, the beating of a single drum like a steady heartbeat.

They seemed barely human, those squares of armoured military might, every head helmeted, every face obscured. Some of the red crests of the centurions were as long as Boudicca's hair. Every long rectangular shield was locked against the shield alongside. It was like hurling water on to a box of bronze, and though Boudicca charged once, twice, a third time, she could not break those disciplined squares.

Then the cohorts began to beat on their shields with their short swords and to push forward, slicing, stabbing, routing, re-forming into squares. They came on with such ruthless certainty that the Britons turned tail and ran.

Boudicca's shrill, grating voice summoned her daughters to her chariot. She pulled them in over the tailboard. They crouched, bleeding, against her legs as she whipped up her horses to a last frenzied gallop. This time her bladed wheels cut down her own people as she fled capture.

She drove as far as the great forest of Epping – in those days a tossing, immeasurable sea of dense green trees older than either Romans or the tribes of Britain. Out of the sunlight she flashed, into its ominous shade. The Romans could not fail to follow. The trail of a battle chariot carrying four women is not hard to trace. Escape only bought Boudicca a little time: a brief respite to be alone with her daughters and to shed the bloody madness of battle.

They came to rest in a clearing where the trees stood too close and the undergrowth too dense for the chariot to pass. White and purple bell-flowers swung from twining stems among the saplings and fallen boughs.

"Remember Caractacus who fought the Romans for ten years in Wales?" said Boudicca. "First they captured his wife and children, then they took him to parade in the streets of Rome. That must never happen to us." The three girls shuddered and lowered their heads. "What do you say, children? Let's gather flowers and make a drink to refresh our flagging souls." So they picked the purple flowers and stewed them into a purple liquor. "Let us drink to Adraste, who shall give us the last victory. And as you drink, remember the prophecies of the Druids. One day these Romans will be gone, swept away and forgotten." Then she kissed her three daughters tenderly, and they all drank. Poison to make them sleep. Poison to put them beyond reach of Roman revenge.

Their bodies were never found.

Boudicca (also sometimes Boadicea) was robbed of her kingdom and humiliated at the same time as outrageous wrongs were being committed in Colchester. Veterans of the Roman army were evicting the British and forcing them to work on reconstruction of the city as well as a new temple to the dead Emperor Claudius, now declared a god. So there was plenty of support for Boudicca's rebellion. A layer of ash has been found under present-day London which dates from her burning it down. Verulamium (St Albans) was also razed to the ground. Her body is variously reputed to lie in Hampstead, in Lincolnshire, in Epping Forest – even under Platform 10 of King's Cross Station.

Running Towards Paradise

300

HIS SANDALLED FEET TROD THE MOSAIC floors depicting all the Roman immortals, but Alban's mind was filled by only one god – a god so immense and magnificent that He overflowed Alban's mind and spilled out of him in a torrent of joy. But these were times when the Roman army, in which Alban was a soldier, was still dutiful to the gods of Rome. Though Alban and his fellow legionaries were born in Britain, they occupied and policed it on behalf of Rome, and were obliged to worship Roman gods – Neptune and Jupiter, Janus and Juno and Diana. Loyal Romans purged Christians like the lice in their uniforms.

When the search party came to the house of Amphibalus, a Christian priest fleeing persecution, they immediately arrested the man they found there. It was not until he was brought for judgement that they realized it was not Amphibalus at all, but it was a Roman in disguise. Alban of Verulamium had taken the priest's place to allow him time to escape.

The judge was incensed that Alban, who served under the Roman eagle, symbol of Jupiter, should so deny the Roman gods. "Make sacrifice to the true gods of Rome!" he demanded, but Alban refused. "I worship only the living and true God." Neither torture nor threats could break his resolve.

"Take him out and put an end to him!" raged the judge, and Alban was led away to die. A large crowd had gathered at the place of execution, on a hilltop beyond the river. They stood speculating on what Alban had done and why. Alban was so eager to keep his appointment with immortality that, instead of walking to the bridge, he hurried straight down to the riverbank. The tumbling water slid to a halt, evaporated, and was gone, leaving him a dry path to cross over. Minutes later he crested the hill and crossed as easily from life to death, his head slashed from his shoulders by a Roman sword.

"Let that set an example to any other Roman who thinks to abandon the gods of Olympus!" said the judge, watching from his window.

It did set one, too. For Alban was happy to die. Roman soldiers had always been ready to die for the Roman eagle, for Caesar, for their honour, but they had never loved their gods enough to die like that: fearless, happy, eager to set out on the road to paradise. Alban was Roman Britain's first martyr. And martyrs make for converts.

During the fourth century, Christianity swept Roman Britain, until it was the predominant religion. When the Roman Empire crumbled and the Roman armies withdrew from Britain, they left behind them a Christian country.

Then the Danes came, under their raven-banner. The Vikings and the Danes arrived in longships, burned down the monasteries, slaughtered the monks, stole the crucifixes and tore up the Gospels. They brought with them their own gods: Thor and Odin, Wotan and Freya – gods who admired bloodshed and awarded paradise only to warriors. The few Christians who survived the rout fled west into Wales and Ireland, leaving the stones of their churches to be re-used for pagan temples or swallowed up once more by primeval forest. Their villages were lived in now by the pagan, blond-haired, blue-eyed Angles.

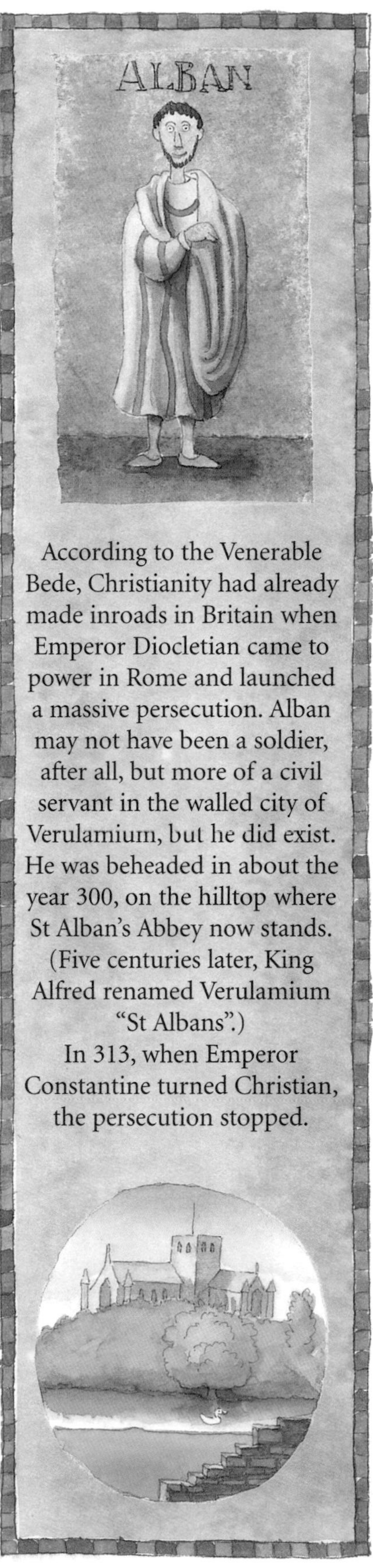

According to the Venerable Bede, Christianity had already made inroads in Britain when Emperor Diocletian came to power in Rome and launched a massive persecution. Alban may not have been a soldier, after all, but more of a civil servant in the walled city of Verulamium, but he did exist. He was beheaded in about the year 300, on the hilltop where St Alban's Abbey now stands. (Five centuries later, King Alfred renamed Verulamium "St Albans".)

In 313, when Emperor Constantine turned Christian, the persecution stopped.

The Hallelujah Victory

429

"Help us! help us!" they begged. "Save us! You know the mind of God, Father! When will He help us?"

Bishop Germanus thought they were talking about their immortal souls, but they were not at all. The Britons he had come to visit were talking of their homes, their wives, their children. "We write to Rome, but they send no troops to help us, and we – God forgive us – we have forgotten all the arts of war we ever knew!"

The Roman legions had been withdrawn from England, as the Roman Empire shrank and disintegrated. For centuries the occupying forces had defended the land, fortified its borders, kept at bay all interlopers and barbarians. But now the Romans were gone, leaving the door to Britain banging open in the wind.

Scenting rich pickings, the Picts and Scots seized their chance – hardy, unconquered people who could fight with all the skill which the southern Britons had forgotten. They launched more and more audacious raids, burned villages, took cattle, killed anyone who stood in their path. "Now they are coming in hundreds – and with Saxons among them – and how shall we stand against them?" they begged the visiting bishop.

"Do as I say, and all may be well," Germanus told the Britons, though secretly his heart quailed when he thought what the future might bring the people of the southern kingdoms.

The people did as Germanus instructed. They took their stand on high ground, on three sides of a valley – well strung out – a laughably small number in the face of the advancing army of Picts and Scots and Saxons.

On came the raiders, shaggy as beasts, silvered over with the glint of axeheads, spearheads, arrowheads, swords. They filled up the valley like a summer brook swelling into a winter river. The noise of their feet, their baggage, their ugly nasal languages rose up unmuffled by distance. Then, at a signal – the slow silent arc of a single arrow – the Britons did as they had been told to do. They opened their mouths and shouted:

"Hallelujah!"

An avalanche of sound tumbled into the hollow, bounded and resounded around, redoubled by the kettle-hollow basin of the place, echoing, re-echoing, as if the Day of Reckoning had come and a million angels were all shouting:

"Hallelujah!"

The second cry met with the first and swelled it, ricocheted around the reverberating rocks till there was more sound in the valley than air, and all of it the one word:

"Hallelujah!"

The men below turned and fled. They thought that all their enemies must have united as never before, congregated around this one valley to ambush and destroy them. And they fled. Not a stroke was struck, never an axe fell, but the Scots and Picts were routed as totally as if God had taken up arms against them.

St Germanus was the Bishop of Auxerre in France. He visited Britain in 429 to argue against a heretical Christian schism, but is better remembered for helping win the bloodless "Hallelujah Victory". The site of the battle, Maes Garmon in Flintshire, North Wales, means "the field of Germanus".

Hengist, Horsa and the Lovely Rowena

449

After the Scots and the Picts came the Jutes, sweeping in like the sea. There was no stopping the relentless push westwards of these Germanic hordes urgent for land, greedy for the rich orchards and fields and vineyards of Kent.

King Vortigern, already plagued by attacks from northerners, saw the forces of Hengist and Horsa closing on his coastline and knew that the Jutes were too strong for him. He did not fall on his knees and pray. He did not reach for his sword either. He saw another way of surviving. Why should he not *ally their power* to his?

Perhaps it was cowardice, perhaps it was cunning, but Vortigern went down to the shore and greeted the brothers, chieftains of the Jutes: "Ah! Just the men I need!"

He pitted Hengist and Horsa against the Picts and Scots, saying he would pay them if they were victorious. (He was secretly hoping they would kill each other and leave Kent in peace.) But the Jutes easily defeated the northerners. And as soon as they had, they returned, palms outstretched for their pay. And on top of money they wanted land. What they could not get by threats, they took by force, and far from sailing away over the horizon, more of their kith and kin began to arrive.

On board one Jute ship was Hengist's daughter, Rowena. One sight of her, and Vortigern's soul was in thrall. For those blue eyes, for that yellow hair, for that tall, willowy form, he would have sold the sun out of the sky, the salt out of the sea, anything that was his or not his to give. In exchange for Rowena's hand in marriage, he gave Hengist the throne of Kent.

Perhaps he knew it was lost already, that it was Hengist's for the taking. But there were those who thought him a traitor. Not least his sons.

Dispossessed of their inheritance, shamed by their father's marriage, Vortimer and his half-brother took up the fight which Vortigern had let fall. They rallied the men of Kent fleeced and scattered by the Jutes, and at the Ford of the Eagles clashed with such a clamour that the river water shivered like broken glass.

Horsa, the brother of Hengist, fell at the hands of Vortimer, and Vortimer's brother fell at the hands of Hengist.

Rowena's blue eyes swam with tears when the news came from Aylesford. "I weep that your dear son is dead," she told her British husband. But in truth, her Jute heart howled for vengeance at the death of her uncle, Horsa, and with misery that the Jutish fleet was even now sailing away in defeat.

Biting her tongue, Rowena awaited her chance. She paid a servant to poison young Vortimer's food and, when he died, wept crocodile tears over his grave.

"Invite my father to come back," she crooned as she consoled her gricving husband. "The time is past for wars. The land has drunk blood enough. Let us make peace, the men of Kent and the men of Jute. Do, I beg you."

So a great feast was arranged between the chieftains of Britain and Hengist's warriors.

"Let there be no weapons brought," said Hengist, "for we shall sit down as friends and hospitality forbids that those who eat together should bear arms."

"Naturally," said Vortigern. "The laws of hospitality are the same the world over."

It was a feast to stretch the powers of the chroniclers who wrote of it. The fire spits bent under the weight of roasting meat. After such a meal, there were many oaths sworn of undying friendship and never-ending peace. "Is not Britain large enough for all of us?" cried Vortigern, face flushed, unsteady on his feet, fingers clumsy in his wife's yellow hair. "Shall we not put the killing behind us?"

Hengist too pulled himself to his feet. He did not seem to have drunk so deep. "Now, men," he said, without raising his voice. And from under their cloaks, from out of their boots, from hidden sheaths and false pockets, the Jutes drew their daggers.

Rowena looked on, unmoved, unafraid. She stretched wide her sea-blue eyes, so as not to miss a single death. No tears fell from her blue eyes.

No dagger was turned on Vortigern, for he was beneath contempt, already shackled to his enemies by love of a woman. Overturning his chair, clutching his misery to him in trembling hands, he fled, calling to Rowena to follow. But she did not. When 300 Britons lay dead on the floor, Rowena raised her glass to the ghost of Horsa and wished him peace in his warrior heaven.

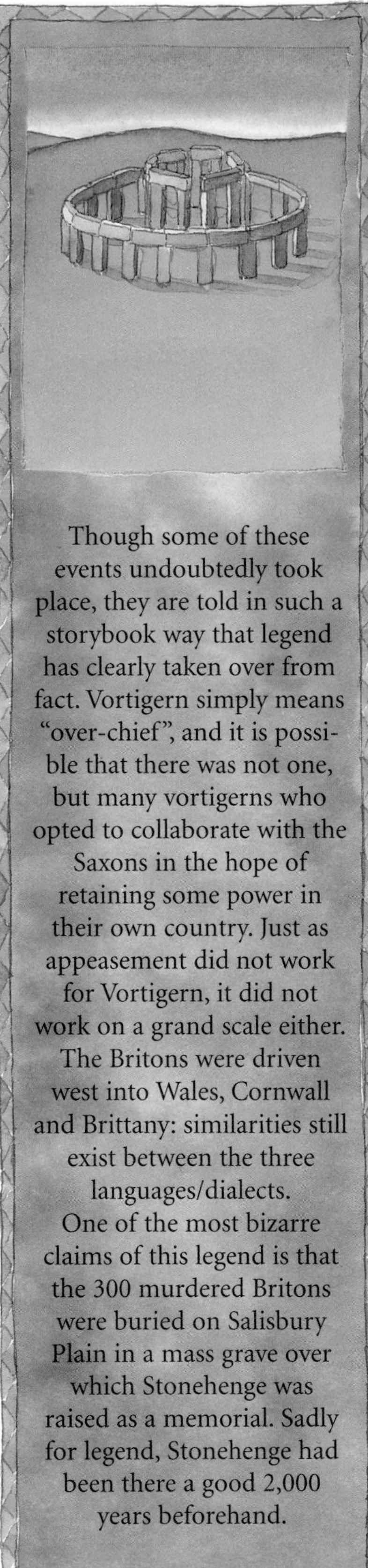

Though some of these events undoubtedly took place, they are told in such a storybook way that legend has clearly taken over from fact. Vortigern simply means "over-chief", and it is possible that there was not one, but many vortigerns who opted to collaborate with the Saxons in the hope of retaining some power in their own country. Just as appeasement did not work for Vortigern, it did not work on a grand scale either. The Britons were driven west into Wales, Cornwall and Brittany: similarities still exist between the three languages/dialects.

One of the most bizarre claims of this legend is that the 300 murdered Britons were buried on Salisbury Plain in a mass grave over which Stonehenge was raised as a memorial. Sadly for legend, Stonehenge had been there a good 2,000 years beforehand.

The Castle Which Could Not Stand

about 450

VORTIGERN WAS DESPERATE, HUNTED LIKE A FOX across the length and breadth of his own kingdom by the enemy he had thought to befriend. Holding his life in his teeth, holding his power in sweating hands, he finally found himself with his back to the Welsh mountains. There he made his stand. Planting his foot on the crest of Dinas Emrys, he commanded, "Build me a castle! You men, quarry. You men, heave. Build me a fortress!" He thought that if he built the walls high enough, both his crown and his life would be safe inside.

But though every day Vortigern's castle grew, by night it crumbled into a pile of rubble. The wind blew dusty mortar into Vortigern's open mouth. "Find me a prophet! Find me out what evil magic is eating away at my castle!" he demanded.

Superstitious advice poured from his wise men. "Your castle will not stand, my lord, until the noble blood of a fatherless boy is spilled on the foundations."

"Find one, then, and split him!"

The countryside was scoured, but though there were many children whose fathers had died, or gone away to war, there was not one who had *never had a father*.

"Who's this?" sneered Vortigern when a brown-eyed boy was at last brought before him.

"His mother entered a nunnery the day her child was born," his advisors told him. "The child was brought up by his grandfather – a magician."

"But who was his *father*?" Vortigern wanted to know.

The child did not answer, but his mother did. "Something between a dream and a nightmare," she said, unashamed. "One night I dreamt of a man wearing a golden crown. He fathered my child, then melted away with the daylight."

The little boy stared at the woman wearing the nun's habit. This was the first time he had seen his mother, and the first he had heard tell of his dream-father. Now, in this moment of discovery, he was to die.

"Bind him and slit him and let his blood flow!" cried Vortigern. "Tonight my castle will not fall down!"

"It will and it shall, while you build it there!" The boy's voice was high, but clear and loud. It captured every ear. "Don't you know what lies beneath this ground?"

The King snorted. "Nothing. Who knows? The ruin of something Roman." (Indeed, there were signs of ancient building, mossy with mould.) The wise men were asked, but the wise men did not know.

"Then I shall tell you," said the boy. "I have dreamed this place, and the future will come of it. Below here lies a pool of water, and at the bottom of the pool, two stone tanks. Unless you drain the pool, you may as well build on quicksand."

A muscle in Vortigern's cheek twitched. Silence hung over his army of builders until at last he spoke: "Look and see. We can kill him after."

They broke up the ground with picks. It fell away into a hollow place beneath, splashing into water. They laid bare a vast man-made basin, a sink of black water, and pumped it out down the mountainside. As the water drained away, two stone vaults the shape of coffins were uncovered.

"Inside each is a dragon," said the boy. "I have dreamed them, and the future will come of it. Wake the dragons if you dare, King Vortigern; they will tell you your fate."

"If anything were ever living in there, it is certainly dead by now," sneered Vortigern, and had his men set to with cold hammers.

The coffins broke like eggs hatching. Out of the first came a red dragon, writhing, the colour of blood. Out of the second came a white dragon, the colour of frost. Their tails intertwined, then they turned on each other and fought. The white dragon was low and slinking: it overturned the red and scuttled for its throat. But the red dragon was leaping lively. It threw off the white one, blinding it with scarves of scarlet smoke. Then, with a lunge, the red jaws fastened on the white throat till its fire was out.

As the vanquished dragon dragged itself back into the crater to die, the red victor leapt skywards. It passed so close to Vortigern that its claws tore his cloak and its hot breath singed his beard. The horror of it rooted him to the spot.

"I have dreamed this fight, and the future will come of it," said the fatherless boy. "The red dragon represents the Britons, Vortigern: the men you betrayed to Hengist and Horsa. The white dragon is the invading horde you have brought down on us. For a time they will triumph over us, but the Britons will drive them out, as you yourself have been driven out. Uther Pendragon will rule after you are dead. The Jutes and Saxons are coming after you, Vortigern, but beyond them, behind them comes an Age of Gold!"

Vortigern's whole army turned and looked across the plain. The sun flashed off some distant metal – a spearhead? a helmet? an army?

"The pit is drained. The dragons are gone. Fill in the hole and start building, you idle dogs!" The King would have liked to cut the boy's throat and silence his prophesying. But there was not a man there who would have been ready to do it. There was magic in the lines of his small hands and in every word he spoke. "What is your name, you with the Devil for a father?"

But this time the boy's mother spoke for him. "My son's name is Merlin."

Vortigern's castle was never finished. Though its foundations were sure, so too was the future. The Jutes killed him, and buried him in a pit. And the Britons rallied under Uther Pendragon. Dragon-headed Uther, they called him, because there was fire in his blood and magic in his eyes. His best friend was Merlin the Druid, Merlin the Magician, and it was to him that Uther entrusted the safety and education of his son: the Once-and-Future-King, Arthur.

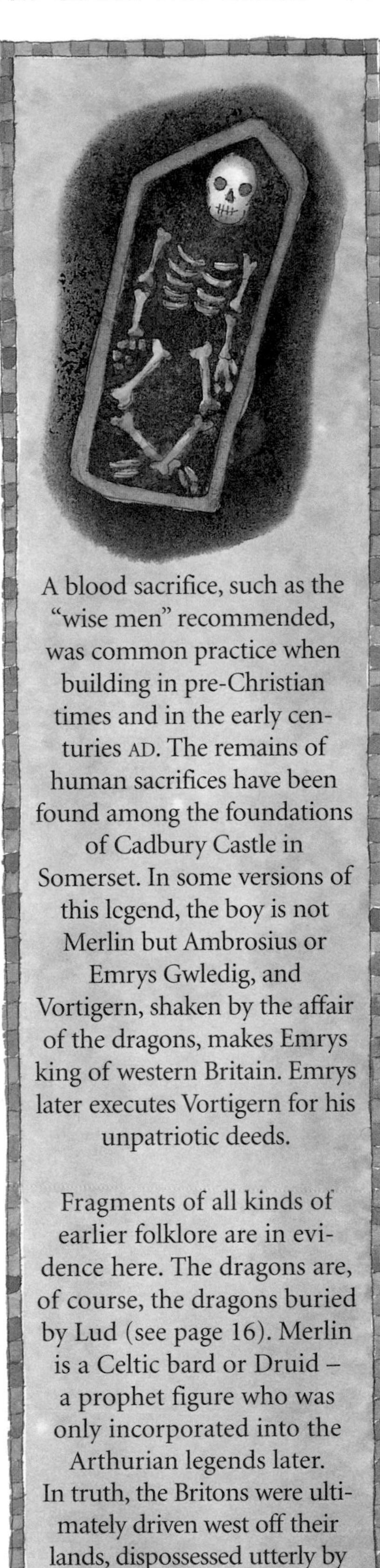

A blood sacrifice, such as the "wise men" recommended, was common practice when building in pre-Christian times and in the early centuries AD. The remains of human sacrifices have been found among the foundations of Cadbury Castle in Somerset. In some versions of this legend, the boy is not Merlin but Ambrosius or Emrys Gwledig, and Vortigern, shaken by the affair of the dragons, makes Emrys king of western Britain. Emrys later executes Vortigern for his unpatriotic deeds.

Fragments of all kinds of earlier folklore are in evidence here. The dragons are, of course, the dragons buried by Lud (see page 16). Merlin is a Celtic bard or Druid – a prophet figure who was only incorporated into the Arthurian legends later. In truth, the Britons were ultimately driven west off their lands, dispossessed utterly by Jute and Saxon invaders.

St David and the Naked Ladies

519-589

Arriving in the Vale of Roses in the west of Wales, St Patrick looked round him and thought, "I shall settle here." But an angel, stooping hawk-like out of a cloudless sky, urged him on his way. "This place is meant for David," said the angel, "and David is not yet born!" So St Patrick pressed on to Ireland and won it for Christ. For fifty years the Vale of Roses stood waiting.

By the time David arrived there, though, to found a monastery, the area lay at the mercy of a brutish man called Boia and his equally brutish wife. David and his monks wanted only to farm the land and to pray, but Boia wanted them gone. He set out from home, blustering and boorish, telling his wife he meant to run them off his land.

When he came back, he was meek and mild, speaking of 'joy', saying he was sorry for his sinful life. He had met David, and he was a changed man.

"Get you up there and tell that blanket-tossed son of a mangy dog to shift his bag of bones off our grazing!" squawked his wife, but Boia only looked at her with faraway eyes and a wistful smile. "They are my brothers-in-Christ, wife," he said.

So she boxed his ears and took matters into her own hands. Summoning her serving maids she told them, "Over there yonder stands a barn of a place full of lonely men, all priding themselves that they can live without wives and sweethearts, all sworn to shun women till their dying day. Get up there in your nothing-at-alls. When those monks see what they are missing, they will break their vows, and give up religion!"

The maids went – big buxom girls, with blushing cheeks and curvy bodies which they flaunted outside David's window. "Come out, saintly David, and see what you be missing by living the single life! There's kisses a-plenty out here!" They perched themselves on gates. They lounged against door posts. They rang the monastery bell and peeped in at the alms window. "Oh, *do* come out and look us over, boys! There are arms out here just waiting to hold you close!"

David saw them, and his mouth set in a hard, straight line. He kept on at his work. He behaved as if the naked ladies were no more of a nuisance than the sheep which roamed about the monastery buildings pushing their noses in at the doors. He outstared their brazen winks. He resisted their beckoning fingers. "The joys of this world, brothers, are no match for the joys of heaven," he told his monks.

And because he resisted the ladies, the other monks were able to do the same. For all the hardship of their solitary life, they loved God and their abbot enough to shun the pink maid-servants of Boia. Why, they had seen sights far more wonderful! They had seen flat ground heave itself upwards into a hill when David spoke, so that the crowds might hear him better. They had seen springs burst out of the ground at his command. They had seen the waters at Bath bubble hot with healing grace after David's blessing. They had seen the sick healed, and barbarians like Boia transformed into gentle lambs. His maid-servants could offer them nothing so miraculous. The girls shivered in the cold, put on their clothes and went home.

In time, Boia and his neighbours had cause to be glad they had not driven David out of the Vale of Roses. Famous for his wisdom and goodness, David made his little, sleepy corner of the world famous. He made it wise with his saintly wisdom, and peaceful by his saintly example. But not till after his death did David do them the greatest favour of all. Even from beyond the grave, he brought them victory over the Saxons.

In huge marauding hordes the Saxons came, and in skirmish after fray they fought the Britons. Though David was a man of peace, and would never have raised up a sword in anger, he gave his neighbours the best advice. "Wear a leek in your caps," he said.

"A leek?"

"A leek. There is nothing so Welsh as a leek, and the Saxons have no understanding of the magnificent nature of a leek."

It would be a badge – a mark by which a Briton, in the whirling madness of battle, could instantly recognize a fellow Briton. A man half-crazed with battle fever, half expecting at every second the slash of a blade to catch him unaware, lashes out at everyone who comes near. But in the great battle of 640, the Britons stuffed leeks in their caps, just as St David had taught them to do, and knew each other instantly on the battlefield. The Saxons (perhaps because they wore no distinguishing badge, perhaps because the prayers of St David confounded them) inflicted terrible wounds on each other and were defeated.

After the battle, the Welsh offered up thanks to St David (though he had been sleeping peacefully in his grave in the Vale of Roses for fifty years), named the day for him and declared David the patron saint of Wales.

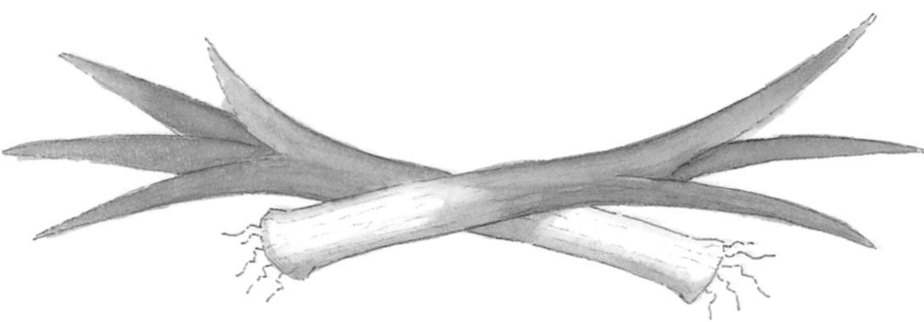

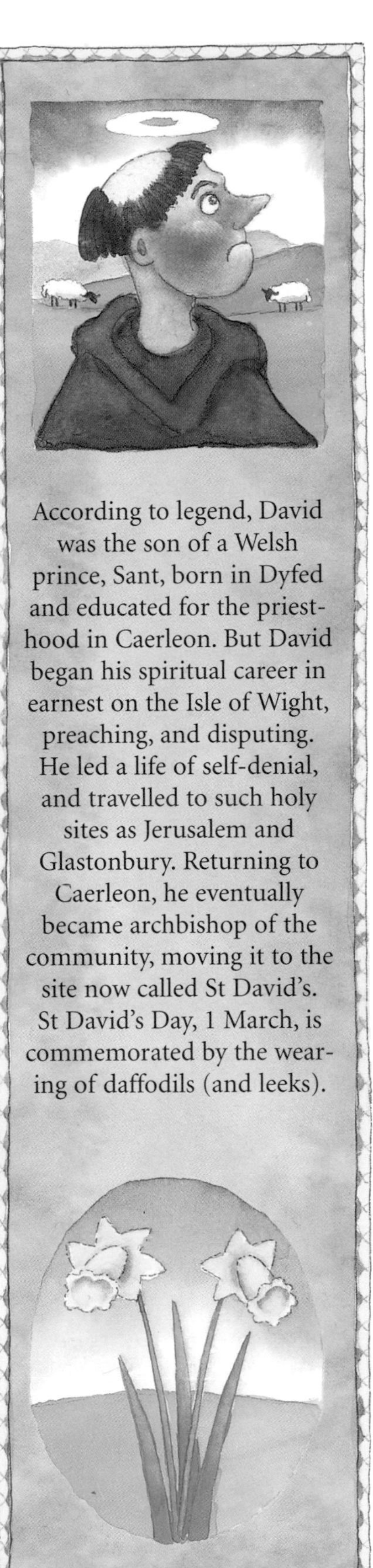

According to legend, David was the son of a Welsh prince, Sant, born in Dyfed and educated for the priesthood in Caerleon. But David began his spiritual career in earnest on the Isle of Wight, preaching, and disputing. He led a life of self-denial, and travelled to such holy sites as Jerusalem and Glastonbury. Returning to Caerleon, he eventually became archbishop of the community, moving it to the site now called St David's. St David's Day, 1 March, is commemorated by the wearing of daffodils (and leeks).

"Not Angles but Angels"

597

WITHIN THE MARKET PLACE IN ROME, SLAVES were just another commodity. Listless and afraid, chained and herded, they were on a par with the penned pigs or the chickens hung up by their feet. They were on sale. They were thirsty, too, under the hot Italian sun, and the flies pestered them. Among them today were foreign slaves whose blond hair glistened and glinted in the strong sunlight – an unusual sight among the swarthy, brown- and red-haired Romans.

Brother Gregory, walking through the market, commented to his companion on the beauty of the blond-haired slave children. "What is their nation?" he asked.

"They are Angles, Brother, from Britain."

"Not Angles but angels," joked Gregory. "They have angelic faces. Are they Christians?"

"No, Brother."

"What is the name of their king?"

"King Ella," came the reply.

"Then Ella-lujah shall be sung in their land!" quipped Gregory and his companion laughed indulgently. Gregory liked to pun. Fortunately, his sense of humour was not the best thing about him.

Gregory was renowned throughout Rome, not for his jokes but for his goodness and charity; he had the ear of the Pope himself. So taken was he with the angelic appearance of those Angle slaves that he went to the Pope now and asked to be sent as a missionary to convert their pagan island to Christianity. The Pope could not spare him – knew that Gregory was loved too much within the city for him to risk martyrdom in God-forsaken Angle-Land. His request was refused.

But Gregory remembered those blond-haired, blue-eyed children – nursed the memory even after the Pope was dead, even after Rome had elected *him* to the highest office in the world. Pope Gregory the Great summoned a Benedictine monk called Augustine and told him, "Take forty monks and travel to England with the good news of Christ!"

Halfway there, the forty lost their nerve. They wrote asking to come home, but Gregory answered them with a letter of such eloquence and fiery inspiration that they forged onward. Armed with a silver cross and a picture of Christ crucified, Augustine landed near Ramsgate, and invited King Ethelbert of Kent to hear him preach.

The King agreed to meet them, but only in the open air, wary of the evil magic that might be practised on him indoors.

Augustine used no evil magic. Even so, within months Kentishmen and women were flocking to hear the Benedictines preach and to be baptized. Soon after Ethelbert himself knelt at Augustine's feet for baptism, one thousand of his subjects were baptized in a single day. In pairs they waded out into the River Swale, one sinking the other beneath the water as Augustine bellowed his blessing from the bank. Whole families walked into the Swale that day and waded out again Christians.

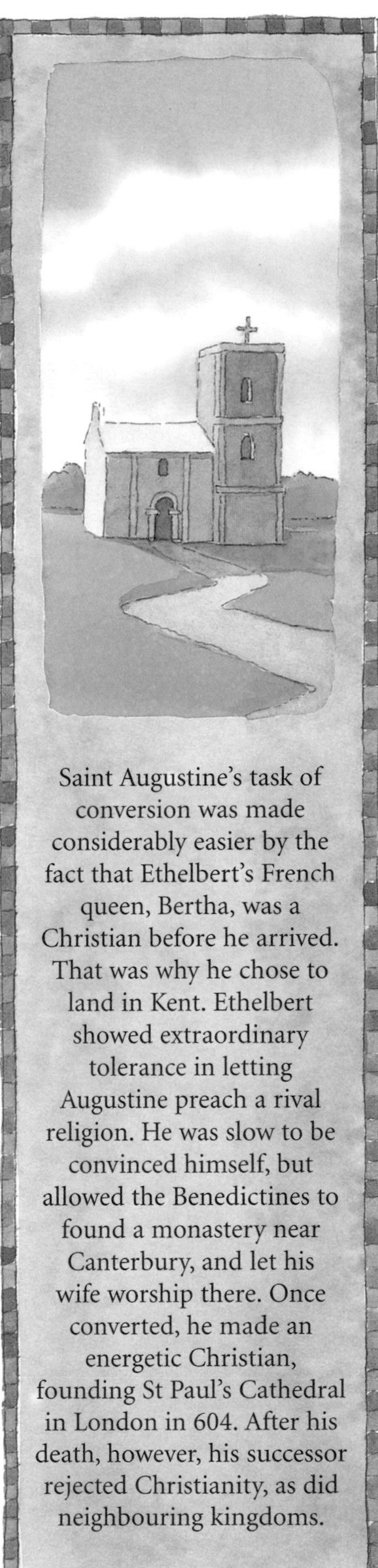

Saint Augustine's task of conversion was made considerably easier by the fact that Ethelbert's French queen, Bertha, was a Christian before he arrived. That was why he chose to land in Kent. Ethelbert showed extraordinary tolerance in letting Augustine preach a rival religion. He was slow to be convinced himself, but allowed the Benedictines to found a monastery near Canterbury, and let his wife worship there. Once converted, he made an energetic Christian, founding St Paul's Cathedral in London in 604. After his death, however, his successor rejected Christianity, as did neighbouring kingdoms.

King Arthur and his Questing Knights

6th century

King Arthur's fabled court at Camelot stood on the fringes of the Summer Land, not far from the Island of Glass. Raised and educated by the prophet-magician Merlin, and armed with a magical sword Excalibur, Arthur set about freeing his kingdom from evil and the forces of darkness. To that end, he assembled the finest knights in the land. So that they would not quarrel about which of them was the grandest or highest ranking, he seated them at a great round table.

Giants and dragons were slaughtered, maidens were rescued and quests were mounted. But the greatest quest of all was to find the Holy Grail.

An image of that cup, which Christ had used at the Last Supper, which Joseph of Arimathea had brought to the Summer Land and hidden in a secret place, which none but the pure of heart would be allowed to find – showed itself one feast-day to the knights of the Round Table. Immediately the knights took it for a sign that they should go questing in search of the real thing.

Sir Gawain searched, but gave up. Sir Lancelot searched, but could not find it because his heart was not pure enough. But Galahad his son, along with Sir Bors and Sir Perceval, came at last to the mysterious castle of Corbenic, where, in a radiance of light, Jesus Christ Himself appeared to them. Amid the sound of English birdsong, Christ gave them bread and wine, then entrusted them with the very cup from which they had just drunk: the Holy Grail.

The happiness of that moment broke Galahad's heart like a loaf of bread; Perceval devoted himself to a life of prayer, and Bors returned to recount the story to his fellow knights.

But the Golden Age of King Arthur was over within a few short years. In gathering together all the good knights, Arthur had driven the forces of evil to unite in a single, menacing army. The fate of Albion had to be settled by one last battle.

In the water-threaded Summer Lands, man by man, the knights of the Round Table fought and died. The black-armoured knights of treachery and sin and greed were all killed, but at terrible cost. Only the good Sir Bedivere was left standing and, lying wounded at his feet, Arthur, clenching the last minutes of his life like sand in his fist.

"Carry me to those woods," he told Bedivere. "There is something I must do before I die." A stretch of water glinted through the trees. Arthur was desperate to reach it, but his wounds were too deep. "Take my sword," he told Bedivere. "Take Excalibur, and throw it into the water."

"*Excalibur?*" Bedivere was appalled.

He stood by the waterside, his feet in the soft, oozing black mud, and the sword in his hands. But the sheer beauty of that shining blade, that elaborate jewelled hilt, seemed far too marvellous to sink in fathomless muddy water.

He hid the sword and went back.

"What did you see when you threw it?" asked Arthur.

"I saw the moorhens run and the ripples spread," said Bedivere with a shrug.

"Then go back and take the sword from where you hid it and *do as I commanded you!*" raged the King, his eyes bloodshot with fury.

Bedivere meant to do it, he really did. He ran to the reeds and pulled out Excalibur. But the sword had such memories for him – such happy memories! Soon Arthur would be dead. Was there to be nothing left to show for the court of Camelot, the Golden Age? Again he hid the sword, and hurried back, fearful the King would die alone.

"What did you see?" whispered Arthur.

"I saw the fish scatter and the reeds shake."

"*Villain! Traitor! Liar! Must I do the job myself?*" Arthur tried to get up, but fell back in agony. Bedivere took to his heels and ran – back to the waterside, scrabbling in among the reeds. Swinging the sword round his head, he flung it, letting fall a sob of effort and misery.

But just before the expected splash, a woman's hand rose from the heart of the lake and caught Excalibur by the hilt. Three times it brandished the blade, slicing the moonbeams. Then Arthur's sword sank, drawn down out of sight.

A Romano-British war-lord named Arturus, living in the west of England, is mentioned in Welsh chronicles, a fighter of notable courage against invading Saxons.

Most Arthurian legends originate, however, from the Age of Chivalry in the eleventh and twelfth centuries, when various "literary" writers recreated him in a complex cycle of stories, none of which is likely to be true. They required a Christian figure of courtly character, pitting himself against evil. There had to be a romantic element – romantic love was just being invented – and a code of knighthood (which did not even exist in the era when Arthur supposedly lived). A body of ancient Celtic myths has become interwoven with the Arthurian legend. In it Merlin is an important figure.

Extensive efforts have been made to site Camelot, but these are driven more by romantic wishful thinking than archaeological probability.

Arthur saw from Bedivere's face that his order had been carried out, his loan repaid to the Lady of the Lake. He sank into semi-consciousness, and Bedivere knelt over him, listening for the King's last breath.

Then the sound of oars behind him made him start to his feet. Through the trees came three women, veiled and with their hands drawn up inside their broad sleeves.

"So. It is time," they said to Bedivere. "He has earned his rest." They carried the King, with the greatest ease, aboard a low black craft moored among the reeds.

"Where are you taking him?" cried Bedivere distractedly. "Have some pity, won't you? Let him die in peace!"

"Die?" said the women. "He is sleeping. After such a life, is he not entitled to sleep? When Albion needs him, he will come back, never fear." Then each woman took hold of an oar and they rowed away, into the veiling vapours which evening had drawn up from the sodden landscape.

And where did they take him? To Avalon. A land of magic.

But where is Avalon? Why, it is the Island of Glass, of course. Or if not that island, some place very like it.

When Bedivere retraced his steps, the battlefield still lay strewn with dead. But the Knights of Arthur were all gone – all gone to Avalon to sleep alongside their king, heads pillowed on blossom petals from the Holy Thorn, sipping, in their dreams, from the Holy Grail, until their next summons to arms.

These days, the waters have drained away from the Island of Glass. But the hill is the same hill, the earth of the hill the same earth, the secrets of the hill the same well-kept secrets. Kestrels still hover, and the magic still clings.

Fleeting Glory

726

"A SHIP! A SHIP HAS struck the rocks, Father!" cried the fisherman's daughter above the howling wind. Dafyd leapt up and ran outdoors. The wind which met him was full of sea spray and cries, and fragments of rigging like twigs blown off a tree.

The ship in the bay lay on its side, surf crashing down on it likc fists. "Help me, with the rowing boat!" Dafyd told his daughter, "or many a good man will drown tonight!"

Twenty men they dragged from the water by the scruff of the neck. Each frozen face spluttered thanks in some strange, un-Welsh tongue. At last the hulk settled and disintegrated under the strengthening daylight. Dafyd sent his daughter over the hill to fetch a monk to speak words over the dead.

Back at the hut, huddled by the fire, one of the survivors in particular seemed to command the respect of the others. All eyes were on him when he spoke.

"Reckon he's the captain," said Dafyd to his wife, "for all he doesn't look much."

The monk laughed at the simplicity of the fisherman. "O ignorant man! Do you not know English when you hear it spoken?" he said, and went to ask this "captain" who he was. A moment later he came reeling back and sat down on a crab pot. "By the saints!" he gasped (in Welsh). "D'you know what you've done, Dafyd? You've only saved the King of Wessex, that's all! You've only rescued King Ine of Wessex!"

"Oh yes?" responded the fisherman dubiously. "And where's Wessex, then?"

King Ine, spared from an early death, spent a great deal of time at his prayers after that. He founded a church on that bleak Cardiganshire coast, in thanksgiving, and he was an altogether devout and Christian king. His queen was equally saintly, and looked forward to the time when (as was the practice in those days) King Ine would resign his crown to a younger man and live out his life in prayer and contemplation.

She was to be disappointed. Ine might be a good king, but he was also a persistent one. Having grown used to power, he did not welcome the idea of giving it up. "Another month or two," he told his wife. "Just until I am content they can manage without me." But the months passed and still Ine held the reins of power, forever travelling from castle to castle, forever checking that his orders were being carried out.

After one particularly lavish night of feasting, he once again set out for yet another corner of the kingdom. He grumbled when the Queen asked them all to turn back. "There is something I forgot," she said.

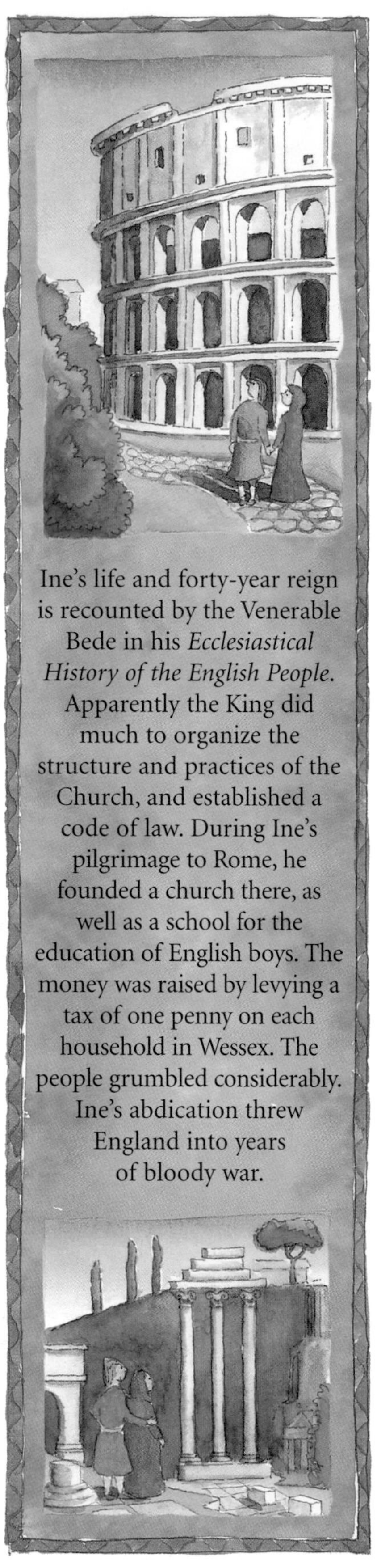

Ine's life and forty-year reign is recounted by the Venerable Bede in his *Ecclesiastical History of the English People.* Apparently the King did much to organize the structure and practices of the Church, and established a code of law. During Ine's pilgrimage to Rome, he founded a church there, as well as a school for the education of English boys. The money was raised by levying a tax of one penny on each household in Wessex. The people grumbled considerably. Ine's abdication threw England into years of bloody war.

"I have things to do. Affairs of state! You really must not delay like this, wife," Ine complained, but the Queen insisted. They retraced their steps to the castle.

The banners and pennants had gone from the walls. The minstrels had been paid off and gone. Litter from the feast lay strewn around the yard and the great hall, and dogs were chewing on bones amid the dirty strewings. Chickens pecked up and down the long table where, the night before, roast swans had stood amid custards and sweetmeats. Worst of all, on the couch where King Ine and his Queen had reclined to eat, a gigantic sow was lying on her side with a dozen piglets suckling.

"Someone will pay for this!" raged Ine. "Is this the esteem I am held in? Who is responsible for this disgrace?" He glanced around him at the carls and serfs, but they only looked at the Queen.

"What's the matter, my lord?" she asked innocently. "Did you expect to leave a trail of lasting glamour behind you, after you were gone? Did you think one night's pomp and splendour would fend off dirt and decay for ever? Our feast last night was like the rule of a good king – one brief span of glory. But everything passes. Everything decays. Every king will one day be reduced to a pile of forgotten bones. Life is so fleeting."

Many men, when lectured by their wives like this, would have called it nagging. But standing there in that squalid hall, Ine suddenly glimpsed the scale of eternity, and the absurdity of kingly pomp. His lifetime was nothing but one grain of sand in a sand dune of lives, and he had already wasted too much of it fretting about detail.

So although Ine realized that his queen had deliberately staged the pigs, the dogs, the litter, he took her lesson to heart. Soon afterwards, he resigned his crown to a younger man. He made a pilgrimage to Rome, then cut off his hair, and lived like a poor peasant for the rest of his life, working with his hands, thinking, praying and, of course, talking to his wife about the things which really matter.

Offa's Shame

794

IT IS ONLY NATURAL THAT A BRIDEGROOM SHOULD be nervous. But as King Ethelbert stepped out-of-doors and walked towards his horse, his legs shook, he staggered and almost fell. The waiting horses bolted, sending wedding gifts and bundles of clothing tumbling to the ground. Thatching slumped from the roofs. It was not Ethelbert who was trembling, but the earth itself. Dust rose so thickly that, for an hour, night returned.

"It is a bad omen, son," said his mother. "Do not go to Mercia!"

The King of East Anglia laughed. "It would be bad luck indeed not to marry the fairest maid in Christendom! When I take the Princess Alfleda for a wife, Anglia shall be united with Mercia and I shall be the happiest of men. If this is an omen, Mother, it is sent to some greater man than me."

Meanwhile, in the next-door kingdom, another woman wept and turned her face to the wall. "I tell you my poor heart will break! I shall never know another moment's happiness if this wedding takes place!"

King Offa slapped his forehead. "But what would you have me do, lady? My word is given! The betrothal is made. My daughter Alfleda is promised to Ethelbert. He is on his way here to marry her, even now! Why should they not wed?"

Pale and anguished, Queen Drida dabbed away tears. "It should be enough that I ask it," she said, and bit her beautiful blood-red lip.

A hundred miles away, sleeping on the cold ground under a snow shower of stars, King Ethelbert screamed in his sleep. He dreamed that his mother stood at the foot of a big double bed, weeping tears of blood. The tears splashed on to the sheets of the bed, while an armed man swung an axe over and over again, splintering the canopy, the legs, the footboard, splitting the mattress till the air was snowy with feathers. He knew it was his bed, too: his bridal bed.

Never before had the spoiled Queen Drida striven so hard to get her way. It made her sulky that Offa begrudged her what she asked. "Alfleda is too good for this yokel king!" said Drida. "There are far greater men over the ocean for her to marry. I will not have her wasted on a fenland peasant!"

"Silence, Drida," said Offa. "I have accepted the man's gifts and promised him my daughter's hand. Say no more about it. My mind is made up."

Queen Drida did hold her tongue – bit into it with sharp little teeth and kept silent. But the ambition did not die within her, nor her determination to stop the marriage.

White-faced for want of sleep, grimy and dishevelled from his journey, King Ethelbert of Anglia smiled broadly at the sight of Offa's castle. Here was the home of his beautiful bride. Tomorrow he would marry Alfleda. He was a truly lucky man.

As he stepped in at the door of Offa's throne room, he hesitated. There was an uneasy atmosphere. The Queen was looking steadfastly at the floor. But Offa opened his arms in welcome, beaming with delight: "Come in, son-in-law! Come in and welcome!" Two long tables groaned under joints of meat, custards, sweetmeats and cakes. Ethelbert took his place at the feast, and Alfleda sat down beside him, birdlike and delicate. The double doors closed against the weather, and a bolt shot home.

Hours later, flushed with wine and laughing with joy, Ethelbert was shown to his room by the Queen. It was luxurious, with a curtained bed, tapestries on the wall and, at the centre of the room, a vast chair piled with down-filled cushions. Ethelbert thanked the Queen over and over again: "Such a welcome . . . such a feast . . . such a fine, comfortable room." This was the last night he would retire to bed alone: tomorrow he would be sharing his dreams with the lovely Alfleda. Weary and overfed, he flung himself down in the great chair.

Lurching backwards and sideways, the chair twisted and buckled. Then it plunged through a jagged hole in the thin planks which had been supporting it. Down it fell into darkness, into the musty, hollow darkness of a hidden well. Ethelbert saw the room's light recede to a smaller and smaller circle, then the chair struck the bottom of the well and splintered under him. The fall broke his bones, knocked all the wind out of him. But finding himself alive, Ethelbert began to yell for help.

He was heard, too. Queen Drida's hired men came out of hiding and ran to the brink of the pit. They brandished triumphant fists, like hunters who have snared a bear. Then as he went on shouting – "Get me out! Pull me up! For pity's sake, help me!" – they began to throw things down on to him – the bedspread, the sheets, the pillows. They ripped apart the bed and threw it down, bit by bit, on to Ethelbert. Soon no more sound came from the well.

"Haul up the body, cut off his head, and bury him somewhere out of the way," said Queen Drida.

Offa no sooner learned what his wife had done, than the servants came running to him in terror, speaking of lights shining in the dark – lights which hovered over a piece of newly turned earth, lights marking a murdered man's grave. Offa went to see for himself, and sure enough, lights hung like altar candles over the place where the body and head of King Ethelbert had been hurriedly crammed underground. In a guilty panic, Offa told the servants to bury the remains somewhere else, before the lights attracted attention. But within hours the men were back, banging on his door, shouting in hoarse whispers that the lights were shining now over the new burial place.

That was when the real terror began – the guilt which troubled Offa's sleeping and waking hours. "Drida, you have made a murderer of me!" he said. "You and your scheming and ambition! How will we ever be clean of this good man's blood?"

The Queen gave a petulant shrug.

Offa covered his head with his hands. "But Drida! Alfleda loved him! She *wanted* to marry him. And now he is dead!"

In the course of his long reign (almost forty years), Offa expanded his kingdom from Mercia to encompass Kent, Sussex, Wessex and East Anglia, making him the most powerful monarch prior to AD 1000. He called himself *rex Anglorum*: the King of the English. Versions of the story of Ethelbert and Alfleda (or Alfrida) vary so widely that there is probably little truth in the details. In another telling, a nobleman called Winebert beheads Ethelbert the moment he steps through Offa's door. But quite possibly Offa did assassinate this rival monarch for political reasons. The murdered King was certainly declared a saint. The achievement for which Offa is best remembered is the building of a 100-kilometre-long earthwork – Offa's Dyke – as a defence against Welsh raiders with whom he spent his whole time at war. After his death, his kingdom fragmented again.

Again that pettish shrug. "She's not my daughter, she's yours. I never liked her. Why should that simpering girl get what she wants? Do I? What has she ever done to deserve a beautiful young man like that? She's always been a thorn in my side, with her sheep's eyes and praying hands and hair like a yard of weak ale. I cannot abide her. Better she should be married to someone far away. On the other side of the . . ."

Offa did not stay to hear more. He ran from the room, sickened by the jealousy of his spoiled wife. He ran to his Bible, but found no comfort there. He ran to his confessor, but his confessor blanched white as a ghost. Offa's conscience was as bad as if he had done the deed himself. His dreams ran red with blood. The eerie, hovering lights beckoned him back time and time again to the place where Ethelbert lay; they even escorted the body as Offa removed it to a place of honour in Hereford Cathedral.

So ignoring his wife's shrill complaints, Offa set off on a journey far longer than Ethelbert's. He set off for Rome, to do penance for the death of an innocent man and to beg forgiveness from the Pope. And when he returned, he could be found, on many and many a day, crouched beside the dead King's tomb, recounting all that he had seen and done in the Eternal City.

The bronze likeness of the young dead King listened, holding his severed head in his lap, erect and serene, though with an expression of wistful sadness, perhaps at all pleasures of life which he had died too soon to enjoy.

The Kingly Martyr

869

INSTEAD OF WHITE GULLS, BLACK RAVENS WERE flying that summer over the eastern coast: the raven banners of Vikings. They swooped in across the ocean and gorged on Christian blood. Monasteries were sacked for the sake of their holy treasures, and villages burned for the sheer pleasure of destruction. Only King Edmund of East Anglia stood between his people and the Vikings. But Edmund's faith burned within him like the candle in the sanctuary which, by day or night, never goes out. He did not believe for a moment that God would suffer the true religion of Christ to be snuffed out by pagans.

So, as the Viking cleavers sliced through the November air, and the banner of the cross fell to an unkindness of ravens, what thoughts passed through the King's mind? He was defeated. His knights lay dead around him. His own life was at the mercy of a Viking warlord.

The Viking leader eyed his prisoner like a bird of prey. His eyes were paler than water. He had a certain respect for the King of this flat, damp, fertile kingdom. "You fought well. You are not dishonoured by defeat, King Edmund. I may yet spare your life."

No change of expression crossed Edmund's battle-weary face, but a flicker of hope must have kindled painfully in his heart.

"Yes, you shall go free – why not?" said his captor, spreading his hands in a gesture of generosity. "Just forswear that milksop religion of yours and honour the Norse warrior gods who overthrew you today."

Edmund's head dropped forward. "I will never renounce my faith in Christ Jesus."

The pale yellow moustache rucked into a sneer, and the Viking slouched sideways in his chair. "Take him out and let the archers put him to some use."

Edmund was dragged roughly away, the guards snatching off his cuirass and shirt as they went. They tied him to a tree, and he saw the Viking archers restringing their longbows. It was late November: his bare limbs jumped with cold.

"There is still time to change banners!" called the man with pale blue eyes. "What has he ever done for you, this Christ? This Jesus Christ?"

"He has blessed my soul with bliss, as I pray He will one day bless yours," said Edmund. "I forgive you this spilling of my blood."

The Viking leader turned away with disgust and vexation. As he went, he could hear the whisk of arrows through the leaves, the thud of arrowheads sinking into the tree's trunk. Then the archers found their distance, and began to hit their mark. It gave him no satisfaction.

The name of Bury St Edmunds bears witness to the final place of the martyred king. His bones were moved there after a miracle cult grew up around his memory. He was probably about twenty-nine years old when he died.

Tradition has it that King Offa, who had no son of his own, adopted Edmund, the son of a Frankish king, to be his heir. Little else is known about him.

When the arrows had finally killed Edmund, his head was cut off, and the Vikings moved on to lay waste to more kingdoms. The King's followers, reeling with horror, despair and fatigue, emerged from hiding. But though they were able to cut down the body bristling with arrows, they could not find his head. For days they searched, but without success.

As they combed Eglesdane Wood one last time, a voice called out: "*Over here!*" Everyone asked everyone else. "Was that you?"

Then the voice came again. "*I am here! This way! Over here!*" Their hair stood on end.

Following the voice, they came to a clearing. Then a dozen men gasped and froze, their hands on their sword hilts. There stood a huge wolf, grey as winter, its front paws straddling the bloody head, its lower jaw resting on the pale forehead of the martyr-King. They waited for it to spring, but the wolf backed grudgingly away from its prize, as though it had merely been waiting for them to come. A page darted forward and grabbed up the head, but the wolf did not move to recapture it, nor to run away. Hastily the King's party beat back through the woods. Walking, they broke into a run as they realized the wolf was dogging their footsteps, keeping the scent of them in its nostrils, watching them with its yellow eyes. But they got back safely to the body of the dead King. Now he could be laid to rest.

They took him to Hoxne. And every time they looked back, the wolf was still following, loping along after the horses, melting into the trees if they reined in.

Word of Edmund's death was spreading – not of his defeat, but of his marvellous courage, his saintly faith. Edmund their king had gone to join the saints. Now there was one more saint in heaven to watch over the people of Anglia.

As the sorry remains, body and head, were lowered into the grave, an uninvited guest stood watching from the church lych-gate. With watchful eyes, the wolf observed the laying to rest of the dead King. Only then did it turn and lope back into the forest whose trees, in the rising wind, whispered a thousand prayers for the soul of St Edmund.

Alfred and the Cakes

878

ALFRED THE GREAT OF WESSEX HAD FOR HIS ancestors three of the ancient Saxon gods: Woden, Sceaf and Geat. So when Saxon Britain began to fall, field by town, to the invading Danes, Alfred and his brother Aethelred went out to fight them. In 871, at the battle of Ashdown, the marauders were routed for the first time.

It was a hard won victory. Though their muscles should have ached with exhaustion, success lent the Saxon troops new energy. They set about hewing and gouging the hillside nearby as they had hewn and gouged the Danes, carving out the shape of a gigantic white horse in the chalkstone, for future generations to see and remember.

But the Danes came back again and again. They killed Aethelred and cowed the Saxons to such an extent that they abandoned their king. Along with a few loyal men, Alfred alone held out against them, a mysterious figure living a shifting, ghostly life, haunting the countryside, emerging from hiding to attack the Danes.

By 878, things were going so badly that Alfred's pocket army was confined to the Isle of Athelney in the middle of the Summer Land. Their shelter was in turf cottages and their food was bread made from acorns grubbed from under the spreading oak trees.

Alfred sought shelter from a local man – a cowherd – and asked whether he might sleep a night or two at his house.

"By all that's holy, my little place ain no fit shelter for a king, sire! But you'z honour me and the wife past all speaking, if you'z see fit to sleep under our roof!"

Denewulf was not exaggerating: his little turf-roofed house was mean and small and bare. But Alfred was simply glad to be out of the rain. He had no fear for his safety among these good people: they were all ready to lay down their lives for the Saxon cause. This cowherd, for instance. He would return the man's loyalty if ever it were within his power to do so.

With much bowing and blushing – "My wife – where is the silly woman? – she'll make you some food – prepare you up a bed" – Denewulf seated Alfred on a rush stool in front of the fire and dashed away again to try to find his wife and tell her the wonderful honour which had befallen them. Alfred spread out his great swordsman's hands to warm them at the grate.

"What you'm doing in here soaking up th'heat?" asked an imperious voice behind him.

Alfred turned round and caught his first sight of the cowherd's wife. "Your husband said I might stay here for a while."

"Oh yes, that be typical of 'im, the lummock." The woman had never seen a king before. She did not see a king now – only some mud-stained, unkempt ragamuffin with leaves in his hair, sitting on her best rush stool. "Well, you'm best make yourself useful. Can you do that?" she snapped. "Shake the blankets? Sweep out the straw?"

The King had never been asked such a thing before. "I expect so."

Alfred was dog-tired, but he was also a gentleman. So he did as he was told, and thanked the lady when she brought him a bite of food. Her manners were not quite those of a royal valet, nor was bread and cheese exactly a banquet, but Alfred was used to less. He realized that the woman had no idea who he was.

He marvelled at the bareness of her existence – the few sticks of furniture, the empty store cupboard, the single cooking pot. But he marvelled, too, at the way she could whip up an egg, a spoon of flour and honey into a cake-mix, and set the little scones to bake on a griddle over a twig fire.

"Now you'm watch them cakes and don't you'm take youz eyes off 'em, or I'll have words to say!" barked the woman. "I have to milk the cows. Someone has to . . . And *no nibbling*, you hear?" were her parting words.

Alfred smiled to himself, then settled down in front of the hearth, legs stretched out, and watched the cakes. Little bubbles rose up to the surface of each scone and popped with a sigh. They swelled, as if with Saxon pride . . .

As he sat, Alfred sank into thinking, remembering the bad times, remembering the good.

One day, in the forests, he had come across a lady in blue standing very still in a downshaft of sunlight. "Are you lost, lady?" he had asked. But when she turned towards him, he had known in an instant, with absolute certainty, that he was looking at Mary, mother of Jesus, at the Holy

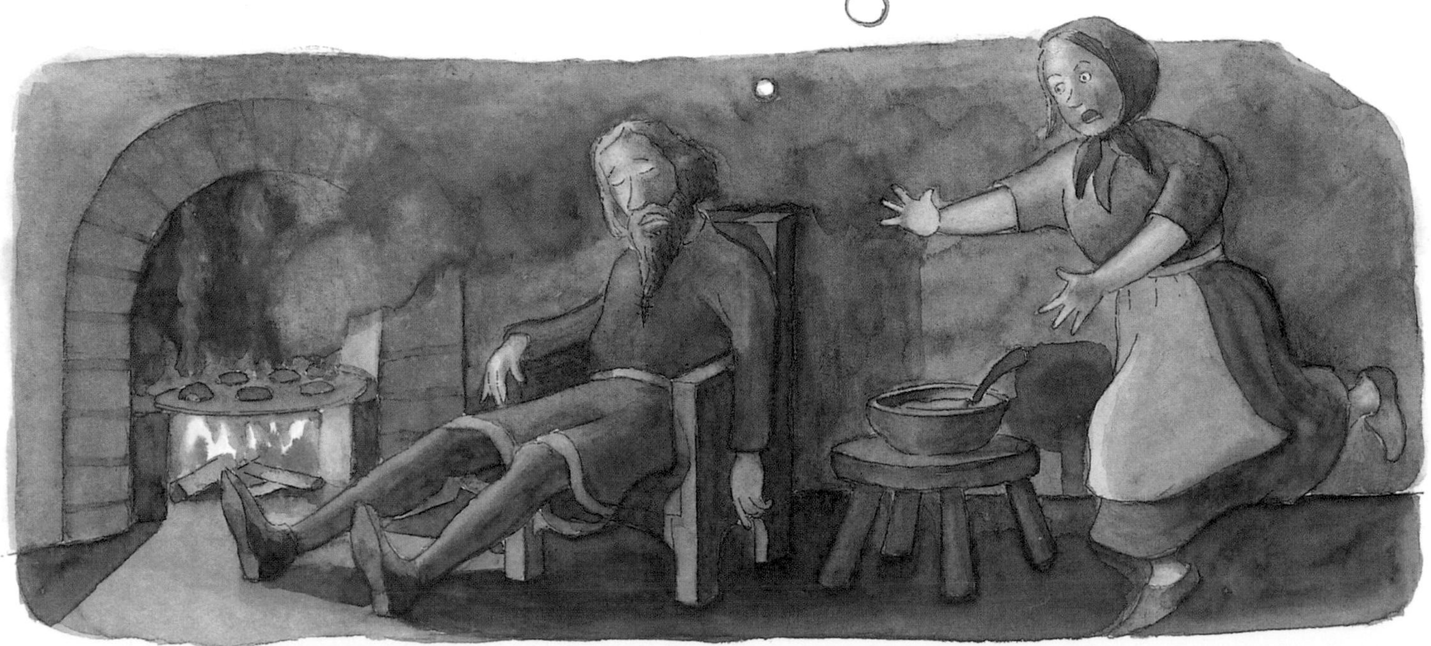

Madonna herself. Speechless with awe, Alfred had done the only thing his wits would allow, and cast at her feet the most precious object he was carrying – his jewelled cloak pin. Before disappearing like a summer mirage, the lady had opened her lips and said . . .

"You goon! You great lazy, idle, good-for-nothing lummock! You let my cakes burn!" Alfred slipped off his stool in waking and peered around him: the hut was oddly dark. It seemed to be full of smoke. "You great hulking fool of a wet Wednesday! What you got for brains, frogspawn or mud?" Six smouldering little cakes reproached him from the griddle, as black and brittle as charcoal.

"I'm –"

"I know what *you* be," the woman went on. "Anyone can see what *you* be! You be your mother's greatest shame and your father's worst mistake! You be a wet cloud looking for someone like me to rain on! What *you* be is –"

"The King of Wessex," said a voice behind her. Her husband, the cowherd, stood in the doorway, paler than the pail of milk he was carrying. But it was not he who had spoken. It was one of the officers behind him, cloaks thrown back off their mail shirts, swords drawn. The woman's mouth froze in mid-word. "Son of Aethelwulf," the officer went on. "Kin to the gods Woden, Sceaf and Geat; Lord of Wessex. What shall I do with her, sire?"

The woman's mouth still spoke its small, silent "O". Her eyes filled with tears. Now she would be hanged, and her hut burned down, and her husband's cattle forfeit to the army. Now she would be cursed by her neighbours, remembered as the shrew who had bad-mouthed the greatest man in England. She fell to her knees and curled her body into a crouching bow. She could find no words to excuse her offence.

Alfred picked up a cake and burnt his fingers doing it. He smiled to himself and then at the others. "Why, help her to her feet, man! She's perfectly right! This good woman left me to mind her cakes, and I let them burn. She's quite right – I am a fool! Shall I hang her for telling me the simple truth? Here, madam." He pulled out his purse. "Here's recompense for the cakes, and a little something for your . . . honest and fearless nature. Now gentlemen! Let's sit and discuss what can be done to pull England from the fire before she burns, shall we?"

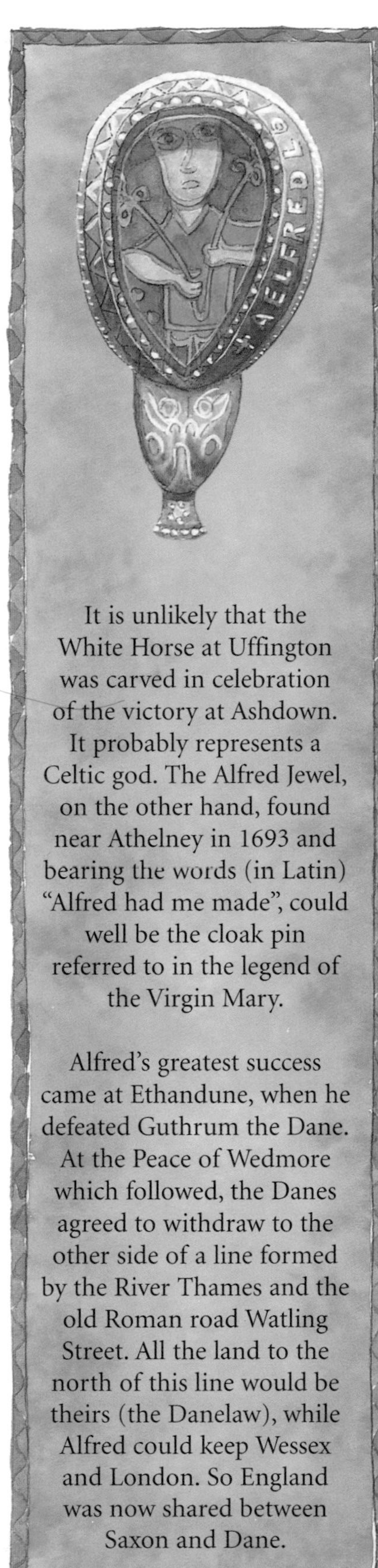

It is unlikely that the White Horse at Uffington was carved in celebration of the victory at Ashdown. It probably represents a Celtic god. The Alfred Jewel, on the other hand, found near Athelney in 1693 and bearing the words (in Latin) "Alfred had me made", could well be the cloak pin referred to in the legend of the Virgin Mary.

Alfred's greatest success came at Ethandune, when he defeated Guthrum the Dane. At the Peace of Wedmore which followed, the Danes agreed to withdraw to the other side of a line formed by the River Thames and the old Roman road Watling Street. All the land to the north of this line would be theirs (the Danelaw), while Alfred could keep Wessex and London. So England was now shared between Saxon and Dane.

Dunstan and the Devil

about 980

THERE WAS A MAN WHO LIVED through the reigns of eight kings, and lent his advice to six of them. Small wonder that kings and nobles held no dread for him. St Dunstan was of the opinion that God was on his side, and that made him a dangerous man to cross. His enemies said he dabbled in the black arts – and that made him more dangerous still.

As a young man, he was by trade a blacksmith – or perhaps it was merely a hobby of his, for later, when King Edmund made him Abbot of Glastonbury, he set up a forge in a little stone cell projecting from the outer wall of the abbey and would go there, by way of relaxation, to forge horseshoes and pokers and scythes. Local people would call on him and ask him, "Make me this, Father Abbot," or "Make me that."

One day an uncommonly pretty woman came and fluttered her lashes at Dunstan, asking if he would make her a toasting fork. While he worked, she moved about the room – a flick of the hips, a flash of the eyes, a smile. But Dunstan kept his eyes firmly on his work. The hammer clanged down. Sparks exploded: there was a smell of sulphur. The woman became still more daring, brushing up against him, fingering his tonsure. It was only as she stepped over a hammer on the floor that her skirts lifted, and Dunstan glimpsed her feet.

Lifting his blacksmith's tongs red-hot from the furnace, he reached out with them – and seized the woman by the nose!

How she shrieked and screamed. But Dunstan did not let go. How she altered into a mottled, bent old crone gripped in the lips of the red-hot pincers. But still Dunstan did not let go. Now she was not even female, but a sooty writhing fellow roaring and trumpeting in the grip of the tongs. But Dunstan still did not let go – no, not even when the Devil himself was dancing in front of Dunstan on his two cloven hooves.

"You should not have let me see your feet," said Dunstan smiling grimly. Then he threw the Devil out of the window, just as the bells rang for vespers.

The Devil was a fool, really, to approach Dunstan in the shape of a woman. For women were not a breed St Dunstan much cared for. In those days, it was the custom for certain orders of priests to marry and have families. But Dunstan thought the whole priesthood should stay unmarried. The arguments had been dragging on, bitter and unresolved, for many years when, one day, a meeting took place in an upstairs room at Calne in Wiltshire.

Opinions were equally split. It was hard to see how a final decision could be reached. Dunstan closed the proceedings. "We shall never agree, so I say, let the decision rest with Christ Jesus Himself!"

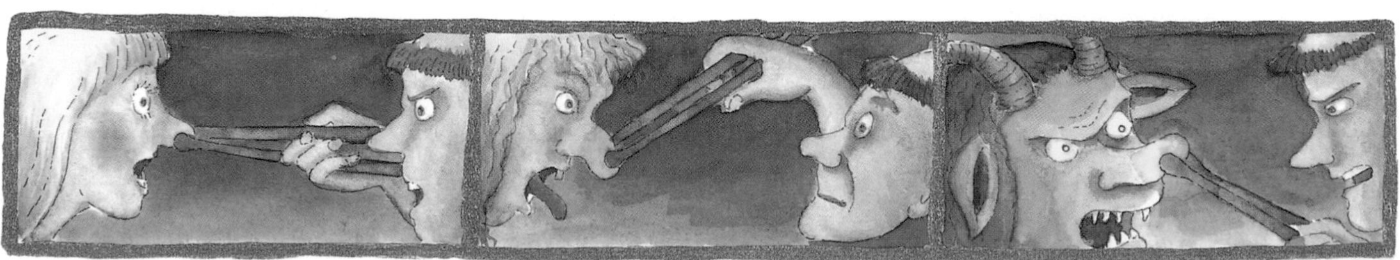

There was an ominous groaning of timbers. Then a large portion of the floor suddenly fell away, and the long central table listed and slid through the hole like a sinking ship, carrying with it everyone on one side of the room.

It was a long drop. In the room below, some lay trapped under the table or under fallen roofbeams. Some staggered ghostly white from the ruins, showered with plaster. Dunstan and his followers, however, were left in the upper room, like angels looking down on the chaos below.

Dunstan's enemies said he had sabotaged the floor. Dunstan said that God had taken a hand. And even if dry rot were really to blame, still Dunstan carried the day. Marriage was forbidden to the clergy.

Not that some monks cared what Dunstan said. Some monks did not give a fig for the holy life or their vows of poverty and virtue. The monks of Middle Fen, for instance. Their lives were as easy and pleasant as they could make them, and they never gave God or religion a thought from one day's end to the next. Their wives and children, sweethearts and friends all lived together in the abbey which stood on an island in the midst of Middle Fen – a rowdy, lawless rabble with wine-stains on their habits and money on their minds.

But Dunstan came down on them like the wrath of God. No sermons or penances. No fines or trials. He simply turned them into eels, every one, and emptied them into the rivers and dikes and ponds and marshes of the fenland. That's why the place is called Ely – the place of eels – and why Dunstan is better remembered than any of the kings he served.

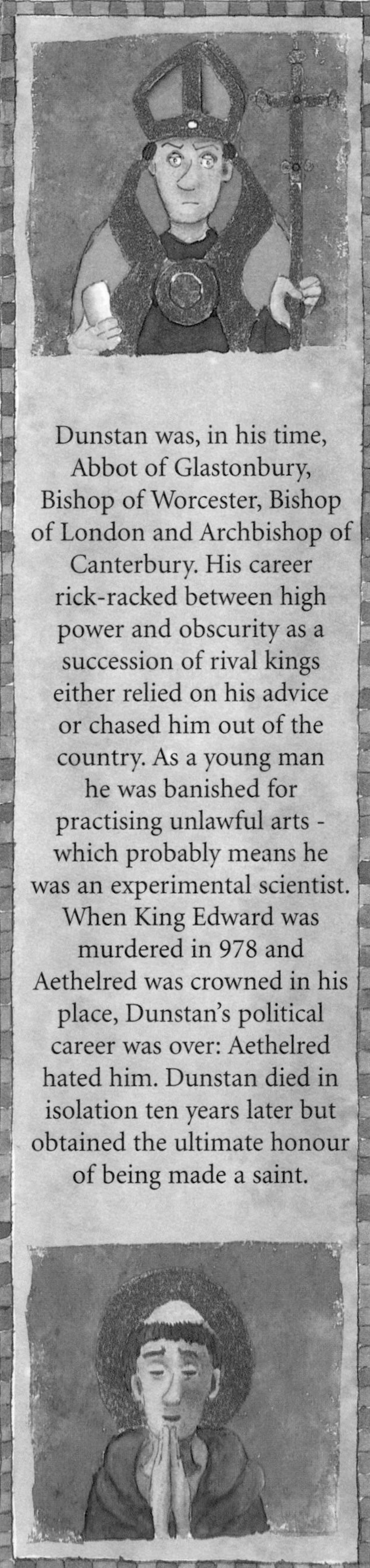

Dunstan was, in his time, Abbot of Glastonbury, Bishop of Worcester, Bishop of London and Archbishop of Canterbury. His career rick-racked between high power and obscurity as a succession of rival kings either relied on his advice or chased him out of the country. As a young man he was banished for practising unlawful arts - which probably means he was an experimental scientist. When King Edward was murdered in 978 and Aethelred was crowned in his place, Dunstan's political career was over: Aethelred hated him. Dunstan died in isolation ten years later but obtained the ultimate honour of being made a saint.

London Bridge is Falling Down

1013 and 1016

"THE VIKINGS ARE COMING! THE VIKINGS are coming!"

The cry had echoed so often up the river reaches, and yet it never failed to terrify. London was the great prize in the game, and London was being captured and recaptured now like a carcass of meat wrangled over by lions.

In 1013, King Swayne the Dane had taken the city from King Ethelred, but Ethelred was determined to take it back. He enlisted the help of King Olaf of Norway, and sailed up the Thames estuary – more dragon-headed ships lunging upstream, more cries of "The Vikings are coming!"

Swayne was ready for them. His men were massed on London Bridge, at their feet lay huge cairns of rock for pelting the attacking ships. There were archers, too, and spear-wielders.

But Ethelred knew the river: it was *his* river. He had foreseen the blockade, and equipped Olaf's ships accordingly, each with a high platform rising from the foredeck.

"He thinks to shield his rowers from the rocks," thought Swayne, peering against the brightness of the river. "It is protection for the rowers."

But as the dragon-prows nosed closer, Ethelred's and Olaf's men swarmed up on to the platforms so as to stand almost on a level with their opponents on the bridge. They stood in pairs, one holding a coil of rope tipped with a grappling hook, the other holding a shield with which to fend off the arrows, the stones, the spears.

Insanely, it seemed as if they would really moor up to the bridge, for they pitched their grappling irons at the bridge's wooden pilings.

Their faces were on a level with the bridge parapet: like sailors in two closing warships, both sides looked each other in the eye. There was a moment's silence, like a pause to draw breath. Then the men on the bridge were hurling, shouting, bloodying their hands on the large rocks in their haste to heave them over on to the ships beneath.

Six, a dozen, twenty of the men on the platforms were dislodged by stones and plunged into the river. Some fell stunned to the decking. But then the rowers swung their legs over the benches and faced the other way. The dragon-headed ships dropped back downstream, but between them and the bridge now ran a dozen stout ropes.

"Heave!" cried Ethelred.

"Heave!" cried Olaf. And the rowers heaved till the muscles stood proud of their shoulders. The ropes twanged taut, spraying silver droplets into the air.

The grappling irons chewed on the wood of the bridge; two broke free and splashed into the river, but the rest held. The strain stirred the wooden pilings of the bridge in their muddy sockets in the river bed.

What with the great weight of stones amassed on the wooden planking and the great press of defenders, the bridge was already overladen. Now, as its pilings were dragged out from under it, London Bridge broke its wooden back.

For a moment it staggered drunkenly on its unsteady legs. Then down into the Thames fell stones and shields, timber and helmets and men. The dragon-headed longships rolled on the huge wave which washed downstream from the splash, and the rowers rested on their oars as silence fell over the wide, grey river.

Within three years another king held London – Edmund Ironside – and London Bridge had been built up again, too strongly for whole galleys of rowers to pull it down. But King Canute was a man who did not pit brawn against brawn. He brought the power of cunning to the problem of capturing London.

Arming his men with picks and shovels in place of swords, he had them dig. He had them dig a channel just a hand-span wider than the beam of his ships. It ran south from the Thames. Then west. It bypassed London, looping to the south, and, when flooded with Thames water from either end, it filled to a depth just a hand-span deeper than the draw of Canute's ships. Long chains of men, heaving like barge horses on cables of rope, hauled the entire navy of Canute round Edmund Ironside's London, and attacked from the west – from inland! – unexpected, unresisted, irresistible.

When King Swayne attacked England in 1013 he was accompanied by his son. A few years later, that son had become king of Denmark, and as Canute the Great came back to finish the job. He was England's first Viking king, capturing the country from Ethelred (or Aethelred) "the Unready" in 1015 – all except for London, which was held by Ethelred's son and heir, Edmund Ironside. Hence this masterly stroke of engineering and military tactics.

Ultimately, Knut reached an agreement with Edmund Ironside to share the kingdom, but Edmund died a month later and everything fell to Knut. To strengthen his claim to the throne, he set aside his so-called "northern wife", Aelgifu, and married King Ethelred's widow, Emma.

Canute Defies the Sea

about 1020

GOOD OR BAD, A KING DRAWS FLATTERERS like a horse draws flies, and King Canute, in his fenland kingdom, had accumulated a veritable swarm.

"The sun is shining today, my lord, because it is glad to see you so well!"

"The kings of all Europe are trembling this morning, your honour, at the thought of your might and wisdom!"

"The Pope himself is surely envious of your saintliness, my lord!"

Canute stood up suddenly. "I dare say I could cross swords with the moon and win," he suggested.

"Oh, no doubt! No question, my lord King!"

"And command the sea itself to do my bidding."

"The seas, my lord King, would be honoured to serve you," said the toadies.

"Then take hold of my throne – you – you – and you! – and be so good as to carry it down to the beach," said Canute, to the court's surprise.

The sea lay vast and grey, breathing shallowly, lapping at shells on the wet sand. Canute had his throne placed a few steps from the water's edge and sat in it. His courtiers stood about, hands clasped on their stomachs, smiles set hard. The tide was rising.

"Hold off, Sea!" commanded Canute, holding up one royal hand. "I, Canute, say you shall not rise today!" His courtiers looked at each other, but went on smiling. "Stay back, thou great wet thing!" commanded Canute, holding up both royal hands. "I, Canute, command it!"

But, of course, the sea continued to lap the shore, and every seventh wave ran higher up the beach, wetting dry sand, turning dry stones. Soon the legs of the throne were awash. The royal feet were distinctly wet. The courtiers, hopping about dismally, kept on smiling.

"O unruly and uppish monster! Do you defy me? Do you dare to invade my kingdom?" protested Canute. A large grey wave wetted everyone to the knees and the backwash dragged sand from under their sodden velvet shoes.

"I really think, your Majesty," began the chancellor, "it's not quite safe to . . ."

"But you told me I was more powerful than the sea!" Canute retorted, and he sat fast, until the throne itself was being rocked by large cold waves, and his courtiers were up to their waists in brine.

"Scurvy ocean!" Canute declaimed. "I see that you have not heard of King Canute the All-Powerful! I see we must wrestle hand-to-hand!"

"No! No, my lord!" cried several of his courtiers, wading through the swell. "Please!"

"You mean to say I am *not* all-powerful?" said Canute with exaggerated amazement. "You mean to say that the winds and waves do *not* obey God's anointed king?"

"I –"

"We –"

"Ah –"

"No? Then in future, I'll thank you not to tell me such monumental untruths, gentlemen. I look to you for your help and advice and measured opinions. I do *not* look to you for flattery, lies and servility. Do I make myself clear?"

"Perfectly!" howled the court in unison as a great wave broke and left them flailing ashore, tripping and gasping, and dipping for their hats in the unheeding sea.

At one time, King Canute ruled three kingdoms – England, Norway and Denmark – and spent long periods overseas. But his twenty-year rule in England was a time of relative stability. After his death, his empire fell apart as his sons fought for supremacy. His first heir died. His second heir, Hardaknut, was hated, unlike Knut who was revered as a wise, religious man.

The story of Knut and the sea was and is frequently mis-told, as if Canute believes the sea will obey him, but only because listeners like to hear of the proud being humbled.

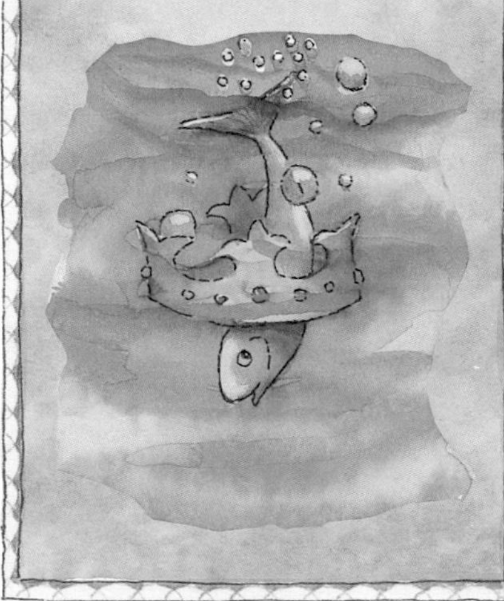

"Macbeth Does Murder Sleep"

1040
(Shakespeare, *Macbeth*)

MACBETH WAS EXULTANT AS HE RODE homeward from the coast. He had fought a whole fleet of Danish invaders and won. At his side rode his friend Banquo, Thane of Lochaber. Suddenly, out of the dank, wreathing mist, three old women appeared. "Hail Macbeth, Thane of Glamis. Hail Macbeth, Thane of Cawdor. All hail Macbeth, soon to be King of Scotland!"

"None of these titles is mine," said Macbeth. "You mistake me for my father even to call me Thane of Glamis." But perhaps these old crones were witches. Perhaps they were blessed with the magic powers and could see events in the future as other people saw fish in a pond.

"Have you nothing to say to me?" asked Banquo, eager for a prophecy of his own.

"No king thou, but a father of kings!" chanted the gnarled, weather-blasted crones. Then they were gone, swallowed up by the mist . . . and approaching, each from a different direction, were two messengers. Macbeth's father was dead: the title "Thane of Glamis" had passed to him. And King Duncan, in acknowledgement of his victory over the Danes, had awarded valiant Macbeth the estates of Cawdor.

Two prophecies come true in as many minutes! The news shook Macbeth more than any battle. For if two prophecies could come true, why not the third? Might Macbeth one day be king? The thought warmed him like a great dog leaning against his belly.

If Macbeth were ambitious, his wife Gruoch was eaten up with ambition. There was royal blood in her veins and it cried out for power. When she heard tell of the three witches, heard of her husband's new titles and saw the hunger in him to be king, she swept aside all his qualms, drowned out the whispers of his conscience, telling him, "Yes! Murder Duncan and be king!"

Duncan and his son, Prince Malcolm, were invited to stay at the castle of the Macbeths, near Inverness. After the old man had gone to bed, Gruoch drugged his bodyguards and, when they were slumped snoring by the King's bed, Macbeth took their daggers and stabbed Duncan through the heart. In the morning, when the body was found, he feigned horror and outrage – and, blaming the guards, killed them outright.

Duncan's son, Malcolm, was not fooled for one moment. He fled – over the border into England, rightly supposing that he was the only person who stood between Macbeth and the crown which he and Gruoch so insanely craved.

The great prize was won, just as the witches had said it would be. The metal crown weighed heavy on his temples . . . but the second prophecy dragged like a sea-anchor on his heart. Banquo's sons would be kings? How? Why not Macbeth's?

He would kill Banquo. No! He would pay for Banquo to be killed: a king does not need to sully his hands. It was done: another obstacle removed, another bloody notch cut in Macbeth's conscience.

But he could not rest easy until he had visited the three old hags again.

He was not disappointed; the three old women were still there on the heath. Their mumbling toothless heads emerged from the rocky dark like tortoises emerging from their shells. "Show me the future!" he demanded. "Is my crown secure? Am I safe from my enemies?"

They looked at him with eyes as yellow as cesspits. "Macbeth shall not be conquered till Birnam Wood comes to Dunsinane."

Macbeth gave a shrill, gasping laugh. Safe, then! Birnam Wood stood several miles from his castle at Dunsinane, and how could a *forest* move? He told his wife. He told his men-at-arms: "I am invincible. Nothing can defeat me till Birnam Wood comes to Dunsinane!"

Meanwhile, in England, Malcolm threw himself on the mercy of Edward the Confessor and scuffed his heels around the English court. He won over to his cause the Earl of Northumberland and a thane called Macduff, wronged and driven out of Scotland by King Macbeth. They raised an army and marched on Dunsinane: Macbeth's spies quickly brought him word of it, but Macbeth only laughed. Cloaked round in his magical prophecy, he was smugly complacent.

A servant came stumbling into the room, eyes bulging, mouth a-jabber. "The wood, sire! The wood . . . !" He almost died, Macbeth's fingers around his throat, for the news he brought: that Dunsinane Wood appeared to be *moving towards the castle.*

Macbeth flung him aside and ran to the battlements. The raw wind stung his eyes to tears as he stared. The prophecy clamoured in his head, indistinguishable from the alarm bell.

In marching through Birnam Wood, Macduff had told every soldier to strip a branch from the trees and to carry it, and so mask the size and nature of the force coming against Macbeth. It would keep him guessing.

But as far as Macbeth was concerned, the battle was already lost. His heart crumpled within him. He looked around and saw that his men, too, remembered the prophecy. It hamstrung them; it set their sword-hands shaking. With one last effort of will, he rallied them to the attack. The portcullis lifted, and they forayed out to meet the enemy they knew would destroy them . . .

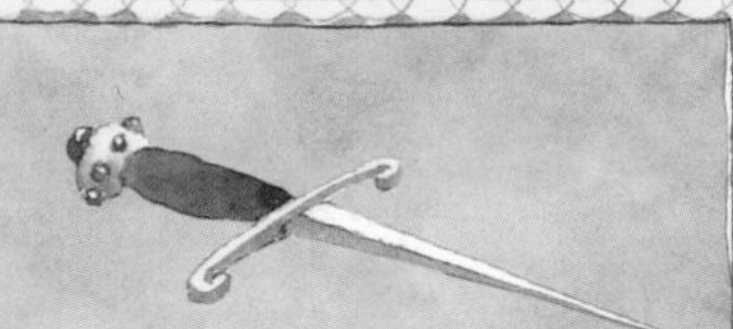

The source of this story is Raphael Holinshed's *Chronicles* of 1577, and it was this book which Shakespeare would have used when he wrote his tragedy, *Macbeth*. It is known that Macbeth seized the throne by murdering Duncan, and that he suffered defeat at the hands of Prince Malcolm. But Holinshed made free with the facts and Shakespeare adjusted them even more.

In fact Macbeth ruled Scotland for seventeen years, and his reign was thought of as a time of prosperity. He gave large sums to charity (possibly to salve a bad conscience) and went on pilgrimage to Rome. And although he lost the battle at Dunsinane, he escaped and survived three further years before he was killed by Malcolm. Shakespeare depicted Lady Macbeth as a woman driven to madness then suicide by her guilt, but Gruoch's true fate is unknown. She simply disappeared.

In the context of eleventh-century Scotland, there is nothing remarkable about the violence of Macbeth's rise and fall. It was the masterpiece Shakespeare wove around the events which immortalized this obscure chapter of Scottish history.

Lady Godiva's Shameless Ride

about 1050

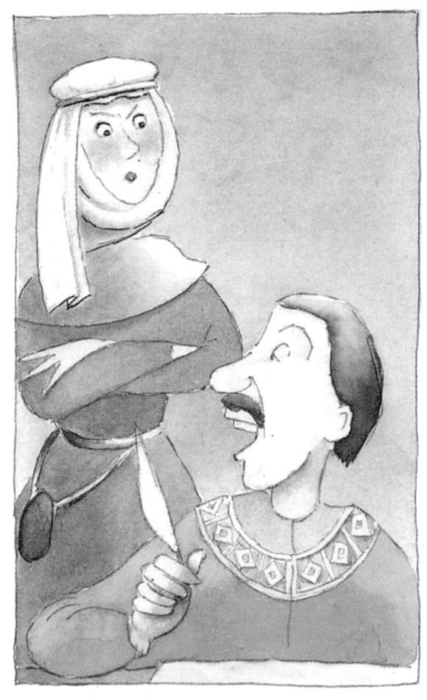

People did not know how Godiva could bear to live with Leofric: his meanness, his little acts of spite, his nasty temper. And she so kind and beautiful! People said what a shame it was that the best wives sometimes marry the worst men.

But Lady Godiva loved her husband. Even though he was not handsome or gentle or even very pleasant, she genuinely loved him. It saddened her that he was so unpopular with the people. Leofric was Earl of Chester, which gave him, for his income, the revenue of the city of Coventry. Tithes, rent, fines, fees and levies, Leofric took them all. If anyone could not pay, he evicted them. Sometimes Lady Godiva would try to help the hardest pressed, with a coin from her own purse, but she had to do it in secret: Leofric looked on charity as throwing good money after bad.

"The Bible tells us we should help the poor," Godiva pointed out gently.

"The Bible tells us to work hard and pay our taxes," said Leofric disagreeably. "They have plenty of money, you take my word. You shouldn't believe their hard-luck stories."

He raised the taxes, until the people complained aloud. Then he punished them with higher taxes.

"Don't do this, husband," said Lady Godiva one day, as he sat composing a new proclamation. "I have never contradicted you before, but this new tax of yours is wrong. It will cause such suffering."

"Keep your place, woman," snapped Leofric. "What do you know of such things?"

"But the people will hate you for this tax. Don't do it, I beg you."

Leofric laughed. "What do I care if they hate me, so long as they pay?"

Lady Godiva breathed deeply. "If you really need this money, I will give it you out of my own inheritance."

That silenced his laughing. "I'll have you know, madam, that your money is already mine to do with as I please. And I do not please to use my *own money* to pay what the people of Coventry owe me."

Lady Godiva was quiet for so long that Leofric thought he had won the argument. But then his wife drew herself up to her full height. "My money may be yours, Leofric, but I think you will agree, my body is my own. If you will not be ashamed, I must be ashamed for you. Withdraw this latest tax . . . or I shall ride naked through the streets of Coventry in token of the people you have left naked to wind and rain."

Leofric snorted with scorn. "*You?* The virtuous Lady Godiva? You would die of shame, and I would die of laughing." His quill nib scratched on the parchment like a rat on a granary wall.

Next Sunday, in every church in Coventry, there was an astonishing announcement made. "Tomorrow, Lady Godiva, wife of the Earl of Chester, will ride naked through the streets of the city. Let her shame fall on Leofric for his greed."

Some priests whispered it, some choked on the word "naked", some never even reached the end before uproar broke out. Soon everyone had grasped the news, including Leofric, dozing sleepily in his scarlet padded pew.

His first thought was to put his wife under lock and key, but Godiva was too quick for him; she had already gone into hiding. "She will never do it," he comforted himself, but he did not sleep well that night, in his big Coventry house.

Next morning, he woke to the sound of hooves on the cobbles below. They rang through the silent city streets. He threw open the shutters and shouted along the whole length of Broadgate: "Don't do this, Godiva! Don't do this to me!"

The rising sun shone on her long, loose hair falling over her bare shoulders, breaking over the horse's rump. She rode bareback, astride her grey mare. From the crown of her head to the soles of her feet, she was stark naked.

Godiva did not feel the cold; her skin burned with shame and anger. This was not the act of some brazen woman carrying out a shocking dare. Godiva was humiliating herself in the hope of humbling her husband. She did not round her shoulders nor cower down over the horse's neck, but inwardly she knew what agonies she would suffer when exposed to the whistles and stares of a market-day crowd.

Was this not a market day?

On market days, the city was busy even before sun-up, crowded with people setting up stalls, opening the front windows of their houses to trade with passers-by; countryfolk walking in from the outlying villages with eggs, vegetables and wicker-work. On market days carts vied for right of way; tinkers bawled and shouted.

So was this *not* a market day?

The streets were so quiet! No carts rattled over the cobbles. No one was setting up their wares in the market place. Godiva raised her eyes. Every house shutter was closed, every door shut. Somewhere a dog barked. Water gurgled down the drain in the middle of the road. But no one shouted, no one pushed a handcart through the alleyways. No one stared.

Leofric came running, Godiva's cloak bundled up in his arms. He tried to throw it over her, but she shrugged it off and it fell into the drain. "Godiva, please! Look at you! You'll die of cold. I'll die of shame! What are you doing to me?"

"You have stripped the people bare with your taxes and your levies," said Godiva looking steadfastly ahead. "The people of Coventry will think no less of me for this. But *your* name will go down in history as the man who swindled Coventry." Her bare heels thudded into the horse's withers, and it broke into a trot.

Leofric looked around him, cringing, anticipating the laughter, the hoots, the crude jokes that would shower down on his lovely wife and on him. These people were nothing but despicable peasants, after all.

He saw the closed windows, the shut doors, the empty alleyways and the silent market place. Every citizen had turned his face to the wall and shut his eyes, sooner than shame Lady Godiva.

Not quite *every* one shut their eyes. Tom Henny rubbed his sweaty hands in glee and knelt down by the keyhole. Tom often went out late at night and peeped through shutters in the hope of seeing a pretty girl undressing. The sight of Lady Godiva naked was going to be sweet as honey! Let the other prudes shut their eyes: Tom would look his fill. He licked his lips as the clip-clop of hooves came closer. He pressed his eye to the keyhole . . .

A sudden unseasonable swirl of wind gusted down the street, lifting an eddy of dust. Tom Henny gave a scream of pain. A piece of grit had embedded itself in his eye. As the hooves clopped by outside, he had no thought of seeing Lady Godiva, dressed or naked. All he could think about was getting the grit out of his eye.

Leofric waited in Cathedral Square for his wife to ride back the way she had gone. "I give in!" he called, as she came into view. He spoke in a loud voice, knowing the town stood listening behind its closed shutters. "You have your wish! I shall not impose the new tax. If that earns me the respect of these decent people, I shall be rich enough."

The town remembered that day – wrote of it in the annals of the county, with a sigh of admiration for Lady Godiva. They saved their scorn for Tom Henny – Peeping Tom, as they called him. He had to endure the silent contempt of his neighbours as, collar up, hat pulled down, he went about, day by lonely day, trying to conceal his one blind eye.

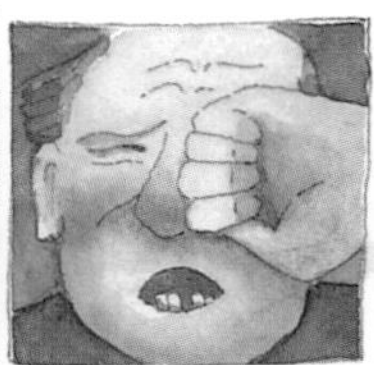

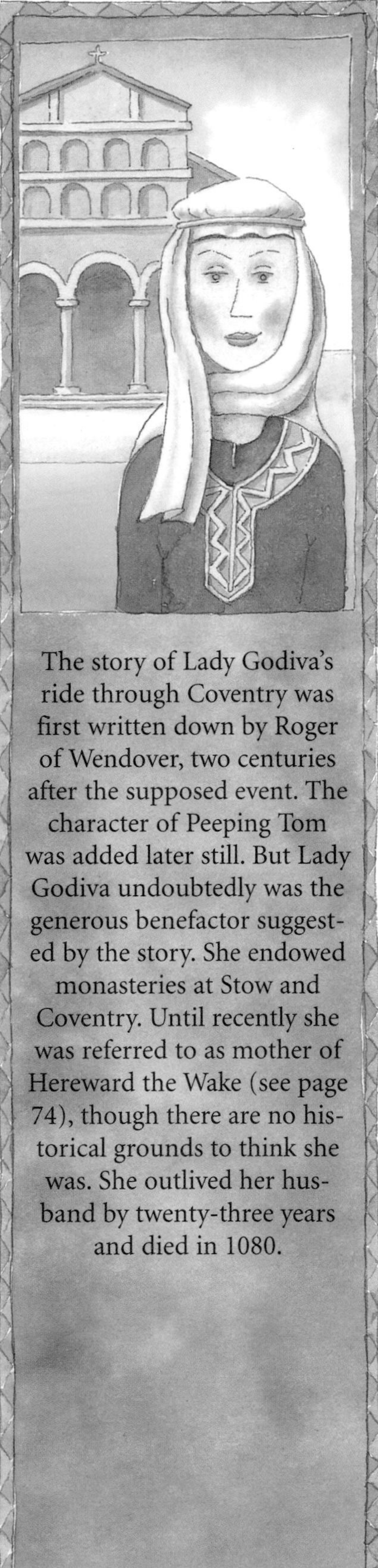

The story of Lady Godiva's ride through Coventry was first written down by Roger of Wendover, two centuries after the supposed event. The character of Peeping Tom was added later still. But Lady Godiva undoubtedly was the generous benefactor suggested by the story. She endowed monasteries at Stow and Coventry. Until recently she was referred to as mother of Hereward the Wake (see page 74), though there are no historical grounds to think she was. She outlived her husband by twenty-three years and died in 1080.

Swearing on the Bones

1064

BEFORE THE DEATH OF EDWARD THE CONFESSOR, promises were flying about more plentiful than starlings around the spires of Westminster Abbey. King Edward favoured Harold, Earl of Wessex, as his successor, but William, Duke of Normandy, had a powerful claim as well. There was bound to be a struggle for power when the old King died. Already the rival candidates were trying to extract promises of support from anyone and everyone.

Then Harold was shipwrecked on the shores of France, and taken prisoner. Duke William was informed, and arranged for Harold to be set free. Indeed, Harold was very glad to escape a stone dungeon floor and sharing his food with rats.

So when the two men met, there was no unpleasantness between them Harold said how grateful he was. William said it was nothing: all that he asked in exchange was that Harold should swear to forfeit his claim and help William to his rightful place on the throne of England. "Here. Your word on it!"

The table was spread with cloth of gold. Wine stains and fragments of chicken speckled it, but William cleared space to set down the Gospels.

Did Harold wet his lips or look shiftily about? Did he hide one hand under his tabard and cross his fingers? No. Harold had lied to better men than this before now. He would lie with gusto, knowing that the throne rightfully belonged to him, knowing that God would turn a deaf ear. Solemnly, he laid his hand on the Gospels – William covered it with his own, sword-hardened palm and Harold swore: "to help William, Duke of Normandy, to win the crown of England".

The hand lifted off his. He felt his freedom already. He could not wait to get back across the Channel. With the flourish of a magician, William of Normandy drew off the cloth of gold; it cracked like a banner on a windy day. His eyes were still on Harold, still fixing him, as a cat fixes a cornered mouse. Two armed men sprang forward, and Harold thought, they are going to stab me.

But the two soldiers only lifted the table top off its trestle legs to reveal, underneath, a big carved,

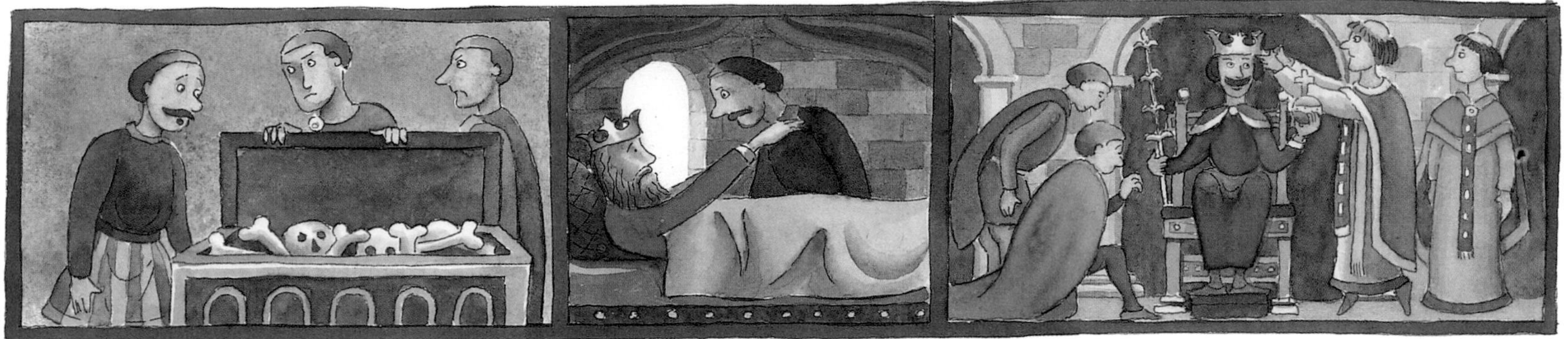

darkwood chest. That too was opened. Inside it lay something which stood Harold's hair on end.

"Bones?" he said.

"The relics of a dozen saints," said William. "Can there be any oath so solemn as the oath sworn on the relics of a saint?"

Harold went pale and shuddered. Not for an instant did he consider keeping his promise, laying aside his claim to the throne. But it was as if, in that moment, the windows of heaven closed and the angels deserted him.

Edward the Confessor did name Harold his heir; the Witan Council of wise men elected him, too, and Harold said nothing in defence of Duke William's claim. In short, he broke his promise, in order to be crowned King of England.

William wrote reminding Harold "of the oath which thou hast sworn with thy hand upon good and holy relics". But Harold wrote back that he had promised what did not belong to him, "a promise which I could not in any way perform". War was just a matter of time.

That year Halley's comet swung low through the sky like a burning tear. What could it mean? Did it foretell disaster?

William mustered his invasion forces, but for a long time the wind blew against him. Indeed, hurricanes smashed his ships and drowned his crews. Perhaps the saints were not on his side after all. Overhead the comet hurtled on through space, bearing the colours of neither side, instead unfurling a blank white banner.

Then the Norwegian King invaded England from the north. Harold had to hurry north to Stamford Bridge and counter the invasion. He fought a masterly battle – defeated the Norwegians, and rode south again, flushed with victory. Perhaps the comet plunging past the earth meant disaster for the Northmen, after all. Or perhaps it acclaimed the coming of Harold the Victor, a king destined to win many such victories.

His fleet was still sailing up and down the Channel, guarding the south coast against William's threatened invasion. Still an adverse wind kept William from setting sail. Harold, rushing south as fast as his battle-weary army could go, smiled every time he saw a weathercock on a church roof.

But then the English navy ran out of provisions and had to put back to port for more. *That* was when the wind came about, when William set sail. Four days after the battle of Stamford Bridge, William of Normandy landed his invasion force at Pevensey Bay.

First ashore were the archers, shaven-headed, in short tunics. Then came the horsemen, in coats of mail, with polished conical helmets, lances and heavy broadswords. Next came the workmen: sappers and armourers, smiths and fletchers. And last of all came William himself.

Tripping, he promptly pitched on his face in the sand and cut himself. Superstitious dread seized on a thousand men. Was this an omen? Had the comet in the sky signalled disaster for the Normans and not, after all, for Harold the Oath-breaker?

With remarkable presence of mind (considering the pain in his knees), Duke William closed his fist around a lump of sandy soil and held it aloft. "Now I have taken possession of England and will defend it with my blood!" he bellowed, and a thousand men let go their pent-up breath in a gasp of relief.

Harold was in no mood to negotiate. Besides, he had already parcelled out England to his own choice of friends, knights and barons: they would never let him abdicate. So the English troops, only returned in the nick of time and exhausted from the high-speed journey, made their stand near Hastings, mustered on top of a hill, behind a wooden palisade. It gave the Normans marshy ground to cover and a steep climb before they could even cross swords with the English.

With horrid fascination the English watched a single rider break ranks and ride forward up the hill: a troubadour-knight known as Taillefer or "the Iron Cleaver". He began to sing – a ballad of heroism and self-sacrifice – and as he sang, he tossed his sword in the air and caught it, again and again, so that its arcing, somersaulting blade sliced the sunlight into spinning shards. It mesmerized the eye – such juggling, such foolhardy panache. With suicidal daring, Taillefer hurled himself on the first two Englishmen in his path, and cut them down, before he himself was pulled down and lost from sight amid the confusion of the first charge.

The Normans were galvanized into action. Time and again they made sallies up the hill, shouting, "God strengthen us!" but were thwarted by the wooden palisade and javelins thrown back with the cry, "God Almighty!" Duke William, leading a charge uphill, felt the horse under him shudder then plunge to its knees, a spear in its chest. But he no sooner hit the ground than he was on his feet again, leading the assault on the palisade. They captured the hill, but not the English standard. That stood at King Harold's side, surrounded by his finest knights, and evening was coming on.

"Shoot your arrows into the sky!" called William to his archers. "Let them fall on the English faces!"

The archers arched their backs, squinted into the evening clouds. They fired their arrows upwards as if they would shoot the very evening star out of the sky. And their arrows fell like rain.

Harold looked up at the sound of whistling in the skies, and saw a hail of death falling on him. It was the last thing he saw. An arrow entered his eye, filled his brain with light and then with darkness. Like a comet plummeting away into unfathomable space, Harold fell: from noise to silence, from glory to oblivion. All around him the English still cried, with futile desperation, "God Almighty!"

But all Harold could hear was the rattling of bones underground.

The full story of Harold's sworn oath, the Norman invasion and the battle of Hastings is told in the Bayeux Tapestry, a long strip of linen embroidered in wool, probably by English needlewomen. The embroidery was commissioned by Bishop Odo, half-brother of William the Conqueror, to commemorate the victory. It naturally presents William in a good light and Harold as an oath-breaker who deserved to lose the crown. The comet is there, foretelling Harold's downfall.

Unfortunately, it is now thought that the figure seen pulling an arrow from his eye may not be Harold at all. So the best "known" fact about Harold (i.e. that he died of an arrow in the eye) may not even be true. No other record exists describing his death.

Hereward the Wake

1070

HE WAS ALWAYS A WILD boy. From the start, Hereward was so wild that they say his own father declared him an outlaw and drove him out to live in the forests and fens. Hereward was a young man full of rage and fire. But when the Normans came and the country was taken out of Saxon hands, Hereward's rage suddenly found a fitting target. He vowed to drive the Normans out of England or make them wish they had never come.

The good Saxon abbot of St Peter's Abbey had been replaced with a Norman one. So Hereward felt free to storm the Abbey and pillage it of every candlestick and cross and chalice. A military campaign needs funds, after all.

But afterwards, a dream rose into Hereward's sleep like mist rising off the fens. He saw St Peter, angry and woebegone, searching, searching under every bush and in the hollow of every tree. He was searching for his treasure. "Oh Hereward, Hereward, what have I ever done to you?" glared the eyes of St Peter.

At first light, Hereward packed up the treasure of St Peter's Abbey and sent it back – every last chalice, plate and candlestick. "My quarrel is with the Normans, not with the saints," he told his bewildered men.

Armed with his sword Brainbiter, Hereward the Wakeful harried the Normans as a fox harries a chicken coop. Suddenly, stealthily, out of darkness or mist, his band of loyal Saxons would fall on barracks or encampments, on castles or shipments of coin, till the Normans were run ragged with chasing him. Elsewhere King William's Norman Conquest was quick, easy, unopposed. But in the fenlands, thanks to Brainbiter and the Saxon who wielded it, the rivers often ran red with Norman blood.

The landscape itself defied conquest. Hidden within its wet wilderness, Hereward and his men were as elusive as fish underwater. At long last, William found out that Hereward's stronghold was on the remote and moated Island of Ely. He determined, difficult as it would be, to put Hereward the "Wakeful" to sleep once and for all.

He would throw a bridge or causeway across the water, so that his army could storm the island. Of course, he needed labourers to build such a bridge, but it never occurred to him that the enemy would volunteer to help build it . . .

Hereward covered his long blond hair with a hessian hood,

shouldered a bag of tools and set off to build bridges for the Normans. Day after day, he sank pilings, raised levees, knocked in nails, dug drainage trenches. He even helped build the tower at one end of the bridge, though he was not sure what it was for.

"Ah! So you are the woman I sent for," said King William, suppressing a shudder of revulsion. "Do you know your task?"

The woman in front of him ran her fingers through tangled masses of greasy, grey plaits. "I must curse the Saxons and blast their souls to ashes." Her voice was so loud that the King involuntarily put his hands over his ears.

"Not that I believe in your magic," he said, paying her in French gold, "but these Saxons are as superstitious as fishwives. They have a horror of witches like you – and you, madam, have made an art of horror, so I hear."

The witch looked at him with contempt and fingered the mummified shrew strung round her neck. "You do your part, and I will do mine," she said.

As the causeway neared completion, William massed his forces, ready to swarm across the water into Hereward's stronghold. Shortly before dawn, the workmen were withdrawn. The French witch mounted the tower like a great black spider climbing into its web, and her ugly voice rasped out:

"A curse on you, Hereward's men! Your luck is held in a sieve! Your blood is curdling in your veins! The hairs fallen from your head are in my cauldron! I have spoken with the spirits. I have warned the worms of your coming! My toads have walked on your faces while you slept: I know your dreams! My cat has scratched a hole for your skulls to lie in!"

Under the causeway, though no one knew it, one workman had remained behind. Hereward clung to the underside of the bridge like a crab in an upturned boat, and between his teeth was a burning fuse. He stuffed kindling into a crevice and lit it. Then he dropped down and waded, chin-deep, back to his island stronghold. The noise of the witch's insane laughter disturbed him. His men were as bold as greyhounds, but he knew what terror the black arts could strike in them. He saw their eyes glimmer in the dark, staring out at that crazy crone. Then he realized that the glimmer in their eyes was firelight. His fire had taken. The causeway was burning.

Two hundred Normans had already started across the bridge before they realized that it was alight. The witch was chanting incantations now, curses in rhyme. She worked herself to such a frenzy of abuse that she was unaware of the panic below, the splash of men jumping for their lives, the groaning of timbers breaking, the roar of fire. Gradually, an orange glare suffused the whole scene. throwing every figure into silhouette, showing the gaunt latticework of her flimsy tower.

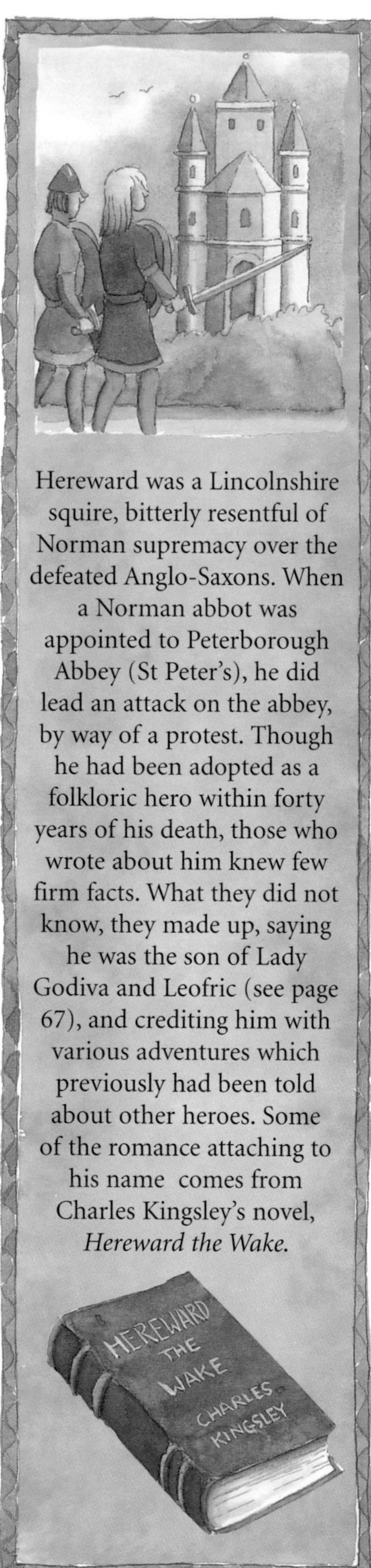

Hereward was a Lincolnshire squire, bitterly resentful of Norman supremacy over the defeated Anglo-Saxons. When a Norman abbot was appointed to Peterborough Abbey (St Peter's), he did lead an attack on the abbey, by way of a protest. Though he had been adopted as a folkloric hero within forty years of his death, those who wrote about him knew few firm facts. What they did not know, they made up, saying he was the son of Lady Godiva and Leofric (see page 67), and crediting him with various adventures which previously had been told about other heroes. Some of the romance attaching to his name comes from Charles Kingsley's novel, *Hereward the Wake.*

No one gave a thought to saving the witch – William's men were too busy saving themselves. When the fire reached her, she screamed curses against Norman and Saxon alike, dancing puppet-like on an orange platform. Then, with a soughing rush of wind and ash, the burning tower listed and toppled into the river. The witch was silenced. The marsh soaked up her black magic. A constellation of burning cinders settled with a hiss on the sodden landscape.

Of course sometimes the wild places of England can be as confusing and dangerous to a Saxon as to a Norman, and more than once Hereward himself went astray. After a daring raid on Stamford, as his band made their way through Rockingham Forest, cloud blotted out the moon and left them blunderingly, helplessly lost.

All of a sudden, a gentle light began to shine ahead of him, and he glimpsed another out of the corner of his eye. Soon, individual flames – disembodied balls of light – were settling like birds on the branch of each tree. A soldier gasped and dropped his shield, but Hereward picked it up and gave it back to him. "Don't be afraid," he said. "It's just St Peter returning a favour." And no mistake, there were candles of phosphorescence glowing on every tree and shield rim – enough to see by, enough to reach a dry bed by an Anglo-Saxon hearth.

Margaret's Prayer

1070-1071

KING MALCOLM WAS NOT A MAN EASILY moved to pity. But when he saw Margaret, her sister and her mother, storm-soaked and exhausted, he was very moved indeed, and the feeling in his heart was nothing like pity.

A ship, bound for Hungary but driven ashore on the Scottish coast, had brought to his doorstep Edgar Aetheling, a claimant to the throne of England. The Norman conquest, rebellion and civil war had erased young Edgar's hopes of ever wearing the crown, and now he was fleeing for his life with his mother and two sisters, Christina and Margaret. Malcolm Canmore, King of Scotland, opened his door to the runaways – gave them food and shelter and warm whisky. But his eyes were always and only on Margaret, the stillness of her hands, the long-lashed lids of her downcast eyes.

Everything about Princess Margaret delighted him, from her soft psalm-singing to the Hungarian lilt of her accent. He was nearly forty and she was twenty-four. He quickly made up his mind to marry her. There was only one obstacle to overcome: Margaret was already promised in marriage: to God.

She had long since made up her mind to be a nun, and all her education had prepared her for a cloistered life. She was altogether out of place at the court of King Malcolm, a barbarous, uncultured man who swore and drank and whose chief joy in life was to ride over the border and kill Englishmen. So her mother and sister were startled when, without explanation, Margaret the pious, Margaret the pure, suddenly abandoned her vocation and agreed to marry Malcolm Canmore.

Pleased as he was, Malcolm was baffled by his new bride. She left his bed at unearthly hours of the night; she ate like a sparrow. She no sooner had money in her purse than it was gone and she was asking for more. She even stole from him! He saw her scribble hasty notes and dispatch them furtively by rider or runner. Even in broad daylight she would often disappear – he had no idea where – creeping out of the house alone, without a word, and not returning for hours.

Malcolm began to suspect the worst. Was she meeting a lover? Was she lavishing her money on some sweetheart? Could this lady, who had been unwilling to marry and stain her purity, really be deceiving him? He vowed to find out. The very next time she slipped away down the back stairs, he followed her, at a distance, to see where she went. He followed her northwards along the winding streets of Dunfermline town. How eagerly she moved, head down, hurrying through the alleyways! At last she ducked in at the dark doorway of a low building.

Hand on knife, Malcolm followed, swearing to kill her then and there if his suspicions proved right. Already he could hear that soft sweet voice of hers whispering tenderly . . .

The place was more of a cave than a room: a gloomy, secret place. Peeping inside, Malcolm crossed himself and dodged hastily backwards, cracking his head on the arch. Smiling now, he bent for a second look.

There knelt his wife in front of a simple altar, her lips moving in fervent prayer.

"Lord God, protect and bless my beloved husband, and grant me the power to work some good upon his nature. He does not mean to be so fierce and brutal. He has a good heart underneath his shouting and cursing. Be good to him! Perhaps he has his reasons. Perhaps he does not enjoy the same happiness as I am blessed with."

Tears of remorse sprang to Malcolm's eyes. How he had misjudged his beautiful queen! Well, he would make things up to her! Perhaps with her help he could even make things up with God! Following his wife home again, he saw what became of his stolen money, too. She gave it liberally to the beggars and maimed old soldiers who haunted the lanes of Dunfermline town.

After that, the court of Malcolm Canmore was a different place. Not that the Scottish lords there were any-the-less wild or warlike, but their days followed a different course. Every morning, nine little orphans were brought to the Queen's private room so that she could sit them on her

lap and feed them with her own spoon. Before every one of her own meals, the Queen would serve twenty-four poor people with food. The chamberlain had the nightly task of finding six poor people, fetching them to the castle, and making them presentable: because somewhere between a triple dose of prayers in the middle of the night and going briefly back to bed, the King and Queen liked to wash the feet of the poor, in keeping with what the Bible taught. During Lent as many as 300 needy citizens would file daily into the great hall, the doors would close, and the King and Queen in person would serve them a meal.

Monasteries and churches were built; religious men came to advise Malcolm on how to breathe new life into Scottish worship. And those hastily scribbled letters? They were indeed to spies. Margaret kept spies all over Scotland, so as to know about the English captives being held to ransom on Scottish soil. As well as ensuring that they were not cruelly treated during their captivity, she frequently paid their ransom herself.

She went on stealing gold from Malcolm's coffers; he often saw her do it. But now it made him laugh, rather than rage. His saintly little queen never ceased to amaze and astound Malcolm. Though she ate less than any of the chickens in the yard, she was tireless in her work. Furthermore, she gave birth to eight strong, healthy babies one after another, and they all lived to adulthood – a miracle indeed in those days.

One thing did not change about Malcolm's life; oddly, Margaret made no attempt to change it. She never said to Malcolm, "For the love of God or for love of me, don't go to war. Don't go raiding over the borders. Don't kill and plunder and burn . . ." Raids and wars were as much a part of her husband's life as the cut of his beard or the shoes he wore. But every day he was away, she prayed for his safe and speedy return. Even when she was ill. Even when the pain cramped her stomach like a sword thrust, she prayed for him and for his people rather than for herself.

She was ill when he set off the last time, with their oldest son, Edward. She was dying when they brought her the news that they were both dead.

If her waiting women expected Margaret to turn her face to the wall in despair – if they expected her to reproach God for rejecting her prayers, she surprised them one last time.

"All praise be to Thee Almighty God, who has been pleased that I should endure such deep sorrow at my departing, and I trust that by means of this suffering it is Thy pleasure that I should be cleansed from some of the stains of my sins." Then in the middle of reciting the Communion prayer, she simply stopped breathing.

Queen Margaret made a radical impact on eleventh-century Scotland. She was quickly declared a saint - Scotland's only royal saint - and though the account of her life by Turgot, her confessor, may exaggerate somewhat, her life patently merited sainthood. Turgot, a monk, was commissioned by Margaret's daughter (later Queen Matilda of England) to write *The Life of St Margaret.* Several miracles were reported soon after her death.

Who Killed Red Rufus?

1100

When he was ill, there was no one more religious than William Rufus. But when he was well, he was the Devil made flesh. He plundered Church coffers and jeered and sneered at its faith. Each time a church post became vacant, Rufus postponed appointing a new man – left the position empty, and took all the revenue himself. Or else he sold the post to the highest bidder. There was not one sincere religious conviction in his whole blasphemous soul. The only music which moved him was the jingle of money and the cry of the hunt.

From the people, he took the great primaeval forests, declaring all the wild life in them his to hunt. And he guarded this royal prerogative with grotesque cruelty, maiming and hanging poachers, razing villages to the ground which were in his way. It is said that the Saxon oaks groaned under slavery to this Norman tyrant. Consequently, this ruddy-faced Rufus was not a man blessed with good friends . . . nor a man short of enemies.

One summer morning in 1100, William-called-Rufus was staying in Winchester, for the hunting. After a huge breakfast, he was preparing to hunt when a fletcher, or arrow-maker, presented him with six new arrows. He admired them, passed two to his closest companion, Walter Tirel, and went outdoors to the waiting horses. As he mounted up, a letter arrived post-haste from a monastery in Gloucestershire: a letter of warning.

One of the monks had dreamed a dream: a woman kneeling in front of the throne of Christ, begging Him to free England from the yoke of King William. The warning rolled harmless off the King's back. He just laughed, screwed up the letter, and spurred his horse to a gallop.

Once inside the forest, the huntsmen split up. William and Tirel set up on either side of a clearing, while the beaters startled a roe deer out of the undergrowth. It sprang between the two men. The King raised his crossbow to shoot, but the arrow glanced off the deer's hide. "Shoot, Walter! Shoot!" shouted the King, and Tirel fired.

With a whistle, a thud, a bolt struck William Rufus in the chest. He was dead before he hit the ground. From everywhere, men came running forward to stare at the body on the ground. Tirel knelt over it. "It wasn't me!" he said.

"The arrow's like the ones he gave you this morning," the royal huntsman pointed out. The stares were all turned on Tirel now – fixed, accusing stares. Without a word, Tirel remounted his horse and galloped south, towards Southampton. He could see that he was going to get blamed, guilty or not.

Hours later, a pair of charcoal-burners were scuffing their way through the woods collecting brushwood and dead twigs when they came across the body of the King, the triple feathers of a crossbow bolt emerging from his chest like a seedling. Of his courtiers and huntsmen and friends – of his brother Henry – there was not a sign.

The charcoal burners bundled Rufus on to their handcart and trundled him out of the green forest gloom, jolting him over tree roots and leaving behind a trail of blood like scarlet periwinkles growing in his wake. “Him bled all the way,” they told the priests at Winchester Cathedral, tipping the King out on to the stone slabs.

But no one was interested. Duke Henry was already there, at the cathedral, arguing with the bishop, trying to lay hands on the royal treasure which was kept there. *He* was now King, he said, the crown had passed to *him*. The argument grew noisy and undignified. The bishop maintained that William’s *other* brother, Duke Robert, was the rightful heir. But Robert was away crusading – not there to defend his interests.

William Rufus, his face smeared redder than red now with his own heart’s blood, lay on the flags of Winchester Cathedral and said nothing at all.

When it came to burying Rufus, the Church had its revenge. They called him an unbeliever, a heretic, a blasphemer. They called him an enemy of the Church and a sacrilegious villain. They deigned to sink him in the ground – under the floor of Winchester Cathedral, no less – but no one spoke a word of prayer over him. No one sanctified his burial or prayed for his soul.

Seven years later the cathedral tower crashed down, shattering sepulchres and statues, fonts and pulpits. Devout folk locally blamed the presence of evil Rufus.

But the people who lived by the forest saw things differently. They said that the forest, older than Christianity, had exacted a blood sacrifice, so that its crowns of green might continue to flourish. In that case, just whose hand fired the crossbow hardly matters.

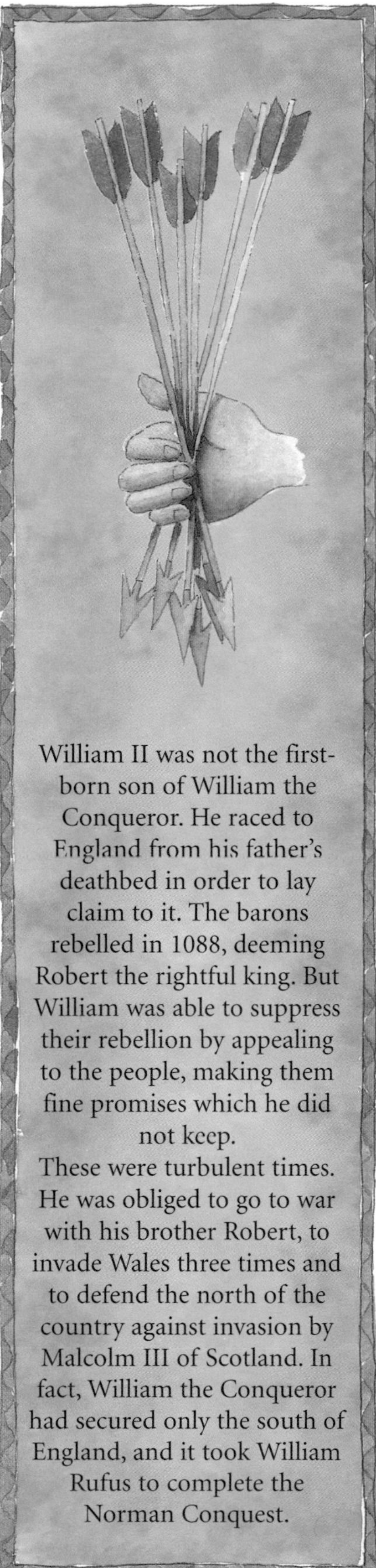

William II was not the first-born son of William the Conqueror. He raced to England from his father’s deathbed in order to lay claim to it. The barons rebelled in 1088, deeming Robert the rightful king. But William was able to suppress their rebellion by appealing to the people, making them fine promises which he did not keep.

These were turbulent times. He was obliged to go to war with his brother Robert, to invade Wales three times and to defend the north of the country against invasion by Malcolm III of Scotland. In fact, William the Conqueror had secured only the south of England, and it took William Rufus to complete the Norman Conquest.

The White Ship

1120

AT LAST THERE WAS PEACE. After years of war between England and France, a peace had been struck, and the future blossomed with promise. King Henry I's heart was crammed with cheerful memories and optimistic plans as he boarded his ship at Barfleur, bound for England. The ship rubbed flanks with another in the harbour – *La Blanche Nef* – the *White Ship* – whose captain had begged for the honour of conveying the King's party home. But Henry's ship was ready, laden and rigged. So, sooner than snub the good captain, Henry had entrusted his children to the *White Ship*, along with the royal treasure. They could follow on the next tide, Prince William and the rest.

Of course, as far as Henry was concerned his children *were* the royal treasure. He was a harsh, demanding father, not above dragging one daughter through a frozen moat to teach her a lesson; but he adored his children. His oldest son, his heir, Prince William, had grown into as fine a young man as any father could hope for. In France he had won his spurs, remembered his manners, charmed the French court. And Maud! How lovely little Maud had looked as she wished him *bon voyage*. Fortunate England that it should enjoy both peace and the promise of such princes and princesses. Fortunate Henry. The sea was calm, the sky generous and big. The King watched Barfleur slip below the horizon, then walked to the prow to watch for the Dover coast.

The tide ebbed and flowed once more. The young people of the royal party, no longer required to be on their best behaviour, drank a little too much and became noisy and excitable. When French priests came down to the waterfront to bless *La Blanche Nef*, the English crew and passengers told them in blunt, colourful English: "Take yourselves off, you sheep-faced bunch of old women!" Even so, long after the *White Ship* had set sail, one of those priests stayed on, looking out to sea, moving his lips in silent prayer. He stood there till the grey of evening turned to night.

On board the King's ship, the look-out cocked his ear and looked back southwards. Everyone heard it: a strange shrill cry carrying over the water. Gulls, they thought. Gulls, thought the King.

The *White Ship*'s eager captain, Thomas Fitz-Stephen, had set himself the task of overtaking the royal ship, proving the excellence of both ship and crew. The prow cut smartly through the waves, unslowed by cross-winds or swell. But the steersman, either drunk or ignorant of the rocky Raz de Catteville, was taking the *White Ship* to her death.

When she struck rocks submerged by high tide, the people aboard loosed a cry – a single scream of horror which travelled like cannonfire across the sea. Within minutes the vessel lay with her keel ripped open, the sea gushing in.

"Hold her to the rocks with grappling hooks!" Captain Fitz-Stephen commanded. "The rocks will hold her up till help comes!" But the rocks only chewed the ship apart, board by board.

"Get the prince away safe!" commanded the captain, and even amid the panic and confusion, one jolly-boat was got off, with Prince William kneeling up, white-faced on the rear thwart.

It was not a sight for a boy to see – his friends, his brothers, his sisters being washed one by one off the tilting deck. The noise was terrible – the howled prayers, the curses, the cries, the submerged rocks grinding on the keel. If the tide had been lower, the rocks themselves would have stuck up out of the water: somewhere to cling. But the rocks were only a darkness now below the water. Swimmers trod nothing but numbing, icy water.

"My sister! I hear my sister!" cried Prince William. "Row back! We must save Maud!" His beloved sister's screams drew him like a magnet.

The rowers did turn back. They were able to snatch Maud from where she clung to the stringy rigging sluiced by icy sea. But the water round about her was alive with swimmers. Like sharks they snatched at the oars. Hands shark-blue with cold came over the side of the boat, the drowning trying to pull themselves aboard. Desperately, the rowers tried to prise the fingers loose, but the boat rolled lower and lower . . . until the sea simply washed in over the back and sucked everything down in the foundering swirl of the *White Ship*.

Captain Fitz-Stephen, surfacing from an eternity of airless cold, grasped a broken spar to keep himself afloat. Two men erupted through the surface nearby and heaved themselves over a piece of flotsam. One was a scrawny young courtier, Geoffrey Daigle, wearing thin, torn silks, one a fat Barfleur butcher in a sheepskin jacket.

"What of the King's son? Are the King's children safe?" called the captain.

"All gone! Drowned and gone!" came the reply, and the captain, his honour already drowned in the Raz de Catteville, let go the spar and slid back down into the dark. Better to die than to live with the shame of what he had done.

Before morning the butcher of Barfleur found himself alone on the ocean, sole survivor of the wreck of the *White Ship*.

It is said that the royal treasure washed up intact on a French beach. Not so the heir to the English throne.

When the news reached England, no one knew how to tell the King. No one wanted to be the man who broke the King's heart. So they found a young boy and taught him to say the words parrot-fashion. "The *White Ship* is gone down, sire. Your children are lost."

When the King heard the words, he rose to his feet and stood silent for a few moments. Then his knees gave way, and he crashed to the ground, unconscious. It is said that King Henry I never smiled again.

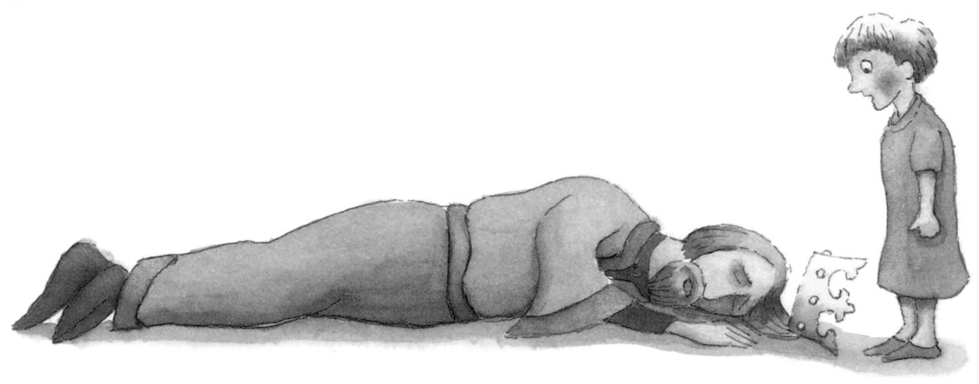

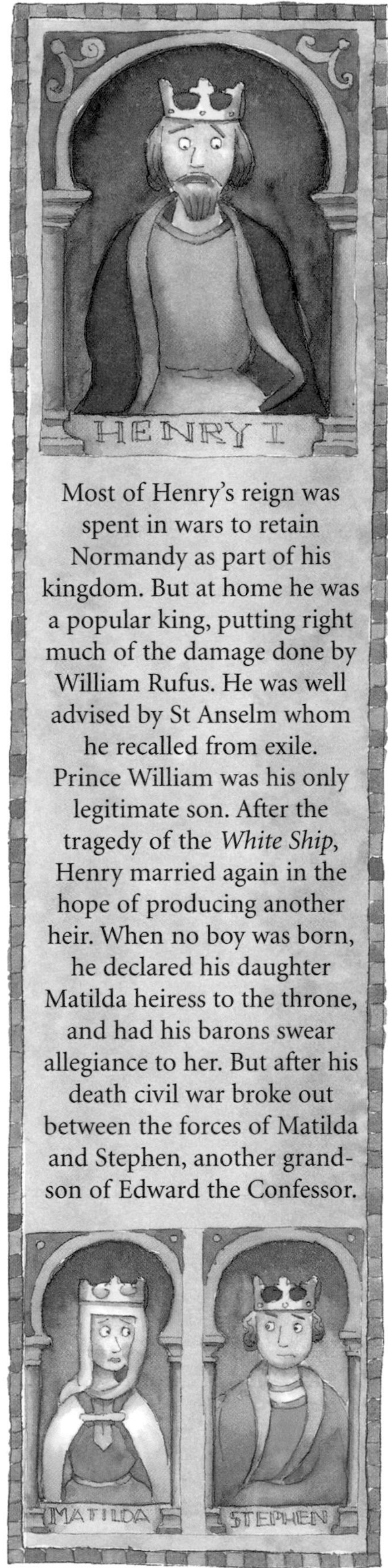

Most of Henry's reign was spent in wars to retain Normandy as part of his kingdom. But at home he was a popular king, putting right much of the damage done by William Rufus. He was well advised by St Anselm whom he recalled from exile. Prince William was his only legitimate son. After the tragedy of the *White Ship*, Henry married again in the hope of producing another heir. When no boy was born, he declared his daughter Matilda heiress to the throne, and had his barons swear allegiance to her. But after his death civil war broke out between the forces of Matilda and Stephen, another grandson of Edward the Confessor.

“This Turbulent Priest”

1170

As young men, Thomas à Becket and King Henry II were the best of friends. They were forever horsing about, vying with each other as to who wore the most splendid clothes or made the most witty remark. Once, the King had pulled off Thomas’s cloak for a joke, and given it to a poor old man, telling Becket that “charity demanded it”.

Thomas was only a low-born commoner, but he showed such genius at any and every job that he rose from soldier to ambassador to chancellor! Henry was happy to work hand-in-glove with clever, witty, tactful, *loyal* Thomas. He even entrusted his son’s education to him.

The Church, on the other hand, was regularly troublesome to Henry. The Church felt less need to obey the King than it did God and the Pope. Henry’s solution was to put someone he could trust in authority over the Church. And who better than Becket?

“I do not want the office,” said Thomas. “You will take your favour from me, and our love will then become hatred.”

Henry should have listened; Becket’s advice had always been sound. But he brushed the warning aside. In 1162, Thomas à Becket was consecrated Archbishop of Canterbury.

He changed then. As if Henry had accidentally spoken some magic word, Becket began to alter. He resigned as chancellor, laid aside the rich clothes, the vanity and splendour of court life, and dressed like a monk, with a hair shirt against his skin. Each night, after supper, he had himself flogged, in penance for his sins. He gave away his belongings – and he gave over his loyalty – the loyalty which, till that time had belonged entirely to Henry II – to God and to the Church.

Suddenly he was the champion of the clergy, defending the Church against any and every attack. Henry found to his dismay that, far from gaining influence over the Church, he was being thwarted at every turn by Archbishop Becket. Henry felt betrayed. Becket’s former friends and colleagues felt betrayed.

The two men clashed most fiercely when Henry tried to make the clergy answerable to the law. At that time, a priest could rob or murder or burn down a house and still escape arrest. Extraordinarily, Becket refused to give up this much-abused privilege. Henry retaliated by confiscating castles and fining Becket for leaving his post as chancellor. He took his son out of Becket’s care.

On the day the King's pages threw mud at him and called him "Traitor!", Becket realized the danger he was in, and took a ship for France. For two years the cold Channel flowed between the two friends, and a still colder hostility.

Then the quarrel was patched up and Becket came home. The nobility still resented him, but not the common people. He was one of them! He was a saintly man who daily washed the feet of the poor! They had tasted his charity, his goodness, his sanctity! They welcomed him home like a conquering hero, thronging Canterbury in the hope of glimpsing the great man.

Becket had not mellowed in the least. He was as pious and as unyielding as ever. Now he began to wield a power even Henry did not possess. He began to excommunicate his enemies.

A king can cut off a man's head, but the man's soul is free to fly up to heaven. An archbishop – by snuffing out a candle, ringing a bell, closing a book – can condemn a man's soul to burn in everlasting fire. How could Henry compete with that kind of power?

Far away, in his French territories, Henry raged at Becket's insolence, pride and thanklessness. "A fellow that has eaten my bread! A fellow that came to court on a lame horse with a cloak for a saddle!" He fumed and fulminated. His chair turned over, and he began to pace the room, throwing his hands about in melodramatic gestures, smacking at his forehead, groaning and gasping with exasperation. "What cowards have I brought up in my court, who care nothing for their duty to their master! Will no one rid me of this turbulent priest?"

Four knights – Sir Reginald Fitzurse, Sir Richard le Breton, Sir Hugh de Merville and Sir William Tracy – looked at one another, got up and left the room. They sailed to England that night.

They rode to Canterbury Cathedral with a band of horsemen, but went inside alone, unarmed. Naturally. It is a sacrilege to wear a sword inside a church.

Becket kept them waiting. When he finally deigned to see them, there were heated words behind closed doors, and then an argument which spilled out into public.

"We bring you the commands of the King . . . Will you come with us to the King and account for yourself?"

"I will not."

"Absolve the bishops you excommunicated!"

"I will not!"

Their voices rang up and down the echoing cloisters of the huge building. "In that case, the King's final demand is that you depart out of this realm and never return!"

"I do not choose to go. Nothing but death shall part me from my Church!"

At that moment, the bell began to ring for vespers. The great cathedral stirred itself for divine service. The nave would be filling with townspeople. The sounds of holy ritual chased the knights outside into the late afternoon. There they threw off their white cloaks – and began buckling on swords.

A friend of Becket's, who had witnessed the argument, shook his head anxiously. "My lord Archbishop, it is a pity you will never be advised. You would have done far better to have kept quiet and answered them mildly."

But Becket was in no mood for advice or soft words. He set out along the cloisters, towards the cathedral, to conduct vespers – found he had left his cross behind – would not go on till it was fetched. Monks flitted past in alarmed disorder. "They are arming!"

"Let them arm. Who cares?" Those were Becket's exact words.

The monks wanted to lock the cathedral doors – they had already locked the hall door.

"I will not have the church turned into a castle," said Becket irritably.

Meanwhile, finding the hall doors locked against them, the four knights could have gone round to the main entrance and got in easily, but they dragged a ladder over to a window and broke in that way, hurrying through the building, hard on the heels of Becket.

Daylight was all but gone. The only light in the nave came from banks of tallow candles: lozenges of gold floating in the cavernous dark. Some monks had run and hidden. Others were determined to protect their archbishop, even if it cost them their lives. "What are you afraid of?" asked Becket, annoyed by their busy comings and goings.

"Where is the traitor? Where is Thomas Becket?" *Becket-ket-ket.* It echoed round the nave. No one answered.

"Where is the archbishop . . . *ishop . . . ishop*?"

That title Becket was ready to acknowledge. "I am here."

Fitzurse had never meant this to happen. He owed so much to Becket. In a low quick whisper he said: "Flee, or you are a dead man."

"I am ready to die. And may the Church, through my death, obtain peace and liberty. I charge you in the name of God that you hurt no one here but me."

There was a noise of running feet: townspeople had heard there was something amiss and began flocking up the nave now, only to find a man with a sword barring their way to the choir. The darkness added to the confusion.

Fitzurse suddenly grabbed Becket and tried to drag him away. Perhaps he still thought to take the archbishop prisoner and avoid bloodshed. But Becket tore loose: "Off, Reginald. Touch me not!"

Then Tracy and le Breton were on him. But Thomas was tall and strong: he threw Tracy to the ground. He called Fitzurse a Judas. Again Fitzurse told him to run. Again Becket refused. In a clumsy muddle of movements, Fitzurse waved his sword and knocked off Becket's mitre; perhaps he was still trying to frighten him. A monk tried to fend off the second, heavy, downward blow, but fell to his knees as the blade broke his arm, and cut deep into Becket's head. A third stroke felled Thomas to his knees, hands raised as if in prayer.

For a moment all was stillness: a candlelit silence. Then Becket keeled over on to his face, with no more noise than a cloak makes in falling from a man's shoulders.

A fourth blow scalped him. The most vicious wound of all was made last, through the open wound. They made very sure the "turbulent priest" was dead.

When Europe heard the news, it quaked like a drumskin. The primate of England murdered in his own cathedral on the orders of his King?

When Henry heard the news, he gasped and wept inconsolably. What a terrible mistake, he cried. His words had been misunderstood! He had never meant his old friend to be murdered!

When he got back to England, he took off his royal clothes and walked barefoot to Canterbury Cathedral in a hair shirt and pilgrim's cloak, to kiss the flagstones where his friend had died. Beside the tomb, he fell weeping on his face and allowed each one of the eighty bishops and monks to lash him with whips: five lashes each.

The watching thousands crowding the streets of Canterbury were impressed. Nothing less would have satisfied them, but they were impressed.

Quite soon there came news of miracles bestowed by the dead archbishop. Pilgrims began to converge on Canterbury from all over the country. After all, Becket the martyr was an easier man to love than Becket the cantankerous archbishop. And the common people had a new voice to speak for them in heaven: a man low-born like themselves, their very own saint.

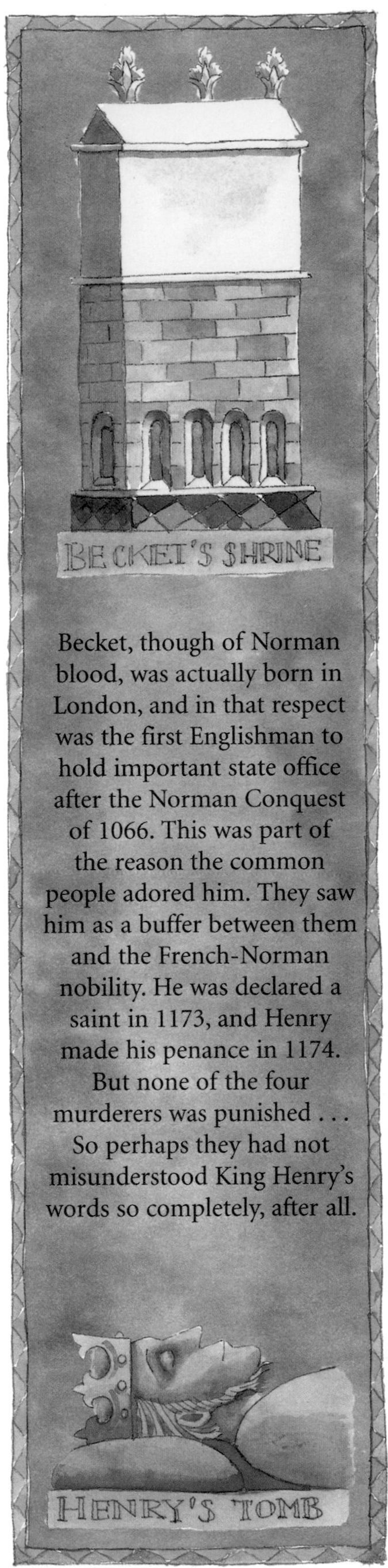

Becket, though of Norman blood, was actually born in London, and in that respect was the first Englishman to hold important state office after the Norman Conquest of 1066. This was part of the reason the common people adored him. They saw him as a buffer between them and the French-Norman nobility. He was declared a saint in 1173, and Henry made his penance in 1174. But none of the four murderers was punished . . . So perhaps they had not misunderstood King Henry's words so completely, after all.

The Fair Rosamond

about 1175

ELEANOR OF AQUITAINE WAS A WOMAN WHO HAD GONE TO THE Crusades, worn eastern robes in the palaces of Constantinople, captured the hearts of a hundred troubadours and broken them all by marrying a second husband, this time for love.

But Henry II was ten years younger than she, and a man of such immoderate passions that, in his tempers, he bit men's shoulders or fell on his face and chewed the straw. It was unlikely, from the very outset, that he would ever give his love to Eleanor alone.

He had a whole gaggle of lovers, but none took so firm a hold on his heart as Rosamond Clifford, known as the Fair Rosamond.

Some said that they had been sweethearts since childhood days, and that Henry had secretly married Rosamond before he ever met Queen Eleanor. But whatever the truth, Henry determined to keep Rosamond both secret from the Queen and hidden from any eyes but his. So he shut her up – a willing captive – somewhere he was sure the Queen would never find her, and he visited her as often as he was in Oxfordshire. Perhaps the Queen suspected. Perhaps she kept watch. Or perhaps it was by chance that she saw Henry striding out one day across his estates at Woodstock Park, and spotted something trailing from his heel. His spur had snagged a thread of silk, and as he walked towards the house, it pulled taut behind him. Where had he been, to have embroidery thread caught around his spur?

He did not see Eleanor standing in the shade of a tree, and when he had passed by, she stepped out and picked up the thread, following it back in the direction the King had come. Through the vegetable garden it ran, around a bush, across a grassy lawn to the maze.

It was notoriously huge and complex, the maze Henry had designed to ornament his park; a knot of paths circling and doubling back on themselves. Eleanor had never entered it, for she was a busy woman and could not spare time on such idle amusements. But she entered it now.

The paths wound to and fro until, without the thread to guide her, Eleanor would have been hopelessly lost. But the strand of blood-red silk led her unerringly to the centre, and at the centre she found a door. Through the door she went, down stairs into a subterranean passage-way which twisted as intricately below ground as the maze had done above. She was not bewildered by the dark and twisting corridors, for she had the thread in her hand. She had long since guessed what she would find at her journey's end.

Soon a glimmer of light showed ahead of her, and the passage opened into a large, well-lit room hung with tapestries. A beautiful young woman with yellow hair leaned intently over her embroidery; at her feet a basket of silks, the red skein half pulled out and unravelled almost to its end. The sewer looked up, thinking that Henry had forgotten something and returned. Her lovely face registered first shock, then fear, then a slightly proud defiance.

"Tell me your name," demanded the Queen.

"I am Rosamond Clifford, ma'am."

"Are you held prisoner here against your will?"

"Oh no, ma'am! It is my joy and duty to –"

But Eleanor had turned her back – gone. Within half an hour she had returned. In the meantime, Rosamond's courage had risen. "Did you ask him? Did Henry tell you? We were married these many years since, and have a son true-born and –"

"I will ask you again," Eleanor interrupted. "Are you held prisoner here against your will?"

"I told you before," said Rosamond. "I am not."

"In that case, you are free to go," said the Queen. She took out from a pouch at her belt a little Turkish dagger, souvenir of the Crusades, also a small bottle of some blue-green liquid. "Shall you die by the dagger or by the poisoned cup? For die you shall, Fair Rosamond, and with you your shame and the shame of my husband, King of England."

There was no crying out, no appealing to Henry to overrule his wife; they were far from the house and deep underground. "Nothing you can do will alter the fact that Henry loves me best!" said Rosamond through her tears. "Nothing in any of your apothecary's bottles will ever serve to make you young again, nor blot out the truth – that you were married first to King Louis and abandoned him so as to be Queen of England! I *love* Henry! I have always loved Henry – not his country, not his title! And Henry loves me. So which of us do you think is his *true* wife?"

But it was fruitless to argue with Eleanor about love. Eleanor knew all about love. Leaving the house, she locked the door behind her. Leaving the maze, she sheathed the little Turkish dagger. For Rosamond had chosen the poison in preference to the blade. Even now she lay amid her tapestries and silks with an empty cup in her hand and a thread of spilled wine amid her yellow hair.

Rosamond Clifford may well have married Henry when he was a boy; he once swore that their son was legitimate. But whether and however Eleanor discovered her husband's secret love, the part about the poison and the dagger never happened. Rosamond died much later at Godstow Abbey near Oxford, where she had been living for many years. Perhaps Eleanor obliged her to enter the convent.

Eleanor of Aquitaine continued to be a sore trial to her husband in all kinds of ways. She tended to support his enemies and favour her sons before her husband. But given their natures, it must have been an extraordinary marriage.

The mazes built in those days would have been elaborate, raised-turf patterns, not the obscuring kind with high hedges, so the story of the thread is also probably a fiction.

The Troubadour Rescues His King

1193

"Hail, King of England, in vain you disguise yourself. Your face betrays you." As Richard awoke, it was a moment before he could remember where he was, or what had brought him to be captured at sword point in this dirty, ill-lit room which smelled of ale. Then it came back to him – his eventful homeward voyage from the Holy Land, his landfall on unfriendly shores, his attempt to reach home, disguised as a peasant. Now, in this flea-ridden inn, alone and friendless in exceedingly dangerous times, he had fallen into the hands of Duke Leopold of Austria.

Richard had made enemies of half the crowned heads of Europe. They tussled over him like dogs over a bone. Duke Leopold waited to see who would offer most for his prestigious prisoner. His enemies either wanted to ransom Richard for cash, or to kill him. His brother, Prince John, was longing to hear that Richard had died on his way home so that he could seize the crown of England. If news could be kept quiet of Richard's capture, there was a chance he would moulder away in some obscure dungeon and never reappear.

Fortunately, the truth got free. Rumours of the King's capture spread far and wide: somewhere the King of England, Richard the Lion-Hearted, lay in chains, his only hope the persistence of his friends in seeking him out.

Blondel was a troubadour – a writer of ballads, a singer of roundelays. Richard was partial to music and verse and to handsome young men. He had encouraged and rewarded Blondel, and Blondel was, in return, devoted to his king. As soon as he heard Richard was missing, he vowed he would travel the world until he had found him.

Day after week after month the troubadour roamed Europe, earning his bread with a song, sleeping under the stars. A musician could go anywhere. So long as Blondel was careful whom he questioned and how many questions he asked, he would not arouse suspicion. And if he kept his eyes open and listened carefully in the alehouses and market squares, he was sure he could track Richard down.

Eighteen months later, having found no trace or whisper of an imprisoned king, he was less sure.

At last, just when he was on the point of despair, he struck up conversation with an innkeeper's wife. She said: yes, there was a rumour – it might only be gossip – you know how people talk – but up at the castle – that gloomy place, aye, up yonder by the river – she had heard tell there was a prisoner locked up in the tower who was of such impor tance that the duke guarded him day and night.

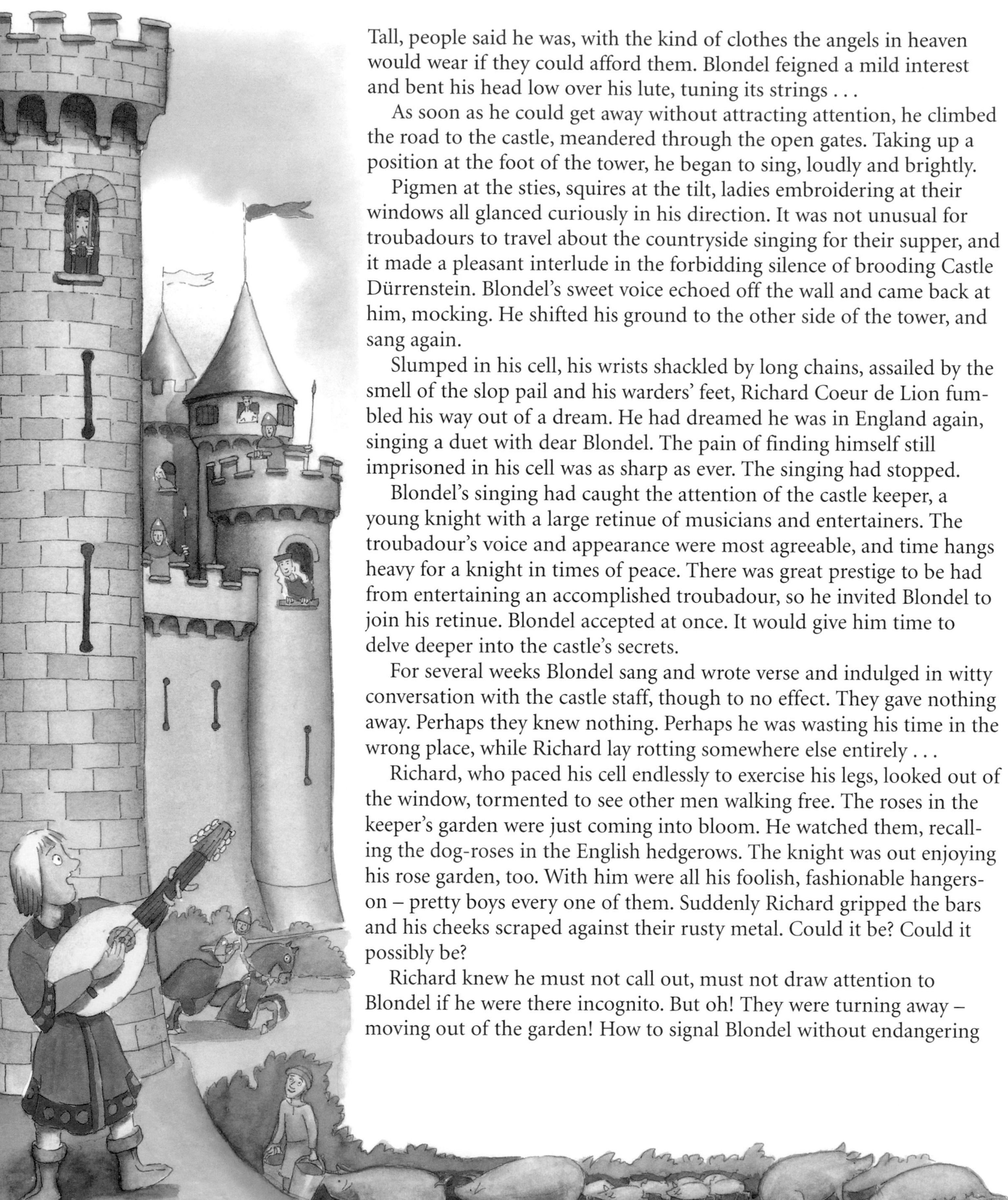

Tall, people said he was, with the kind of clothes the angels in heaven would wear if they could afford them. Blondel feigned a mild interest and bent his head low over his lute, tuning its strings . . .

As soon as he could get away without attracting attention, he climbed the road to the castle, meandered through the open gates. Taking up a position at the foot of the tower, he began to sing, loudly and brightly.

Pigmen at the sties, squires at the tilt, ladies embroidering at their windows all glanced curiously in his direction. It was not unusual for troubadours to travel about the countryside singing for their supper, and it made a pleasant interlude in the forbidding silence of brooding Castle Dürrenstein. Blondel's sweet voice echoed off the wall and came back at him, mocking. He shifted his ground to the other side of the tower, and sang again.

Slumped in his cell, his wrists shackled by long chains, assailed by the smell of the slop pail and his warders' feet, Richard Coeur de Lion fumbled his way out of a dream. He had dreamed he was in England again, singing a duet with dear Blondel. The pain of finding himself still imprisoned in his cell was as sharp as ever. The singing had stopped.

Blondel's singing had caught the attention of the castle keeper, a young knight with a large retinue of musicians and entertainers. The troubadour's voice and appearance were most agreeable, and time hangs heavy for a knight in times of peace. There was great prestige to be had from entertaining an accomplished troubadour, so he invited Blondel to join his retinue. Blondel accepted at once. It would give him time to delve deeper into the castle's secrets.

For several weeks Blondel sang and wrote verse and indulged in witty conversation with the castle staff, though to no effect. They gave nothing away. Perhaps they knew nothing. Perhaps he was wasting his time in the wrong place, while Richard lay rotting somewhere else entirely . . .

Richard, who paced his cell endlessly to exercise his legs, looked out of the window, tormented to see other men walking free. The roses in the keeper's garden were just coming into bloom. He watched them, recalling the dog-roses in the English hedgerows. The knight was out enjoying his rose garden, too. With him were all his foolish, fashionable hangers-on – pretty boys every one of them. Suddenly Richard gripped the bars and his cheeks scraped against their rusty metal. Could it be? Could it possibly be?

Richard knew he must not call out, must not draw attention to Blondel if he were there incognito. But oh! They were turning away – moving out of the garden! How to signal Blondel without endangering his life? Richard cleared his throat. He had had no cause to sing for a year and a half, but now he began a song – a song he and Blondel had sung together a dozen times, a song he had no difficulty in remembering.

"If everything were as I wish it,
We would not divided be;
He in the east and I in the west
And in between, the sea."

Smiling despite himself, he fixed his eyes on his troubadour's face and willed him to hear.

A spasm passed through Blondel, which he hid with a sneeze. Unwrapping his lute from its cloth bag, he began to strum it. Supplying the chords at first, then joining in the descant of the song floating down from the tower, he moved away little by little from the group of squires and jongleurs. He was singing louder now, joining in split harmony with the singer in the tower, just as he had done a dozen times sitting at Richard's feet.

"The time until his ship comes home,
Is time most pitiful to me;
He in the east and I in the west,
And in between, the sea."

When the song ended, Blondel calmly wrapped up his lute again and sauntered back to the others. Tomorrow he would tell the knight that he was leaving – on a pilgrimage or a Crusade. Then he would quit Castle Dürrenstein and head for England.

He knew now where the King was being held. Prince John might try to persuade the people his brother had died, but Blondel knew differently. He could tell the churchmen and barons and ministers and diplomats where to find their true king. All the way home, that knowledge gave rise to new songs which the troubadour sang to the seagulls from the deck of the cross-Channel packet.

Although it is true the Duke of Austria captured Richard and imprisoned him at Dürrenstein, the King was soon moved to Castle Triefels in Germany where he was tried and offered freedom in exchange for an astronomical ransom. Great doubt has to be cast on the truth of the Blondel legend, though the troubadour probably was part of Richard's retinue. £100,000 was raised in ransom – a sum which beggared England after years already spent financing Richard's crusading. The Lion Heart, spoiled, reckless, full of vices and never home, was hardly his country's best friend.

The Three Outlaws

about 1200

THE MEN OF THE NORTH COUNTRY could not come to terms at all with King John's claim to own the Forest of Englewood. It is one thing to say that the cows in a field belong to the farmer who raised them. It is quite another to say that the deer, the partridge, the wild pig and rabbits belong to one man, simply because he says so. The men of the borderlands continued to hunt there as their fathers and grandfathers had always done.

But the sheriff and justice of Carlisle were eager to prove themselves loyal officers of the King, so they hanged one man after another for killing the King's deer.

Sooner than hang, accused men slipped away into the forest and lived as outlaws, never able to visit their homes or families again. And the three bravest who ever took shelter under the greenwood trees were Adam Bell, Clym of the Cleugh, and William Cloudeslee.

One night, by the campfire, William said, "It's half a year since I saw my wife and children. Tomorrow I think I'll take a walk into Carlisle Town and pay them a visit."

"Don't be a fool, Will!" exclaimed Adam. "The sheriff has your house watched! It's too dangerous. Doesn't the little pig-boy bring you messages from home? Be content!"

But Will's mind was made up. He mingled among the last travellers of the day and arrived just before the city gates shut for the night, making his way from shadow to shadow, to rap on the shutters of his house. His wife's pale face appeared at the window.

"Will! Are you mad? What a risk to come here!" But she slipped the latch, and Will Cloudeslee was once again in his wife's arms, his children dangling from his belt and wrists and jerkin. He could hardly credit how much and how little things had changed. Alice was as beautiful as ever. His children had grown so big! Old Meg still sat by the fire.

"She's *still* here?" Will whispered.

"Of course! You said she could stay, when she had nowhere else to go. She took you at your word!" Alice whispered, laughing. "She's part of the furniture now."

Will greeted the old lady by the fire, asked after her health, then turned his attention to his family.

Everyone thought Old Meg was bed-ridden; a harmless, helpless old woman. So they never thought she could slip out of her shadowy corner, out of the house and away down the alley. Never for a moment did it occur to them that a guest treated with such kindness might betray them for a quick profit. Old Meg went straight to the sheriff. "If I give into your hands that outlaw William Cloudeslee, what will you give me?"

Old Meg sold Will to his enemies for a piece of scarlet cloth, then creeping back to her place by the fire, she sat with the parcel crammed under her dress, warming her wicked knees.

At around midnight, Alice glanced out of the window, and saw the glimmer of chain mail. Armed men. "You are betrayed, Will," she said. "Run!"

But it was too late. The sheriff's men surrounded the building and there was nothing for it but to stay and fight, or surrender and be taken. "Get into the bedroom," said Alice picking up an axe. "I'll guard the door while you use your bow."

Will looked at her across the heads of their children. "I do not deserve you," he said.

The sheriff sneered when he saw his best men running to shelter from Will's flying arrows. "Burn the place down! That will put an end to his archery."

The town's people, brought from their beds by the commotion, gave a roar of protest as they saw burning faggots stacked against the house. "What about the man's children? What about his wife? For shame!"

The sheriff simply narrowed his eyes against the smoke, covered his nose against the stench of burning.

Will fought on till the sound of his children's crying blinded his own eyes with tears. "I won't have your lives on my conscience!" he called to Alice. "Pull the sheets off the bed and tear them in strips . . ."

Alice would have chosen to stay with her husband, but for the sake of her children she allowed Will to lower them all to safety down ropes of knotted sheets. The people in the street rushed forward in such numbers to help them down that the sheriff's archers were knocked off their feet. The burning house overhung them like a breaking wave of fire.

Remembering Old Meg, Will ran to save her, too. But the old crone only boggled at him, with mad, soot-rimmed eyes, and clutched a parcel to her stomach. She would not let it go – not even to put her arms around his neck. Back he ran to the window, firing arrows till the flames singed and broke the bowstring. Then he stepped out on to the sill. So much chain mail was gathered in the street below that it looked like silver sea into which he leapt . . .

"Who is the gallows for?" the little pig-boy asked the morning watchman.

"For William Cloudeslee, the outlaw," came the response.

The boy ran with the news all the way to the greenwood. "Adam Bell! Clym of the Cleugh! Where are you?" Then, crouched by the camp fire, he told them their friend was condemned to hang at noon.

"That doesn't give us long," said Adam thoughtfully. "Can you get us into Carlisle, boy?"

"Not till the gates open again! The sheriff has ordered them kept shut till Will is dead!"

"Ah, but they will open for a *King's messenger*, I know," said Clym, whose plan was already taking shape. "You and I, Adam, shall pretend to be messengers bearing a letter for the sheriff. There's only one small difficulty . . ."

"What? The guard? The gatekeeper?" Adam was eager to help.

"No. The fact that I'm not a *writing* kind of man."

Fortunately, Adam Bell could both read and write. With a tree stump for his table, he penned an impressive-looking letter which they rolled up and sealed with candle-tallow. Forest bark served in place of the royal seal. "A fitting seal for a king who thinks he owns the forest," said Adam Bell.

"No one enters until the outlaw is dead," said the gatekeeper for the third time.

"Then you'd best tell the hangman to prepare for a second hanging!" roared Adam Bell, "for by this hand, the King will have you hanged if you delay his messengers another minute!"

The gatekeeper blenched. He looked at the letter they wagged in his face, but he was not a reading sort of man, and he could not have told the royal seal from a lump of candle-tallow. So he opened up, and the two men strode in.

As he went to hang the keys back inside the gatehouse, an arm circled his throat and a hand relieved him of the keys. The "King's messenger" he had just admitted said, "I think *I* shall be gatekeeper of Carlisle today, and you shall be Clym of the Cleugh. Bind him, Adam, and see that he doesn't escape."

William was carried to the gallows bound hand and foot, lying face down in the execution cart. The streets were full of angry murmurings. "What has the man done but shoot a deer? Shame on the sheriff for his spite! Shame on the justice for his heartlessness!"

William was lifted to his feet, and a noose placed around his neck. The ropes round his ankles were freed so that he could climb the ladder to the gallows. The sheriff of Carlisle stood at his window rubbing his hands with glee. Beside him stood the justice, saying, "One fewer outlaw to trouble the King's deer . . ."

Those were the last words he spoke. Two arrows flew across the town square and plunged into the hearts of both sheriff and justice.

Then chaos. Adam cut Will's bonds, and Clym cleared a path across the square with his sword. The guards, slow to realize what was happening, had to push the crowds aside to give chase through the narrow streets. Under their feet they found the city pigs, let loose from their sties to trip them up. The three outlaws had plenty of time to unlock, open, close and relock the city gate. They stood on the outside breathless and laughing.

Clym slung the keys over the top of the gate. "I resign as gatekeeper!" he called. "I think I'll go back to an honest profession as outlaw!"

When they reached Englewood they found a visitor in their camp. She stood amid the green-clothed men, children clinging to her skirts, weeping as if her heart were broken. "And all for my sake!" they heard her say.

"Alice?" said Will Cloudeslee.

She stared at him as if he might be a ghost. "But I thought . . . I thought you must be dead!"

"Who, me? Never!" Then he drew his wife aside, kissed her and made her this promise. "Go home, my love. Wait for me seven years, and I shall return to you a pardoned man. Adam and Clym and I shall go to London and win the King's forgiveness. Until then, Alice, keep me alive in your thoughts and prayers, and I shall keep to the greenwood like the nightingale keeps to the tree – out-of-sight but singing, my dear, out-of-sight but singing."

Cuckoos

about 1212

THE KING'S OWN MESSENGERS WERE ACCUSTOMED to causing a stir. Usually, when they rode into a town or village, people rushed out of doors to stare, local dignitaries hurried to fawn and flatter them, the inn prepared a splendid supper. But when King John's messengers rode into Gotham, nobody paid the smallest notice.

Four men came quarrelling down the road carrying between them a great length of picket fence. "It's your fault," said one.

"Well, how was I to know?"

At a shout from the royal messengers, the men with the fence all bumped into each other and stumbled to a halt. "We been trying to catch the cuckoo up yonder," explained one. "Sings in that bush on the hill. Pretty as a picklejar."

The man behind him joined in: "We knocked in this fence right around it! Got that bush so surrounded there was no getting out . . ."

"We had him, didn't we? We had him surrounded!" said a third eagerly.

"Then the cuckoo up and flew off," said the fourth sorrowfully dabbing his eyes.

King John's messengers looked at one another. One tapped his forehead with one finger. "You, sirs, are cuckoos yourselves if you didn't think of that . . ." began the chief messenger. But he was left talking to himself as the four cuckoo-catchers bumbled away down the road.

A man without trousers and wearing a jacket with wet coat-tails came sprinting down the street holding a big eel at arm's length. Dashing straight past without so much as a glance at the King's messengers, he ran to the village pond and threw the eel into it with a triumphant shout of, "There now! Drown and good riddance to you!"

Intrigued, the messengers asked what had happened. The villager looked at them with a slightly crazed grin and said, "I'm sorry you had to see that, but the vile beastie ate all the fish in our lake. So we held a trial and found it guilty and condemned it to death-by-drowning. That there was the execution."

"But eels can" – The royal messenger did not finish. Clearly the man was a lunatic if he thought he could drown eels – just as his neighbours were lunatics if they thought . . .

A woman carrying a bag of oatmeal came bustling out of the inn, calling back over her shoulder: "I'm just off down to the river to cook your porridge, Jack!" She curtsied as she passed the troupe of royal messengers. "River's bubbling nicely this morning!" she observed (as someone might comment cheerily on the weather). "Must be right hot to bubble like that! Porridge will be cooked in no time." They could not help noticing that her ears were painted green.

"They're all mad!" whispered the banner-bearer. "Are they dangerous, do you think?"

"You, sir! Come hither!" called the chief messenger imperiously. "You, farmer!"

"Oo? Me, sirrah?" A farmer leading a sway-backed old horse out of town, with two bags of grain slung across the saddle, shot them a hunted, guilty look and started talking before they could stop him. "I know what you're going to say! I know, and it's all true! This old horse shouldn't have to carry those heavy sacks, should she? Not after the lifetime of service she's given me! Well, neither shall she, sirs! Neither shall she! I'll spare her! You have showed me I am a cruel and unfeeling man!" So saying, he tugged the sacks off the old horse and tucked one under each arm. "I'll carry them myself, so I will!" Then he clambered awkwardly astride the animal's back, still clutching the sacks, and clicked his tongue for her to walk on.

"Let us hurry back and tell the King. This is no fit place for him! The village is full of half-wits! I swear there's not a soul living here but he's mad!" And so the royal messengers left at a gallop, sleeping in the forest sooner than stay in Gotham overnight.

When they had gone, the good gentlemen of Gotham converged on the Cuckoo Bush Inn for a pint or two of ale. "Reckon that put paid to them," said Farmer Giles.

"Reckon it did," said the carpenter.

"No hunting lodge hereabouts for King John, then," said the innkeeper's wife, brushing oatmeal off her dress. Everyone spat on the floor in unison.

"No Gothamites banned from their own forest, just so some king can enjoy his sport in sole splendour," said the man busy wiping the smell of eel off his hands.

"There's wisdom in what you say," said the innkeeper's wife with a wink. "But then Gotham was always blessed with a wealth of wise men."

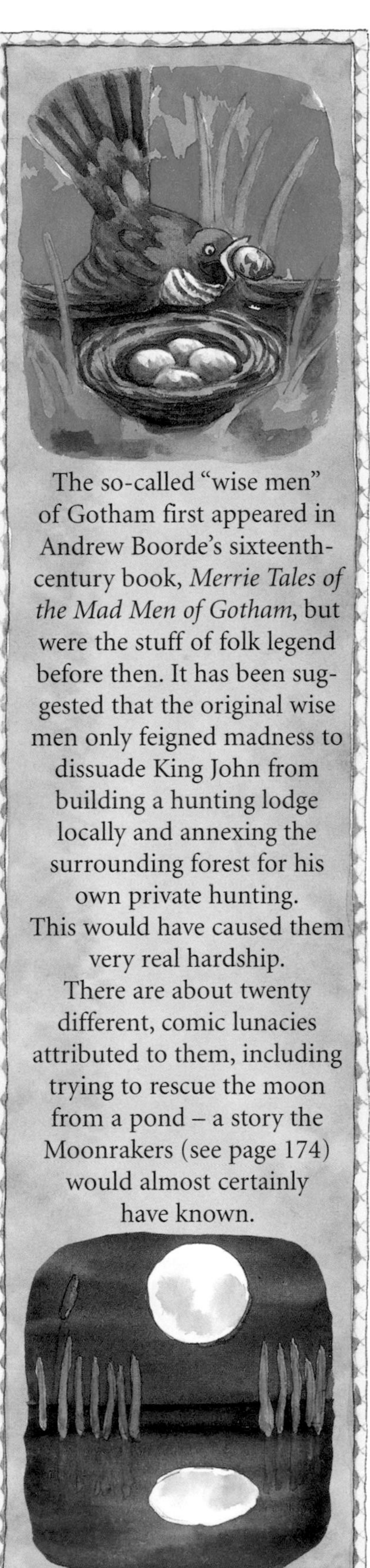

The so-called "wise men" of Gotham first appeared in Andrew Boorde's sixteenth-century book, *Merrie Tales of the Mad Men of Gotham*, but were the stuff of folk legend before then. It has been suggested that the original wise men only feigned madness to dissuade King John from building a hunting lodge locally and annexing the surrounding forest for his own private hunting. This would have caused them very real hardship. There are about twenty different, comic lunacies attributed to them, including trying to rescue the moon from a pond – a story the Moonrakers (see page 174) would almost certainly have known.

Lost in the Wash

1216

PERHAPS IF HE HAD BEEN MORE HANDSOME, MORE successful, more popular, King John would have minded less about clothes and jewellery. As it was, he carried his wealth of showy possessions with him everywhere he went. Even when the King of Scotland invaded and John set out to fight him, he took with him a baggage train of personal belongings, including the Crown Jewels.

Pushing too far south, into the Cambridgeshire fens, the Scottish invaders overreached themselves; John was easily able to turn them back, without heavy loss of men. But it left him in inhospitable fenland – a damp, shivering landscape which he hated. He had been feeling unwell lately, which made him even more irritable and impatient to get home. The sooner he and his men marched north and inland to Nottingham, the happier he would be.

And there at his feet, invitingly flat and golden, lay the vast sands of the Wash, a bite-shaped indent in the eastern coast of England. John studied the map. "If we cut across here," he said, drawing a jewelled finger across the Wash, we can take fifty miles off our journey and be out of this pestilential county by nightfall."

So out on to the hard-packed sand threaded a long line of horses and carts, banners, dogs and wagons. John slouched in his saddle: this salt air would be ruining the vellum of his books and the silver-gilt embroidery on his robes. A vast mackerel sky gave an impression of rippling water overhead. There was spray in the air, such as marks the turn of the tide. The tide.

Some of the wagons were having difficulties – sinking into the wet sand, bogging down. The sandy, featureless plain grew more beautiful by the minute, with little twisted cords of silver, and a bluey tinge reflected from the sky. It was no longer clear where the beach ended and the sky began. The horses' hoof prints were filling with water, making a line of silver stitches across the brocade tan of the sands.

Then the mist came down – a white pall of water droplets which hung on the men's eyelashes and beards and wetted them to the skin. The distant cottages on which they had taken a bearing dissolved like lumps of sugar in milk, and the gulls fell suddenly silent.

A horse floundered and fell to its knees. Its back arched as though it were leaping invisible fences, but its feet did not move – could not move. Soon only its head was straining and tossing, while the quicksand swallowed it up. A cart turned over with a crash of breaking crockery.

The tide did not roll in. It seemed to well up from below ground. The orderly line of troops and baggage carts broke up in panic. More horses pitched nose-down, their riders flying, hands-out, into the soft, receiving sand. Suddenly they could barely hear one another above the noise of the sea. "Look to the Crown Jewels!" shouted King John. "Look to my royal treasure!"

But men were running for dry land now (though they could not see it), jumping from island to island of damp sand, while the channels in between became wider and deeper. Soon there were no more dry patches, and the soldiers were all knee-deep and floundering, the sea pushing against their thighs, dragging the sand from under their boots. Here and there, groups of men trapped by quicksand bawled for help, but the sea piled up behind them, filling up the bottom segment of the sky.

The carts were afloat now, mostly on their sides. They banged against the horses, and mounted knights cursed and abandoned them. The sea came looting its way through the bags and baggage of the royal party, snatching here a coronet, there a jewelled glove. It leafed through the pages of the King's library. Chests too heavy with gold to float bubbled pearls of air, then sank underwater and into the sand. Gold chains looped and knotted themselves to the seaweed, and gem stones glistened in one last brilliant cascade before joining all the other, unremarkable pebbles on the seabed.

The loss gripped at John's chest so hard that he thought his heart was failing. Every time he thought of his ermine and scarlet wool, he groaned with physical pain. Dozens of good men had disappeared without reaching the shore, and the survivors sat about, shocked and shivering. But John thought of each piece of beautiful treasure, the buying of it, the price he had paid, the exquisite craftsmanship, the pleasure it had given him – and misery made him clutch his stomach and howl like a dog.

They pushed on to Nottingham, where John consoled himself by gorging on preserved peaches and cider. Within a fortnight, he was dead of dysentery, unmissed and unmourned, with an epitaph which damned him as "the worst King in English history".

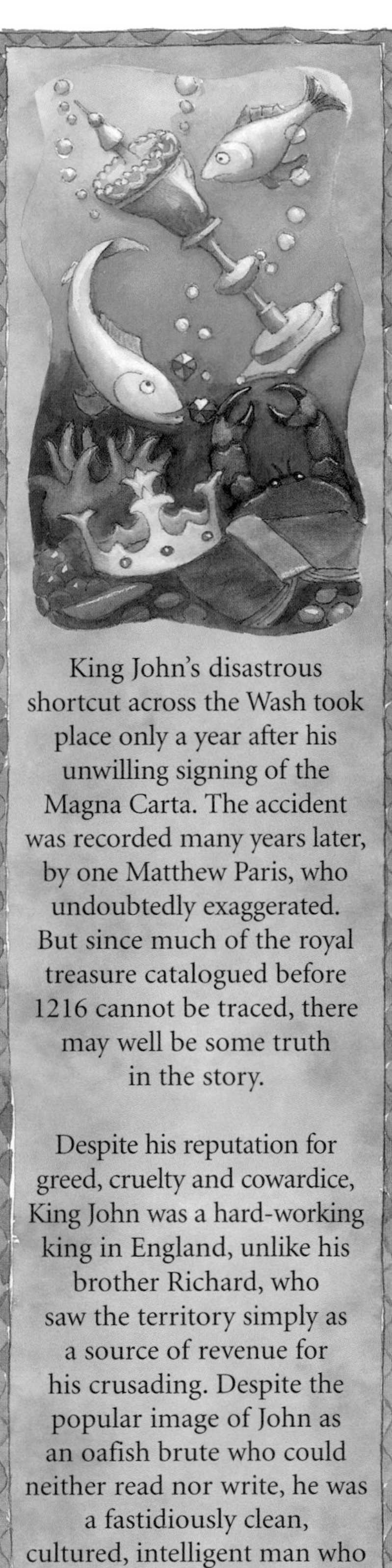

King John's disastrous shortcut across the Wash took place only a year after his unwilling signing of the Magna Carta. The accident was recorded many years later, by one Matthew Paris, who undoubtedly exaggerated. But since much of the royal treasure catalogued before 1216 cannot be traced, there may well be some truth in the story.

Despite his reputation for greed, cruelty and cowardice, King John was a hard-working king in England, unlike his brother Richard, who saw the territory simply as a source of revenue for his crusading. Despite the popular image of John as an oafish brute who could neither read nor write, he was a fastidiously clean, cultured, intelligent man who possessed a large library of books. He travelled the country checking on the honesty of his officials.

"Wrap Me Up In A Cloak of Gold"

1255

TWO DOZEN BOYS WERE playing football with a pig's bladder. Someone skied the ball. It flew high over a wall, then they heard it bounce ringingly on the paved courtyard inside. Both teams scattered.

"What about my ball?" called little Sir Hugh. "I want it back!"

"Not going in there!" his friends shouted as they ran.

"Mother said to keep away!"

"A fairy lives there, says mine!"

Hugh, too, was afraid of the beetling stone walls and the big dark mansion beyond. But he stayed rooted to the spot, thinking about his ball. A gate creaked. A lady came out. She was dark-haired and beautiful, with a fine aquiline nose and dark eyes. He noticed that her gown was green – the colour fairies wear: an unlucky colour – but she smiled pleasantly enough. "Come in, little Sir Hugh. Come in and fetch your ball."

"I can't! I won't!" he blurted. "I mustn't! Not without my friends." His own rudeness embarrassed him, but the lady took no offence. She simply reached out, took Hugh by the hand and led him indoors. The gate banged shut behind them.

She smiled while he fetched his ball, smiled while he apologized for his rudeness. "Would you like some sherbet, Hughie?" she asked.

She led the way along stone corridors, through wood-panelled rooms hung with tapestries. At last they came to a windowless chamber lit by candles. "Sit down, Hughie. See, there is a golden chair for you to sit on."

"I should be going."

"Ah, but have some sweets before you go. Boys like sweets." She held out to him a plate of sugar bonbons, and he sat in the ornate golden chair, his feet swinging clear of the ground. The sweets were good . . . but they made him sleepy – they, or the incense burning in the room, or the soft glimmer of the candles. He only screamed when he saw the knife.

"No use screaming," said the lady in the same soft voice. "The walls here are a yard thick. No one will hear you." She scooped him up out of the chair as easily as if he were a baby, and laid him face-up on her dressing-table. Sleep, like a dozen strong hands, stopped him struggling.

"Let me say my prayers, at least!" he whispered.

But she stabbed him, then and there, in the throat, so that the blood ran down. The football, rolling out of his hands, bounced – *tch tch tch* – down a flight of stone steps. Sinking her fingers in his golden hair, gripping both ankles in one large hand, she carried him to the well by the high wall, and dropped him down it.

When little Sir Hugh did not return home, his mother went looking for him. His friends told her about the football and helped her search, sorry now that they had run off and left their friend alone. The town watch called at the big dark mansion behind its high perimeter wall, but the lady there only smiled pleasantly: no, she had not seen the boy.

His mother became more and more distracted. The river was dragged; the huntsmen checked their traps in the greenwood. But there was no trace of the boy. Then a servant lad, passing by the well, heard singing without knowing where it came from:

"Mother, mother, make my bed.
Make for me a winding sheet.
Wrap me up in a cloak of gold.
See if I can sleep."

The lad stopped passers-by: "Listen: can you hear that?"

Hugh's mother came and listened, white-faced, by the well, her hands clasped over her mouth to contain her terror.

"Mother, mother, make my bed.
Make for me a winding sheet.
Wrap me up in a cloak of gold.
See if I can sleep."

The body was grappled up from the bottom of the well and given a Christian burial wearing a cloak of gold. The well fell silent then, though no one dared drink from it. Many more ball games were played up against the high stone wall, but never again was a lost ball retrieved. Never again did the lady in green open her gate and invite a child in – for she had been tried for murder and burned to dust in the market place, along with all her kith and kin.

Although this horror story features an evil fairy, it started life as a piece of anti-Jewish propaganda in which the murderer was a Jew. The ritual murder in 1255 of nine-year-old Hugh of Lincoln was the reason given for hanging several (probably innocent) Jewish men in the city. The thirteenth century was a time of great religious intolerance. Pogroms – ethnic massacres – were common. Any wild rumour or blatant lie was an acceptable excuse to seize Jewish property, torture, murder and evict innocent Jews, while the Church looked on approvingly. The sensational details of the Lincoln murder were soon adapted into a variety of folk tales and ballads in which the anti-Jewish element gradually disappeared. Parents through the ages must have found this story useful for impressing on their children: "Never take sweets from a stranger".

"A Prince Who Speaks No Word of English"

1284

When English money shall become round
Then the Prince of Wales shall be crowned
in London.

Thus ran the ancient prophecy of the bard Merlin. So when King Edward I issued new coins worth a halfpenny and a farthing, the Welsh stirred like a field of daffodils in a rising wind. Their leader, the mighty Llewellyn, led an insurrection against the newly-crowned King of England. Wild Welsh mountain men raided the western counties of England, and the bards swore to conquer London.

Edward had spent time in Wales and knew the terrain. He imported mountaineers from the Pyrenees, expert in mountain warfare. He armed a thousand pioneers with hatchets to hack their way through Welsh defences, and sent a fleet to attack Anglesey. To his dismay, Prince Llewellyn found himself alone and hunted.

To baffle his pursuers, he had a blacksmith re-shoe his horse with the horseshoes back-to-front, so as to leave misleading hoofprints. But the blacksmith ran squealing to the English, and they were soon on his trail again.

Crossing the River Wye, Llewellyn set the bridge alight behind him, leaving the English milling helplessly about on the opposite bank, unable to cross. But they simply trekked downstream until they found a place shallow enough to ford.

Still, Llewellyn did not have far to go to join the Welsh forces massing nearby, and lead them into one last, decisive battle. So hiding in a barn, he waited for his pursuers to give up and return to prepare for the battle. When everything fell silent, he ran outside, only to come face-to-face with a single rider, lance levelled . . .

Adam de Frankton wiped the tip of his lance on the grass and rode on to join his regiment. The battle went against the Welsh, who seemed confused and disorganized: only afterwards did the English discover why. Frankton rode back to the farmyard where he had stuck the running Welshman like a boar and left him bleeding to death. He found the man dead but, discovering the signet ring on his finger and the letters in his pocket, realized he had killed Prince Llewellyn! The Welsh had fought without a leader. It was no wonder they had lost.

"How does the prophecy go?" said Edward toying with the bloodstained letters which Frankton had brought him. "'Then shall the Prince of Wales be crowned in London?' Well, then. Cut off Llewellyn's head and carry it to London. Impale it on the walls of the Tower – and crown it as befits a traitor."

What did those blood-soaked letters recovered from Llewellyn's body say? Would they tell him which chieftains were loyal and which were not? With calm deliberation, Edward tossed the letters unopened into the fireplace and watched them burn. "They would only make me suspicious of men I would rather trust," he said.

It took more than one battle to subdue Wales. While Llewellyn's head, crowned with a wreath of ivy, glared out across London, Edward spent months in Wales, building fortresses, holding talks with surly chieftains. His wife Eleanor, to be close by her husband, lived first at Rhuddlan, then at newly completed Caernarvon Castle.

One day in April 1284, Edward was again in conference with Welsh chieftains – some restive and resentful, some resigned to defeat, some undecided what to make of this conciliatory Englishman who beat them in battle but still wanted their friendship. Today the King's thoughts were plainly elsewhere. When a messenger arrived, Edward pushed back his chair and hurried from the room.

He returned grinning, his face flushed with pleasure and with an announcement to make: "Meet me in one week at Caernarvon, my lords," he said, "and I will present you with a prince born in Wales who can speak no word of English nor ever did any wrong to man, woman or child!"

Until Edward I's "prophetic" issue of half-penny and farthing coins, the practice had been to cut pennies into halves and quarters. This encouraged the crime of "clipping" whereby people shaved slivers of silver off every piece of money which came their way. Introducing small-denomination coins and so doing away with the excuse to cut coins was one of Edward's first acts of reform in a long, intelligent reign.

The baby's mother, Queen Eleanor of Castile, bore Edward eleven children and shared his work for thirty-six years; the couple were devoted to each other. When she died in Nottinghamshire, Edward transported her body back to London, raising a stone cross wherever her body rested on the journey. Three of these nine Eleanor crosses still exist. Unfortunately, the "Welsh-speaking" Prince Edward, in whose birth everyone took such delight, proved a grave disappointment as King Edward II. Forced to abdicate, he died in prison, probably murdered.

The Welsh were taken aback – delighted. What could it mean? A Welsh-speaking prince? The conference broke up excitedly and in a new mood of optimism.

It was a hushed, expectant gathering of shaggy, battle-scarred, weather-beaten, warriors, wrapped in Welsh-wool cloaks who crowded into the courtyard of Caernarvon Castle in the May sunshine to meet their new prince. Edward emerged to meet them, his queen at his shoulder. Cradled in his arms was a new-born baby. "According to my promise, I give you a prince born in Wales, who can speak no word of English!" and he lifted the baby high, for everyone to see.

The Welsh might have taken it for an insult – a joke at their expense. They did not. Edward was not deriding them. The baby Prince Edward was to have a Welsh nurse and Welsh servants, guaranteeing that his first words would be Welsh. Wales was no longer an independent country; it was a mere principality within Edward's kingdom. But conquerors have treated their vanquished foe far worse. One by one, the warlords came forward and, taking the baby's tiny hand between huge, gnarled fingers, kissing it through bushy beards, they swore an oath of loyalty to the English King.

A year later, Edward's first-born son, Alfonso, died, and the infant Edward became heir to the throne. At twenty-four he was crowned in Westminster Abbey.

So what of Merlin's prophecy?

When English money shall become round
Then the Prince of Wales shall be crowned in London.

Robert the Bruce and the Spider

1306-1314

"ROBERT THE BRUCE, LOST, STOLEN OR STRAYED!" read the English proclamation jeeringly, for the so-called King of Scotland had been gone all year and those trying to hunt him down could find no trace.

Dispossessed of his country by the English and driven to live as an outlaw, he and his companions were on the run, propping up branches for shelter, sleeping on animal skins, eating rabbits, berries and fish. With winter coming on, Robert the Bruce deemed it better the ladies should go to Kildrummie Castle, into the care of his young brother Nigel, while he and his few companions headed further north.

The news that reached them was all bad. Though Bruce kept his comrades entertained with stories of questing knights and poems about the heroes of Scotland, his spirits sank lower and lower. Every day, relations and friends were being captured, imprisoned, put to death. Perhaps he should abandon any dreams of driving the English out of Scotland. Six battles he had fought with the enemy, and six times his fortunes had fallen still lower.

One night, sheltering in a dilapidated hut on the island of Rathlin, he lay looking up at the roof. A spider hung there from a single thread, trying to swing from one rafter to the next so as to establish a web. Again and again it tried, though surely the distance was too great. Four, five, six times it tried. What perseverance! Did it never know when to give up? Why did it not scuttle away into a corner and weave there? Bruce found himself oddly caught up in the efforts of the spider. His eyes hurt with watching it so intently. I too, have made six attempts, he thought. If this creature tries again – if it succeeds – then, by all that's holy *so will I!*

The little gossamer thread was barely visible, and yet from it now hung the rest of Bruce's life. He forgot to swallow. He forgot to blink. The spider gathered its legs into a single black pellet. Swinging across the dark chasm of the roof, the little trapeze artist reached its goal and began, without respite, to construct a gossamer kingdom between the rafters.

In that moment, a surge of determination swept through Robert the Bruce which drove out all his weariness and despair. He would live to see the English driven out, and to be acknowledged King of Scotland! "And when I do, I shall make a pilgrimage to Jerusalem to give thanks. This I swear, Lord!"

The spider brought no sudden change in Bruce's luck. He learned that Kildrummie Castle had been taken, and the ladies there – his sister and wife – had been shut up like wild beasts in wooden cages, and hung over the battlements. Another sister had been placed in a nunnery. And his young brother Nigel – no more than a boy – had been hanged. But now, instead of increasing his despair, such news only fuelled Bruce's zeal for revenge. Even though the people were too terrified to answer his call to arms, and two more of his brothers were captured and hanged, Robert the Bruce would not give up hope.

He gained the friendship of Black Douglas, terror of the Borders, and at last highland and lowland lairds began rallying to his cause. More and more castles were captured by his growing army.

At Stirling, King Edward sent against him the greatest army ever led by an English king. When it came into sight, Black Douglas reported back to Bruce that it was the "most beautiful and most terrible sight". Sixty thousand men, better mounted and better armed than the Scots, came on like cloud shadow over the landscape.

Bruce said, "If any man of you is not ready for either victory or death, let him leave now!" But not one man quit the field. The odds were against them two to one, but everyone knew that on this battle the future of Scotland rested: its independence, its nationhood, its pride. The lines were drawn up for the battle called Bannockburn.

"They are kneeling to beg forgiveness!" cried King Edward, thinking the Scots were going down on their knees in hope of mercy.

"Yes, but they are asking it from God, not from us," said an English baron. "They are praying. These men will conquer or die."

The English cavalry moved off, formidable in their fine armour, on their huge horses, speeding from a walk to a trot, from a trot to a canter. Helmet crests and pennons flickered as if a grass fire were devouring the plain . . . And then all of a sudden they were stumbling and pitching, their horses tripping and going down. Knights fell from their ornate saddles and lay pinned to the ground by their weight of armour. Bruce had had his men dig 10,000 holes to the depth of a man's knee –

10,000 artificial rabbit holes in which a galloping horse could step and break a leg. Many of the horses and many of the knights did not stir, for Bruce had also strewn the plain with spiky calthrops which lie always with one lethal point upward.

Bruce's cavalry rushed the English archers: after that the English military advantage had gone. King Edward fled. The attendant who escorted him safely off the field (valuing his honour more than Edward did) turned back and threw himself into the mêlée to die fighting. But as the royal banner retreated, so the English ranks broke and ran, all the heart gone out of them.

The battle of Bannockburn established Robert the Bruce as King of Scotland. But the Pope said he would only acknowledge Bruce if he went on Crusade to the Holy Land.

No penance could have pleased Bruce more, remembering the vow he had made on Rathlin. He longed to see Jerusalem. But illness had dogged him down the years, and now it caught up with him. Leprosy prevented Bruce from keeping his promise to the Pope. So he sent for his best friend and bravest fighter, Black Douglas, and asked him, "Keep my promise. When I am dead, go to the Holy Land in my place. Carry my heart with you, and bury it in the Holy Sepulchre where Christ lay down and rose again to life."

Black Douglas did as he was asked. Though Robert the Bruce was buried, wrapped in cloth-of-gold, in Dunfermline Abbey, his heart, sealed in a lead casket, was worn around Douglas's neck the day he joined battle with the Infidel.

He had travelled only as far as Spain (then occupied by Moorish Moslems). Cut off from his troops, Douglas saw no escape. So he wrenched the casket from round his neck and hurled it forward, overarm, crying, "Pass onward . . . ! I follow or die!"

The descendants of Douglas emblazon their shields with a bleeding heart surmounted by a golden crown to commemorate this last great act of loyalty and devotion.

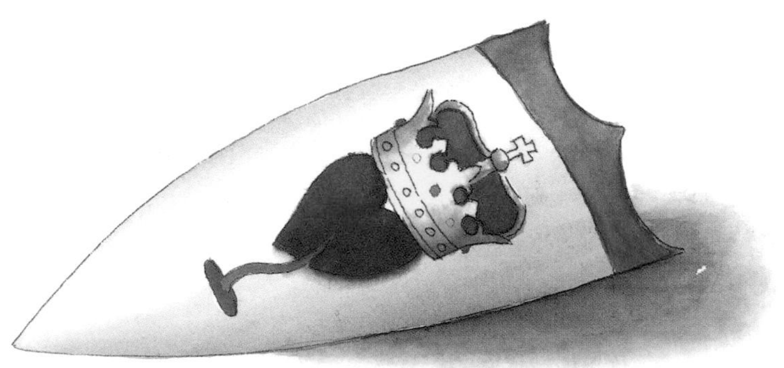

King Edward II took with him to Scotland a Carmelite priest called Baston, renowned for his skill as a poet. The intention was that Baston should record in verse the King's glorious victory over the Scots. In the event, Baston was taken prisoner, and Robert the Bruce persuaded him to celebrate the Scottish triumph instead. His poem still exists.

After the battle of Bannockburn, the "wild men" of Scotland grew more and more audacious, annually raiding Durham and Northumbria. Peace was only struck when Bruce's young son, David, became betrothed to an English princess.

The Brawling Scottish Wench

1338

WITH A USURPER ON THE THRONE OF Scotland, hammered in place by English armies, the Scottish people seethed with indignation and resentment. Their loyalty was to the child king, David II, and despite a catastrophic defeat at Halidon Hill, when 10,000 Scots fell under a sleet of English arrows, individual strongholds still held out against the English invaders.

Away on the coast, its feet in the ocean, its face turned to the land, Dunbar Castle came under siege by the English. The lord of the castle was away, fighting in the cause of the young King David, leaving his wife in sole charge. But his wife was more formidable than many a knight; his wife was Agnes, daughter of Randolph. With her swarthy skin and the hairband worn low across her eyebrows, she had the look of a war stallion champing at the bit. And they called her Black Agnes.

William Montacute, Earl of Salisbury, pitched camp so as to isolate Dunbar on its rocky promontory. Then he brought up his great machines of war – his trebuchets. These gigantic catapults lobbed boulders in great arcs of destruction, demolishing whole sections of battlement, crumbling masonry like Scottish shortbread.

"Watch for the white flag," said Salisbury, confidently expecting Black Agnes to appear pleading for her life.

And indeed, shreds of fluttering cloth did appear on the battlements. A group of women moved slowly along the parapet flicking napkins. But not as flags of surrender. They were *dusting* the castle walls, flicking away grime and chippings, as though Salisbury's trebuchets had simply spoiled their housekeeping! Even some of the English troops gave a gasping laugh of admiration at such cool audacity.

Salisbury was not amused. "*Bring up the sow!*" he bellowed.

Now the "sow" was a siege engine with a sloping, arrow-proof roof which enabled workmen to get close up to a castle wall and work in safety, digging to undermine the wall. The roof protected them from archers on the battlements. Up trundled the sow now, concealing dozens of English solders beneath its roof of timber and hide.

Black Agnes peered over the wall.

"Beware, Montacute, your sow is about to have piglets!" she called down.

Again a gasp from the English camp. For a gigantic heap of debris – masonry, boulders from the beach and sundry castle rubbish suddenly lurched forwards into view, toppled from behind by crow bars. Tons of rock cascaded over the battlements on to the sow below. Agnes had predicted the exact spot at which Salisbury would attempt to break through. She had arranged the perfect answer to Montacute's sow. The hide roof smashed and splintered under the falling rock. The men beneath it screamed and went down, or ran for their lives squealing like demented piglets. "Oh look!" said Agnes, two hands clasped at her breast. "See the English piggies run!"

Earl Salisbury was spitting with rage.

Consequently, when a traitor came to his tent by night – a servant from the castle – the earl rubbed his hands with malicious delight. *Now* I have you, Black Agnes, he thought. "You say you can give the castle into my hands, man?"

"For gold enough," said the servant, "I can do King Edward that service. Come to the gate at midnight, and I'll tell you how."

With only his squire for company, William Montacute went at midnight – and, to his amazement, found the portcullis of Dunbar Castle raised just as high as a man's head! At this time of night, Agnes would be in her night-gown, sleeping. There was not even a sentry on watch! What could be easier? "Go on, go on in," he urged his squire.

With a rattle and a clank, the portcullis fell, its mesh of bars jarring the drawbridge on which Earl Salisbury was standing. On one side stood his squire, round-eyed with terror, fingers poking through the cullis, whimpering. On the other stood Salisbury. He had been within one pace of stepping into Agnes's trap, and though the trap had been sprung too early, he took to his heels now and ran, pursued all the way back to his tent by the ringing, rasping laughter of Black Agnes watching from the battlements.

Scottish minstrels were soon writing ballads about Black Agnes. One verse ran:

That brawling, boisterous, Scottish wench
Kept such a stir in tower and trench,
That came I early, came I late,
I found Black Agnes at the gate.

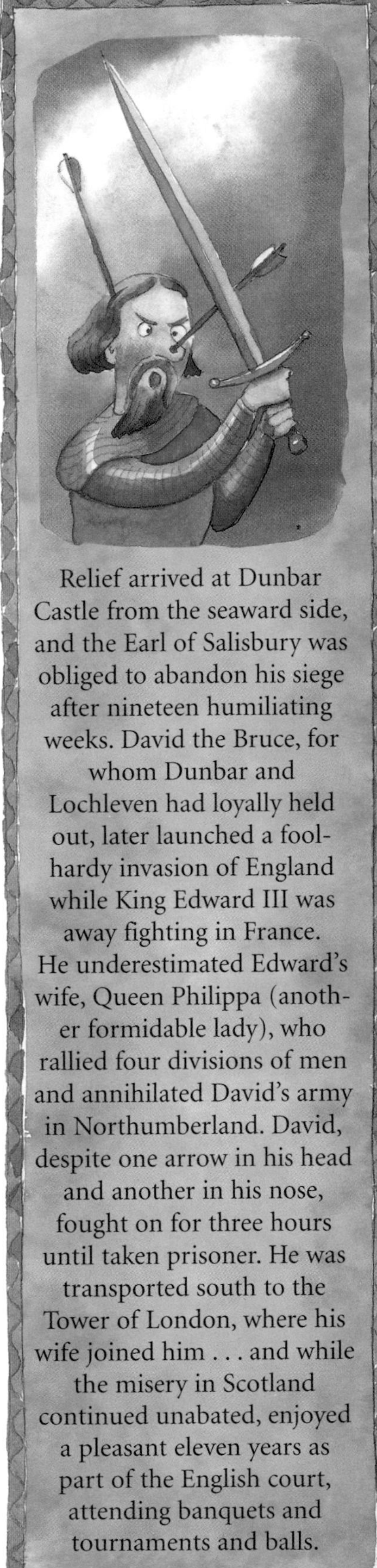

Relief arrived at Dunbar Castle from the seaward side, and the Earl of Salisbury was obliged to abandon his siege after nineteen humiliating weeks. David the Bruce, for whom Dunbar and Lochleven had loyally held out, later launched a foolhardy invasion of England while King Edward III was away fighting in France. He underestimated Edward's wife, Queen Philippa (another formidable lady), who rallied four divisions of men and annihilated David's army in Northumberland. David, despite one arrow in his head and another in his nose, fought on for three hours until taken prisoner. He was transported south to the Tower of London, where his wife joined him . . . and while the misery in Scotland continued unabated, enjoyed a pleasant eleven years as part of the English court, attending banquets and tournaments and balls.

The Black Prince Wins His Spurs

1346

HE WAS ONLY SIXTEEN, and barely able to contain his pride, as his father, the King, dubbed him a knight. For almost as long as Prince Edward could remember, England had been at war with France, but this was to be his first military expedition and the biggest of the war – a foray into northern France, with the chance of rich pickings.

Then, somehow the King overreached himself and suddenly he was in retreat, chased by the full might of French nobility and half of Europe with them. Sixteen-year-old Prince Edward did not regret the turn of events, but it looked as if his first campaign was going to end not quite according to plan.

King Philip of France and 68,000 men were marching to confront a mere 7,800 English and Welsh. But Prince Edward's worst fear was not of dying. It was of being sent away to a place of safety: heir to the throne, too precious to lose, too young to be trusted with his own life. To his great relief, it did not happen. Instead, his father invited him and the other knights and earls to dine in his tent on the eve of battle, and to offer up prayers. No mention was made of preserving his life.

The Prince determined to observe and learn. There would never be a bigger or better lesson in kingship and military command. So he watched everything. He saw how his father, armed with only a white wand, surveyed his troops, encouraging them, making jokes, telling them to eat well and take a glass of wine. He saw how the archers – the great bowmen of England – settled down to sleep under their blankets, in the teeming rain, helmets by their feet. He ran his unpractised eye over Crécy Hill, struggling to interpret his father's strategy.

He swelled with pride at being given command of 3,800 men; he bridled a little at being given the Earl of Warwick and Sir Godfrey de Harcourt to help command them. But he was glad enough of their wisdom and advice when, out of the morning rain, the French army came lumbering into view – a solid mass of armour and silks and saddleclothes, of bannerets, nodding horses and slogging footsoldiers, all bearing down on Crécy Hill.

His thoughts then were a wild confusion of prayers, fears and hopes, dense as the flock of ravens and crows which circled over the battlefield. And yet some part of his brain went on seeing with icy clarity.

He saw the French advancing – then the French heralds darting to and fro trying to tell them to halt: King Philip had not yet formed his battle plan. The army would not or could not halt: its numbers were too vast to absorb the command.

He saw the Genoese crossbowmen in the front – 1,800 of them – fumbling with their weapons in the downpour, the strings too wet to be strung. He noted, by contrast, the steely composure of the English bowmen as they rose to their feet, undaunted by their night on the muddy hill. From under their helmets they drew dry bowstrings, calmly and deliberately strung their longbows – and fired.

As in a dream, Edward saw that sleet of arrows, that whistling storm within a storm. For lightning was crackling between sky and earth and the air was smoky with rain. At noon the sun went out: darkness ate it away bit by bit: a dread omen for one side or the other. Then the Genoese were running from the storm of arrows, running and being hacked down by their own side for getting in the way, clogging up the road.

Now the French knights were within range of the arrows. Riderless horses capered and reared in terror, though those behind kept pushing forward, unaware of what was happening at the front. Forward went the Prince's Welshmen – the Cornishmen too – with their gruesome long knives – *snicker-snack*! – dealing out death in the midst of the milling confusion.

The clouds drew back to reveal the sun, restored after its eclipse, shining full in the face of the French, blinding them. *There* was the strategy of Crécy Hill! Prince Edward flushed full of hot pride in his father who rode now helmetless through the field.

One tiny scene of heroism fixed itself in the boy's mind: the old blind King of Bohemia riding into battle between two French knights, their bridles tied together so as to steer the old man's horse. Flank against flank they rode, Bohemia's white plumes nodding proudly as he rode to certain destruction, fighting the noisy darkness until it overwhelmed him. Edward rose in his saddle to see what became of the three . . .

Then suddenly, as if from nowhere, two French regiments were closing on his own flank. They had skirted round the chaos in mid-field to attack the Prince of Wales.

After that, Edward felt nothing except the hot churning hysteria of battle – lashing out, kill-or-be-killed. All those strokes and parries practised for tedious hours in the tilt yard came back to him now. But for every Frenchman he killed, two more seemed to materialize. Out of the corner of his eye, he saw the Earl of Warwick dispatch a herald to fetch help.

But help did not come. The King refused to send it. "Is my son dead, then? Or unhorsed, or so badly wounded that he cannot defend himself?"

"No, thank God, but he is in great need of your help!" panted the herald.

"Then go back to those who sent you and tell them not to send again nor expect me to come. Let my boy win his spurs, for I am determined that the glory and honour of this day shall be given to him!" Some who heard him asked themselves: what manner of man refuses help to his son?

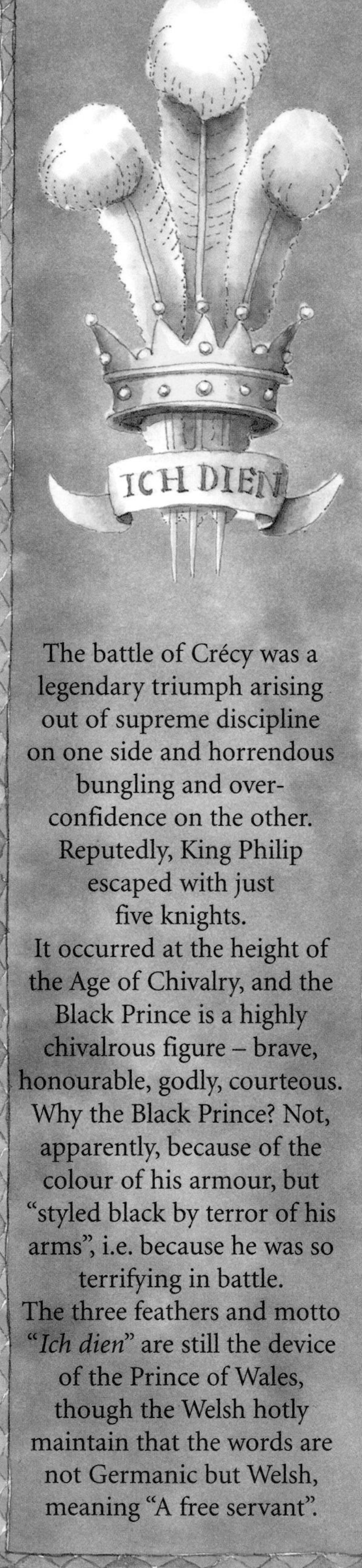

The battle of Crécy was a legendary triumph arising out of supreme discipline on one side and horrendous bungling and over-confidence on the other. Reputedly, King Philip escaped with just five knights.

It occurred at the height of the Age of Chivalry, and the Black Prince is a highly chivalrous figure – brave, honourable, godly, courteous. Why the Black Prince? Not, apparently, because of the colour of his armour, but "styled black by terror of his arms", i.e. because he was so terrifying in battle.

The three feathers and motto "*Ich dien*" are still the device of the Prince of Wales, though the Welsh hotly maintain that the words are not Germanic but Welsh, meaning "A free servant".

The troops arrayed on Crécy Hill did not break rank, or chase after the French when the French scattered, or rush down to plunder the dead. Disciplined to the last, the bowmen stood longest, until night was resting on their bowtips, and hymns of thanksgiving were flocking into the darkening sky along with the ravens and crows. Bonfires were lit; an army of torches were lit from the bonfires.

Those who had seen the prince fight were full of admiration, calling him his father's son, dubbing him "the Black Prince". The King came looking for his son, his hood of mail pushed back. Those nearby said that there were tears in his eyes. "Sweet son," he said, rushing to embrace the boy, searching every inch of his face. "You are indeed my son, for you have acquitted yourself most loyally this day and you are worthy to be a king!"

"The victory was all yours, Father."

"Nay, yours, son, yours!" There was a wild relief in the King's face which hinted how hard it had been for him not to send help.

From the prince's hand drooped three ostrich feathers, specked with blood. He had recovered them from the helmet of the fallen King of Bohemia, along with the old man's device: "*Ich dien*". "I serve".

"It shall be my device now," he said, "and the coat of arms of every Prince of Wales to come."

Then the battle-fever drained out of him and he was left white-faced and weary, with trembling limbs: sixteen again, for all his glittering spurs.

“Oss! Oss!” “Wee Oss!”

1347

THE FRENCH INVADERS CAME, THINKING IT would be easy to help themselves to the wealth of Padstow.

Across the Channel, Calais was under siege, and the fishermen and shopkeepers, the craftsmen and farmers of the little Cornish port had built two ships by their own efforts and set sail to help King Edward capture the city. No sooner were they gone than a fleet of French ships, knowing Padstow lay unprotected, sailed the other way, thinking to take over the town.

But they had not reckoned with Ursula Birdhood.

“Fetch out your red cloaks and your scarlet petticoats!” Ursula told the women of the town, “and meet me at Stepper Point!”

If Ursula was a witch, she was a wholesome witch, and if there was magic in her, it was of a very ancient kind. And her magic was small alongside that of the ’Obby ’Oss, dancer-in of the May!

Every May Day, from before daybreak till long after dark, the Padstow Hobbyhorse dances through the streets, twirling and leaping on its twin thin legs, its black cloth body flapping, its black conical body as pointed and jaunty as a witch’s hat. And all the while it dances, it drives out winter and fetches in spring.

Now the French were invading, with swords sharp as winter and faces cruel as February, and nothing but a handful of women to keep them out. By the time Ursula Birdhood and the women of Padstow reached the headland at Stepper Point, a crescent of French warships was dropping anchor in the bay.

If those women were frightened, they sang the fear out of their throats. If their legs were shaking, they danced the fright out of their legs. In a deep, gruff voice, Ursula Birdhood began to sing and everyone joined in the familiar words:

“Unite and unite and let us unite
For summer is acome unto day . . .”

A drum took up the beat – a jogging, syncopated beat, like a horse trotting over broken ground:

“And whither we are going we will all unite
In the merry morning of May!”

They sang the Night Song and after that the Day Song, even richer with magic:

“O where is St George
O where is he O?
He is out in his long-boat all on the salt sea O.
Up flies the kite and down falls the lark O . . .”

This same story – of dancing women in red scaring off a French invasion – is told in at least one other place, across the Severn Estuary, in Wales. So it is unlikely both versions are true, but all the more likely that something of the sort did happen *somewhere.*

Age-old songs can become altered over the years into gobbledegook. One Padstow verse which runs:

'Aunt Ursula Birdhood she had an old ewe
And she died in her own Park O'

But until 1850 the 'Obby 'Oss dancer *was* accompanied through the streets of Padstow on May Day by a character representing "an old woman in a red cloak". Was she Aunt Ursula? The horse itself has its origins in a Celtic religion older than Christianity, and brings fertility and renewal. It used to be thought that if the 'Oss threw its skirts over a young wife, she would give birth within the year.

The Padstow celebration is one of the most exciting and genuine folk rituals still observed in England. Most were suppressed or "adopted" by Christianity, or frozen out by disapproving Victorians.

Out at sea, the Frenchies saw the flicker of red cloth on the top of Stepper Point, though the singing was too far off to be heard.

"Il y a quelqu'un!"
"La! En haut!"
"Les soldats anglais?"

They pointed, shouting.

Then, indistinct among the red glimmer of moving figures, they saw another shape – one which struck far more fear into their superstitious souls: a big flapping creature, black and headless, conical as a witch's hat and madly leaping on tireless legs – a creature they could make no sense of, unless . . . unless it was . . .

"*Le Diable! Le Diable hors d'Infer!*"

Had the English won the Devil over to their side, and were they even now whipping up magic on Stepper Point headland to sink the French, to crack their hulls like eggshells, to whisk their souls away like spray off the white wave tops? From time to time a single unheard voice exhorted, "Oss! Oss!" – but the dancers shouted their answer loud enough for the cry to cross the water: "*Wee Oss!*"

The French weighed anchor and sailed away. Ursula Birdhood watched them go, standing on the headland, red cloak streaming out behind her, one hand knotted in the tail of the nodding, skittering Hobbyhorse of Padstow.

The Garter

1348

THE DANCERS PROMENADED UP AND DOWN, forming circles, forming lines, interweaving like the threads of the silken banners overhead. Surrounded by the heraldry of fifty ancient families and the crested helmets of warrior knights, the dancers themselves formed a kind of heraldry, bright with colours and chivalric splendour.

Then the Countess of Salisbury's garter slipped, slid down and came off altogether, to lie on the marble floor. Nobody could miss it. A page tittered. A gossip pointed. And the music ended just as King Edward saw it too.

Splendid in a quartered doublet of silk-lined velvet, he made a low sweep of his hand, a flourishing bow to his dancing partner, and his fingers scooped up the offending garter.

The countess flushed a vivid red. The silk stocking, which the garter had been holding up, wrinkled unceremoniously round her ankle. Was the King going to make some coarse joke? Humiliate her in front of her friends and inferiors? Would this model prince really do such a thing?

Edward pointed a toe and slipped his own foot through the garter, sliding it up as far as it would go round his manly calf. The crowd did not know if it was a joke. Two or three nervous giggles erupted from the courtiers. King Edward, turning his leg this way and that, heel in, heel out, looked up sharply. "Shame on him whose thoughts are shameful!" he said.

"*Honi soit qui mal y pense.*"

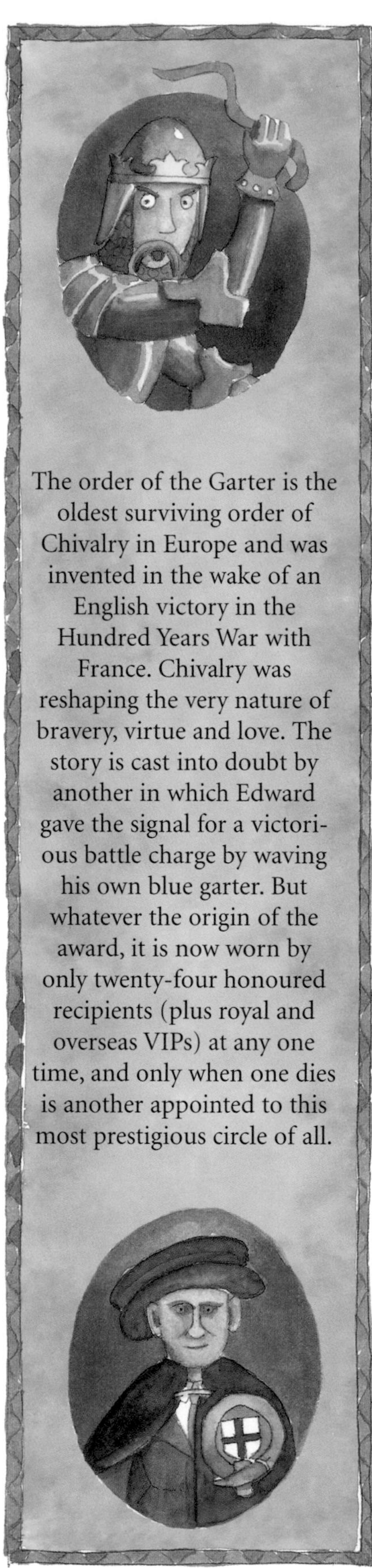

The order of the Garter is the oldest surviving order of Chivalry in Europe and was invented in the wake of an English victory in the Hundred Years War with France. Chivalry was reshaping the very nature of bravery, virtue and love. The story is cast into doubt by another in which Edward gave the signal for a victorious battle charge by waving his own blue garter. But whatever the origin of the award, it is now worn by only twenty-four honoured recipients (plus royal and overseas VIPs) at any one time, and only when one dies is another appointed to this most prestigious circle of all.

It was the kind of slogan noble houses were adopting the length and breadth of Europe, in the great race to invent a new, more civilized nobility: devices, mottoes, heraldic beasts, liveries, crests and honours. Some flattering duke jotted down the King's words in a commonplace book. The music struck up again and the countess, still pink with a mixture of embarrassment and pleasure, joined fingertips with the King once more. The slow, prancing geometry of the next dance began.

The lady's garter flashed and flickered on the King's calf – elevated now to the status of colours on the lance-point of a jousting chevalier. By the end of the dance the King had pursued his chivalrous thought still further. Again he thrust forward his leg and declared: "Only the greatest in the land shall wear such a garter! Let it be awarded only to my most favoured subjects! Only the most esteemed and chivalrous men in the kingdom will share with me this honour, this privilege of wearing . . . *the Garter!*"

And so the Order of the Garter began – at a time when English pride was at its height, when it lay in the power of a king to grant everlasting glory.

Dick Whittington

1358-1423

ONCE UPON A TIME, A POOR boy called Dick lived in a village in the middle of nowhere. He had no mother or father to feed or clothe him, no future, so it seemed. "You should go to London!" said a neighbour. "They say the streets there are paved with gold!"

So Dick set off to walk, thinking London must be just over the hill. A hundred hills later, he found himself in narrow streets, among high houses and the shouts and bustle of London. His poor sore feet found no golden pavements to walk on – not so much as a golden pebble. And his stomach was empty.

He got work scraping pots in the kitchen of Captain Fitz-Warren, a rich merchant. Though Dick could eat the scrapings, the cook was a cruel bully. Dick slept in an attic so overrun with mice that with his first sixpence he bought a cat. That cat was a good friend to Dick, and he came to love it . . . almost as much as he came to love Captain Fitz-Warren's daughter, Alice. Sweet, kind, beautiful Alice. "If I weren't me and you weren't you, I would marry you one day!" he used to say.

"Who knows what you might be one day," Alice would say in reply.

But the cook's cruelties were too much for Dick to bear, and one very early morning he and his cat ran away. He might have walked all the way home, had he not stopped to rest on a milestone at Holloway. Across the fields came the distant ringing of Bow Bells in Cheapside – a familiar enough sound – except that today he seemed to hear words among the clamour: "Turn again, Whittington, thrice Lord Mayor of London!"

At once, Dick ran back the way he had come, and was busy scrubbing the kitchen floor before the cook even woke.

That day the house was all at sixes and sevens. Captain Fitz-Warren was setting sail. All kinds of people had invested in his voyage, hoping for huge profits when the merchant sold his cargo in distant parts. "Why not invest something yourself, Dick?" asked the merchant.

"Me? But I have nothing, sir," said Dick.

"You have that cat of yours! I need a cat to keep down the rats on board my ship."

Dick did not want to be parted from his friend, but at the last moment, he agreed.

Disaster! Captain Fitz-Warren's ship ran aground on the shores of a country where no one wanted or needed his valuable cargo. The caliph there had everything a man could desire: gems and silk, sherbet and oysters, palace walls clad in beaten gold.

One thing more the caliph had. Rats. His realm, his palace, even his throne-room swarmed with rats, because there were no cats in the whole land. When Puss saw the rats, he slew them by the dozen, by the tens of dozen, while the caliph watched in wonder. "For this cat I will pay three sacks of diamonds!" he declared.

Dick's fortune was made. With the proceeds, he became a respected London merchant and before long he was elected Lord Mayor of London – not once but three times. Bow Bells rang once again for Dick Whittington – on the day he married Alice Fitz-Warren.

The True Story

Sir William Whittington of Gloucestershire had three sons but, when the youngest was still a baby, he was outlawed. The two older brothers sent Dick to London to be apprenticed to a distant relation, Sir Ivo Fitzwaryn. Sir Ivo was a mercer – a dealer in fabrics – and Dick's first job, at thirteen, was to stand outside his master's shop shouting, to attract customers. "What d'ye lack? What d'ye lack?"

From early morning till Bow Bells rang at eight, Dick learned his trade. They were eventful times. He saw John Wycliffe tried for heresy, saw Wat Tyler's rebels come flooding over London Bridge, saw the plague carry off 30,000 people in a single year.

They were fashionable times, too – times when the rich spent lavishly on clothes. There was no better time to be a mercer. The London mercers had money to spare, so became the bankers of the day as well, growing even richer from lending money.

By the age of twenty-nine Richard Whittington had £10 of his own to invest. At thirty-five he was an alderman and sheriff. King Richard II appointed him Mayor of London (there was no Lord Mayor then). His fellow Londoners re-elected him time after time.

Mayor Whittington invented street lighting, commanding every citizen to hang a lantern outside his door at night. He invented the public drinking fountain, too. He was the terror of dishonest tradesmen, prosecuting those who gave short measure, watered beer, overcharged or sold shoddy goods. He rebuilt his parish church, built almshouses for the poor, began a vast library . . . and lent King Henry V £60,000 towards the cost of fighting a war in France.

He entertained Henry and his new bride, Princess Catherine of France, to a feast more splendid than any ever seen before, warming the banqueting hall with three blazing fires of costly cedarwood and cinnamon. Queen Catherine clapped her hands in delight at such sweet-smelling, extravagant fires.

"Ah, but I shall feed them with something more costly still than cedarwood!" declared Sir Richard, and promptly tossed into the fire all record of moneys he had lent King Henry. "Thus do I acquit your Highness of a debt of £60,000" he said.

Henry was staggered. "Never had a prince such a subject!" he cried.

"Never had a subject such a prince," said Whittington with a gracious bow.

Whittington *did* marry his employer's daughter, Alice. But they had no children. So when the great man died a widower, his immense wealth was bequeathed to London – to rebuild Newgate Prison, to restore St Bart's Hospital, to put windows in the Guildhall, to found a college . . . and his library of books was given to the Greyfriars. He had many "cats" (for the word means a cargo-carrying sailing boat); but as to the furry kind – well, they leave no pawprints on the pages of history.

Say "Bread and Cheese"

1381

"When Adam delved and Eve span, who was then the gentleman?" John Ball asked the question in market squares all over Kent, and no one could answer him. Everybody is descended from Adam and Eve. So how come some people have become knights and barons, the rest starving serfs, taxed and oppressed by their so-called "betters"? Ball was a "Lollard". He wanted to end the feudal system. The people of Kent were eager to help him.

At Dartford, the cry was taken up by Walter the Tiler (or Wat Tyler).

Unlike Ball (an educated priest with strong religious beliefs), Tyler was a hooligan and a murderer. But the people followed him, like children following the Pied Piper. Joining forces with John Ball and a thatcher named Jack Straw, Tyler began to march towards London trailing behind him a growing army of protesters. Some just wanted to tell the young King their grievances; some wanted to bring down the old order, some simply a chance to pillage the city and cut a few throats.

Out of other counties came other columns of marchers. The citizens of London, faced with this flood of angry rebels, slammed the gates of London Bridge, to keep them out.

"Tell them to gather on the Thames shore at Rotherhithe on Thursday, and I will speak to them," said King Richard.

He was only fifteen, but appeared calm as he and a company of barons sailed down-river to meet the rebels. At the sight of him, the huge crowd on the bank raised a noise "like all the devils in hell", and surged towards the river. It was impossible to judge their mood. "Don't go ashore, your Majesty!" the barons begged. "It's too dangerous!"

So the boy-king stood up in the prow of the barge. "What do you wish?" he shouted.

"Come ashore, and we'll tell you!" the mob shouted back.

The Earl of Salisbury stood up, rocking the boat. "Gentlemen, you are not properly dressed for conversation with a king!" As the barge pulled out again into mid-stream, the crowd muttered angrily, and headed for London. Finding the gates of London Bridge shut, they threatened to burn down the suburbs and take the city by storm.

Could they be fought off? The Lord Mayor was doubtful. The City itself was full of rebel sympathizers – maybe as many as 30,000 living *inside* the gates might rise up, too, if it came to a battle. Slowly, creakingly, the gates were swung open, and the mob surged across – hundreds of hungry men. Sooner than be plundered of everything, grocers and bakers hurried into the street to distribute food.

A mob is a mindless, savage beast. This one went through the city looting, setting fire to the homes of lawyers, courtiers and churchmen. They burned down the Savoy Palace, the house of the Knights Hospitallers and the Marshalsea Prison. It was a night for settling old scores. Wat Tyler searched out an old employer who had crossed him once, and hacked off his head.

His power-crazed army grabbed people in the street, shaking them by the throat and screaming: "Say 'bread and cheese!' " When times are hard, the poor and the ignorant always blame foreigners for their troubles. Any trace of a foreign accent and they killed their victim. "Say 'bread and cheese!'"

"Brod unt cheess."

"Kill him! Kill the foreigner!"

Sixty-two innocent Flemish citizens were murdered that night for the crime of speaking with an accent. Meanwhile, inside the Tower of London, Richard II and his Council discussed the best way to deal with the revolt.

"When they're all drunk or asleep, we can go out and kill them like flies!" it was suggested. "Not one in ten has a weapon, and we can muster – what? – 800 armed men!"

But the Earl of Salisbury shook his head. The mob must be appeased, soothed with kind words. "If we should begin to kill them, and not go through with it, it will be all over with us and our heirs. England will become a desert."

So Richard sent word telling the rebels to meet him at Mile End meadow where he would discuss their demands.

Only half the mob believed him. The rest were too busy cutting throats. Waiting till the gates of the Tower were opened and the King's party gone, Ball and Tyler and Straw sped across the drawbridge, scouring the maze of apartments and staircases for the people they hated most. They slashed the bed of the Princess of Wales. They beheaded the Archbishop of Canterbury, killed a prior, a friar and a sergeant-at-arms, and mounted their heads on poles to decorate London Bridge. Then on to Mile End meadow.

Tens of thousands of peasants from every county in England confronted Richard as he rode out to speak with the leaders of the Peasants' Revolt. Some of his pages and courtiers were so scared that they turned their horses and galloped away, abandoning the young King. But his nerve held.

"My good people. What is it you want and what do you wish to say to me?"

"We want you to make us free for ever," said a man nearby.

"I grant your wish," said Richard.

Just like that. An end to serfdom. An end to one man "owning" another.

It took the wind out of their sails. It defused the moment. It turned the mob back into a dignified assembly of loyal subjects. "Go home now," said Richard. "Leave two men behind from every village, and I will have letters written, sealed with my seal, for them to carry home. I shall send my banners, too, as proof that you have my authority."

Thirty secretaries were summoned to write those precious letters, and as each one was sealed and delivered, large numbers of protesters turned for home, saying, "All's well. We have what we wanted."

Not Wat Tyler. Not Jack Straw. Not John Ball, nor thousands of others. They had the City of London at their mercy, and were not going to leave till it was stripped bare. Still more peasants were converging on London, and the looters had no wish to share their plunder with newcomers.

Almost by chance, King Richard and sixty out-riders came face-to-face with the vast, drunken mob at Smithfield. Fresh in Richard's mind were the horrors he had found at the Tower – those four headless bodies, the blood, the trail of destruction leading from room to room. And yet the words of the Earl of Salisbury were still ringing in his ears: ". . . England will become a desert."

When he recognized the King, Tyler gave a terse laugh and fumbled for his stirrup, to mount. He was keyed-up, drunk on stolen wine and lack of sleep. "Stay here. Don't stir until I give you a signal. When I make this sign, come forward and kill everyone except the King. He's young and we can do with him what we please."

Then he rode forward – so impetuously that his horse ran its nose into Richard's. "King," he blurted out, "do you see all those men there? They are all under my command and have sworn to do whatever I shall order." He wanted the King's letters, he said – would not leave London without them in his hand.

"That is what has been ordered. They will be delivered as fast as they can be written." The fifteen-year-old King answered calmly.

But Tyler was hysterical, overwrought, wanting to prove what power he wielded. "Give me your dagger!" he told the King's squire. The squire refused, but Richard told him to give it up. "Now your sword!" demanded Tyler. The squire refused.

The Mayor blustered: "How dare you behave thus in the presence of the King!"

Richard remembered those four headless bodies, all that blood. "Lay hands on him!"

A sword struck Tyler so hard on the head that he fell. The royal party milled around, their horses blocking the crowd's view. A squire dismounted and finished Wat Tyler where he lay. Messengers rode off to the city for reinforcements.

Then the body was spotted. "They have killed our captain! Let's kill the whole pack of them!" The mob drew a single breath. Arrows were laid to ash-wood bows, and the crowd began to move, like volcanic lava, bubbling, seething. What happened in the next few seconds would decide the fate of everyone there.

"No one follow me!" said King Richard, and urged his horse towards the furious crowd. Rising in his stirrups, he yelled: "Gentlemen! What are you about? You shall have no other captain but me. I am your King!"

It was a startling gesture from a boy of his age. Thousands drew back from the brink. Some hotheads wanted to cut down the King, but hesitated, uncertain.

That hesitation gave time for several thousand armed men to ride, pell-mell, out of London, and reinforce King and court.

John Ball and Jack Straw crept away, hoping to hide.

"Let's charge, and kill them where they stand!" urged one of Richard's knights, but the King would not hear of it. There was no need. The balance of power had changed. King Richard was demanding the return of his banners, the handing back of his letters. And the people were passing them forward – banners and letters – giving up their passports to freedom.

In front of their eyes, Richard tore up the letters, crushed the waxy seals, and they stood and watched him do it – docile, cowed, leaderless. Like sheep they scattered. Like sheepdogs at their heels, new proclamations chased them out of town. Anyone not resident in London one year or more was to be gone by Sunday or lose his head.

As they streamed over London Bridge, three severed heads grinned down at them from the top of poles: not the archbishop nor the prior nor the sergeant-at-arms, but Wat Tyler, Jack Straw and John Ball. On the various roads to London, thousands of peasants still thronging to join in the Peasant's Revolt heard that it was over – and turned back.

Who was in the wrong? Wat Tyler and his murderous louts? The King and Parliament, with their broken promises? After the peasants returned home, every letter was revoked, every charter withdrawn. Even more hardships were heaped on the peasants. Large crowds were forbidden to gather. Richard II imposed his authority by marching around the country with an army of 40,000 men. The nobles were no more ready to set serfs free than to give away their own knives and forks. Property is property, after all.

In some regions, the Peasants' Revolt was not so easily snuffed out. There were risings all over the country, and nobles shut themselves up in their castles and trembled. But order was gradually restored by the usual means: battles, trials, beheadings; in Essex, 500 peasants were killed.

"A Little Touch of Harry in the Night"

(Shakespeare, *Henry V*)
1415

FROM THE FRENCH CAMP FLOATED THE NOISE OF blacksmiths hammering home rivets, a minstrel singing, men laughing; banners of red-and-yellow light. But within the English camp there was hardly a sound, hardly a light showing. Six thousand exhausted men had walked through teeming rain 260 miles from Harfleur, with too little to eat and disease dogging them every step of the way. In the morning they would have to confront the army barring their road to Calais and escape. And the well-equipped French outnumbered them four-to-one. There did not seem much to sing about, as the rain teemed and the dark pressed suffocatingly close.

"Who goes there?" The sentries were jumpy.

"Friend."

"Whose regiment?"

"Sir Thomas Erpingham's." The cloaked figure moved closer, hood pulled forward against the filthy weather. The sentry let him pass and join a group of men sitting round a damp little fire.

"It's all right for the King," one was saying. "He wants to win the throne of France, so we have to come here and die."

"Is that how you see it?" said the hooded stranger equably. He took a sip of ale, before passing his tankard on round the group. "I would have thought the King had a heavy burden to carry. He's the father of his men. He has to provide for them, pray for them, look after them . . . All those wives and children depending on him to bring home their menfolk – that's a terrible responsibility for any man."

"Yeah, but tomorrow he'll be up there on his big horse on top of a hill somewhere, watching us get trampled by the French cavalry."

"Oh, why? Was Harfleur like that?"

Another answered instead. "No! No, at Harfleur, Harry was right there at our elbow, fighting like a demon!"

"Yeah, you can say that for the saucy rogue," admitted a sergeant grudgingly.

"Harry's not afraid to get his hands dirty."

They turned to speak more, but the stranger was moving away. For a second the firelight caught his face and the sergeant's hand shot out and gripped the man alongside him. "Oh no! You know who that was, don't you? You know what I just done? I only went and called the King of England a saucy rogue to his face!"

Henry walked on, moving between the dim red circles of dying campfires like a meteor through the dimness of space, calling out greetings to those he knew by name. Some recognized him, even bare-headed and without his surcoat of leopards and lilies. The King was a tall, erect figure, with a long, straight nose and strong jawline. His voice was sometimes soft and soothing, sometimes bright and laughing, depending on the nature and needs of his men. He played dice with some, exchanged memories with others, broke bread with them, listened to their jokes. He did not sleep that night, but the following morning his men were less weary because of it.

Only then did he begin to speak of glory.

His sword was drawn as he spoke, rallying them, encouraging them, praising their valour and skill as warriors. The men farthest off craned to catch every last word. Henry invited all those who wanted to leave, to go with his blessing – but warned them that they would miss out on the glory, miss out on being part of the greatest battle ever fought. No one got up to leave. When he had finished, there was no more talk of dying under French hooves, no more lolling in the mud nursing belly aches and fear. Henry had his men mustered and ready while the French were still quarrelling about who would lead the charge.

So sure of victory were the swaggering French knights, that they bragged to one another: "I shall capture the English banner!"

"I shall take a thousand prisoners!"

"They haven't above 900 men-at arms! The rest are nothing but poxy archers!"

Their horses pranced and capered under them, so unruly that their commander could not apply his battle plan. They even managed to trap 3,000 of their own crossbowmen behind them, leaving them unable to fire on the enemy for fear of hitting French knights.

At mid-morning, with a shout from Henry of, "Banners advance! In the name of Jesus, Mary and St George!" and with a blare of trumpets, the

English trudged a half mile towards the enemy. When the French banners were just within range of the archers' arrows, the English halted and sank long, sharpened stakes into the sodden ground, points outward.

With a single unearthly note, the bowstrings of the English longbowmen loosed a swarm of arrows, blackening the sky. Death fell on the French like a plague of locusts.

Enraged by such unexpected casualties, 1,000 knights spurred their lumbering great horses into a charge. But the ground in front of them was boggy, and the English archers could fire off twelve arrows a minute – metre-long arrows whose tips could pierce armour. By the time the French cavalry reached the longbowmen, 850 out of 1,000 were dead. The survivors rode on to the wooden stakes, or were pulled from their saddles and done to death by the archers. Riderless horses and fleeing French knights turned and galloped back the way they had come – trampling their own foot-soldiers.

The first line of French infantry finally surged up. But they were so tightly massed that they had no room to swing their weapons. They could only mill about, gasping for breath. The English archers threw down their bows and fell on them with swords and axes. Unaware of the disaster at the front, more French men-at-arms came marching up from behind. The first line, now trapped, could neither advance nor retreat. More Frenchmen died of being crushed, than of wounds inflicted by the English.

The aristocratic knights, in their heavy, ornate armour lay in the mud, helpless to get to their feet, trampled by horses and running feet, drowning in mud. In three hours, 10,000 Frenchmen died – half of all the noblemen in France were either killed or captured.

The cost to the English was a mere one hundred men.

King Henry V, frivolous and unpromising as a young man, changed completely after his coronation in 1413, into a sober statesman. He believed so fervently in his claim to the French throne that he pawned the Crown Jewels to fund a war, and borrowed hugely from such people as Dick Whittington (see page 119). By tireless warring, by the astounding victory at Agincourt and by marrying Catherine, daughter of the mad old King of France, he secured both England and France for his son.

Undoubtedly, English chroniclers of the battle exaggerated the difference in casualty figures. But the events recounted here are not simply some patriotic invention of Shakespeare's. His play *Henry V* (1599) was based on "fact" – the chronicles of Hall and Holinshed. Henry V, king for only nine glorious years, was dead at the age of thirty-four.

"Hang on the Bell, Nelly!"

1460

"AND THIS BE THE sentence OF this court; that you be taken from this place and, at the sounding of the curfew bell, hanged by the neck until you are dead. And may God have mercy on your soul."

The young man standing between his guards sagged a little at the knees, and a young women in the court cried out, "*No!*" But the judge did not so much as look up. He had passed the death sentence so often before. In these days of war, death was commonplace.

This was the time of the Wars of the Roses. The young man – Neville Audeley – was a Lancastrian. In attempting to visit his sweetheart, Nell, he had been unlucky enough to fall into the hands of Yorkist troops. His only crime was to be on the wrong side in the wrong place, during an endlessly bloody civil war which had torn apart families, and pitted neighbours and towns against one another. Once, Neville had given Nell roses, but all she had left now were the thorns embedded deep in her heart.

There was hope, even so. Neville was the nephew of the Earl of Warwick, and his uncle had influence. A word at court, a favour owing, and the earl might just win a reprieve for his nephew. But court was far off in London, and there was so little time! To Neville, gripping the bars of his prison cell, it seemed that the sun was crossing the sky with the speed of a cannonball, bringing his death hurtling towards him.

"Time to go," said his gaoler, jangling the keys in the lock.

"But my reprieve! What of a reprieve?"

"What of it? If it comes after curfew, they may paste it on your tombstone." He tied Neville's hands and led him down a dank stone passageway.

The day outside was already grey with age. There were a few townspeople still on the streets, despite the closeness of curfew. They would have to hurry home to put out their fires while the bell tolled . . . while Neville kicked out his life to the sound of St Peter's church bell. I shall never hear the last stroke of that curfew bell, he thought to himself, as he set his foot on the bottom rung of the gallows ladder.

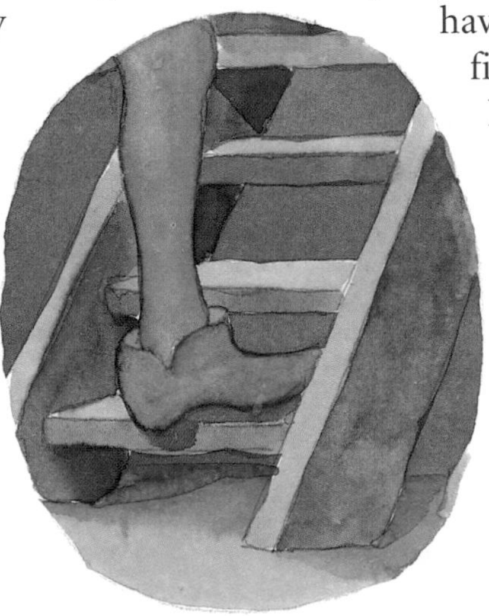

He searched among the crowd for Nell, but to his utter dismay she was not there. Where was she, his "little Nell"? Where was her sweet, encouraging face? It would have lent him such courage to catch one last glimpse of her. With her there, he thought he might at least have put on a show of bravery.

"For shame!" someone yelled. "He's only a boy! Hold off, hangman. There'll be a reprieve come for sure! He's Nelly Heriot's sweetheart! He's only a lad!"

But the hangman worked to the letter of the law, and the law said that Audeley must die on the first stroke of curfew. The belltower of St Peter's cast its shadow across the square, dwarfing the town gibbet. The bell-ringer stepped out smartly, squinting up at a corner of sky to judge the correct time. He was a very punctual man.

Up on the gallows, the noose around his neck, Neville waited for the bell to chime. He listened so intently that he could hear the starlings roosting, a horse stamp in a stable, a cook scrape a spoon around a pot. There was a dull thud he mistook for his heart breaking. Too late now for a reprieve. No hope now of seeing his Nelly again.

Inside St Peter's, the bellringer tugged again on the rope, but again there was no sound. He swung his whole body weight on the rope's end, but it was as if the bell had been struck dumb. Had frost broken off the clapper? Had the rope become entangled in the rafters? He pulled with a will – strong, rhythmic heaves: nothing but silence throbbed out into the darkening sky.

Beneath the gallows, the crowd began to stir restlessly. Surely the curfew should have rung by now? Had a reprieve already come? Or did St Peter himself refuse to sound the death knell of this poor young man? His eyes blindfolded, his hands losing their feeling with the tightness of the ropes, Neville could not judge what time had passed. Still he strained his ears for the sound of the bell. But half an hour went by, and it did not ring.

Then, with a noisy commotion which startled everyone, a rider galloped into the square.

"Reprieve! Hold off! Reprieve! A reprieve from the King!"

At the foot of the ladder, the crowd swept Neville Audeley along with them in a mad stampede for the church. The streets were dark: it was way past curfew, and yet curfew had not rung! Now they were free to satisfy their curiosity as to why.

As they got there, the bellringer had just finished climbing the long succession of ladders to the top of the belltower. He peered ahead of him in the shadowy belfry, mobbed by bats. At first he mistook the pale figure for a ghost. Then he saw it for what it was.

Nell had climbed up the tower and, despite the dizzying drop below her, leapt out to clasp the bell's huge clapper, wrapping her arms and legs around it like a lover, cloaking and muffling it with her clothing and hair. A hundred times and more the bell rope had swung her against the great brass wall of the bell, and yet she had not let go. Sickened by the motion, battered and bruised by the crushing impact, she had still refused to let the bell sound, refused to lose her grip, refused to die.

Half insensible, she refused even now to let go until the people called up to her through the wooden platforms of the tower: "He's safe! Your sweetheart is safe!" Only then did she allow her hands to be prised from its clapper, and permit the bellringer to carry her down the tower across his shoulder. ". . . must not ring . . ." she repeated, over and over, without opening her eyes, ". . . must not ring tonight . . ." until, at the church door, Neville's kisses finally silenced her.

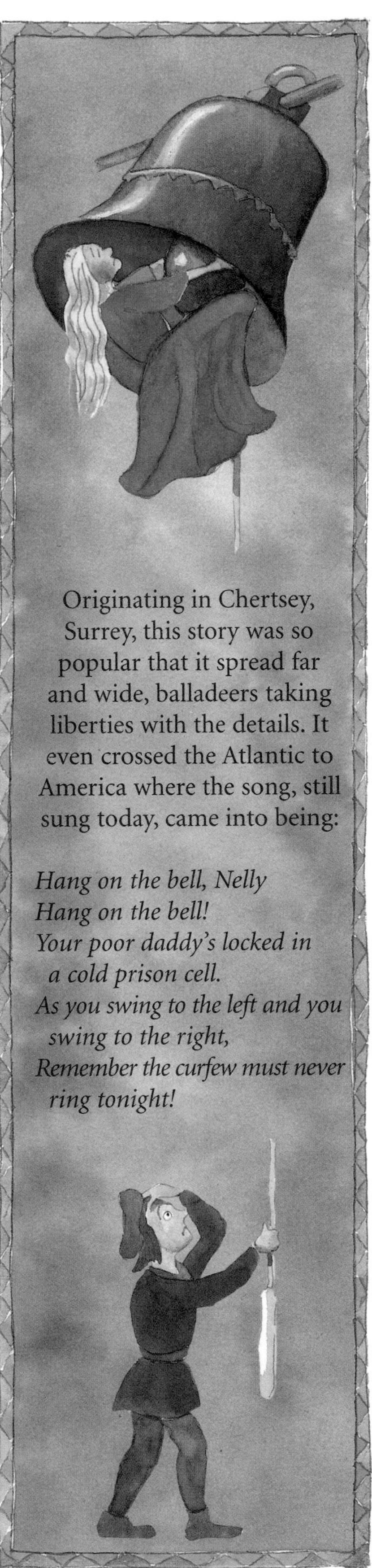

Originating in Chertsey, Surrey, this story was so popular that it spread far and wide, balladeers taking liberties with the details. It even crossed the Atlantic to America where the song, still sung today, came into being:

Hang on the bell, Nelly
Hang on the bell!
Your poor daddy's locked in
a cold prison cell.
As you swing to the left and you
swing to the right,
Remember the curfew must never
ring tonight!

The Princes in the Tower

1483

"MOTHER, MOTHER, WHO ARE THE BOYS IN the velvet coats who came to the Tower today with all those servants and fine baggage?"

"That is Prince Edward, my dear – king as shall be – and his brother Richard. Their father is newly dead of a fever, and soon Edward will be crowned. Think of that!"

"Poor souls," said Mary.

"Why do you say that? The Tower of London isn't all dungeons and guardrooms, you know. The state apartments are very fine."

"No, no. Poor boys to have lost their father, I mean," said Mary.

"Mother, mother, *when* is Prince Edward going to be crowned? I see him and his brother playing in the gardens and on the battlements, but the coronation never comes . . . They look sadder than they did. Only today I heard a servant call out: 'My Lord Bastard!'"

"Ah, child. There'll be no coronation now. It is held that Edward was born illegitimate. He cannot be king. Their uncle is crowned instead: King Richard III."

"Poor boys," said Mary.

"Mmm, but to be king at twelve, and to carry the whole weight of government on those narrow shoulders. It would have been a hard life for the boy."

"No, not to lose the crown, I mean," said Mary. "Poor boys, to be called such names by their own servants."

"Mother, Mother, why do the princes never play in the Tower gardens any more? I see them at the windows, looking out, and they look so sad and pale."

"I think, child, that their palace has become a prison, and they are kept locked up tight, for fear some politicking nobleman argues that Edward is true King. So many factions. So many ambitious men. The world is a wicked place these days, my dear."

"Poor souls," said Mary.

"To be squabbled over like a hand of cards? Yes, my dear."

"No, no. Not to be able to play out-of-doors, I mean," said Mary.

"Mother, Mother, where are the princes? I never see their faces at the window any more."

"Sshsh, my dear. No more questions. Best to keep silent in these wicked times."

"Tell me. I want to know. What has become of the princes?"

"Very well. I shall tell you what is said. They say that the King – King Richard, that is – gave the orders. He chose the most ambitious man at court, and told him, 'Do it.' James Tyrrell was eager to 'oblige' the King in anything. So he summoned two men, his keeper of horse, John Dighton and Miles Forest who looks after – looked after the princes."

"The boys were asleep together in the one bed, their arms tight round each other. Forest took hold of a feather pillow, Dighton another . . ."

"Oh Mother, no!"

". . . and they pressed the pillows over the boys' faces. The sleepers woke, of course, and struggled, but what could two little boys do against two grown men? After a while they stopped struggling. Forest and Dighton hid the bodies, and it was as if those little princes had never lived."

"King Richard did that? But why?" asked Mary. "He already had the crown! Why did he need to kill them?"

"Hush, child, speak lower. If he did order it done, then it did him no good. Richard himself is dead – killed in battle – and there's a new king crowned. A Tudor king. King Henry VII. He says that Richard killed the princes in the Tower. So keep quiet, little child, and say no more. These are not times to question what we are told."

"Poor souls," said Mary.

"Yes. They were only children. No older than you, after all."

"I did not mean the princes, Mother. I meant us. To live like pawns in a chess game and never know enough to tell black from white."

The Wars of the Roses (1455-87) was a time of turmoil, with factions forming alliances, then betraying each other. The crown kept changing hands. That is why it is so difficult to arrive at the truth of what happened to the princes in the Tower.

Some 200 years after their disappearance a box was unearthed by builders. It contained the skeletons of two children aged about ten and twelve – probably, but not certainly, the princes. The bones were interred in Westminster Abbey.

After defeating Richard III at the battle of Bosworth, Henry Tudor set about systematically blackening Richard's name. All at once Richard was a hunchback, a child killer, a psychopath. (Shakespeare, living under a Tudor monarch, helped greatly in this reshaping of history, casting Richard as the arch villain.) Historians think Henry (whose own claim to the throne was not strong) might equally have ordered the killings. So might Henry Stafford, Duke of Buckingham, who may have been waiting his chance to usurp both Henry and Richard.

A Recipe for Simnel Cake

1487

TAKE ONE COUNTRY, NERVOUS AND UNSETTLED.

Take one king, newly crowned and with a shaky claim to the throne.

Add ambition. Take a gamble.

Take one fifteen-year-old: Lambert Simnel.

Spread thickly the rumour that *he* is the rightful heir to the throne.

Whip up the Irish and a few English lords.

Raise an army.

Lambert Simnel was pretending to be the Earl of Warwick.

The priest called Father Symonds had tutored Lambert well. By the time he turned up in Ireland, he carried himself like an earl, could speak intelligently about affairs of state, and seemed to be acquainted with all the lords and ministers of court. He was handsome and pleasant, and people instantly warmed to him. They listened with bated breath to the thrilling account of his escape from the Tower of London, where wicked King Henry VII had locked him up.

The Irish sank to their knees and paid homage. They also swore to put this wronged boy back in his rightful place: the throne of England.

In fact, Father Symonds was banking on the fact that the Earl of Warwick had been murdered by King Henry. Secretly. Unwitnessed. What could the King say, then, when this "escaped Earl of Warwick" suddenly appeared to claim his rightful crown? "You are an impostor; I have already murdered the real Earl of Warwick"? Hardly.

And Father Symonds' obedient, talented protégé had managed to convince the Irish. Lambert Simnel knelt at the altar rail of St Patrick's Cathedral, Dublin. The crown was placed on his shining blond hair, and a fanfare acclaimed him Edward VI, *rightful* King of England.

There were only two drawbacks Father Symonds had not foreseen. In point of fact, Henry VII had *not* murdered Edward, Earl of Warwick: he was still alive! Secondly, Edward, Earl of Warwick, was *not* a handsome, intelligent, well-informed young man. He was a gormless ninny, as everyone knew who had ever met him.

King Henry fetched out the real earl, and paraded him through the streets of London, saying, "Speak to him! Anyone may speak with him! Ask him who he is!" It seemed a simple way to prove that the rumours from Ireland were all nonsense.

"Ah, well yes, he *would* produce an impostor," argued Father Symonds, "and pass him off as the real earl. But we know the real one, do we not? We have met the true Edward Plantagenet!"

Some believed him in all sincerity. Some simply *chose* to believe him since, to them, any usurper was preferable to the upstart Henry VII.

Francis the First Viscount Lovell, for instance, was ready to throw in his lot with the young "King Edward VI". So, too, was the Earl of Lincoln.

But Lincoln had met the real Edward Plantagenet many times in the past. So what expression crossed Lincoln's face when he met the boy impersonating him? Surprise? Amusement? Whatever thoughts went through his mind, he bent and kissed the hand of Lambert Simnel, and his face betrayed not a qualm, not a doubt.

Perhaps Father Symonds miscalculated. Perhaps, by the time he found out the Earl of Warwick was still alive, he was in too deep to turn back. Perhaps he staked too much on the unpopularity of Henry VII. The English lords who rose up in support of "King Edward VI" brought with them a few household armies; the Irish brought daggers and short swords. Altogether, they were no match for the army which came against them at Stoke. King Henry fought his rival for the throne, and won.

Lincoln was killed and Lovell fled, their hopes and fortunes dashed. Lovell made for his house at Minster Lovell, and hid in an underground room. "Lock the door and make it secret," he told a servant. "I have not been here, you understand? You have not seen me – or the King will have my head before the week's out!"

Father Symonds and Lambert Simnel did not slip so easily through the King's fingers. They were caught at once, and people winced to think what hideous punishment awaited them.

To everyone's astonishment, Henry VII, far from loosing the full might of royal justice on his enemies, seemed mildly amused by the whole affair. He invited the rebel lords to dine with him, and as they sat there, a serving boy came to serve them each with meat.

They looked once, they looked twice. An earl choked on his bread and grabbed for a cup of wine. It was! It had to be! The last time they had seen this boy, they had bent their knees and bowed their heads and sworn everlasting fealty to him and his descendants. It was Lambert Simnel. Henry had cut off neither his head nor his hands. "I have put him to work in the scullery," said Henry brightly. "He turned the spit where your meat was cooked tonight, so if it is underdone, you can blame – well, you may blame the King, I suppose!"

Lambert Simnel must have given satisfaction in the King's kitchen, for within a few years he had risen to the post of royal falconer.

There is a tradition that Lambert, while working in the King's kitchen, invented the Simnel cake one Eastertime. A spicy fruit cake, flavoured with almonds, he topped it with eleven marzipan balls, in token of the eleven faithful disciples. The twelfth was missed off, of course, because Judas, the twelfth disciple, betrayed Jesus. And nobody likes a traitor.

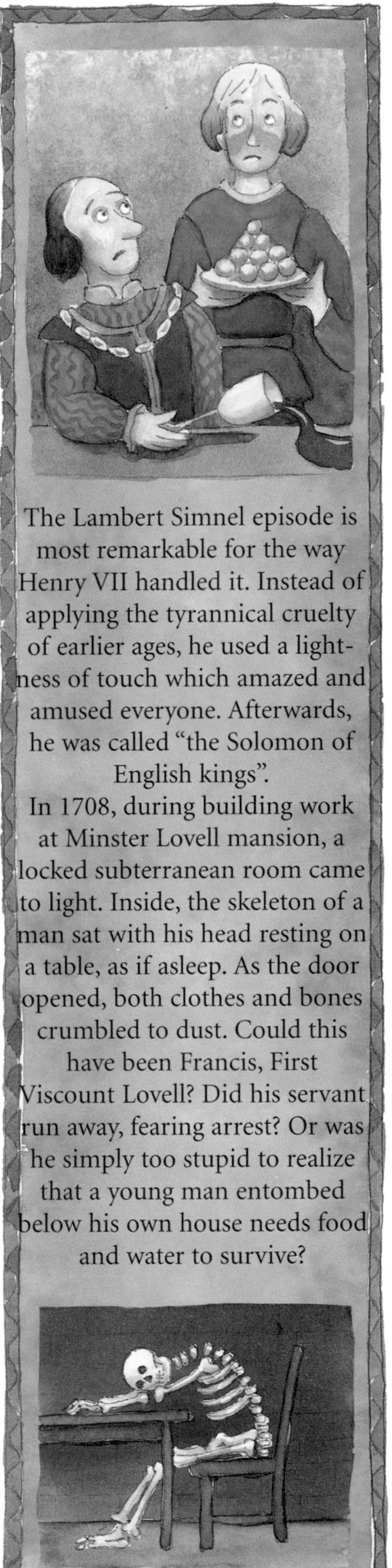

The Lambert Simnel episode is most remarkable for the way Henry VII handled it. Instead of applying the tyrannical cruelty of earlier ages, he used a lightness of touch which amazed and amused everyone. Afterwards, he was called "the Solomon of English kings".

In 1708, during building work at Minster Lovell mansion, a locked subterranean room came to light. Inside, the skeleton of a man sat with his head resting on a table, as if asleep. As the door opened, both clothes and bones crumbled to dust. Could this have been Francis, First Viscount Lovell? Did his servant run away, fearing arrest? Or was he simply too stupid to realize that a young man entombed below his own house needs food and water to survive?

The Faery Flag

1490

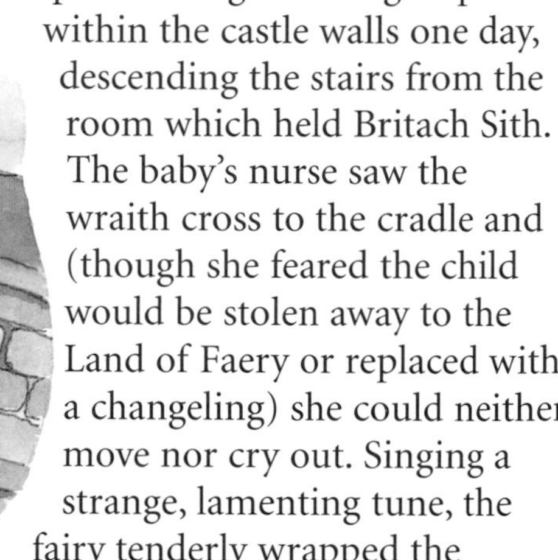

THE WIFE OF THE FOURTH LAIRD of the MacLeods led him by the hand to a bridge near Dunvegan, and kissed him on the cheek. “Twenty years I have been a wife to you, MacLeod,” she said, “and twenty years I have kept secret my birth and parentage.”

“What do I care where you come from or who your parents were?” he said bluffly. “You've been a good wife to me. Better than most.”

“That's because I am different from most. I am a fairy,” she said, “and being a fairy, I came only for a while. I must go back now to my land. But before I do, I have a present to give you, in token of the love that has been between us.” And she gave him Britach Sith: “the Faery Flag”. “If ever the clan of the MacLeods is in mortal danger, unfurl this banner, and the tide of fortune will turn. Three times its magic will come to your family's aid.” Then she stepped away from him, over the parapet of the bridge, and disappeared like the spray of the water beneath.

Now the bold MacLeods are not people to ask help of anyone, especially the fairies. And though the fourth laird treasured the banner, at Castle Dunvegan – a memento of his faery wife – he never unfurled it. Nor did his children.

But a hundred years later, when a future laird was born, a slight, diaphanous figure was glimpsed within the castle walls one day, descending the stairs from the room which held Britach Sith. The baby's nurse saw the wraith cross to the cradle and (though she feared the child would be stolen away to the Land of Faery or replaced with a changeling) she could neither move nor cry out. Singing a strange, lamenting tune, the fairy tenderly wrapped the baby in the flag and began to rock him in her arms. Then she laid him back in the cradle.

After she had gone, her tune stayed lodged in the nurse's brain like a splinter in a finger. Singing it, she found she had the power to soothe the loudest crying. Never again was a nurse employed to care for any heir to the MacLeod estates unless she had learned the faery lullaby from her predecessor. And yet still no human hand had unfurled the banner for its real purpose – to summon aid. The MacLeods were Scotsmen, and Scotland is a land of granite.

In battle, the Faery Flag was guarded by twelve of the finest men, each one holding a rope tied to the flagstaff, so that Britach Sith might never fall to the enemy. But what enemy could stand, anyway, in the face of the ferocious MacLeods, beards piled on their chest, red hair flying?

None but the MacDonalds.

At Glendale, MacDonalds as numberless as the thistles on the braes, came clamouring down to the noise of drum and fife, and hemmed in the MacLeods.

"The Faery Flag! Unfurl the Faery Flag!" came the cry, and the Twelve Finest unfurled the banner from its pole-head with a century of creases kinking its silken design.

Perhaps the sun came out to shine in the MacDonalds' eyes. Perhaps magic threads entwined themselves in the hearts of the MacLeods. Either way, before sunset, the glen was strewn with dead MacDonalds, and the day belonged to the MacLeods.

Back and back came the MacDonalds intent on revenge, numberless as the tics on the heather. At the battle of Waternish, thirty years later, the MacLeods of Clanranald once more faced destruction at the hands of their age-old enemy.

"The Faery Flag! Britach Sith or we die!" came the cry, and the little silken bundle at the head of the flagstaff licked out like a dragon's tongue over the heads of the Twelve Finest.

Suddenly, the MacDonalds' charge faltered and stumbled to a halt, the men behind cannoning into those leading. Claymores dropped from hands weak with fright, and the hardest men of the glens turned tail and fled. For marching down on them they saw an army of 10,000 men, bright with raised weapons, russet with jutting beards and wild red hair. Whether the light had tricked them or whether magic fibres of the flag had strangled their courage, the battle was a rout, and victory went to the MacLeods.

Many wars have washed over the purple hills of Scotland and stained the glens with blood. And many more MacLeods have travelled to dangers farther afield. But the Faery Flag has yet to be unfurled a third time. It lies folded within Castle Dunvegan, awaiting the third and last cry of "The Faery Flag! The Faery Flag! Unfurl the Faery Flag!"

Some believe the Faery Flag to have come to Scotland with the Norwegian king, Harald Hardraade, when he set out to conquer England in 1066. He flew a flag which he called Land-Ravager, a magic flag which, once unfurled, supposedly brought destruction to any enemy. On his journey south to fight King Harold, he lost Land-Ravager somewhere among the lochs and glens of Scotland.

Even in this century, during the First and Second World Wars and on battlefields far away from the braes, men of the MacLeod clan carried photographs of Britach Sith over their hearts. Some of them even came home again, their photographs as creased and tattered as the flag itself.

Tyndale's Crime

1536

LET ME TELL YOU ABOUT TYNDALE. WHO AM I? Nobody much. In fact, I won't tell you my name, or I'll be in trouble with the authorities again. But to my mind, William Tyndale was one of the great men of all time. And now they've burned him. Like a log of wood, they've burned him.

He studied at Oxford and Cambridge; he was a brilliant scholar – could speak five languages! His colleagues had nothing but good to say about the man. But when he set about translating the New Testament from Latin into English, for the common people to read, suddenly he was a criminal. He had to go abroad to get it done.

"If God spares my life, ere many years I will cause the ploughboy to know more of the Scriptures than you do," he told his learned colleagues before he went.

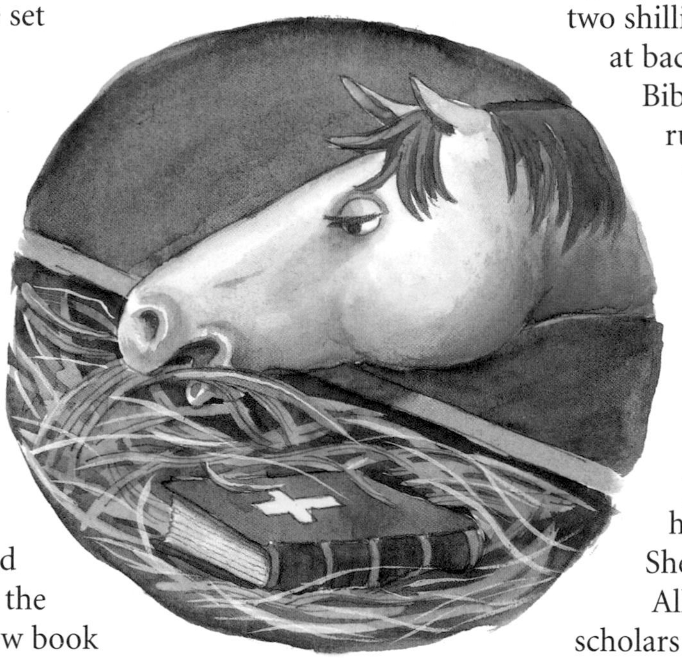

Even abroad they hounded him. Some villain overheard the printers talking about the new book they were working on: Tyndale's New Testament. "What a revolution this will stir up in England!" the printers said, and this eavesdropper thought, Revolution? Here's news the authorities will want to know about.

When they raided the printers, only the first ten sheets had been run off. But William was too quick for them. He had those ten sheets rolled up in his pack, and he was away to another city before they could lay hands on him.

He was in danger the whole time, every day of every year, but he pressed on with his work. Two editions were printed finally – one large, for reading aloud in public, one small enough to fit in a man's pocket. Anyone's pocket. Yours and mine.

He needed help, naturally, to distribute them. An association of European merchants, regularly travelling to and fro across the Channel in the course of their business, hid Tyndale's little printed Bibles among their goods. The books sold for two shillings, in shady corners and at back doors – black-market Bibles, selling like smuggled rum. There were 6,000 in the country before the bishops even knew what was happening. Everyone wanted one. *I* wanted one. I don't ever remember wanting a thing so much, or prizing anything so dearly as that parcel slipped into my hand one rainy day on Sheep Street.

All the clever men, the scholars and bishops bleated that it was an "ignorant piece of work", riddled with errors. What did a few errors matter to the likes of us who had always been shut out from understanding, because nobody taught us Latin? We knew it was an excuse. We knew they wanted to keep God to themselves – not share Him about. "Pearls trampled under the feet of swine," was how they put it. We didn't care. We had the Word of God in our own hands at last, in our own language. My old mother learned to read, specially to be able to read Tyndale's Bible.

When they couldn't track down the printing presses, they bought up thousands of finished copies and burned them in great bonfires. But the more they burned, the more people wanted to know what it was they were missing.

So the King made it illegal to own a Tyndale Bible.

Troopers searched high and low, in bread ovens and mangers and haylofts. Anyone found owning a Bible or reading one was put in prison for a month. I was one.

It was Shrove Tuesday, 1527. There were six of us. They dressed us up in penitential robes and gave us candles to carry, and faggots of wood. And there was this great parade through the streets – a public humiliation. We had to kneel on the ground and beg forgiveness from the people for our "crime". Then we were led three times round a bonfire – had to fuel it with those faggots of wood – and they made us throw our Bibles into the flames.

It was like throwing my very heart, I can tell you. It's hard to put into words, but I hated myself for doing it. Tyndale had given us this great book and here I was, destroying his years of work, *apologizing* for the joy he had given me. Of course I never meant a word of what I said that day. But I said it, even so. Like the apostle Peter denying Christ three times, to save his skin.

And now they've thrown Tyndale himself into the flames. Do you want to know his last words, before they strangled him at the stake and set him alight? "Oh Lord, open thou the King of England's eyes." That's what he said.

Well, you can burn a man and you can burn his books. But the truth won't burn, no more than water or milk. Fifty thousand copies of Tyndale's Bible have come into this country since the presses started up in Belgium. They might as well try to gather up the stars as to keep all those out of the hands of the people. It can't be done. Look here, hidden behind this panel in the wall: here's proof. Hold it. Open it. Read it. They will never stop up God's mouth – not now He's able to speak to us face to face, in Tyndale's English.

Tyndale's translations were not the first. As far back as John Wycliffe in the reign of Richard II, the Bible had been available in English. But copies of that had been hand-written and cost the great sum of £30 apiece, so they were scarcely meant for ordinary people.

Though Tyndale's translations were suppressed (of the first 15,000 volumes imported to England only three or four are left in existence) King Henry VIII was forced to acknowledge a need for a Bible in English. He therefore authorized a new translation – and the Great Bible came into existence.

These beautiful, large-format volumes were chained to church pulpits and read out at weekly services. People flocked to hear them in such vast numbers that the nobility and clergy must have taken fright. Within a couple of years Henry passed a law forbidding anyone to own or read or listen to readings from an English-language Bible unless they were of noble birth or a member of the clergy. Ordinary people were once again shut out. Two more reigns came and went before they were allowed access to the Word of God.

The Ghost of Anne Boleyn

1536

WHEN THE OLD QUEEN DIED, ANNE BOLEYN and her train of ladies wore yellow dresses, in celebration. "Now am I a queen indeed!" she said gleefully.

She had already won the heart of King Henry VIII away from his wife of eighteen years; in order to marry Anne, he had divorced Catherine. But now everyone would regard Anne as the true queen – even those who had questioned Henry's right to set aside his first wife. All that remained was for Anne to give Henry a child – a male heir – and their happiness would be complete.

She gave him a daughter – Elizabeth – but then Catherine had achieved *that* much. No, no. What Henry really wanted was a son, and Anne would give him that, too. Already she was pregnant again.

Turning the handle of the door, Anne entered, already shuffling the handful of pretty phrases which she would deal the King if she found him there. Henry was there, but to her surprise, not alone. One of the ladies-in-waiting was sitting on his knee, giggling at some witty remark of his, her fingers sunk lovingly in his beard.

At the sight of Anne, Jane Seymour flinched; her cheeks flushed red. But Henry's big, fat-chopped face looked oddly calm, oddly undisturbed. He made no hasty move to slide the wench off his lap. "Be at peace, sweetheart," he said to Anne, "and all shall go well with thee."

Anne Boleyn stirred herself from frozen astonishment to shrill hysterics. One hand went to her round belly, the other to her forehead. She was hot. She was cold. Tears pricked behind her eyes. She felt sick. The roaring in her ears told her she was about to faint.

The shock of finding her husband with another lady sent Anne into labour much too soon. The baby she was expecting – a boy – was born dead. Afterwards, Henry shouted at her for allowing "the loss of his boy". Anne reproached him for being the cause. But Anne had seen him wear that expression before – when people had counselled him against divorce, when people had spoken up for the ex-queen. Henry might just as well have shut the visor of a helmet: his face was all steel.

His love for Anne went out like a snuffed candle. All the fun had been in the chase and the wooing. Now he had seen another pretty face and he wanted to have it. Anne Boleyn was headstrong and gave herself airs. Saucy little Jane Seymour was far more agreeable, far more accommodating. No one had been able to stop him changing wives before – indeed his toadying ministers had smoothed the way to it. And if he could do it once, what was to stop him doing it again? The toadies would arrange it.

So he cut Anne Boleyn adrift.

There are always a ready supply of people who will say anything for money, or because they have been told to. A good lawyer can whip up a whisper of gossip – the smallest, spiteful rumour – into a mountain of damning evidence. Before long Anne was accused of being unfaithful to Henry with a whole host of men – even her brother. Accusations were flung like clods of mud, until the truth disappeared altogether. Henry had no interest in the truth – only the outcome. The Queen must die, so that he could marry Jane Seymour.

He un-married Anne. He un-queened Anne. He sent for a swordsman to cut off her head.

Getting up at two in the morning, she said prayers till dawn. Later, she sent for Sir William Kingston and said, "I hear I shall not die afore noon, and I am very sorry therefore, for I thought to be dead by this time and past my pain."

"The pain will be little," he said, his eyes fixed awkwardly on the carpet at her feet.

Anne nodded. "I have heard say the executioner is very good," she said, putting both hands round her throat, "and I have a little neck."

In the morning of 19 May 1536, Henry VIII went hunting in Richmond Park. He was restless and excitable as he stood beneath the shade of a large oak tree and the eager hounds turned and leapt and yelped on their leashes. Across the park came a dull roar – the signal gun being fired at the Tower of London.

"Aha! The deed is done!" cried Henry jubilantly punching the air with both fists. "Uncouple the hounds and away!" Next day, when he became betrothed to Jane Seymour, he wore a white silk suit – a sort of fancy-dress intended for gala days.

But Anne Boleyn's spirit was not so easily done down. Her headless ghost leads a nightly procession of phantom knights and ladies through the Tower, down to the chapel of St Peter-ad-Vincula within the Tower's precinct, where her body was interred. And every 19 May, a ghostly coach drawn by four headless black horses drives up to the gates of Blickling Hall where Anne was born. In it sits a ghost, her severed head resting in her lap. Meanwhile her father's accursed spirit is chased by a pack of shrieking demons over forty Norfolk bridges from midnight till dawn: an everlasting penance for giving his daughter into the hands of a murderer.

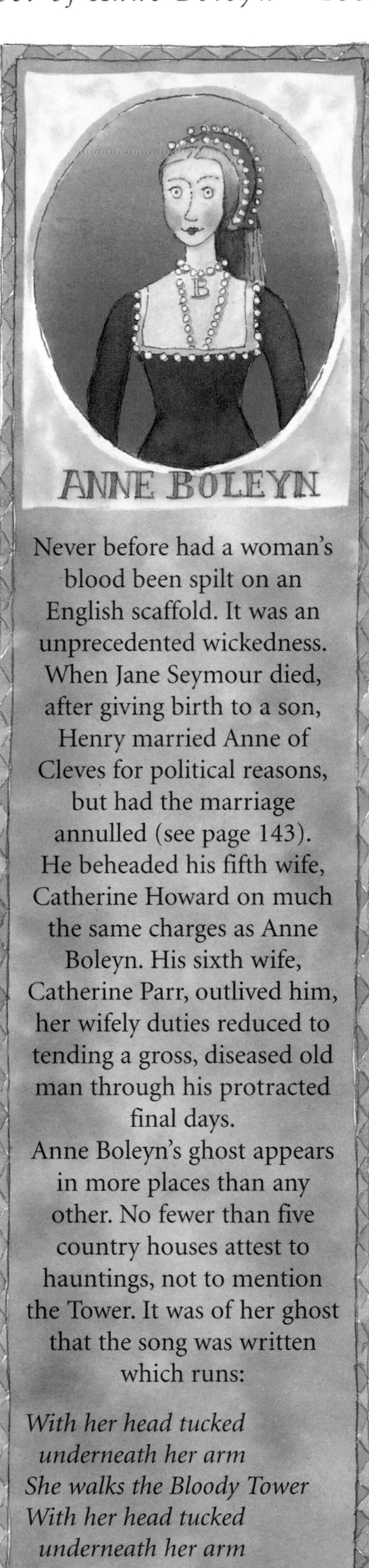

Never before had a woman's blood been spilt on an English scaffold. It was an unprecedented wickedness. When Jane Seymour died, after giving birth to a son, Henry married Anne of Cleves for political reasons, but had the marriage annulled (see page 143). He beheaded his fifth wife, Catherine Howard on much the same charges as Anne Boleyn. His sixth wife, Catherine Parr, outlived him, her wifely duties reduced to tending a gross, diseased old man through his protracted final days.

Anne Boleyn's ghost appears in more places than any other. No fewer than five country houses attest to hauntings, not to mention the Tower. It was of her ghost that the song was written which runs:

With her head tucked
underneath her arm
She walks the Bloody Tower
With her head tucked
underneath her arm
At the midnight hour . . .

"Little Jack Horner Sat in a Corner"

about 1537

LITTLE JACK HORNER sat in the corner of the inn, the Christmas pie on the table in front of him. He was deeply depressed. What would become of the animals, he wondered; of the fish in the ponds, of the crops in the fields, of the books on the shelves, of the wines in the cellar? What would become of the tenants who rented their land from the monasteries, of the church plate and the saintly relics? And what would become of him, if the abbey ceased to exist?

He knew the answer to all but the last. Everything would go to the King – that insatiable, Godless villain, Henry VIII, who had set about disbanding holy communities a thousand years old. Perhaps during Jack's service the odd teaspoon or bottle had found its way into his pocket, but on the whole he considered himself an honest, loyal, hard-working servant. But where would loyalty and hard work get him if the monastery were dissolved? He would lose his position, his livelihood, his home. Would his master still employ him when that master became plain "Richard Whiting, Gent", rather than Abbot of Glastonbury?

Horner eyed the pie. Well, perhaps the bribe would work after all, and Glastonbury would be spared. Jack did not hold out much hope. He had heard what happened to other monasteries – their treasures confiscated, their statues smashed, their monks turned out of doors. Jack failed to see how one Christmas pie was going to persuade the King of England to spare Glastonbury. Even this one.

Jack had helped to "bake" it. He had fetched the deeds from the abbot's great oak chest, rolled them tight and bent them round until all twelve fitted inside the pie dish. Then he had watched as the baked pastry lid went on. It was like the old nursery rhyme: "four-and-twenty blackbirds baked in a pie" . . . Only this pie had twelve surprises inside it: the deeds to twelve manorial estates owned by Glastonbury Abbey. The bribe was supposed to persuade King Henry not to close down the abbey.

"That's a fair pie you have there," the inn-keeper said, startling Jack Horner who was lost in thought. "You'll not be wanting supper, then?"

"Yes, yes!" said Horner. "The pie's not mine. It is a present for the King. Bring me something hot, please, and a mug of porter."

After the first, Jack drank several more mugs, and the more he drank, the deeper he sank into brooding melancholy. What did the King of England want with twelve Somerset estates? What had he ever done to deserve them? Loyalty and hard work ought to count for something! Jack Horner clumped an angry fist down on the table. The pie jumped. Its pastry lid came loose.

The fingers of Jack's other hand went up to his mouth. What had he done? One corner of a deed showed white like a piece of tripe. Little Jack Horner glanced around the dimly lit inn. No one was looking. The document slipped out of the pie easy as winking. The pastry slipped back into place. Then, with trembling fingers, Jack broke the wax seal, pulled the ribbon . . .

Mells in Somerset.

It was the best estate of all the twelve. The plum. Horner knew its spreading beech trees, its stew ponds and hayricks, its skylines and rambling manor house. He closed both hands around the document and kissed it.

Well? Weren't eleven manors bribe enough for anyone? King Henry would never know there had been twelve to start off with. If the abbey were dissolved, then better that Mells should be kept back. If Henry spared it – well, then, Jack would always return the deed to Abbot Whiting, and be thanked for saving it.

A log settled in the grate and Jack guiltily crammed the parchment under his jacket. It lay over his heart, muffling the quick beat. He tried to summon the landlord, but the voice cracked in his throat. He breathed deep and tried again. "Landlord! A drink for everyone here, and have one yourself!"

Drinkers looked around, smiling. Horner felt a glow of pleasure.

"Thank you kindly, sir, and who shall I tell folks is treating them?"

"Tell them: 'a man of property'. Tell them: 'the Master of Mells', my good man. Jack Horner of Mells in the county of Somerset."

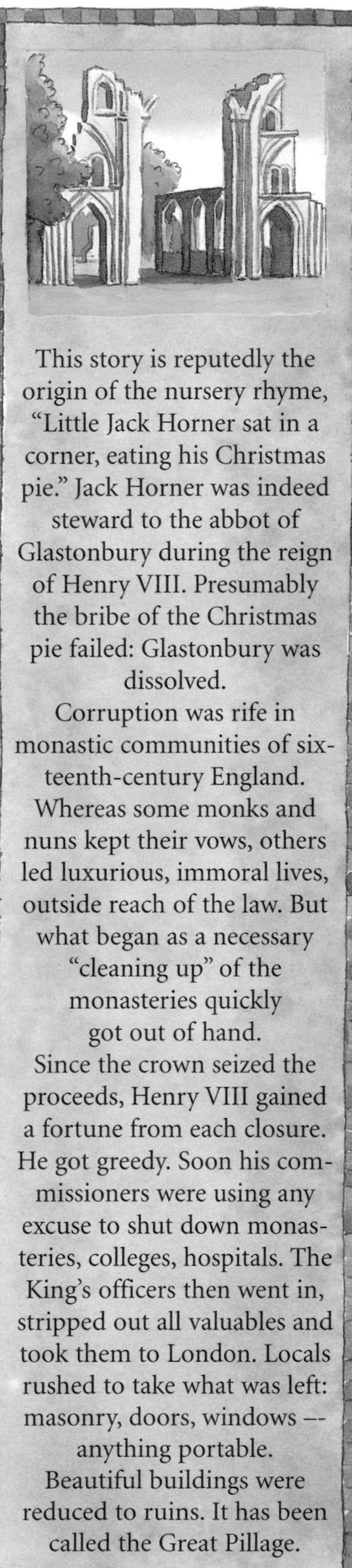

This story is reputedly the origin of the nursery rhyme, "Little Jack Horner sat in a corner, eating his Christmas pie." Jack Horner was indeed steward to the abbot of Glastonbury during the reign of Henry VIII. Presumably the bribe of the Christmas pie failed: Glastonbury was dissolved.

Corruption was rife in monastic communities of sixteenth-century England. Whereas some monks and nuns kept their vows, others led luxurious, immoral lives, outside reach of the law. But what began as a necessary "cleaning up" of the monasteries quickly got out of hand.

Since the crown seized the proceeds, Henry VIII gained a fortune from each closure. He got greedy. Soon his commissioners were using any excuse to shut down monasteries, colleges, hospitals. The King's officers then went in, stripped out all valuables and took them to London. Locals rushed to take what was left: masonry, doors, windows — anything portable.

Beautiful buildings were reduced to ruins. It has been called the Great Pillage.

The Flanders Mare

1540

HENRY RESTED HIS HANDS ON HIS BELLY, AND contemplated the two paintings. What a masterly painter Holbein was! And what a statesman Cromwell had been to track down two such handsome girls! Lutherans, too! A marriage to one of these princesses would endear him to half Europe, as well as filling that cold space in his life left by the death of his third wife.

Poor little Jane. He mourned her even now – even though he detested wearing black. At the cost of her own life, she had given him a boy child, a male heir, and for that he would always thank her. But a man cannot be expected to do without a wife; not a man of such royal appetites as Henry VIII. One more glance at the portraits, and Henry made his choice: the older girl, Anne. What though she could play no music? There are more important attributes in a wife.

Anne was wooed, and Anne was won, though not by Henry in person: he left all that to his diplomats. Anne was sent for and Anne came, crossing the Channel in the depths of winter. The closer she came, the more impatient he grew to see her. So, summoning seven gentlemen of about his own age, he told them to put on grey overcoats and saddle up: they were all riding to Rochester. Behind their obliging smiles, he glimpsed a certain unwillingness, given the filthy weather, but he just could not wait another moment to see his future bride! Henry, too, called for his horse to be saddled and for a grey overcoat to wear.

Eight anonymous gentlemen, all in grey, rode to Rochester, where Anne of Cleves had paused on her journey to London. What a surprise she would have, that beauty from Flanders, when her betrothed suddenly appeared and presented her with a New Year present of tippet and muff, and along with them his undying devotion!

The surprise was mutual.

What did the princess think, still queasy from the crossing, when she first saw her bridegroom? A mountain of bejewelled lard, sweating cheeks bulging through a square beard, eyes piggy with outrage. When she reverently fell to her knees

before him, she could smell a whiff of disease from his lap and legs and feet.

What did Henry think when he first saw his bride? Nothing that could be put into words. He simply stared at that pock-marked face, that stocky body, that nose. The hands she thrust into his were dry as pigskin. When she spoke to him in some ugly, guttural language he did not understand, he could not get away quickly enough.

Thomas Cromwell would pay for this.

"Alas! Whom shall men trust? She looks like nothing so much as a great Flanders mare!" blared the King.

The official meeting of bride and groom at Blackheath scarcely went any better. Admittedly, inside a brocaded tent, with music and quantities of warmed wine within reach, Henry found it easier to be civil. But no one had the right to be as ugly as that! He felt duped. He had been sold a pup. Thomas Cromwell must get him out of this marriage or face the consequences.

The lawyers picked over the princess's life as if checking for nits. But though she had been betrothed as a child to someone else, the law said it was not enough of an impediment. Furthermore, the King's allies would be seriously offended if the wedding were called off. "Is there then no other remedy but I must put my neck into the yoke?" bayed the King.

Cromwell would pay with his: one neck for another. Even as Henry placed the wedding ring on Anne's finger, he was thinking how to be rid of her. She was, after all, his fourth wife, and a man who takes four wives can always take a fifth . . .

The wedding over, the bride was quickly dispatched to Richmond "for the good of her health". Her ugliness was a crime, pure and simple: a kind of treason. He owed it to his people to be rid of her. Besides, Henry had seen a face he much preferred.

Archbishop Cranmer, having just performed the marriage, dutifully listed all the reasons why it should be dissolved. Convocation declared it null and void. Parliament stifled its groans and passed a Bill to the same effect. All eyes turned on Cromwell, who had masterminded the marriage: yet another over-ambitious man brought down by trying too hard to please: yet another casualty of the King-who-liked-marrying.

Meanwhile, Anne of Cleves was approached in private, by flattering, diplomatic men, and offered the chance to retire peacefully from her position as Queen and wife. They promised that her position at court would be that of the King's sister; no one would have precedence over her, except for the

King's daughters and his future queen. And she should have £4,000 a year to live on.

Anne of Cleves sat in the window of Richmond Palace, one hand spread across her throat as she listened. She did not reply at once. Perhaps she was trying to choke back tears of disappointment. "You may tell the King I live only to please His Majesty, and will act according to his wishes – though I hope I may be allowed sometimes to see the Princess Elizabeth who has become most dear to me."

The French ambassador caught her eye. The smile was so fleeting that he thought he must have imagined it, and yet so dazzlingly happy that, for a moment, the ex-Queen of England had appeared truly beautiful.

Six months later, the King was paying a visit to his ex-wife. The servants listening at the door heard laughter all afternoon. The Lady Anne had acquired a good grasp of the English language, and the King was as relaxed as anyone had ever seen him. Plainly, Henry and Anne were finding each other the best of company. She was witty and clever, well read and well bred. Best of all she was a good listener. While she sewed, the King talked, describing events at court, scandals uncovered, visitors up from the country, the word from overseas.

"Do you suppose they might be reunited?" whispered a lady-in-waiting sentimentally.

"He must lack company – a sick old man like that, surrounded by toadies."

"Do you suppose he has come to claim her?" whispered an equerry.

But the King swept out again and left, he in excellent good humour, she waving brightly from the window till he was out of sight. The Lady Anne seemed greatly cheered by the visit. Perhaps Henry had let slip that he was secretly married already to Catherine Howard.

Discussing remarriage, after Jane Seymour's death in childbirth, Henry asked Francis I of France to assemble a selection of pretty candidates for him to choose from. "It is impossible to bring ladies of noble blood to market, as horses are trotted out at a fair," retorted Francis. That is how Hans Holbein came to paint two pictures – of Anne and of her sister Amelia – so Henry could "view" them without committing himself.

Unfortunately, Holbein omitted the smallpox scars which pitted Anne's face, and painted a flattering portrait. Cromwell's agents abroad, anxious to bring about the alliance, also reported nothing but good. Thomas Cromwell, when he saw the King's reaction, tried to duck the blame, but when he could not extricate Henry from the marriage, went to the Tower and was beheaded in July 1540. This is the man who had helped Henry become supreme head of the Church.

The Staircase

1560

THE QUEEN, HER HEAD ON ONE SIDE, contemplated the portrait being held up by two equerries. The man in the picture was handsome – dashing, even. “Hang it at the foot of my bed, where I can see it when I wake!” she said.

Elizabeth I was going through the motions – pretending to be contemplating marriage to yet another eligible suitor. This time it was an archduke – the man in the portrait. Before him there had been King Philip of Spain, the eldest Prince of Sweden, the Earl of Arran . . .

But those well acquainted with Elizabeth knew she cared nothing for any of them. She was not stirred by the archduke in the portrait, nor by any Spaniard, Swede or Scotsman. Elizabeth was in love with Robert Dudley, her master of the horse.

His relatively lowly station did not matter (a commoner can soon be made a baron or an earl), nor did his father’s execution for treason. No, there was only one small impediment to Elizabeth marrying her true love: Robert Dudley already had a wife.

“The Queen is only waiting for her to die,” wrote the Spanish ambassador in his letters home.

But why should Dudley’s wife, Amy Robsart, die? A young woman in the prime of life? It was said by some that she was ill. Others said that she was all too healthy for Dudley’s liking and that he was wondering how to change that.

Amy Robsart sat in the big dark house on Cumnor Hill. The servants had all gone out to the fair in nearby Oxford: she had insisted on them going, despite her pain and low spirits. Every night she rubbed the apothecary’s lotion into her breast, but it seemed to do no good. Perhaps the pain came simply of a broken heart. For she was a woman whose husband did not love her – a woman who, just by continuing to breathe, blocked her husband’s path to success and happiness. That was why she had not refused the wine at dinner, even though she feared it might be poisoned.

Not that Robert would do such a thing. Oh no, surely not her Robert who, in marrying her, had promised to cherish her. But the Queen – ah, the Queen's wishes could creep like ivy into every last crevice of her kingdom. Amy could feel those wishes entwining her, dragging on her, sapping her strength. A loyal subject ought to help the Queen to happiness, rather than hinder her.

The big dark house creaked and rustled around her, its corridors, landings and stairs unlit. It was not her own house. It belonged to a friend of Robert's. And Robert was away at court, as usual, dancing, paying compliments, exchanging witty remarks with the Virgin Queen. The pain in Amy's chest grew worse. The trees on Cumnor Hill put their heads together and whispered – gossip and rumour, rumour and gossip.

Robert Dudley was out riding with the Queen when the messenger arrived from Cumnor. Terrible news, a tragic accident. "What has happened?" asked Dudley.

"It's your wife, sir. Found yesterday, sir. A tragic fall, sir. The stairs . . ."

Amy Robsart lay spread-eagled at the foot of the staircase in the house at Cumnor Hill, her neck broken, her feet bare, her skin as pale as her night-dress. The coroner's jury brought in a verdict of accidental death. In the dark, unfamiliar house, she had tripped and fallen. The other possibility – that she had committed suicide – could not be put into words, for that would have meant a suicide's burial in unconsecrated ground.

The public, however, were in no doubt as to what had happened. Dudley had wished his wife dead and now she was. In the public imagination, Robert Dudley was a murderer, and people hated him for it. The rumour-mongers whispered:

"Have you heard? The Queen is secretly married to Dudley!"

"She is making him Earl of Leicester."

"She means him to rule England with her!"

"A murderer in the arms of our Queen!"

But they were all wrong. The truth was that Amy Robsart's suspicious death had made such a marriage impossible. Dudley was so unpopular now that Elizabeth would antagonize the whole country, her ministers and her allies by marrying him.

Concealed behind the red curls, the porcelain-white skin, the coquettish flirting, the bright, bird-like eyes, was a steely, calculating brain. If Elizabeth had ever considered marriage to the beautiful Robert Dudley, she shut her mind to it now. Love was sweet, but politics were crucial. Marriage to her, she proclaimed, "was a matter of the weal (well-being) of the kingdom". She would only marry if it were in the country's best interests.

She did indeed make Robert Dudley Earl of Leicester, and as he knelt before her to receive the accolade, she tickled his neck playfully and giggled. The courtiers turned to one another with raised eyebrows and meaningful looks. But they were entirely wrong. The earldom was intended to make Robert Dudley a fit suitor for a queen, but not Queen Elizabeth. She had suggested he should woo the troublesome Mary Stuart, Queen of Scots.

Elizabeth was Queen first, woman afterwards. She did not marry the man in the portrait, nor the Duke of Anjou, nor Emperor Charles IX, nor the Duke of Alençon, nor the Earl of Essex, nor any of the other suitors who wooed her. She was in her mid-twenties and yet she had no illusions left. She was a queen, and whoever smiled or bowed or sent her gifts or poetry or portraits was thinking chiefly of her crown, not her beauty.

She was a kind of staircase ambitious men wanted to climb.

Elizabeth never married, although Parliament and the country urged her to, and she assured them she would. She liked to keep suitors dangling for as long as possible, for while a suit continued, she was in a very strong position to negotiate.

Did Amy Robsart kill herself? Was she murdered on her husband's orders? Or by Sir William Cecil, the Queen's Secretary, who frowned on the romance and knew the scandal would force Elizabeth to shun Dudley? Or did Amy just trip in the dark and fall, her spine breaking easily because of the breast cancer which some say was already killing her? The truth will never be unearthed now.

Robert Dudley took a second wife in 1573 and married again, bigamously, in 1578. Elizabeth was fleetingly furious with him, but relented and, despite his poor military record, appointed him commander of forces against the Spanish Armada in 1588. That same year, however, he suddenly died: poisoned. Rumour had it that poison meant for his wife had somehow found its way into his own food.

Walter Raleigh Salutes the Queen

1580

IT WAS NO WEATHER FOR FINERY. BUT QUEEN Elizabeth shone like the sun wherever she went (as she never tired of being told). So Walter Raleigh pulled on his finest shirt, with its wide, stiff ruff of pleated cotton at the throat. His manservant helped him into the stiff, bombasted brocade doublet and short-hose, then pulled the laces tight. (The bright lining showed through the slashed panels of the plump hose like segments of Seville orange.) He drew on his own pale, silvery, silk stockings and secured them with tasselled garter-ribbons above his knee. Then he slid his arms into the painted leather over-doublet and his feet into his new low-heeled, calfskin shoes which he fastened with ribbon bows. He buckled on his embossed swordbelt, then, last of all, swung round him his brand new cloak – a masterpiece of panned, piped, interlined, gilt-clasped, silver-corded velvet. Raleigh was about to meet the Queen of England for the very first time.

Magnificent as Raleigh looked, his outfit paled into shabbiness beside the Queen's finery. As she descended from her coach, the small boys who had chased three miles in its wake caught their breath and gasped. She was as marvellous as a galleon new-rigged, as an angel among shepherds. Her pale kid shoes might as well have belonged to a fairy-tale princess.

But this was not London. It was a country town. This was countryside overshadowed by forest, overhung with cloud, overrun with mud. Elizabeth hesitated and looked around her, with obvious unease, skirts bunched within her two fists, to lift them clear of the dirt. Across her path lay . . . a large, brown puddle.

A cold, spitting rain fell on Walter's hair as he took off his hat and bowed low. A cold, reproachful blast of wind ruffled his cuffs as he unfastened his splendid cloak. Then, with a bull-fighter's flourish (but the careless expression of one who does such things every day) Walter Raleigh laid down his cloak. He laid it down over the puddle – it made a soft, velvety squelch – inviting the Queen to walk over it rather than dirty her shoes.

The sight of that handsome velvet cloak lying in the mud made even Elizabeth catch her breath. She stared for a moment as the cloth grew sodden and settled, then she turned a dazzling smile at the owner. The glance lengthened as she took in his dashing good looks, his exquisite tailoring. Then she stepped on to the cloak, as carefully as a skater stepping on to the ice of a pond. Momentarily, the crowd glimpsed the pale prettiness of her shoe.

The cloak lay ruined, soaked. But as Walter said, with a shrug, to any who mentioned it, that was a small sacrifice to please a queen. Even the beaux and coxcombs strutting in the Queen's wake held handkerchiefs to their noses and whispered among themselves that it was "cleverly done", even they admired the panache of it – the grand, chivalric flourish of it. Raleigh was a made man.

It is not known with any certainty whether the incident of the cloak actually took place – several towns lay claim to it – and whether it was this which first endeared Walter Raleigh to Queen Elizabeth I. Certainly he became a great favourite of hers after joining court at the age of thirty. She heaped gifts of land on him and sent him on various missions of exploration and conquest. But she never seems to have found him reliable enough to entrust with high office. He could not intrigue as well as those around him and eventually lost his head for treason.

The cult of Elizabeth's beauty gave rise to music, literature and art, even after Elizabeth herself, vain to the last, had decayed into a sad, painted old lady with rotten teeth and a flame-coloured wig. At the end, she sat up in a chair for three days and nights for fear, if she went to bed, death would lay hands on her.

Francis Drake and a Game of Bowls

1580-1588

THE SUN ROSE BRIGHT AND CHEERFUL, BUT THE bride did not. Lizzie Sydenham put on her wedding finery with a heavy heart. Her mother and father greeted her with little cries of admiration and happiness – "Fancy! Our little Lizzie a bride!" – but she could not smile.

Even so, she knew better than to say, "I don't want to marry. I do not love this man." So she took the nosegay of flowers from her mother and stepped out of doors for the short walk to church. What good would be served by defying her parents' wishes?

Her one true love was oceans away, attempting the impossible, trying to sail around the world. If he were not already dead, it would take several miracles to bring him safe home. Her parents said Francis Drake was a nobody, a rough, coarse, low-born pirate, for all the gold, silver and pearls he had stolen in the Spanish Main. Lizzie did not believe it, but when, after years of waiting, Francis still had not come home to claim her, what else could she do but accept the respectable, unremarkable gentleman waiting for her now at Stogumber Church? Suddenly, something made her look up.

It happened so fast: there was no dodging aside, no ducking down or turning to run. She stopped stock still, and with a massive thud which shook the ground and raised a spew of dust, a great round stone ball landed at her feet. It struck so hard that it half sank itself in the dirt. The little wedding party stared.

Lizzie's father said that it must be masonry from the church roof. Her mother said someone was trying to kill them. But Lizzie simply handed back her bouquet and said, "I shan't marry today. Francis has fired a cannon ball across the world to forbid it. He wants me to wait for him, so I shall."

And she did. Nothing would persuade her to break her vow. When Francis Drake sailed into Plymouth harbour, and all the church bells in the West Country welcomed him home, Lizzie Sydenham stood waiting.

The rock was not a cannonball at all, of course. Nothing so ordinary. It was a meteorite. While Drake's little vessel the *Golden Hind* sailed round the world, a fragment of debris from an exploding star had been voyaging through the vastness of space, to land at Elizabeth Sydenham's feet. The Spanish said Sir Francis Drake had a drum with which he could summon up the wind. They said he had a mirror in which he saw the future. They said that he had sold his soul to the Devil for mastery of the seven seas. But then the Spanish were superstitious, and their captains preferred not to admit that any Englishman could get the better of them. Ever since Drake had sailed up the River Tagus to Cadiz, and burned the King of Spain's warships, they had called him "El Draco" – "The Dragon" – a beast of fire and destruction.

With Spain's fleet – its "Invincible Armada" – massing for war on the other side of the Channel, the English themselves liked to think that Drake possessed magic powers. They told how he had *made* the entire English fleet, sitting on a cliff one day, whittling a twig. Every splinter had turned by magic into a ship on the sea below.

The Spanish, on the other hand, had felled an entire forest, to build their fleet.

When the Armada finally attacked, the English admirals – Drake, Hawkins, Frobisher and Lord Howard of Effingham – were playing a game of bowls on Plymouth Hoe, a grassy flatness overlooking the sea. The pleasant knock of wood against wood was interspersed with talk of strategy, and jokes about Spanish beards.

Suddenly there was a shout, and a look-out came pelting along the Hoe: "They're coming! They're coming! The Spanish fleet is sighted! They're coming!"

Snatching up gloves and sword belts, peering out to sea, the various commanders started for their ships at a run. There were crews to turn out, gangplanks to raise, ropes to cast off, anchors to weigh, drums to be sounded, wives to kiss goodbye . . . The fate of the country was about to be decided.

"Hold hard, friends, hold hard!"

They turned back. Drake stood just as before, a cluster of bowls at his feet. "Plenty of time to win the game and beat the Spaniards too!" he said, in his slow, Devonshire drawl. And he bowled – slow and steady and true.

The other men walked back, laid aside their gloves, took their turns. Over the horizon a hundred topsails, like puffy white clouds, moved into sight. Crowds gathered along every quay and jetty and cliff, standing on tiptoe, craning their necks to see. But the English commanders finished their game before strolling sedately to their ships and giving battle-orders, for all the world as if they were ordering dinner.

The English ships were smaller, quicker and more manoeuvrable than the lumbering Spanish galleys and galleons. They could dart in close, loosing cannonfire and arrows. Drake used fire-ships, too – filled with kindling or gunpowder, helms lashed on collision course, while down below, the fuses burned . . . Fire ships wrought havoc among the Spanish fleet, blasting them out of the water or burning them down to their keels. El Draco could indeed breathe fire.

Even so, the Spanish sea captains believed that their honour depended on victory, and their honour was worth more to them than their lives. They fought with frenzied heroism, until blood ran in

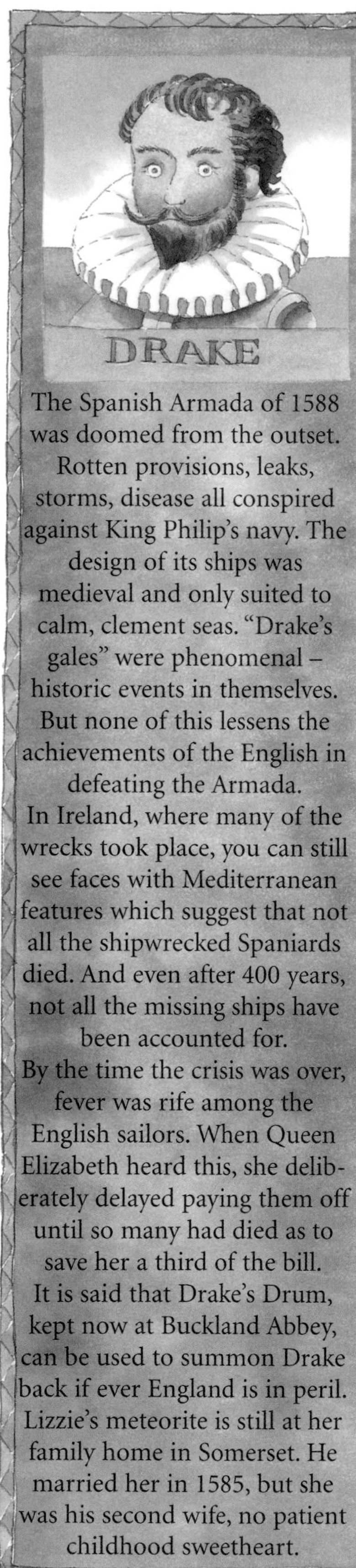

The Spanish Armada of 1588 was doomed from the outset. Rotten provisions, leaks, storms, disease all conspired against King Philip's navy. The design of its ships was medieval and only suited to calm, clement seas. "Drake's gales" were phenomenal – historic events in themselves. But none of this lessens the achievements of the English in defeating the Armada.

In Ireland, where many of the wrecks took place, you can still see faces with Mediterranean features which suggest that not all the shipwrecked Spaniards died. And even after 400 years, not all the missing ships have been accounted for.

By the time the crisis was over, fever was rife among the English sailors. When Queen Elizabeth heard this, she deliberately delayed paying them off until so many had died as to save her a third of the bill.

It is said that Drake's Drum, kept now at Buckland Abbey, can be used to summon Drake back if ever England is in peril.

Lizzie's meteorite is still at her family home in Somerset. He married her in 1585, but she was his second wife, no patient childhood sweetheart.

streams from their gunports and their ships foundered under them. Their commander-in-chief, the Duke of Medina Sidonia, was an incompetent, but they fought on despite him, till ammunition ran out on both sides, and the noise of battle fizzled into silence.

Then the Spanish beat north up the English Channel, planning to skirt the north coast of Scotland and sail home. That is the day, legend says, when Francis Drake went ashore, and danced with the witches and demons on a windswept clifftop, summoning up a storm.

Gales came in from the west. Damaged, leaking ships, manned by injured, hungry crews, wallowed lower and lower in the water. The storms, which raged for a fortnight, drove ships on to rocks, on to sandbars, into unfriendly harbours, or simply swamped them in deep water, leaving not a trace. Of 130 ships which set sail, just over half reached home, and of 27,000 men only some 9,000 survived to feel the Spanish sun on their faces. Then they lay in their mangled ships and died of fever, as though fate had damned every last man.

On his journey home overland, the Duke of Medina Sidonia was pelted with stones by small boys for his disgraceful failure.

Drake went home to Lizzie. But ambition for gold and glory soon sent him back to plundering the Spanish Main. He died there, and was lowered to his eternal rest in the vaults of the sea.

The Long-Expected End

1587

MARY SPRINKLED sand over her letter, to stop the ink running, then shook off the surplus. It made a noise like voices whispering.

She had pondered long and hard whether to answer the letter from Anthony Babington. He was a dear, devoted, devout young man, but rash and passionate. He said he was planning to assassinate Queen Elizabeth and put Mary in her place.

So long as she did not actually *acknowledge* his suggestion, she could not be accused of conspiring with him. But surely a letter would be safe enough hidden inside the empty casks which left Chartley House?

Letters from her friends and supporters arrived in the full casks, and her own left in the empty ones. It was a fine, convenient arrangement and a great comfort to a woman kept under house arrest for the best part of twenty years. Mary folded the letter, and allowed her hand to rest on it, trembling. She had just given her consent to his assassination plot.

Mary Queen of Scots was Elizabeth's second cousin, a Catholic and a serious nuisance. She threatened the nation's stability. Every Catholic would have liked to see Elizabeth dead and Mary crowned in her place. Elizabeth, for her part, would have liked to see Mary dead and out of the way.

And yet they were cousins. Elizabeth must not seem unnaturally cruel to her own flesh and blood. It was a problem. Best if Mary should be discovered committing some gross act of treason, plotting some coup. So Elizabeth put her secret service to work, spying on Mary, keeping a watch on her and her friends, vetting all her visitors – intercepting all her mail.

So when Babington wrote to Mary of killing the Queen, and Mary wrote back, encouragingly, Sir Francis Walsingham, head of the Queen's secret service, read both letters. After all, it was he who had organized the business of the wine casks.

Mary was damned by that letter to Babington. Babington and his fellow conspirators were doomed men. Their plot gave Elizabeth just the excuse she had lacked all these years. Now she could put Mary to death.

In September, Babington and thirteen other conspirators were dragged through the streets of London on hurdles, face-up to the sky, to a scaffold of dizzying height where they were hanged, drawn and quartered.

Elizabeth's Council clamoured for Mary to be imprisoned at once in the Tower of London, but Elizabeth sent her to Fotheringay Castle instead – yet another secure house in the long line of comfortable prisons. At Fotheringay she was in the charge of Sir Amyas Paulet.

Tearfully Elizabeth received loyal deputations from her people calling for the death of the treacherous Mary. With great shows of unwillingness, she finally allowed herself to be persuaded. Mary was guilty of treason. Wild delight met the announcement, with church bells ringing all day and bonfires lit in the streets. Elizabeth's adoring public bayed for Mary's blood. All Elizabeth had to do was agree.

Mary's son James pleaded for her life – but not very hard. He was in line to become King of England, and nothing must jeopardize that. He would be a fool, he wrote to a friend, "if I should prefer my mother to the title".

Elizabeth signed the death warrant . . . but would not give instructions for it to be sent. "What a great relief it would be to me," she murmured aloud, "if some loyal subject were now to kill Mary . . ."

Amyas Paulet, Mary's prison warder, refused to take this heavy hint. He wrote back that he would not "make shipwreck of his conscience without law or warrant".

And so the warrant was sent – oh, quite against Elizabeth's will – an abuse of trust (she said), a wicked flouting of her will! She had never intended it to be sent! The man responsible would pay!

Even so, on Tuesday, 7 February, a hand knocked gently on the door of Mary's apartments and a gentleman informed her, with great civility and courtesy, that, "Tomorrow morning, ma'am, you must die."

Mary spent the night praying, then in the morning dressed entirely in black with a veil of white lawn over her auburn hair. At forty-four, her former beauty had faded. Years of enforced idleness, sitting over books or embroidery or letters had made her portly, with a fat face and double chin. Her shoulders stooped. And yet it was a dignified, fearless figure who was led into the great hall of Fotheringay Castle to be confronted by a scaffold draped in black, two executioners, a huge axe.

Her servants were beside themselves with grief, trembling, sobbing, swooning. Though Mary wept at being parted from them, her sole companions for so many years, she told them to be glad, not sorry. "For now thou shalt see Mary Stuart's troubles receive their long-expected end."

William Davison, Elizabeth's secretary (and innocent scapegoat) was accused of sending the death warrant to Fotheringay against Elizabeth's wishes. He was tried, fined and imprisoned in the Tower. No one seriously expected the sentence to be carried out, but Elizabeth insisted on it. Mary's perfidious son, on his mother's death, became King James VI of Scotland. When Elizabeth died childless (even though James was widely believed to be a secret Catholic), he became King James I of England, too.

The executioners tugged inexpertly at her clothing. She smiled: "I was not wont to have my clothes plucked off by such grooms." Then she knelt at the block and prayed in Latin: "Into your hands, O Lord . . ."

The axe fell; the room flinched with a single spasm at the noise of it. There was a ghastly moment of unforeseen horror. The head was not off! The axe man took a second stroke.

He lifted the severed head up for all to see . . . and the auburn wig and the blood-stained white lawn came away in his hand, letting fall a head of close-cropped grey hair with two ringlets over the ears.

"God save the Queen!" said the headsman.

"Amen!"

"This be the end of all the enemies of Her Majesty!" said the Earl of Kent. But the communal cry of "Amen" broke off, as the skirts of the dead woman began to stir.

Out at the hem nosed a little dog, whimpering and afraid. One of Mary's dogs. It trotted into the pool of blood between head and shoulders, and lay down, whining, inconsolable. Nothing could erase that image from the minds of those who saw it.

No more could Elizabeth's raging and protests and loud public regrets erase the impression that she had got her wish at last: Mary Queen of Scots was extinguished and Queen Elizabeth could sleep easy in her bed.

The City of Raleigh

1587

THE FIRST ENGLISH COLONISTS TO CROSS THE Atlantic landed on Newfoundland, squabbled, fought, fell ill and gave up. Setting sail again for England, their ship went down with everyone aboard. So much for conquering the New World.

Roanoke Island, at first sight, seemed a far more promising place to begin. It rose out of the curved horizon, green and clad in trees. There were rumours of gold and pearls.

One hundred and seven settlers built a fort there. But instead of planting crops, they went hunting for gold. They quarrelled with the local people and ran desperately short of supplies. When a hurricane struck, they were so terrified that they begged a visiting ship to take them home. Sir Richard Grenville, calling at Roanoke, found no one there. He did his best to revive the settlement by landing fifteen men with enough provisions for two years.

In due course, Sir Walter Raleigh arrived with another group (this time including women and children). It was their task to found the "City of Raleigh" in this land called "Virginia" after the Virgin Queen Elizabeth. But where were Grenville's fifteen sailors? There was not a trace – except for one skeleton of a murdered man!

Undaunted, the settlers took over the deserted fort, built timber cabins, cleared land and planted it. A baby girl was born – she too was called Virginia. With just a few more supplies from England, the community would be able to survive the whole year round!

"I'll go myself and get them!" said John White, elected leader of the little community.

But when he reached home, he found that England had troubles of her own. War with Spain was brewing. The novelty of the New World had worn off, and nobody was interested in the troubles of a handful of settlers. It was two frustrating years before he could lead a relief expedition.

It was an anxious voyage for White. How many more children would have been born? Would tornadoes have struck? Or hostile natives? As the ship sighted land, the cheerful sight of rising smoke was a great relief to him.

Then he realized that the smoke was a forest fire, nothing more. The ship fired its guns to attract attention. John White leaned eagerly over the rail, to see which of his friends would come running down to the beach: Mary, Ananias or even Virginia.

No one came.

It was getting late and there was a heavy sea running. Not until the next morning did the captain send two boats ashore. One overturned in the surf and seven people were drowned. But the survivors scrambled ashore. A trumpeter blew several blasts on his damp trumpet, and the rest broke raggedly into song.

There was no reply to their singing. Though they sang till their voices cracked, no one came. There was no one left to come.

Not a trace remained of the settlement. Not only had the people disappeared, but the cabins, too! Books lay around like dead birds, fluttered by the wind. But there was no Mary, no Ananias, no little Virginia Dare.

There were no graves, either, no skeletons or bloodstains. John White took heart from that. "They have moved on. It was agreed among us: if a move was decided upon, they would leave word: a message carved on a tree – a cross beneath it if danger had driven them to it. Look for a sign. Look for a message!" And he ran from tree to tree, searching. "Over here! Make haste, there's something here!"

There carved in a tree were just three letters: C R O. What did it mean? There was no cross underneath, but then perhaps the person who carved them had been prevented from finishing. Anyway, what sense could be made from three letters: C R O?

John White said, "Croatoan. They have gone to Croatoan Island. The Croatoans are friendly. I am greatly joyed. It means my friends are safe!"

And with quite extraordinary confidence in those three crude letters, he set sail again for England. Incredibly, he did not make for Croatoan Island or enquire any further. It was as if the people with whom he had been entrusted had simply gone on ahead of him to somewhere he could not follow.

The next time English ships happened to anchor off Croatoan Island, they found no trace of any English prisoners or settlers. Six expeditions Sir Walter Raleigh sent in search of the citizens of the City of Raleigh: they found nothing.

And yet 100 years later, Croatoans sided with the English in the War of Independence, saying that they had taken all their laws and religion from English settlers. Some had blue eyes, fair hair and beards. They told a legend at their firesides, too, of a little white maid who grew up into a beautiful woman, and then changed by magic one day into a white deer. Was that child Virginia Dare, born in hope, christened in thanksgiving, lost while the world was looking the other way?

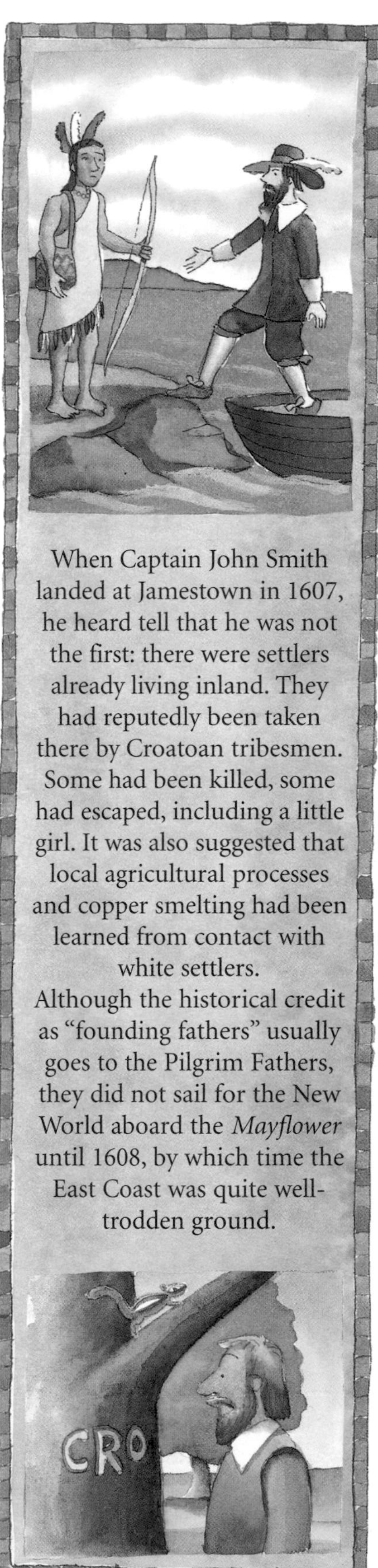

When Captain John Smith landed at Jamestown in 1607, he heard tell that he was not the first: there were settlers already living inland. They had reputedly been taken there by Croatoan tribesmen. Some had been killed, some had escaped, including a little girl. It was also suggested that local agricultural processes and copper smelting had been learned from contact with white settlers.

Although the historical credit as "founding fathers" usually goes to the Pilgrim Fathers, they did not sail for the New World aboard the *Mayflower* until 1608, by which time the East Coast was quite well-trodden ground.

The Spanish Galleon of Tobermory

1588

NOT FOR THE FIRST TIME AND NOT FOR the last, love came in a dream. Viola, the King of Spain's daughter, dreamed of a man, and his face was so fine and his whole bearing so kingly that she swore to find him, even if it meant sailing the world round. Past Scotland she came, to the island of Mull.

Her galleon, the *Florencia*, dropped anchor in Tobermory Bay, for the cliffs had the same ragged edges as in her dream. There indeed she found the man she had dreamed: MacLean of Duart. Viola thought her happiness would never end, that MacLean would marry her and make all her dreams come true. The man himself was hugely flattered. There was only one snag: MacLean of Duart already had a wife – a fiery Scottish wife who did not mean to lose her husband to the lady in the bay.

Wife MacLean took matters into her own hands, took a keg of gunpowder, too, and went aboard the *Florencia*. "Leave my man be, ye black-eyed hussy!" she told Viola. "Have ye not men enough in your country that you must come stealing ours?"

"I must go where my heart leads," said Princess Viola. "I was meant to marry MacLean: my dream told me so."

Wife MacLean left the ship – left, too, her keg of gunpowder and a slow-burning fuse. Not all the Northern Lights on Midsummer Eve ever lit up the Hebridean skies like the explosion which rocked the galleon *Florencia* that day and scattered her to the four winds. The mast was shot like a harpoon at the whaley moon. Pieces of plank skimmed over the water. Only one soul escaped . . . the ship's cook, who was blown, by the force of the explosion, all the way from ship to shore.

Had the cook died in his galley, perhaps the fate of the *Florencia* might have remained a Hebridean secret. Instead, word reached the King of Spain, who was filled with such spitting wrath that men fled him like a keg of gunpowder.

"Get you to Mull!" he told his trusted sea-captain. "Kill the man MacLean, his wife and all his children! Kill his dogs and cats and the birds in his chimneys! Kill his servants and kinsmen and neighbours! Break down his walls and burn every blade of grass on Mull, for he has robbed me of my daughter, lovely as any dream!"

When MacLean of Duart saw the Spanish man o' war drop anchor in Tobermory Bay, his big stomach quaked and his heart beat so wildly that all thought of Princess Viola fell out of it. "See what ye have done, ye foolish wife!" he whispered.

But his wife squared her square shoulders and stuck out her several chins. She summoned all of the eighteen witches of Mull, and pointed to the ship in the bay. Like frogs all hopping into the one pond, the eighteen witches of Mull pooled their eighteen magics, pooled their curses, pooled their worst of wicked spells. Above the bay, they spread their arms, their feather-white shawls. Eighteen seagulls flew out to sea, circling and soaring, screaming fit to chill the blood of any fiery Spaniard.

The wind too began to scream, like a million gulls, and the waters of the bay swirled. The ship's mast turned like the spoon in a mixing bowl. Then down went the ship, confusing sea foam with rich Spanish lace.

When the storm was spent, not a trace remained of the captain or his ship. Within a matter of years, only the ghost of a memory survived, faint as any dream.

A galleon *Florencia* probably did explode and sink in Tobermory Bay on the Hebridean island of Mull in 1588. It was one of the ships of the Spanish Armada sent by Philip of Spain to invade and conquer England. Defeated by Drake, scattered by storms, the fleet struggled to reach home by sailing round the coasts of Scotland and Ireland: many were lost on the way. The Scots and Irish, being Catholic, should have been sympathetic towards the bedraggled Spanish. But in those days, shipwrecks were a ready source of booty, and shipwrecked mariners were not encouraged to survive.

News of the sea battle waged between England and Spain in the English Channel must have been very slow to reach the Hebrides. Even then it would have had precious little significance for the inhabitants of Mull. It is hardly surprising, then, that this local legend grew up to account for the galleon's visit in a more romantic way.

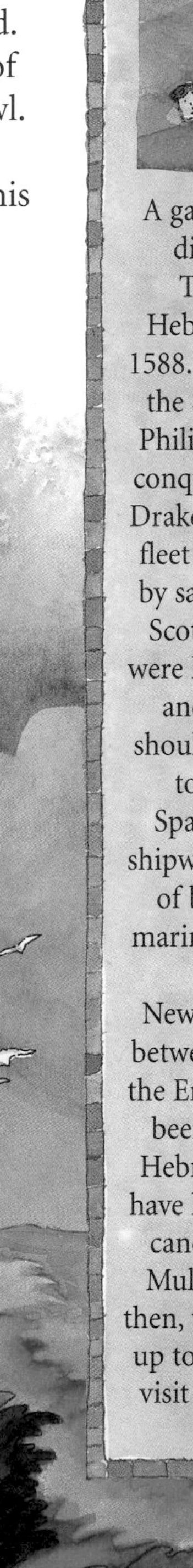

The Theatre that Disappeared

1598

Richard Burbage tried every line of argument he knew. He began good humouredly, in comic vein: "Where will the groundlings throw their apple cores if not at us actors?"

He pulled himself up to his full height (which was not great): "Is this not the Age of Poesie? And are we not the finest of a fine profession, speaking verse of genius, holding up to humanity the bright likeness of its image?"

He tried again: "My father built this theatre! It is the oldest and most visited in London – yeah, in the kingdom!"

He even tried darkest tragedy, and he was famous for his tragic roles. "And wilt thou see us cast upon the mercy of the rude winds? Hoist up upon the shoulders of misfortune for want of a house over our untousled heads?"

But the landlord only crossed his arms, pursed his lips and scowled. "I say the lease is up and that's an end. You actors can take your theatricals, Richard Burbage, and shift yourselves off my ground. The Theatre is closed, and there's an end!"

Burbage threw an arm across his eyes and struck the pose of a man betrayed by fate. But when he took his arm away, the landlord had gone. He was standing alone in the street. Tugging down his doublet, he replaced his hat at a rakish angle and squared his stocky shoulders. "Very well, you wish the Theatre gone, do you? Then go it shall!" he said under his breath.

He went in search of his elder brother, Cuthbert, and told him to hire a cart. "A big cart. Better still, five carts. Then find John and Francis and Will – everyone who's sober. We have work to do." And as the light faded and the streets emptied, a caravan of carts negotiated the narrow lanes of London, southwards towards the river.

Lying in bed the next morning, the owner of the land, north of the city walls, where the Chamberlain's Company had acted night after night, mused on the value of the Theatre, now that its lease had expired. There was not much to be done with a circular building open to the elements in the centre. Cock fighting, perhaps, or a bear pit. Boxing, even. But all those were lewd and Godless pastimes and attracted lewd and Godless people . . .

His wife threw open the window and emptied out the night-soil. She stayed there, pot upraised, her head outside, beyond the sill.

"Close the window, woman. I am in a draught. Did you hear that traffic last night? Horses and carts all night long."

His wife drew her head back inside, but still stood holding the pot at shoulder height. "It's gone," she said.

"What's gone?"

"The Theatre. It has . . . walked in the night."

"Fallen down, you mean?" He ran to the window, the noises of early-morning London rising up like starlings to circle his head. But there in a cityscape he knew as well as his wife's bumpy profile, was a hole. Where, the day before, the Theatre had stood lay a heap of thatching, a snow of plaster, and wattle enough to fence a field. All the timber uprights, and joists and beams and benches, all the barge boards and staging and duck boards and doors had gone, loaded aboard the Burbages' carts and trundled away in the night, southwards over the river.

The landlord's mouth opened and shut, opened and shut, but he knew no poetry with which to express his feelings. He was, after all, neither a theatrical man nor a poet.

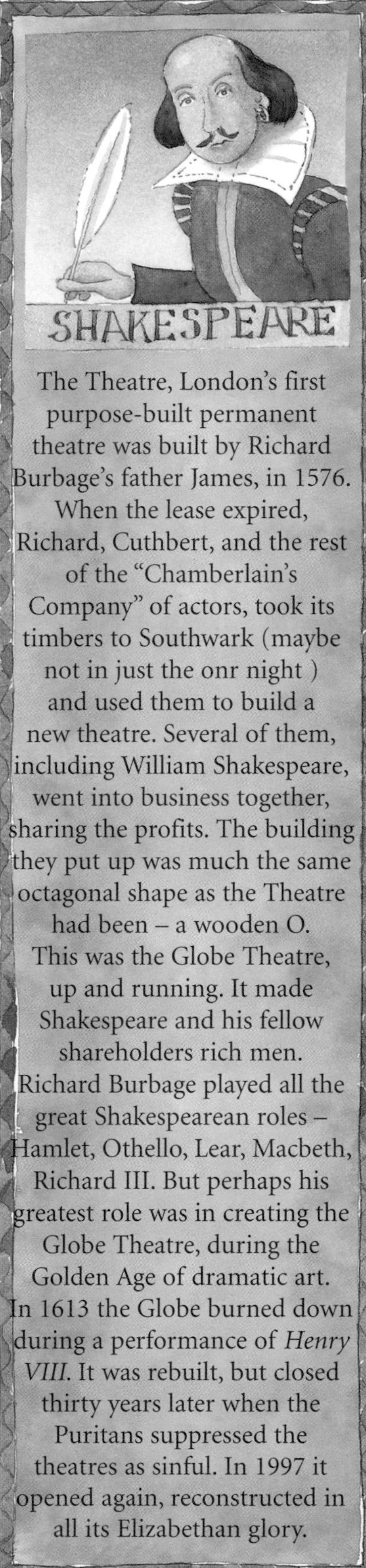

The Theatre, London's first purpose-built permanent theatre was built by Richard Burbage's father James, in 1576. When the lease expired, Richard, Cuthbert, and the rest of the "Chamberlain's Company" of actors, took its timbers to Southwark (maybe not in just the onr night) and used them to build a new theatre. Several of them, including William Shakespeare, went into business together, sharing the profits. The building they put up was much the same octagonal shape as the Theatre had been – a wooden O. This was the Globe Theatre, up and running. It made Shakespeare and his fellow shareholders rich men. Richard Burbage played all the great Shakespearean roles – Hamlet, Othello, Lear, Macbeth, Richard III. But perhaps his greatest role was in creating the Globe Theatre, during the Golden Age of dramatic art. In 1613 the Globe burned down during a performance of *Henry VIII.* It was rebuilt, but closed thirty years later when the Puritans suppressed the theatres as sinful. In 1997 it opened again, reconstructed in all its Elizabethan glory.

Gunpowder, Treason and Plot

1604-1605

GUY FAWKES LIT THE fuse of the gunpowder and doubled back the way he had come. With an enormous thud, the charge went off, shattering the great slabs of the city wall into flying flint. Guido Fawkes had done it! His fellow troopers cheered, and the officers puffed out their cheeks in admiration at his cool, reckless courage.

That was at Calais. They made him a captain for his bravery at Calais. Everyone said there was no better explosives man in the Spanish army than Guido Fawkes of England.

He was still abroad eight years later when his old friend, Thomas Winter, came looking for him. He had a job for Guido – a job for a good explosives man. This time, however, Guido would be striking a blow for his religion – a blow for Catholicism, which England had suppressed with fire and sword for half a century. This time the target was Parliament.

The plot had already been hatched before Captain Fawkes joined it. In April conspirators met at the house of Robert Catesby, a tall, fair-haired man seething with indignation at the plight of English Catholics. King James (that worthless Scots popinjay) would gather, with all his lords and ministers, in the Lords' Chamber of the Palace of Westminster for the State Opening of Parliament. One explosion would put paid to the whole pack of them!

This was no rash, spur-of-the-moment piece of mischief. The conspirators gave themselves nine months to prepare. Thomas Percy, a white-haired, respected gentleman with influential friends, managed to secure a small house right alongside the palace. The cellar lay hard up against the cellars of the Lords' Chamber. All they had to do was tunnel through and lay the charge.

From May to December no one lived in that house but Guido Fawkes – or rather "John Johnson", for that was what he called himself.

December

All those days of waiting, doing nothing: for a man of action like Guido it was a torment. Then one December night, eleven men came to the door, darkly dressed, hats pulled down, spades and adzes and picks hidden under their clothes; also food and ale enough for a fortnight.

Down in the cellar they began to dig – not with great ringing, noisy blows, but with quiet gouging and grubbing and boring. They dug till their hands bled and their backs refused to straighten, but the tunnel progressed with ridiculous slowness.

"At this rate we shan't be through in time for the opening of Parliament!" Catesby fretted.

On 7 February it was announced by the town criers that the parliamentary session had been postponed indefinitely. The men in the cellars fell on each other's aching shoulders and laughed with relief. Time for a rest! Extra time for the tunnel to be finished! God must be on their side . . . but then they had known that all along.

That night, Guido Fawkes and Robert Keyes went across the river to a lock-up in Lambeth. It was dark, and no one saw the two men furtively transferring barrels to a nearby rowing boat. They had chosen a moonless night to row their gunpowder across the Thames to Westminster.

They dug by lantern light, those eleven desperate men, thinking to scratch their way through yards of solid rock. Then all of a sudden, in the middle of the day, came a rushing sound like water or an avalanche.

The diggers in the tunnel fell on their faces. Those nearest the cellar turned to run. What was it? Running feet? Were they found out? Or was the tunnel caving in on their heads?

It was neither. The rushing noise continued. "John Johnson" ran outside into the street. There stood a wagon being filled with coal. The noise was of coal being shovelled out of a room *above* their tunnel – a room they had never even known existed! The coal merchant's vault must lie *directly below* the Lords' Chamber. They had never needed to dig a tunnel – only to secure that vault and pile their gunpowder there!

The tunnel was abandoned. God must truly be on their side – but then they had never doubted it.

Percy managed to rent the place. Spring and summer drifted by, with "John Johnson" caretaker now of a coal-dusty vault. One by one, thirty-six kegs of gunpowder were transferred from their hiding place to the alcoves of the cellar.

October
In one week the hall above would be plush with ermine robes, glittering with coronets, crowded with Protestant statesmen.

Of course there would be Catholics, too. In among the elder statesmen would be good Catholic men, like Lord Monteagle. It upset the conspirators, of course it did. Catholics kill Catholics? Still, it could not be helped.

Perhaps someone thought it could. For Lord Monteagle received a letter – unsigned – advising him not to attend Parliament on 5 November, if he wanted to avoid an "unseen blow". Monteagle read and re-read the letter, then sat tapping it against his lips, wondering what it could mean, what to do with it, who should see it . . .

4 November
It was time for Guido Fawkes, their explosives expert, to stack the kegs, lay the fuses and lie in wait to light them. The other conspirators dispersed – some were already in the Midlands, ready to raise up the revolution in the wake of the bombing. Fawkes was cock-a-hoop. Sir Robert Cecil, Secretary of State, had ordered a search of the cellars, but his incompetent men had found nothing! The way was clear. The time was ripe.

Coal dust glittered like jet in the light from his candle. Guido made himself as comfortable as he could in the cold and clammy dark. His breathing was shallow, his heartbeat steady. This for Guido was a simple act of war. Below ground, he could not hear the church clocks striking midnight.

Tramp tramp tramp. There was the scrape of pikes against stone, a jangle of keys; dancing yellow lantern light sprang into the vault. So sure was Robert Cecil about the letter Monteagle had showed him that he had ordered a *second* search. This time his troopers saw the kegs at once. Then they saw, standing against the far wall, the dark figure of a tall man. He did not struggle as they bound his wrists.

They manhandled him all the way to the King's bedchamber, shouting questions in his face, punching and kicking him. But the man from the cellar gave only his name: "John Johnson".

November

Though the others fled, Sir Robert Cecil seemed to know exactly where to find them. Fawkes refused to name them, but they were tracked down anyway, within three days. They rushed out of doors, swords in hand, and three were gunned down: Catesby and Percy killed by a single bullet.

The gaolers broke Fawkes on the rack. It startled them how long he held out, but in the end, a man can be made to confess to anything on the rack.

He was the last to die. His fellow conspirators had all died traitors' deaths when Fawkes was led out to execution. But the crowd were still in good voice, taunting and jeering. "Traitor! Coward! Murderer! Villain! Devil!" Their hatred and disgust knew no bounds. They would savour his agonizing death: hanged, cut down alive, disembowelled, quartered, and only then beheaded. Guido could barely climb the ladder; the rack had crippled him. But shakily he reached the top, the hangman, the noose.

Whispering a prayer, he jumped from the ladder. His neck snapped. The crowd groaned. The villain had cheated them! He was already dead, and they had been robbed of an afternoon's entertainment.

Guido Fawkes, now referred to as Guy, was born Protestant, but converted to Catholicism after his widowed mother married a Catholic country gentleman. Full of religious zeal and a love of adventure, he left England in 1593 and went to fight in Catholic causes in Europe. He was thirty-five when he died.

In 1606 Parliament decreed that 5 November should be kept as a day of thanksgiving for their deliverance. But the burning of a guy on Bonfire Night is a later, Victorian addition to the festivities.

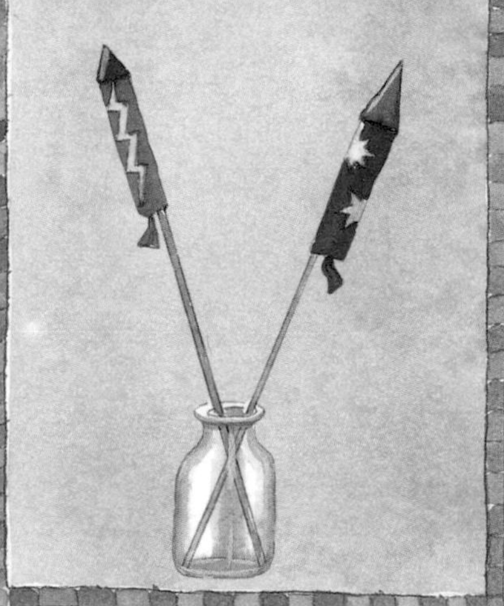

Chicken and Bacon

1626

"KNOWLEDGE IS POWER," SAID FRANCIS BACON, and being an eloquent and sought-after lawyer, he knew the taste of both. Unfortunately, Bacon spent money as he spent words – in extravagant torrents. In order to pay his bills, he was quite prepared to prosecute former friends, marry for money, and accept bribes. It has to be said that though Bacon wrote volumes about virtue, he did not possess much himself.

His glittering legal career came to an end in the Tower of London, imprisoned for dishonesty, and though King James I generously set him free, the last five years of his life were spent writing, studying and pleading for reinstatement.

Everything interested him – from law to poetry, science to politics. And when it came to science, he did not stop short at dry theory: he believed in experimentation and irrefutable proof. Knowledge, he said, came as the fruit of experience.

Riding in a coach one bitter March day, with Dr Witherborne, the King's doctor, the two got talking about the rotting process in food.

"I have observed that the cooler the pantry, the fresher the food," mused Witherborne.

Bacon was not feeling well that day, but a sudden idea so intrigued him that he quite forgot his aches and pains, and leapt down from the carriage. Beating on the door of a cottage at the bottom of Highgate Hill, he fetched out a timid, startled woman. "I want to buy a chicken!" demanded Bacon.

"Yes, sir! Of course, sir! Got a nice little hen-bird out back . . ." She wrung the hen's neck and brought it to him, swinging it limply by its head.

"Could you pluck it, my good woman?"

The woman plucked it, while Bacon stamped about in the garden gathering up fistfuls of snow and cramming them into the pockets of his frock coat. "And draw it?" he called. The woman pulled out the chicken's giblets and washed the carcass at the pump.

Then Bacon sat down on a stool in her cottage and began to ram handfuls of snow into the chicken.

"Are you gone entirely mad, Bacon?" enquired the King's doctor politely.

"I find myself asking," replied Bacon, grunting and red in the face with exertion, "whether *snow* cannot be used to preserve meat, as well as salt. What would you say?"

Excitement carried him through; he completed the stuffing. But when it was done, and the chicken sat pinkly lopsided on the table, leaking snow, Bacon found he did not feel at all well. Staring at hands blue with cold, he murmured, "I must lie down a while, Witherborne."

The doctor offered to take him home – it was only a few miles – but Bacon could not face the journey. "Take me to Arundel's house. It is only a step down the road."

The Earl of Arundel agreed, yes, of course Bacon must be put to bed in his house, and told his maid to run warming pans over the sheet in the guest room. But it had been a long while since the guest bed was slept in. The warming pan raised a gentle steam off the damp sheets, and while Bacon lay clutching his chilled stomach, the bed cooled around him.

Within a couple of days, his cold had turned to bronchitis, his bronchitis to pneumonia. He was running a temperature, alarming the maids with feverish talk of knowledge and power, chickens and immortality.

The last piece of knowledge to be grasped by the great genuis of Francis Bacon was brought to him minutes before his death. It did not concern the nature of God, the afterlife or any of the usual things which prey on the minds of the dying. It concerned the well-being of a frozen chicken sitting on a plate in a pantry downstairs.

"It is not decayed one jot," Dr Witherborne whispered in his ear, and a serene smile spread across Bacon's face. He died in the powerful knowledge that refrigeration does indeed preserve food.

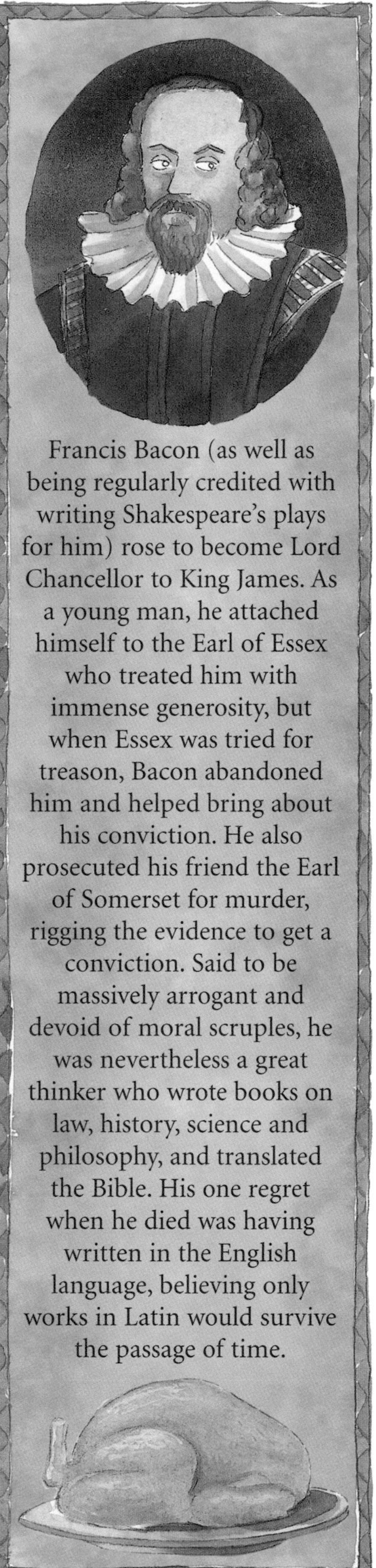

Francis Bacon (as well as being regularly credited with writing Shakespeare's plays for him) rose to become Lord Chancellor to King James. As a young man, he attached himself to the Earl of Essex who treated him with immense generosity, but when Essex was tried for treason, Bacon abandoned him and helped bring about his conviction. He also prosecuted his friend the Earl of Somerset for murder, rigging the evidence to get a conviction. Said to be massively arrogant and devoid of moral scruples, he was nevertheless a great thinker who wrote books on law, history, science and philosophy, and translated the Bible. His one regret when he died was having written in the English language, believing only works in Latin would survive the passage of time.

Jenny Geddes Strikes a Blow

1637

King Charles I believed that he had been placed on earth by God to rule His people. He knew he was in the right. In fact Charles did not even feel the need of a Parliament in order to rule.

John Knox believed that Jesus Christ was the only intermediary between an individual and his God. In church even a king had no higher role than his fellow men: he certainly did not have the right to set bishops in authority over the people. Knox had studied under the great preacher Calvin, and he knew he was in the right. What is more, he had utterly convinced the people of Scotland.

So, when nearly a century later, Charles I ordained that Scottish worship should fall into line with the Church of England, acknowledge him as head of the Church and submit to his bishops, Presbyterian Scotland seethed. *Bishops* dictate to Presbyterian ministers? *Bishops* lord it over Scottish congregations, wearing their fancy garb and offering up prayers for an English king? *Bishops* stand up in the pulpit of the High Kirk of St Giles', where John Knox had stood and preached Reformation? It seemed they must. One Sunday, the music began and the procession of ministers headed by a bishop glided serenely into position between the altar and the people.

The whole nave of St Giles' rumbled with resentful murmurings.

Jenny Geddes was just a poor market-stall holder, not a trouble-maker. But the sight of those rich, white robes encrusted with precious wire and gemstones, and the bishop's droning, patronizing sermon, put her into such a towering rage that she leapt to her feet. Snatching up the three-legged stool she had brought to sit on, she hurled it at the bishop in the pulpit – a wild, inaccurate throw – shrieking, "Ye'll nae say your mass in my lug!" The stool bounced and clattered and broke.

But nobody ever saw where it landed. For by then the kirk was in uproar. The congregation surged to its feet with a kind of angry cheer. The bishop, mouth ajar, struggling for words to condemn such blasphemy, saw a tide of angry faces, saw that the tide was rising – moving forward – coming after him! Clutching his robes in both fists, he turned to run down the pulpit steps, but already he was surrounded. Half carried, half chased, he and his fellow ministers were thrown out of the High Kirk of St Giles' like cats out of a fish shop. The Scots valued their religion above their king, and if Charles wanted to send any more bishops into Scottish kirks, then he would have to send an army first!

Soon after that, a document was drawn up entitled the "Solemn League and Covenant", plainly stating the way in which the Scottish Church should be governed. Scots flocked from far and wide to sign it – to declare themselves "Covenanters", willing to lay down their lives in defence of their religion.

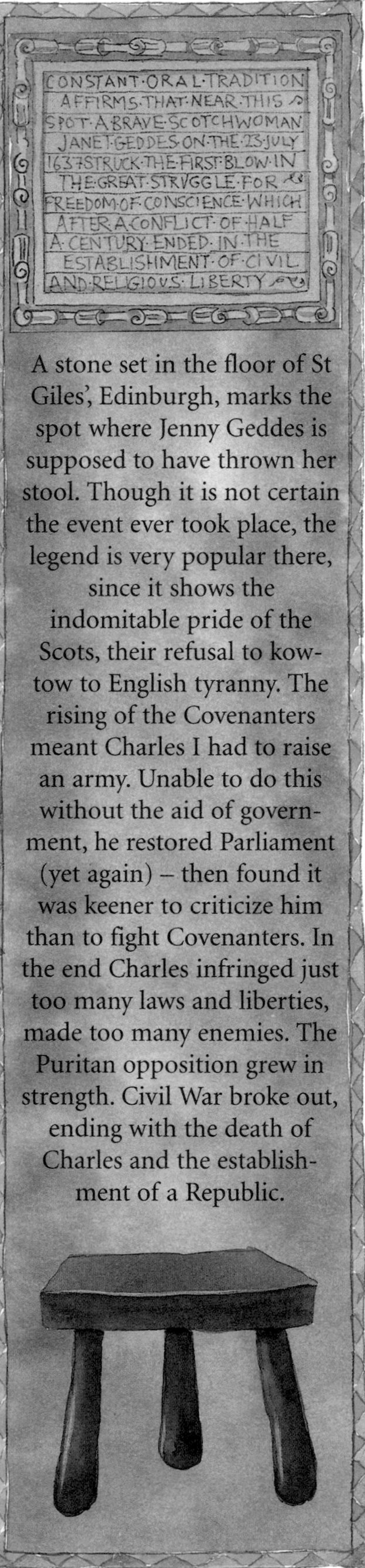

A stone set in the floor of St Giles', Edinburgh, marks the spot where Jenny Geddes is supposed to have thrown her stool. Though it is not certain the event ever took place, the legend is very popular there, since it shows the indomitable pride of the Scots, their refusal to kow-tow to English tyranny. The rising of the Covenanters meant Charles I had to raise an army. Unable to do this without the aid of government, he restored Parliament (yet again) – then found it was keener to criticize him than to fight Covenanters. In the end Charles infringed just too many laws and liberties, made too many enemies. The Puritan opposition grew in strength. Civil War broke out, ending with the death of Charles and the establishment of a Republic.

The Witch-Finder General

1646

MATTHEW HOPKINS COULD BARELY believe his good fortune as the names poured from Elizabeth Clarke's lips. Names and confessions and a fascinating glimpse of things forbidden. Elizabeth Clarke was a witch; he had never doubted it. Was she not bent and deformed – a yammering old woman whose very face scared small children? Wringing a confession from her, he had felt the hot, mouth-drying thrill of prising open a human soul like a shellfish and exposing all the vileness inside. What a pleasure it had been to hear her damn herself with talk of "familiars" and "spells" and satanic rites! Thirty-two names she had given him. Thirty-two witches – imagine! Thirty-two fewer servants of the Devil, thanks to his energetic, brilliant interrogation of this wicked old crone.

Before she and her friends were even swinging from the gallows, Matthew Hopkins was riding north from Chelmsford to rid Norfolk and Suffolk of witches too.

The pious Protestant people of East Anglia greeted "Witch-Finder General", Matthew Hopkins, much as they would a rat-catcher. They were prepared to pay good money to be rid of the evil in their midst. Yes, they knew of an old woman who lived alone with a black cat or two and said her prayers in Latin. Yes, they had known carts stick in mud, a cow fall in the river, a child die who had been well only days before. They gave him names by the score.

Matthew Hopkins accepted £6 from the people of Aldeburgh for cleansing the town of witches. They cheerfully pointed the accusing finger. It was not for them to enquire *who*, exactly, had designated Matthew Hopkins Witch-Finder General. It was not for them to question his motives or methods. He was doing God's work, wasn't he, rooting out servants of the Devil?

He said he carried "the Devil's list of all English witches". And besides, he had the needle. Hopkins was a pricker, and a pricker is a valuable man to have around when there are witches. No easy matter, sometimes, to find the "witch's mark" – that red, sunken place on the body which, when pricked, feels no pain. Hopkins knew where to look – the soles of the feet or the scalp of the head. Then out would come the needle – three inches of spike on a handle, like a bradawl. And in it would go, without a cry of pain from the accused.

The actual torture of a prisoner might be forbidden . . . but that was no drawback to a man gifted in the art of *persuasion.* Starvation. Solitary confinement. Forcing someone to sit cross-legged for days at a time . . . there are many ways of making a person confess. In Kings Lynn they paid him £15 for the work he did.

Why, in Brandeston village, the *entire village* denounced their vicar as a witch, so how could there be any doubt? It was just a matter of obtaining a confession. So John Lowes was locked up and kept awake day and night for a week, forced hourly to run up and down his cell until he agreed to say anything. Anything. Everything. How he had bewitched cattle. How he had sunk that ship in calm weather . . . So what, if he did retract it all afterwards? These witches will say anything to save their necks . . . How those parishioners wagged their heads as Lowes was led to the gallows. *They* knew him for what he was; *they* were not going to shed any tears at the man having to read his own burial service to himself because, as a witch, he was denied a clergyman.

By the time Matthew Hopkins got to Stowmarket, his fee had gone up to £23.

In Bury St Edmunds, all told, he had sixty-eight people put to death.

His real triumph came when he hanged nineteen women in a single day.

What things they confessed to! What sensational pictures they drew – of dancing demons, Satan dressed as a bridegroom, cows jumping over stiles, men flying over weathervanes on the backs of black dogs. What a spectacle they made for the crowds to watch as they struggled with the hangman, swearing their innocence! The people of East Anglia were kept in a state of glassy-eyed hysteria, as Matthew Hopkins prowled among them, pointing the finger, jabbing with his needle.

After he retired – after that jealous wretch, John Gaule, slandered him, and his health broke down – did Hopkins lie awake at night and wonder about the pains in his chest, the blood in his lungs, about the cold sweat and colder nightmares that crawled over him? Did he wonder whose curse was gnawing on him; of those 400, which witch had done for him?

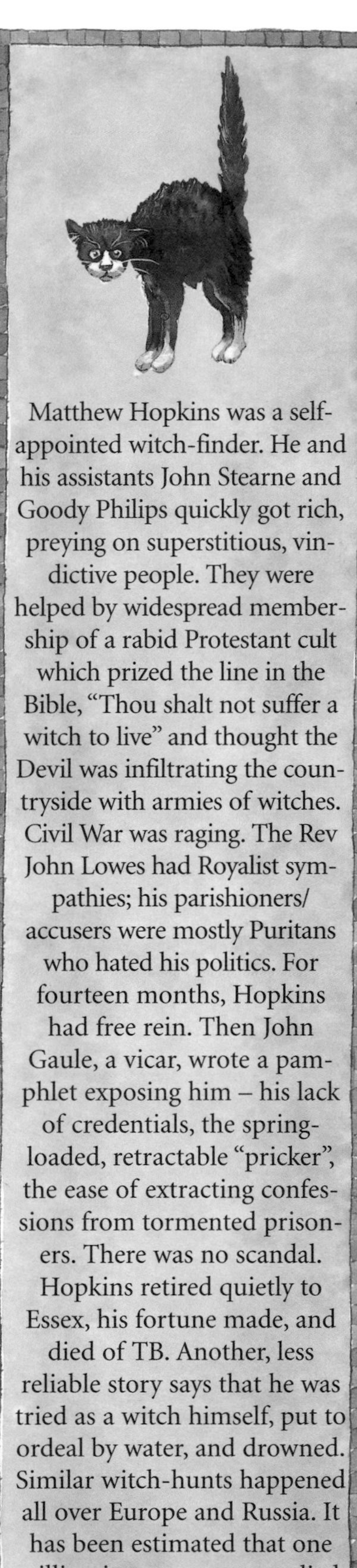

Matthew Hopkins was a self-appointed witch-finder. He and his assistants John Stearne and Goody Philips quickly got rich, preying on superstitious, vindictive people. They were helped by widespread membership of a rabid Protestant cult which prized the line in the Bible, "Thou shalt not suffer a witch to live" and thought the Devil was infiltrating the countryside with armies of witches. Civil War was raging. The Rev John Lowes had Royalist sympathies; his parishioners/accusers were mostly Puritans who hated his politics. For fourteen months, Hopkins had free rein. Then John Gaule, a vicar, wrote a pamphlet exposing him – his lack of credentials, the spring-loaded, retractable "pricker", the ease of extracting confessions from tormented prisoners. There was no scandal. Hopkins retired quietly to Essex, his fortune made, and died of TB. Another, less reliable story says that he was tried as a witch himself, put to ordeal by water, and drowned. Similar witch-hunts happened all over Europe and Russia. It has been estimated that one million innocent women died.

Cromwell and the Goosefeathers

1649

OLIVER CROMWELL WAS A MAN OF THE FENS. HE knew the lores and traditions of those flat, wet, wilderness lands, and he knew their uses. When he needed men to fight King Charles I, he had only to show a goosefeather to the men of the fens and they were obliged to join him – obliged by age-old tradition to offer help and protection to anyone carrying a split goosefeather.

Little by little, battle by battle, Cromwell and his Roundheads got the better of the King and his Cavaliers in a Civil War which saw the country hacked into bloody factions.

Once or twice the trick with the feather recoiled on him. At Snow Hall in Norfolk, it seemed that Cromwell had King Charles cornered, but the King's party escaped through the fens, showing a split goosefeather to the Norfolk Roundheads who barred their way. What could the sentries do? They were fenland men. They honoured the ancient symbol, and let the King slip by, though it left them in fear and trembling of their lives. What would Cromwell say when they admitted to letting the King go?

He said little. Though victory had been snatched from him, and the war prolonged by wearisome months, he listened to the sentries' explanation, took the split goosefeather from their trembling fingers and said, "Better that the King should go free than that old customs should be broken."

Of course his religious zeal gave Cromwell perfect confidence in the ultimate outcome of the war. He knew it was only a matter of time before he defeated Charles. Victory came at the battle of Naseby, and within the year the defeated Charles was brought to trial for his life.

The trial was never going to be fair, but it was no more unfair than the times decreed. Besides, only one outcome was possible in the circumstances. Charles Stewart, one-time King of England, was found guilty and condemned to death by beheading.

The night before the execution, Cromwell sat eating supper when there was a knock at the door. It was a messenger from the King.

"His Majesty scorns to ask mercy," said the messenger, "but demands the right and privileges owing to one who presents this!" And he threw down a split goosefeather on to the table.

Even after supper had been cleared, Cromwell went on sitting at the table. All night long he sat there, twirling the broken feather between his fingers, his eyes looking unseeing into the darkness.

It snowed during the night – soft, white flakes, as though the sky were moulting, and a multitude of downy feathers fell on Whitehall, blurring the outline of the scaffold. Charles put on two shirts that morning, so that any trembling from the cold might not be mistaken for fear.

"I go from a corruptible crown to an incorruptible, where no disturbance can take place," he said, mounting the scaffold. Then he told the executioner the signal he would make when he was ready for the axe to fall, and knelt down at the block.

Afterwards, the King's remains were coffined on the spot and carried away. Cromwell went to see the body – stood for a long time holding the lid raised, gazing at his dead adversary. There was no trace of triumph in his eyes, no hatred or gloating satisfaction. There was no guilt, either. "His body was made for long life," was all he said. Then he laid a single, split, white goosefeather on the King's breast and closed the lid. His conscience was clear. After all, he had granted the King a kind of safe passage: he had set his soul free.

Cromwell and his New Model Army defeated Charles I in the Civil War of 1642-9 and established a Commonwealth, with him as Lord Protector. He was a clever statesman and military leader, but as much a dictator as any king and a dyed-in-the-wool Puritan, abolishing such jolly pastimes as dancing, the theatre and Christmas. When Charles's son, Charles II, was restored to the throne, and the Commonwealth was over and gone, Cromwell's body was made to pay for what he had done. It was dug up from Westminster Abbey and hanged from the gallows at Tyburn. The head was cut off and impaled on a pike, on the roof at Westminster Hall. Twenty years later, in a storm, it rolled down the roof and landed at the feet of a guard who took it home and hid it up his chimney. Passing from hand to hand, bought and sold like stolen goods for 250 years, it was at last presented to Cromwell's old Cambridge college and given a decent burial.

The Moonrakers

1650s

When Wiltshire wool was the finest in the world, some of the richest men in England were the wool merchants who set up business in Swindon. But they were foreigners – men from Holland and Flanders – and on spring days, when lambs were gambolling in the field, the woollenmen would sit sipping Wiltshire wine and sighing. Come autumn nights, too, when the fleeces were baled, the woollenmen still sat sadly, staring into empty glasses and sighing. They longed for a taste of home, for proper Hollands gin – but they were not prepared to pay the crippling tax that the British Government added to the price of imported liquor. A cask of "Hollands", with import duty, cost a week's profits.

And so, these men of business, and merchants and movers of goods, set about quenching their thirst. They diversified. That is to say, they opened up a new line of business. From the moonlit decks of little ships sailing up the Solent came shadowy figures to the weed-slippery coves of the Hampshire coast. They carried mysterious bundles which they hid under the stooks on haywains, and from there the cargo bumped inshore to church crypts and village lock-ups, to pigeon lofts and dry wells and disused outbuildings. Along hollow hedges and down old lead mine-shafts came casks of Hollands gin, travelling north in a series of overnight stages, to the thirsty woollenmen of Swindon.

Don't picture a handful of dubious-looking characters with eye-patches and a beltful of pistols. These smugglers were not recruited from among rogues and vagabonds. Hundreds of ordinary people were soon employed, year in, year out, in fetching home the Hollands. For a quid of tobacco or a little brandy cask (duty-free, of course), a vicar might allow the use of his crypt or turn a blind eye to the sound of carts at midnight. For a bunch of lace, the innkeeper's wife might lay out supper after hours, and watch the wall while the "Wiltshire gentlemen" refreshed themselves on their journey. And the excisemen, though they might ride patrol, and offer rewards, and lie in ambush on moonlit nights, rarely made an arrest. Smuggling was no crime in the eyes of true-born Englishmen. This was easing the springs of contentment. This was the occupation of gentlemen and right-thinking citizens.

Consequently, when the dewponds and duckponds of England greened over with summer algae, their depths often concealed a cask or two of Hollands bound for Swindon – casks which lay there for one night, then moved on northwards. One night, the smugglers of Cannings village grew over-bold, and went out when the moon was full, to the village pond, armed with rakes and an easy conscience.

"Where is it, Sam?"

"Over left of centre, Will. There, just where the moon is . . ."

Out of nowhere, the excisemen were on them, galloping up with muskets and dark lanterns and barking commands: "Stand still! His Majesty's Excise! Show your faces! Name your business!" There was an incriminating silence. "Just as I thought! Smugglers!" said the captain.

Then Jack Brown jerked his rake at the pool and began lurching from foot to foot as if he were two-parts drunk and three-parts simple. "S'a moon, maisters, that's what. Moon's falled in the pond, see maisters? Gonna rake it out an' be rich frever'n'ever!"

"Amen!" said Sam Baker, rolling his eyes and letting his hands dangle like a fool.

"Rich! Rich! Yeah! Wanna share, maisters?" asked Will recklessly. "Ye help us get her out, an' ye can 'ave a share, right enough. Must be worth plenty, woun't you say? Peece o' the moon?"

The excisemen looked at the moon's reflection in the pond. They looked at the fools on the bank splashing away with their rakes, trying to rake the moon out of the pond. "More brains in a duck egg," said the captain of the patrol. "Sergeant, let's leave these buffoons to drown themselves. Raking for the moon, indeed! They're stark mad!" And they rode off, laughing at the stupidity of Wiltshire yokels.

They should have known better. There is no such thing as a stupid Wiltshireman. Within half an hour, another three barrels of best Hollands had been dragged out of the pond and were on their way north.

For 200 years the Wiltshiremen ran Hollands gin, French brandy and tobacco, duty-free, to grateful customers. Somewhere along the way, the smugglers came by the name of Moonrakers. It was a title no right-thinking Englishman disdained to wear, a name whispered with pride and relish.

The villages of All Cannings and Bishops Cannings both lay claim to the story of the Moonrakers, but plenty of other Wiltshire villagers consider it theirs. In fact "Moonraker" has become a term to describe any Wiltshireman. In other versions, the villagers pretend to think the moon's reflection is a cheese which they want to drag out and eat. And since the story turns up in other forms and other countries – *Brer Rabbit*, for instance – it may well be a story-teller's invention. Rudyard Kipling immortalized the work of the Wiltshiremen in his poem "A Smuggler's Song" and the famous lines:

Five and twenty ponies
Trotting through the dark –
Brandy for the Parson,
'Baccy for the Clerk;
Laces for a lady, letters for a spy,
Watch the wall, my darling,
while the Gentlemen go by!

The Royal Oak

1650s

CHARLES I’S SON HAD HIMSELF CROWNED IN Scotland, and rode south to be avenged on Cromwell for killing his father, and to take up his father’s place on the English throne.

It was a misguided idea. Cromwell was ready for him. At the battle of Worcester, 4,000 died and over 7,000 more were captured within five hours. Charles Stuart was forced to flee for his life. At three in the morning, after the battle, he and a handful of supporters reached a Catholic house where they could finally snatch a bite to eat and take stock of their dire situation. Cromwell would be scouring the country for Charles – to put an end once and for all to the Stuart royal line. The King must disguise himself and get away to France.

So they buried his fine clothes in the garden and cut his long, ringleted hair short. The would-be King of England was rechristened Will Jones the woodcutter.

“Don’t walk so upright and dignified,” they told him, “and try to talk like a peasant.”

The rain poured down all day. Charles stood dismally in a wood, with a billhook in his hand, getting drenched to the skin, while bands of Roundhead cavalrymen beat at the door of every royalist house in the Midlands.

At nine o’clock, under cover of darkness, Charles Stuart and a man called Penderel set off for Wales on foot. The old patched shoes they had given “Will Jones” were too small and the King’s feet hurt. The coarse woollen stockings chafed the King’s feet raw. Penderel chivvied him on to the next safe address – only to be informed that the countryside was rife with Roundheads: they must turn back. But at least the King was able to beg a pair of soft green stockings.

In wading across a stream, those green stockings filled up with sand. The King sat down, refusing to go on. Tactfully, respectfully, Penderel insisted, until the hunted King reached Boscobel House in Shropshire, and was given into the care of one Colonel Carlos with instructions to get him to the sea.

“There are Roundheads everywhere,” Carlos told him. “Any minute they will come here to Boscobel, searching. It’s best we hide somewhere outside.”

So, provided with a ladder, a cushion and some bread and cheese, King Charles II and Colonel Carlos climbed into an oak tree. Roped with ivy, dense with leaves and peppered with acorns, the oak took the King to its noble heart. He was so exhausted that he fell asleep almost at once, his head cradled on Carlos’s arm. The colonel’s arm went numb; his legs roared with cramp, but he dared not move: if the King stirred in his sleep, he might easily fall off the branch and plummet to his death.

Down below, the clop of horses, the rattle of weapons announced a party of Roundheads searching the forest. Carlos prayed. The King woke and prayed, too.

"Did you see a tall man, richly arrayed – a man running for his life, perchance?" asked a voice directly beneath the tree.

"I did so, sir!" said a girl's voice, eager and bright. "Going that way, two hours since."

The horses galloped away into the distance: the Roundheads had been sent on a false trail.

A reward of £1,000 was offered for the capture of Charles Stuart. And yet he passed safely from one household to the next and no one betrayed him. When the King expressed a longing for roast mutton, his host and hostess went out and stole a sheep so as to grant the King his wish: Charles cut and cooked the chops himself, finding the novelty of it hilarious. On the road south, an innkeeper called out: "God bless your Majesty wherever you go!"

Later on, "Will Jones the woodcutter" was transformed into "Will Jackson the servant" and had to share a horse with a maid. Awe-struck at having to wrap her arms around the King's royal person, Mistress Lane frequently forgot to treat him like a scullion. Once, they rode directly into the middle of a troop of Roundheads . . . but passed unnoticed.

Once on the journey, "Will Jackson" was told to wind the spit over the kitchen fire, to brown the meat. In his ignorance, he wound the handle the wrong way. "What manner of man are you that you don't know how to wind up a jack?" demanded the cook.

Charles thought quickly. "Where I come from we can't afford to eat roast meat," he said piteously. "And when we do, there's no jack to cook it on."

When the horse cast a shoe, they had to stop at a forge and listen meekly while the blacksmith talked on and on about "that rogue Charles Stuart". In fact Charles Stuart even joined in, agreeing with the smith.

A ship lay at Shoreham bound for France. As Charles, exhausted and careworn, climbed gingerly into a sailor's canvas hammock, the ship's captain rushed below decks. "I know very well who you are!" he said. The King, too weary to rise, boggled over the side of the hammock at the captain, who fell on his knees. "And I would lay down my life to set your Majesty safe in France!"

Lying in that hammock, listening to the creak of the ship's timbers, his cabin rocking gently around him, Charles pondered how to reward such people – all those brave, loyal souls who had been willing to risk their lives and lands to help a defeated man escape his enemies. One day he would return to England and occupy his rightful place as king. No more need for hiding like an acorn buried in the ground. He would flourish like a mighty oak, giving shelter to his people.

When the story of Charles's escape became known, the acorns of the oak tree at Boscobel were planted far and wide. From the acorns grew oaks, and by every oak an alehouse or inn. On Oak-Apple Day, the King's health was drunk at those inns. Long after Cromwell and his Commonwealth were gone and forgotten, the Royal Oaks flourished. And even after the oaks perished, the story survived.

The Tyburn Dancer

1660s

THE DRIVER BANGED ON THE COACH ROOF. "YOU ladies may want to draw the blinds! We are coming to Hounslow Heath, and the gibbets are not a pretty sight to look on!"

Even with the blinds closed, the passengers on the post-coach could hear the creak of ropes, the jingling of chains, as hanged men swung in the breeze. Hounslow Heath was forested with gibbets, for any highwayman hanged at Tyburn had his body returned to the scene of his crime and hung up in chains . . . and the heath was a favourite haunt of such men.

"Foul beasts," said Lady Cynthia, fanning herself furiously.

Lord Babbacombe patted her hand. "Destroy 'em like the vermin they are, I say!"

"Isn't there something rather romantic about them?" said Lady Dorothea. "Living by moonlight, on the brink of disaster?"

"Not when they strangle a defenceless woman for the crucifix round her neck," said her husband. "That's what happened last week, close by here."

Lady Cynthia whimpered.

"Let 'em all dance at a rope's end, I say!" declared Lord Babbacombe.

As if in answer, a voice just beyond the closed blinds cried, "Stand and deliver!"

The coach lurched to a halt. The driver swore. Lady Cynthia swooned clean away, and Lord Babbacombe tried to hide underneath her spreading skirts. Dorothea's husband – a man of considerable wealth – hurried to prime his pistol, but the priming pin fell into the dark bottom of the coach and rattled out of sight.

The door opened, and there stood a man, prodigiously tall in his tricorn hat, one foot up on the running board and a pistol in each hand.

"Permit me to introduce myself. Claude Duval, native of France and gentleman of the English countryside. Your money, if you please, sirs!" Then he saw Dorothea. "If your hand is already spoken for, lady, I must settle for your jewels," he said, and somehow succeeded in bowing, without his pistols so much as wavering.

"Sir, my heart belongs to my husband here, but your manners commend you," said Dorothea looking him boldly in the eye. "I have heard your name spoken in the most exulted circles, Monsieur, though I had hoped never to meet you myself."

The eyebrows above the mask rose a little, and the mouth below it smiled. "Madam, pray do not fear for your safety. Your beauty is such that I could ask nothing more precious from you than the honour of a dance."

Dorothea did not turn to her husband for advice: her eyes remained fixed fast on Duval. "But where is your music, Monsieur?" she asked.

He made a flamboyant gesture with one pistol. "We have the music of the spheres, do we not, Lady?"

"In that case, I shall pay your toll, Monsieur Duval."

There was no moon: highwaymen do not work by moonlight. But the stars shone on that stately pavane. The men by the coach watched open-mouthed as the two figures paced out a dance in time to Duval's humming.

"They say a woman was murdered last week, by one of you 'gentlemen', for the sake of the crucifix around her throat," said Dorothea pertly.

"Do not bless him with the name of 'gentleman'," said Duval. "The dogs who do such things are beneath contempt, and I will shoot him myself if he ever crosses my path! May the lady's ghost hang round his neck till doomsday."

"And where, pray, will your ghost be seen after you are dead, Monsieur Duval?"

"Why, dancing on Hounslow Heath, God willing, with a woman of grace and spirit!"

"Just so long as you never dance on Tyburn Tree," she said, and for the first time that night a shiver of clammy fright went through her.

When the dance ended, Claude Duval took the gems from around Lady Cynthia's neck, a watch and purse from the man hiding under her skirts. He asked of Dorothea's husband just £100 – a tenth of what he might have demanded. But from his dancing partner he took nothing. "I consider myself in your debt, Lady," he said, thrusting the pistols back into his waistband and bowing with a flourish of his tricorn. "My life is far sweeter for meeting you tonight!" Then he whistled for his horse, mounted and rode away.

Afterwards, Dorothea thought of him often and wistfully, though her husband never mentioned the incident, or allowed her to speak of it. When she opened the newspaper one morning and read that Duval was betrayed, arrested, condemned to hang, her own words clanged in her head like a funeral bell: "Just so long as you never dance on Tyburn Tree."

Screwing up her courage, Dorothea hired a chaise to take her to Tyburn. But as she approached the place of public execution, she tapped on the coach roof and called for it to stop. All around the gallows washed a sea of satin and lace, a raft of elegant hats, the susurration of a hundred sighs. Half the ladies in London seemed to have come to make their farewells to the French gallant.

Later, when the notorious Claude Duval had kicked out his last dance at the end of the hangman's rope, been hung up in chains, cut down and buried, a headstone appeared mysteriously to mark the place. It read, "Here lies Claude Duval. If you are a man, beware your purse, if a woman, your heart. He has made havoc of both."

Unknown to Dorothea, her husband had repaid his own debt of honour for the gentlemanly fashion in which Duval had treated both his wife and his wallet.

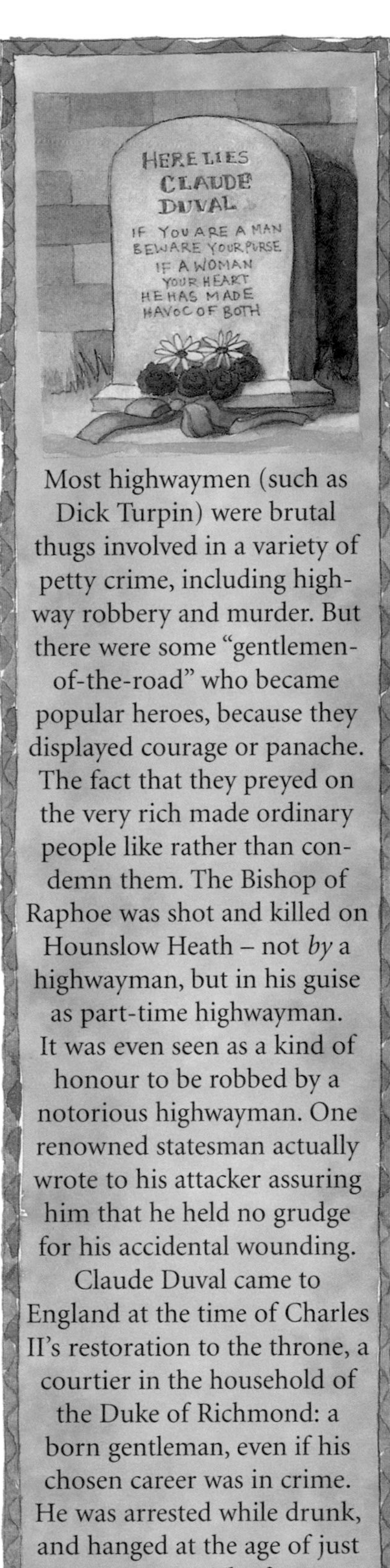

Most highwaymen (such as Dick Turpin) were brutal thugs involved in a variety of petty crime, including highway robbery and murder. But there were some "gentlemen-of-the-road" who became popular heroes, because they displayed courage or panache. The fact that they preyed on the very rich made ordinary people like rather than condemn them. The Bishop of Raphoe was shot and killed on Hounslow Heath – not *by* a highwayman, but in his guise as part-time highwayman. It was even seen as a kind of honour to be robbed by a notorious highwayman. One renowned statesman actually wrote to his attacker assuring him that he held no grudge for his accidental wounding. Claude Duval came to England at the time of Charles II's restoration to the throne, a courtier in the household of the Duke of Richmond: a born gentleman, even if his chosen career was in crime. He was arrested while drunk, and hanged at the age of just twenty-seven. The famous epitaph on his grave at Covent Garden no longer exists.

The Village that Chose to Die

1665

THE FIRST INSTINCT was to run: to pack up bags and bedding and children into a cart and to get away. And when the first cases of plague hit Eyam Village, some did go. There were a few deaths in the autumn, then a season of happiness, when the village seemed to have been spared. In the spring, it came back: the Black Death – moving through Eyam like a stray cat scratching at every door to be let in.

The people went along to the church that day with their minds full of plans and fears. Where should they go? To which relative? Not the plague-stricken London, that was sure. They had only half an ear to lend William Mompesson, their priest. But then they realized what he was saying.

"The plague travels about the country in the blood of those fleeing it. In trying to get away, folk take a death sentence to another community of souls, condemning them too, to die. When a fire breaks out, we protect the houses round about by making a firebreak and starving the fire of new timber. That's what we must do here. As we are Christians, we must be prepared to die in order that others may live. For Christ says, 'Greater love hath no man than this . . .'"

Stunned, the people of Eyam gaped at him. He made it sound so simple. Isolate the disease so that the disease might die out. He was asking them to stay in Eyam, to make no move to get away; to cut themselves off and let the plague burn itself out within the available people – within their children, their loved ones, themselves. Three hundred and fifty people, waiting for an inevitable and terrible death. And yet the man had such an air of certainty. Amid all the confusion and terror, he *knew what to do*. They must simply stop struggling – deliver themselves into the hands of God and the plague.

Of course they did everything within their power to avoid infection. Some smoked pipes all day long, some wore charms and bunches of herbs, some carried nosegays to keep off the stench of death. But the people of Eyam followed the instructions of their priest. As travellers neared the village a sentry would call out, "Go back! We have the plague in Eyam. Go round us, and remember us in your prayers!"

Supplies of food and quicklime and tobacco and so forth were brought to the boundary stone or the well and left where the payment lay, in vinegar-washed, sterile coins. The curious came for a while, to shout questions across the river. But soon no one came. For all Eyam knew, the rest of the world had died.

If William Mompesson thought that God would spare the people because of their selflessness, he was mistaken. One by one they fell ill, each one suffering days of tormenting pain and wretchedness while neighbours watched from a distance, much as people might watch a rabid dog die in the street. The lucky ones died suddenly, after a few hours of raging fever. Sooner than move bodies through the streets, families dug graves in their gardens, ready for when they were too ill to dig them. Mrs Hancock buried her husband, three sons and three daughters in the field beside her house, within the space of eight days.

The church was locked – too good a breeding ground for the disease – but William Mompesson kept on holding services, out in the open air, under a scorching summer sky endlessly smutted with flies and the ash of fumigating fires. He had raised this dwindling little congregation of patient saints halfway to heaven. William Mompesson had done that much for them, and that was more than any surgeon or apothecary could have done.

On 7 September 1665, George Viccars, a tailor in Eyam, in the Peak District, received a parcel of cloth from London, and in it a cloud of fleas, thought to be the source of the epidemic. He was first to die. Three-quarters of the population of Eyam died of bubonic plague within a year. Unlike other "plague villages" which were totally abandoned during the Black Death of the fourteenth century, Eyam survives to the present day. Meanwhile, in London, nearly 70,000 deaths were attributed to the Great Plague.

The Great Fire of London

1666

IT WAS NOBODY'S DOING, NOBODY'S FAULT. Suddenly, at two in the morning of Sunday, 2 September, a pile of firewood stacked against the wall of the baker's shop in Pudding Lane burst into flames. (It was the back wall of the oven, and so of course the bricks grew hot.) Mr Faryner the baker woke to find the room full of smoke and, when he reached the head of the stairs, could see at once there was no escaping that way. The whole of the ground floor was alight.

"Wife! Wife! Wake up unless you want to burn in your bed!"

They climbed out of a dormer window in the roof and spread-eagled themselves against the roof tiles, feeling for the gutter with their feet. The air was full of smuts and smoke. At the window the maid sobbed: "I can't! I can't do it, Mr Faryner! I'll fall! It's too high!" There was no turning back for her – no reasoning with her as she grew more and more hysterical. The baker pressed on, balancing his way along the guttering, while down in the street a crowd of neighbours gathered, stupid with sleep. They watched till the screaming figure of the maid fell back from the window, replaced by leaping spectres of flame.

For an hour the baker's shop alone burned – a bad blaze but not the first in a city of wooden and wattle houses. Neighbours fearing for their own property fetched out buckets of water, but there was no organized attempt to isolate the fire. A brisk wind was blowing. Above the heads of those watching, burning straws and cinders and ash floated in search of kindling.

By morning, the whole street was ablaze.

Lord Mayor Thomas Bludworth was a dithering, indecisive man. He would not order the pulling down of undamaged shops and houses to make a firebreak. "Who will pay for the rebuilding?" he asked querulously. For hours he hesitated, while the fire leapt from roof to rooftop and strung the narrow streets with yellow buntings of flame.

Cellars packed with fuel, barrels of pitch, winter supplies of tallow exploded, throwing burning clods of wattle high into the air and showering the streets with tiles. Families in the path of the fire began to bundle their belongings together into chests and bags and to move their children out of doors. Here and there, gangs of men banded together to fight the fire, but all they had were buckets of water and hand-held squirts. They might as well have spat on the flames. King Charles II, looking out over London, saw the daylight choked by a rising mass of black smoke. "Tell the Lord Mayor he may have all the soldiers he needs!"

"How did it begin?" was all the Lord Mayor wanted to know. "Who's to blame?"

"Foreigners!" people told him. "Fire raisers! Revolutionaries!"

Mr Faryner the baker was summoned to tell what he knew of the fire. Anxious that no one should blame him, he remembered mysterious, suspicious circumstances – the fire starting far from the bread oven, for no good reason. And it had spread so fast and so far! There must have been arsonists operating all over the city!

People powerless to stop the fire turned their energies to finding the culprits. A Frenchman was knocked down with an iron bar for the crime of being foreign. A woman holding her apron gathered up in front of her was set upon by a mob screaming, "Look! Look! She has fireballs hidden in her apron! She's carrying fireballs! Arsonist!" The woman sprawled senseless in the open drain, and a dozen fluffy yellow chicks scattered out of her apron and ran cheeping hither and thither.

At last, the Lord Mayor gave permission for a firebreak to be made, and soldiers with billhooks began pulling apart whole streets of houses, while the householders screamed prayers and abuse and clutched their children close or dragged their furniture clear of the tumbling masonry. But it was too late. The fire leapt their firebreak, a surf of sparks spilling onwards to set alight wash-lines, hay-carts and more thatches.

Down at the river, the watermen had mustered every watertight boat and barge in the city and were busy evacuating families and goods downriver. The river was a red glare, the smoke an artificial night, but the watermen were pitiless in demanding their fee. As the hours passed, and they found they had more trade than they could handle, they demanded higher and higher sums. Huge purses of money changed hands so that a dresser and a harpsichord should float with their owners downstream, out of danger. Already there were tables and benches afloat on the tide, safer in the water than out of it.

Crowds jostled at the waterside for a chance to board, children up to their knees in mud, women balancing on jetties and landing stages, men haggling and swearing. In among them, pickpockets were lifting a fortune in watches and silk handkerchiefs, an unattended valise here, there an unguarded roll of cutlery.

The goldsmiths and silversmiths of the city converged on the Tower of London, to deposit their valuables in the stone vaults and impregnable dungeons of the ancient fortress. But would even the Tower keep out the fire now shredding to rags the London skyline? Church spires were toppling like trees, stone buildings crazing, crumbling, crumpling, their stones bursting like bombs.

The booksellers of London chose St Paul's Cathedral as a safe place for their stock, for it was built in stone and lead and bronze – not kindling like the houses which jostled round it.

Many people also looked for sanctuary in the various churches, only to be harangued by preachers wild-eyed with zeal. "This is the judgement of the Lord! Yea, He hath poured out brimstone on the heads of the unrighteous!" They were out on the streets, too, the evangelists, bellowing in the ears of the milling crowds, their spittle gleaming in the firelight: "God sendeth down destruction on this City of Sin, on this generation of sinners!"

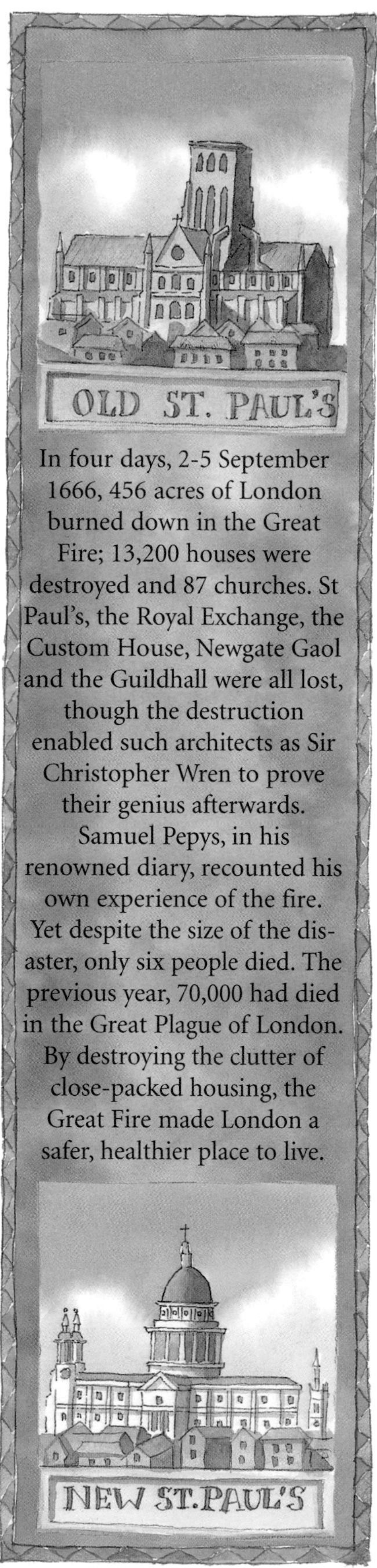

In four days, 2-5 September 1666, 456 acres of London burned down in the Great Fire; 13,200 houses were destroyed and 87 churches. St Paul's, the Royal Exchange, the Custom House, Newgate Gaol and the Guildhall were all lost, though the destruction enabled such architects as Sir Christopher Wren to prove their genius afterwards. Samuel Pepys, in his renowned diary, recounted his own experience of the fire. Yet despite the size of the disaster, only six people died. The previous year, 70,000 had died in the Great Plague of London. By destroying the clutter of close-packed housing, the Great Fire made London a safer, healthier place to live.

Certainly hell did seem to have risen close to the surface of the world that day. In places the ground was too hot to walk on, and the air seared nose and throat and lungs. Rats and mice driven from the burning buildings squealed like demons along the streets. At one time, an area two miles long and one mile wide was alight and burning. The army was blowing up buildings with gunpowder now, adding to the din.

At eight o'clock on Tuesday night, a cry went up which turned the booksellers' hearts to printer's pulp. St Paul's was burning. Lead streamed molten out of its roof, pouring down in cataracts of incandescent silver, splashing on to the faces of the saints and madonnas, obliterating the bronzes on the floor: "Here lies the body of . . ." Into the vaults it poured, making a bonfire of the books and pamphlets and maps and Bibles in a blaze which leapt back up to the carved angels on the hammer beams. The great bells, set swinging and ringing by the hot updraught, began to lose their shape, to soften and bow, to sag, to melt in brilliant torrents.

In the Inner Temple, the beautiful, ancient buildings wavered in the heat-warped air – a golden rain of sparks falling on their roofs. A sailor called Richard Rowe, accustomed to going aloft in rigging, clambered on to the roof of the great hall, as lawyers in wigs and gowns gaped up at him, clutching precious documents. All he had was a pillow, and as he straddled the roof ridge, he beat at flames which scuttled like rats across the tiles.

The great fire had reached the limit of its strength. The explosions had finally starved it of new food. Now, here, at the Inner Temple, it lost the fight against a single man and a pillow. Richard Rowe saved the great hall, to the choking cheers of lawyers and judges, clerks and secretaries. As he sat there astride the roof, all he could see as far as the levelled horizon was smoking devastation.

Outside London, in the parks, 100,000 people huddled bewildered and homeless amid the few worldly goods they had managed to save – a cradle, a wheelbarrow, a sedan chair. The King organized relief supplies of food to be fetched in from the countryside, and personally administered the billeting of the homeless in pubs, inns and churches. Before long, he was commissioning brave new buildings, planning a more open, elegant city than the one which had grown up hugger-mugger, in squalor and overcrowded filth, over 1,000 years. But those who had lost their homes simply roamed about the ruins, picking over the ashes of their houses, counting the cost.

Colonel Blood Steals the Crown Jewels

1671

One day, while Mr Talbot Edwards, the deputy keeper, and his wife were taking tea, a clergyman and his wife called at the Tower and asked if they might view the Crown Jewels.

It was not an unusual request. Old Mr Edwards was accustomed to giving his little informative talk as he displayed the royal sceptre, the sword of state, the jewelled gauntlets and coronets and, of course, the coronation crown. He had been doing it for years.

Such an agreeable couple, Mr and Mrs Edwards agreed afterwards – especially when the gentleman called a week later with a pair of gloves for Mrs Edwards "in gratitude for her great kindness". Seeing the pair of pistols hanging on the wall of the apartment, the clergyman admired them so much that he begged to buy them, then and there!

The friendship flourished. So it seemed the most natural thing in the world that their clergyman friend should bring along two acquaintances – visitors to London – to view the Royal Regalia. That was the morning of 9 May.

Beginning his well-worn talk, Mr Edwards laid out the gems and collars, diadems and weapons on the table in the Jewel Room. "And this, gentlemen, is the coronet worn by . . ."

Suddenly, Talbot Edwards – who was past eighty – found himself enveloped in darkness – a cloak over his head, a wooden bung pushed into his mouth to gag him.

"Give us the crown, the orb and the sceptre and no one will get hurt!" the clergyman hissed in the old man's ear.

But Edwards took his responsibilities to heart. The shame of losing the treasures in his charge to a band of tricksters and brigands was more than he could bear. He began to struggle and moan and kick and wrench himself to and fro in their grasp. They struck him once with a wooden mallet, then when he still struggled, struck him again and again.

"Keep him quiet, can't you?" Colonel Blood snarled.

They stabbed Edwards to silence him.

Colonel Blood beat the crown of England out of shape and crammed it under his cloak. Another man dropped the orb down the front of his baggy breeches. But the sceptre of state was too long to fit up a sleeve or down a trouser leg. They flung it on the table and began to file it in two.

Then a sharp whistle from their look-out on the floor below warned of danger: visitors for the Edwardses! The keeper's son and son-in-law were coming up the stairs! Edwards' visitors opened the door of the apartment to be met by a stampede of masked men, a volley of shouts and swearwords. They were shoved aside, but quickly realized what was happening, crying, "Stop the thieves!"

There was a warder on the drawbridge. Running towards the commotion, he was confronted by the small black circle of Blood's pistol barrel pointing in his face. He saw the hammer lift, the spark flash, then fear swallowed him up in a black unconsciousness he mistook for death. The shot had missed, but Blood and his cronies were through the iron gate and running for the tethered horses.

Talbot Edwards' son put on such a sprint that he crashed into Blood and bowled him off his feet. The crown clattered to the ground, gems and pearls jarred from their settings and rolled away like so many pebbles.

The news was shouted from street to street clear across London: "Have you heard? Someone's tried to steal the Crown Jewels! . . . A band of brigands! . . . They broke the sceptre! . . . They murdered the guards! . . . But they've been caught! . . . And now Blood is refusing to speak to anyone but the King of England himself!"

To everyone's surprise, King Charles II granted Blood an audience.

But did the colonel throw himself on the King's mercy? Did he plead insanity or swear that he had been forced to commit the crime against his will? Far from it.

"Yes, I did it!" said Blood. "I would never deny it to save my life. It was my plan and it was only by the greatest bad luck that it failed. I'm no more sorry than I was when I kidnapped the Duke of Ormonde! No more sorry than when I lay in hiding at Battersea and aimed a gun at you, Charles Stuart, as you went down to bathe in the river."

The audacity of the man, the knowledge he had come so close to being assassinated all but silenced the King. "What stopped you shooting me?" he asked at last.

"My heart was checked by an awe of majesty which caused me to spare the King's life," said Blood. "I shall never name my accomplices. If any of us die, the rest are sworn to be avenged for that death. But if your Majesty were to spare us, the pardoned men would doubtless be ready to do the King great service. We have already proved our daring, you'll agree."

"Take them back to the Tower," said the King, and his court waited, with horrid glee, to see what terrible retribution would overtake the villainous, the shameless, the arrogant Colonel Blood. As if the King could be intimidated by empty threats! As if the King would use the services of such unmitigated rogues!

Within days, Blood was free. Not only free, but his estates were restored to him along with an income of £500 a year. Talbot Edwards lived, but received almost nothing for his loyal service – a pittance in comparison with the rewards Blood received from the King.

So did the King so much admire daring and audacity that he was ready to let an unrepentant criminal go free? Or was he scared of revenge attacks following Blood's death? Or did Blood and the King share some secret which placed the lout beyond reach of the law? Rumour spread that he had done the King some huge favour so murderous and wicked that he held the King in the palm of his hand, free to say what he liked, do what he pleased, rather than swinging at the end of a hangman's rope.

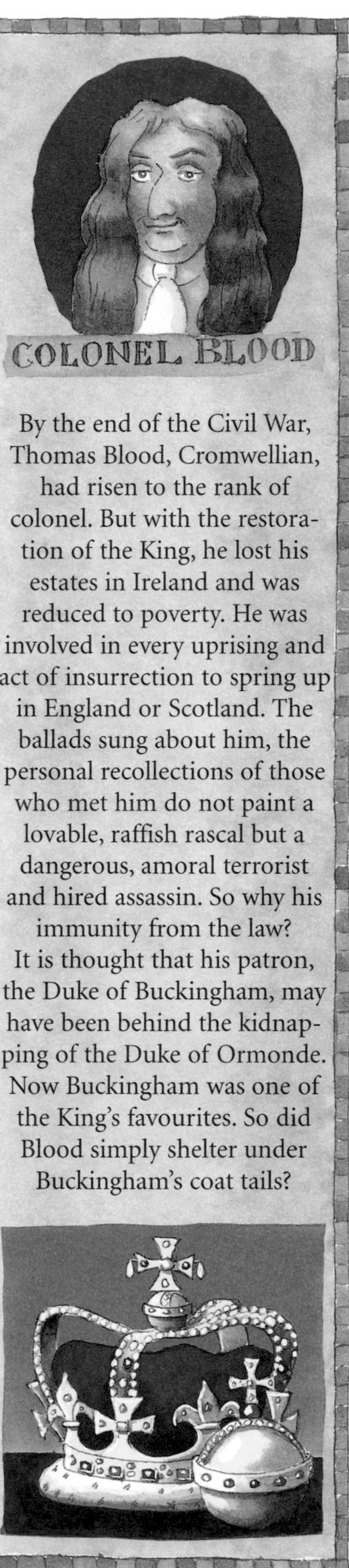

By the end of the Civil War, Thomas Blood, Cromwellian, had risen to the rank of colonel. But with the restoration of the King, he lost his estates in Ireland and was reduced to poverty. He was involved in every uprising and act of insurrection to spring up in England or Scotland. The ballads sung about him, the personal recollections of those who met him do not paint a lovable, raffish rascal but a dangerous, amoral terrorist and hired assassin. So why his immunity from the law?

It is thought that his patron, the Duke of Buckingham, may have been behind the kidnapping of the Duke of Ormonde. Now Buckingham was one of the King's favourites. So did Blood simply shelter under Buckingham's coat tails?

Run for Your Life!

1685

WHEN KING JAMES II PUT DOWN REBELLION in the West Country, he wanted to make sure that no one ever dared to question his kingship again. So he employed Judge Jeffreys to make an example of the rebels, and the judge went to it with a will. He hanged men by the hundred.

Young Hughie was famous. Throughout Somerset he was renowned for the speed and distance he could run. Champion of a hundred races, Hughie of Westonzoyland was both sprinter and marathon runner and could outpace running dogs and outstay an army horse.

"They say you can run, boy," said Judge Jeffreys, supercilious under his black cap.

"I can."

"And I say you can't. A wager on it. What do you say?"

"I have nothing to wager," said Hughie, wary of the gleam in the judge's eye.

"Wouldn't you wager your *life*, boy, that you could outrun a runner of mine?"

"That I would!" Hughie was over-quick to accept the bet. There among the numberless nooses, the trees dangling with hanged men, the muttered prayers of Catholic priests over Protestant prisoners, he grabbed at the chance to live. He knew he could outrun any man in the county. To win his life he was ready to run as he had never run before.

"Then fetch out a horse and tie him to the stirrup!" commanded the judge. "If he tires before the horse, he shall hang. If the horse tires first, I shall rethink my verdict." And before Hughie could draw a good, deep breath, someone slapped the horse across the rump and it sprang forward.

The animal was unnerved by seeing movement in the corner of his eye, by the noise in his swivelling ear of a man's laboured breathing. At first the two of them jostled one another – man and horse, horse and man. The jeering spectators fully expected to see Hughie dragged to his death.

But Hughie timed his strides by the hoofbeats, stretched his gait to match the sway and thrust of the big fetlocks, and soon the pair were running side by side, leaving their captors staring after them. In a panic, soldiers mounted up to give chase and keep the prisoner in sight.

Across the green curves of Somerset, Hughie and the stallion ran; across the green swelling hills, across pillaged farms, past burned buildings and the wreckage of gun carriages. Horse ran and man ran, and if once the pace slowed, there were plenty of shouts from behind to spur on the frightened beast.

In time the horse became accustomed to his running-mate, and Hughie, far from hating the beast, found more in common with its pounding, pungent bulk than with the men hooting and whooping behind. He made of himself a machine, his legs the mill-paddles, the ground the water driving them. "I will run for my life or die running," he told himself.

He thought of Anne, his sweetheart, her sadness at thinking him dead, her joy in finding him alive, his life won back like a trophy. *She* was the trophy at the end of the race. *She* was the goal which kept him running when his legs burned like twin fuses and his lungs were two tattered flags, when his head rolled on his shoulder heavy as a cannonball.

The stallion had no such goal. That is why, in the end, he tired. After three hours of running, his breath broke in his windpipe and his sweating flanks heaved. He slowed to a canter, to a trot, to a walk, then pitched down so that Hughie fell on top of him.

To Hughie's surprise the noise, swelling louder and louder as his pursuers caught up, was of breathless cheering. Miles earlier, the jeering had given way to admiration – wonder, even – at the strength and courage of a young man who could outrun a horse. They took off their hats in salute to him. They carried him back to the judge eagerly, with the news loud in their mouths: "He did it, sir! He did it! The horse tired first! He did it!"

The news of the rebels' defeat by the King's army reached Westonzoyland fast. So did the story of the race: man against horse, horse against man, and how their Hughie had won it. At the village inn they drank a toast to their champion runner: the man who could win any race in the county and who had given them back their pride as West Countrymen, even in defeat. They rattled at Anne's shutters and crowned her with may, because until Hughie came home, his sweetheart was the next best person to crown. She came down to them and danced, in celebration.

Then the news arrived that Hughie was hanged.

The judge had never meant to keep his side of the bet. The race had been, for him, no more than a moment's entertainment in a long tedious day. In Westonzoyland, joy turned to outrage, then to gnawing, blistering despair. While village thoughts turned again to killing and rebellion and revenge, Anne slipped quietly away.

A ghost runs now across the Summer Land: not a boy's athletic ghost timing its paces to the beat of ghostly hoofbeats, but a little pattering ghost wearing a crown of may. Because Anne drowned herself at the news of her sweetheart's death. Now her ghost gasps and sobs and stumbles breathlessly on, everlastingly trying to outrun her grief.

On 11 June 1685, the Duke of Monmouth, illegitimate son of Charles II, landed at Lyme Regis, hopeful of wresting the crown from his uncle, King James II. Over 4,000 West Countrymen mustered to his Protestant cause. For a month – the so-called "Duking Days" – these rebels held Somerset, and Monmouth was proclaimed King in Taunton market-place. But when James brought his full wrath to bear, his army easily defeated the rebels at the battle of Sedgemoor. Monmouth was captured, and cravenly and unsuccessfully begged for his life, even at the cost of turning Catholic. Meanwhile the notoriously harsh Judge Jeffreys was sent to Taunton to try captured rebels. His "Bloody Assize", estimated to have hanged 200 men, transported 800 more to the West Indies and whipped and fined countless others. His barbarism inflicted wounds on the West Country for which neither he nor James, his paymaster, were ever forgiven.

Glencoe

1692

THE THING WAS TO GET IT OVER AND DONE WITH, then put it out of mind. The thing was to say: these are not people, these are MacDonalds. War hardens a man, and after a few years in the army, he can stomach almost anything. It is a lot to ask of a man, even so, to eat another man's food, to sleep under his roof, to accept his hospitality, then to murder him.

Still, King William was determined to be rid of the "Auld Fox" MacIan and the rest of the MacDonald clan once and for all.

So we were billeted on them, with the excuse that the garrison at Fort William was too overcrowded to hold us. As we marched into the glen – 120 men of the Earl of Argyll's Highland Regiment – McIan's sons appeared and asked if we came as friends or foe. "As friends," said Glenlyon. "As friends".

For fifteen days we lived in their poor wee houses, in that great valley called Glencoe, where a river of wind flows always cold, and where the snow fortifies the mountains into castles high as the sky. The Master of Stair had said it must be done in winter, because it was the one time the Highlanders could not elude us and carry their wives, children and cattle to the mountains.

They did not suspect anything. After all, the "Auld Fox" had pledged his allegiance to King William, so he thought he had nothing to fear, even though we were Campbells. (The Campbells and MacDonalds have hated each other for as long as I can remember; that's why Stair chose us for the job.) Also, we had accepted MacIan's hospitality, and that should have guaranteed our goodwill. That's the unwritten law of the Highlands.

So we played cards with the MacDonalds, we drank with them, exchanged stories with them. We sat down to suppers cooked by the women, and our knuckles knocked against their knuckles as we reached into the same bowl for our food. The children tugged at our uniforms, wanting to be sung a song. Their mothers hushed them to bed: "Do nae fash the officer: he needs his sleep."

But there wasn't to be any sleep. At nightfall we were summoned outside and given our orders by Glenlyon. We did not go back in to our beds. When they saw us checking our muskets, the MacIan boys asked: "What's happening?" But Glenlyon only laughed and told them we were going out next day to tackle a local band of robbers.

The time was set for five in the morning, when the clansmen would be asleep or just stirring. So we waited, watching the moon move over the glen through tangles of snow-cloud, a thistledown of snow blowing.

Come five o'clock we went to it. Bayonets fixed. No shot to be fired, that was the order. But some of us were jumpy – or squeamish – and we used our guns. The MacDonalds would have woken anyway, I know. The screaming would have woken them soon enough.

We killed more than thirty. You wouldn't think that would take long. And yet the screaming seemed to go on for an eternity. Sometimes I hear it still in my sleep. Men, women, children. Everyone under seventy years, the order said, and don't trouble the Governor with prisoners. If they locked the doors against us, we set the house alight and burned it down, with the people inside. Women. Children. Fourteen in one house.

In the confusion, some got away, out of the village. It didn't matter. It's so cold up there, the snow lay so deep, and them in their shirts for sleeping, barefoot, without cloak or blanket: we knew they would freeze to death on the mountainsides.

In the house where I had stayed, nine clansmen were gathered round the morning fire when we went in shooting. Four died where they sat. We split up and went after the women, the bairns, the old folk. I came face-to-face with the owner of the house, the one whose knuckles had brushed mine as I reached for bread at supper. Odd how, in all the din – the smashing of furniture, the screaming, the shooting, the curses – there seemed nothing between us but silence. A blanket of silence. Then the man said, "Let me die in the open air, man, no under ma ain roof."

I had steeled myself against the usual things: "Let me live. Spare my wife. Pity the bairns." This seemed such a small thing to ask: "Let me die in the open air."

"For your bread which I have eaten," I said, "I will." So we pushed him out of doors with our musket butts, and he stood there in the dark, his face underlit by the snow. We levelled our muskets.

Then he up with his plaid – that piece of tartan they all wear for a cloak – and threw it in our faces and ran. We fired after him, but the snow swallowed him up. Maybe he lived. Maybe he froze to death, being without his plaid. Part of me hopes he got clear.

The Glencoe massacre was an atrocity brought about by one man's obsessive loathing of the MacDonald clan: Secretary of State for Scotland, Sir John Dalrymple, Master of Stair. Stair had already persuaded King William to put to the sword anyone who would not pledge allegiance to the crown. But MacIan *had* signed. Even so, Stair succeeded in sending 120 Campbells, commanded by Captain Campbell Glenlyon, to massacre the clan. More than thirty were killed, another 300 fled into the blizzard. Chieftain MacIan was shot in bed by a man he had invited to dine; his wife died of her injuries. His sons escaped. The legend of the woman and child was added later – echo of Snow White. Another legend tells of the Campbells led astray by mountain spirits on the way home.

The British public were so shocked by the massacre that Stair was shunned for a time . . . but was ultimately made an earl. Politically, the massacre was a disastrous move, unifying Highlanders and Lowlanders in bitter hatred of the English.

But Glenlyon saw it happen and came down on us raging. "There's two more run into the forest yonder!" he bellowed at me. "Get after them and finish them both!"

From the edge of the wood I could hear them crashing through the deadwood; clods of snow slumped down from the trees, showing the way they had gone. Besides, I could see their footsteps in the snow – one set deep, one set so small and light that it scarcely dented the snow. Pretty soon the snowy trees swallowed up the roar of burning buildings behind me, the crack of muskets. It was silent where I found them: a silent, grey, hollow world pillared with bare tree trunks. A woman and a child, too exhausted to go any further, clung to one another gasping, their breath curling into the air like musket smoke. I fired once, reloaded, fired a second time.

Twigs and snow tumbled down on to me from where the musket balls had holed the leaf canopy overhead. The woman looked at me, her hand clamped over the child's mouth to keep him from screaming. We neither of us said one word.

Then I pulled the shawl from round her shoulders, turned on my heel and headed back. On the way, Providence set a wolf in my path, and I killed it and daubed the shawl with blood. I had to have something to show Glenlyon.

All in all it's not a night's work I'm proud of. If you ask me, I'd say the killing was folly as well as a sin. When word spread, even the sassenachs* pitied the MacDonalds, whereas up till then Highlander and Lowlander had scorned one another. We Campbells were shamed by it. That's my opinion.

I don't tell people I was there. I don't say, "I was at Glencoe." You only have to mention the word and men shudder. I shudder: almost as if the snow blew inside me that night, and lodged where it's never going to thaw. At five in the morning, I lie awake and shiver.

*Sassenach (literally Saxon) is an abusive term for a Lowlander or non-Scot.

The Lighthouse and the Storm

1703

Henry Winstanley designed playing cards and lived in the depths of the country, miles from the sea. So he was not the most obvious contender for the task of building a lighthouse. But whereas others tried and gave up, Winstanley maintained it was perfectly possible and that he was the man to do it. In 1696 he mustered carpenters and engineers and, with his meticulous plans rolled up under his arm, sailed out to the Eddystone Rock to start work.

Ever since vessels first set sail from the English coast, the Eddystone Rock had been a menace to sailors. On a calm sunny day, it looked like nothing – a jag of rock jutting high enough out of the sea for gulls to perch. But in a fog, or when the waves ran so high as to hide it altogether, the Eddystone Rock could rip the keel out of sloop or merchantman or fishing smack. Countless sailors had drowned in the waters around it, and their sunken ships were now crewed by conger eels and shoals of ghost-white cod.

The task would have been hard enough, even under ideal conditions trying to work on a weed-slippery, spray-wet rock while battered by wind and sea, trying to sink foundations sufficiently deep to raise up an indestructible tower twenty-five metres tall. As it was, Winstanley had to contend with dangers of a different sort.

Press gangs roaming the inns and kitchens of the south coast in search of able-bodied men saw work begin on the Eddystone Rock and rubbed their hands with glee. When a press-gang paid a visit there, the builders would have nowhere to run. Winstanley's workmen were coshed and bound and carried off to serve as seamen in the Royal Navy – pressed men – leaving nothing but a scattering of tools and timber. Winstanley recruited fresh men, but there was an understandable shortage of volunteers.

During construction, Winstanley often chose to sleep on site rather than waste time coming ashore. One night, he and his builders were woken by the rhythmic splash of oars, the thud of a rowing boat pulling alongside the rock. French troops, in cockaded hats and with muskets primed, came scrambling over the moonlit reef, barking unintelligible commands at the sleepy, bewildered English. For a few minutes it seemed as if the entire construction team would be murdered where they huddled.

Winstanley tried to reason with them: "Look, I know we're at war, your country and mine. But you French *need* this lighthouse just as much as the English! Does the rock sink only British ships? Does it drown only English seamen?"

Despite his protests, Winstanley's builders were stripped naked and cast adrift in a rowing boat. But at least *they* stood on English soil next day, whereas Winstanley found himself in a French prison. The Admiralty were incensed. They arranged for a mutual exchange of prisoners – and put Winstanley back to work building the Eddystone Light.

At last a core of stone was grafted on to the rock, and on to that a wooden tower, with a windowed chamber at the summit where hung a kind of three-tiered chandelier, crammed with tallow candles. The night those candles were first lit, Winstanley's face glowed almost as bright with pride in a job well done.

"It'll never stand up!" people said.

Praise for Winstanley's handsome lighthouse was guarded. A great many people said it would fall down within days. "I only wish," Winstanley answered them, "that I may be in the lighthouse in circumstances that will test its strength to the utmost."

November 1703 ended amid filthy weather. Then, on the twenty-sixth, a gale struck the south of England more ferocious than any recorded before or since. People woke with the impression that the world was coming to an end, and when they looked out of their windows, they were certain of it.

In London 700 boats and barges were ripped off their moorings and piled up in matchwood mountains against the bridges. The roofs were ripped off houses like so many fish-scales, whirling the contents into the sky, pelting those outdoors with furniture, masonry and tiles, cats and food and roofbeams. Churches collapsed as though built of biscuit crumbs. A flood tide, inflated by the wind, swept up the river and swamped the City, washing over the venerable stone floors of Westminster Hall, setting afloat the bodies of those killed in the maelstrom. Off the coast, three warships foundered with 1,500 men aboard, and 200 sailors were glimpsed, stranded and drowning on the Goodwin Sands.

The face of the English countryside was scarred by those two days of the Great Storm. Whole villages foundered, whole copses were uprooted, barns folded flat. At least 8,000 people died, though the chaos and horror were so great that no true count was ever made. Tens of thousands were injured.

In the depths of the Essex countryside, in the parish of Littlebury, one house stood pretty much unscathed. Hardly any damage befell the home of Henry Winstanley, engraver, inventor, designer of playing cards and lighthouses. A small silver replica of the Eddystone Lighthouse fell from a table: that is all.

Winstanley was not home to see it, however. He was out on the Eddystone Rock, visiting his lighthouse which had recently been increased in height to thirty-seven metres.

On the morning of 28 November, the Great Storm subsided. When the people of Plymouth looked out to sea, they could see the horizon once more, though the sea was still white with rollers. They looked towards the Eddystone Light, fully expecting to see it wrecked, its pulleys and winches snapped off like tree branches, its lattice windows smashed. But they saw none of this. In fact, they saw nothing. Not a trace. Every stone and plank and nail and candle of the Eddystone Lighthouse had disappeared, as surely as if it had never existed. And with it had gone its creator.

A new light was built five years later, and stood for almost fifty years before catching fire. The lead roof, in melting, poured down in a glittering torrent – directly into the gaping mouth of the lighthouse keeper. His slow, agonizing death is commemorated in the local museum by the lead ingot which solidified inside his stomach. But of Winstanley, nothing remains but rumours mouthed by silent conger eels and ghost-white cod.

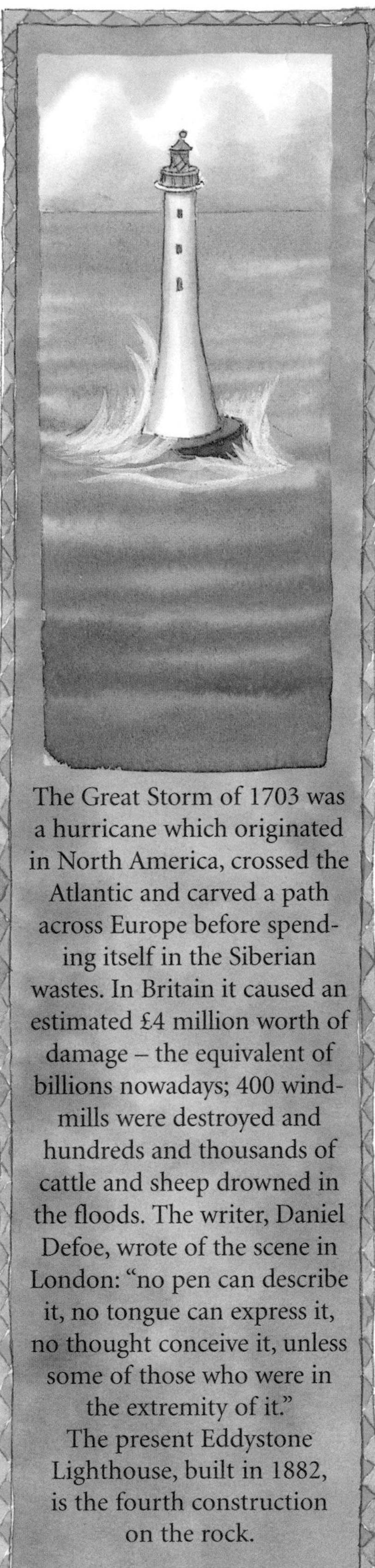

The Great Storm of 1703 was a hurricane which originated in North America, crossed the Atlantic and carved a path across Europe before spending itself in the Siberian wastes. In Britain it caused an estimated £4 million worth of damage – the equivalent of billions nowadays; 400 windmills were destroyed and hundreds and thousands of cattle and sheep drowned in the floods. The writer, Daniel Defoe, wrote of the scene in London: "no pen can describe it, no tongue can express it, no thought conceive it, unless some of those who were in the extremity of it."

The present Eddystone Lighthouse, built in 1882, is the fourth construction on the rock.

The Bubble Bursts

1720

STRANGE AND FAR-OFF LANDS have always held most magic for those who will never go there. In the early days of the eighteenth century, South America was imagined as a faery mound shot through with precious ore. It had gold, and everyone dreams of laying hands on gold.

The South Sea Company *did* exist: it was not imaginary, nor was it set up with a view to defrauding anyone. Real ships *did* sail, from time to time, between England and South America. There *was* some money to be made. But that has nothing to do with what happened in the City of London during the winter of 1719.

Rumours spread that British cargoes landing in South America would be exchanged for outlandish quantities of gold and silver. Investors in the South Sea Company stood to increase their money a hundredfold. Here was no shady, crooked enterprise: the Government itself held South Sea Company stock! Here was an opportunity for people of all kinds to get rich fast. Even when war broke out, ending trade agreements, people went on believing the South Sea Company would somehow continue to bring home vessels wallowing under tons of gold.

There was a stampede to invest. The value of shares soared: money was pouring in – not from South America but from eager investors all over England. A kind of investment fever broke out, which saw all manner of people thrusting their savings at the company's brokers, begging to be allowed to share in the bonanza. A few cautious voices warned against it: no company could or would pay profits of the kind talked of.

But the directors of the South Sea Company realized just how deep they could dip into the pockets of the gullible. When the share price began to drop, and uneasy crowds gathered outside the offices, well-dressed men strolled among them still beaming with confidence. They had *been* in Peru and Chile. They had *seen* the gold ingots piled up in the streets like bricks. Any fool could see how much those shares would soon be worth!

Fools there were in plenty. The share prices soared again. New shares were released – at a price. Hurry, hurry, hurry. Only the quick will get rich . . .

'Change Alley in the City of London was a scrum of people, from dawn till dusk, buying shares from trestle tables. A blizzard of application forms! Quill pens were at a premium; so was ink and somewhere flat to write. A man bent double by disease was charging a penny for the use of his back as a table. He went home with a big bag of pennies – solid, round, brown pennies – and kept them under his bed. A frenzy of greed had gripped the country – a kind of trance which no amount of shouting or cool reason could penetrate.

Those with wit enough saw the game for exactly what it was – a hysterical dash to buy worthless pieces of paper for absurd sums of money. Those with no conscience set up joint stock companies of their own, and issued shares, selling them in 'Change Alley. Why invest in South American gold when you can invest in a process to make sea water drinkable? Or in a perpetual motion machine? Or in re-floating treasure ships wrecked off the coast of Ireland? Why not put your money into making planks from sawdust or importing donkeys from Spain? Fortunes were to be made overnight: did it not say so on the handbills? One day a notice went up offering shares in the ultimate deceit:

> A Company for Carrying on an
> Undertaking of Great Advantage,
> But Nobody to Know What It Is.

The shares sold. Share-fever was such that people could hardly help themselves any more.

To those who did not have £100 to invest right away, came a new temptation: £100-shares in return for a down-payment of £2. Only £2 down and you could be holding a share document worth £100, then and there! Who could fail to be tempted? In the course of a day, 1,000 of these shares were issued, in a room crammed from door to window with pushing, impatient people, all chinking their golden guineas. At the end of the day, the office was locked. The broker washed the ink from his fingers, emptied the day's takings into a carpet bag, and caught the boat for France. He had invested one day of his time and earned £2,000.

Very soon afterwards, Mr Knight, treasurer of the South Sea Company, packed a bag, disguised himself, and also made his way to the Thames. A vessel was waiting to take him to Calais. The value of South Sea shares was dropping. Nothing could hide the truth this time. An airy idea had been inflated to impossible size, and now the South Sea Bubble had burst. There was nothing in it – nothing but hot air and greedy hopes.

Thousands were ruined, their savings gone, their dreams sunk in the South Sea. It almost brought down the Government. It threatened to topple the King from his throne. Public despair was so great that the sighs must have been heard as far away as South America.

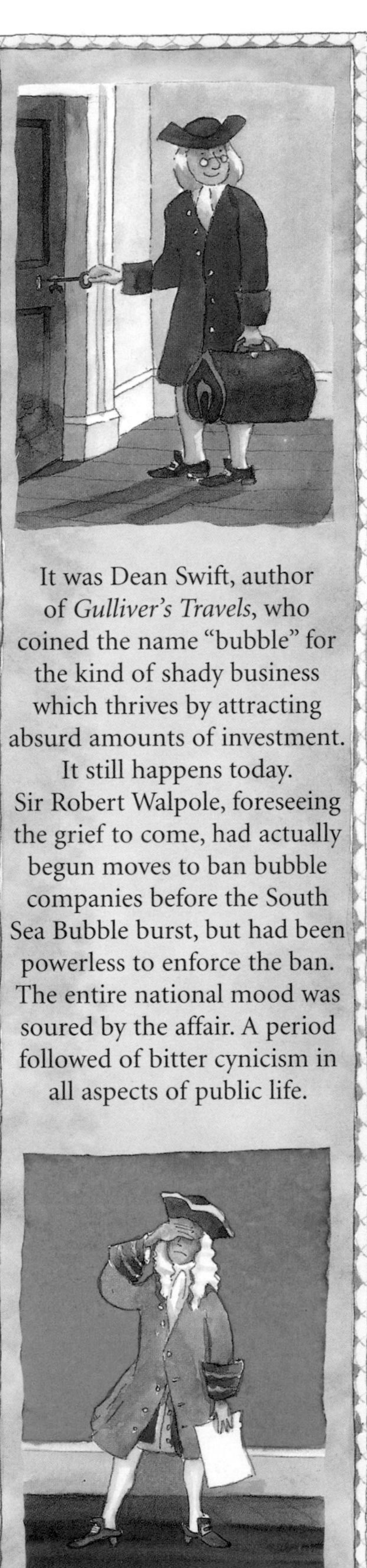

It was Dean Swift, author of *Gulliver's Travels*, who coined the name "bubble" for the kind of shady business which thrives by attracting absurd amounts of investment. It still happens today.

Sir Robert Walpole, foreseeing the grief to come, had actually begun moves to ban bubble companies before the South Sea Bubble burst, but had been powerless to enforce the ban. The entire national mood was soured by the affair. A period followed of bitter cynicism in all aspects of public life.

Makers and Breakers

1730s

In the bright, large-windowed cottage in Bury, the weavers worked away on their looms, passing the woof through the weft, tapping each strand into place, their cloth growing inch by laborious inch. And as they worked, they talked of John Kay and his invention.

"Looms twice the width of these . . ."

"Double the quantity in a working day!"

"And better quality, they say!"

But their tone was not full of admiration. The flying shuttle made a weaver's task easier and produced better, broader woollen cloth, but they did not want to handle one, to master the magic of threading and throwing the ingenious shuttle.

"Should not be allowed."

"Canna be left to go on."

"Must be stopped."

"Putting skilled men out of work!"

And the mood of seething resentment came bubbling to the boil. Then, when all the useful daylight was gone and all that remained were warps and wefts of moonbeams, the weavers and their neighbours converged on Kay's house and attacked. They broke all his windows.

He was baffled, bruised and bewildered. "Why can they not see? This is their future! This is for their good!"

But the weavers hated him. They looked around them and saw all the old ways dying out, the woollen trade becoming an empire in the hands of a few wealthy industrialists, its workers forced to work harder, longer, for less. That shuttle would take food out of their children's mouths. That was how they saw it.

It was just the same when Kay moved away to Colchester – then to Leeds. Oh, his flying shuttle caught on (it was too good an invention not to) but the manufacturers who used it did not pay him anything, behaving as if they had invented it themselves.

When he started up an engineering business, the mobs again gathered to throw bricks through the windows, smash his looms. Lonely and dejected, he went back to his home town of Bury, where he lay awake nights wondering what he had ever done for these people to hate him so much. "Because a thing is new must it be bad?"

One day, the mob surrounded his house. He could hear them jeering and swearing, racketing about, their women cursing, the children bright-eyed at the prospect of destruction, excitement, violence. John Kay apologized to the friends who were visiting him. "I hope nothing unpleasant will spoil our . . ."

A shoulder thudded against the door. A window caved in, in an explosion of breaking glass. The mob poured in, like the sea into a foundering ship. John tried to save his latest models, his books, his few possessions, but saw them sunk beneath a flood of flying fists, kicking clogs, jostling shawls and wooden clubs. The satisfying sound of splintering wood made these people deaf to reason. A mob has no ears.

He fled upstairs, where his friends had already had the good sense to hide. But the mob's leader broke off and looked around. "Let us find Kay. Where is Kay?"

Kay's guests flapped open a folded woollen sheet and threw it over their friend. Then before John could protest, they bundled him up into a shuttle-shape parcel and, lifting him between them, galloped down the stairs. Passing for looters robbing the house, they got Kay away unharmed – though not undamaged.

He was a bitter man. Desperate to earn a living, he left England for France, but did no better there. Just once, he came back, to seek justice against those mill owners who had stolen his invention. He got none. Those opportunists soured him far more than the ignorant louts who had almost killed him. For the manufacturers had known just what they were doing when they tricked him out of his percentage. Besides, the wreckers – those frightened vandals who had wanted to dam the tide of progress – would quickly be swept away by it. Within a few generations, they would be living huddled in urban slums, working on deafening machines for twelve hours a day, their children crawling up and down beneath the looms, their lives reduced to figures in a ledger: profit and loss. Theirs was the loss; theirs and John Kay's. He died destitute in France.

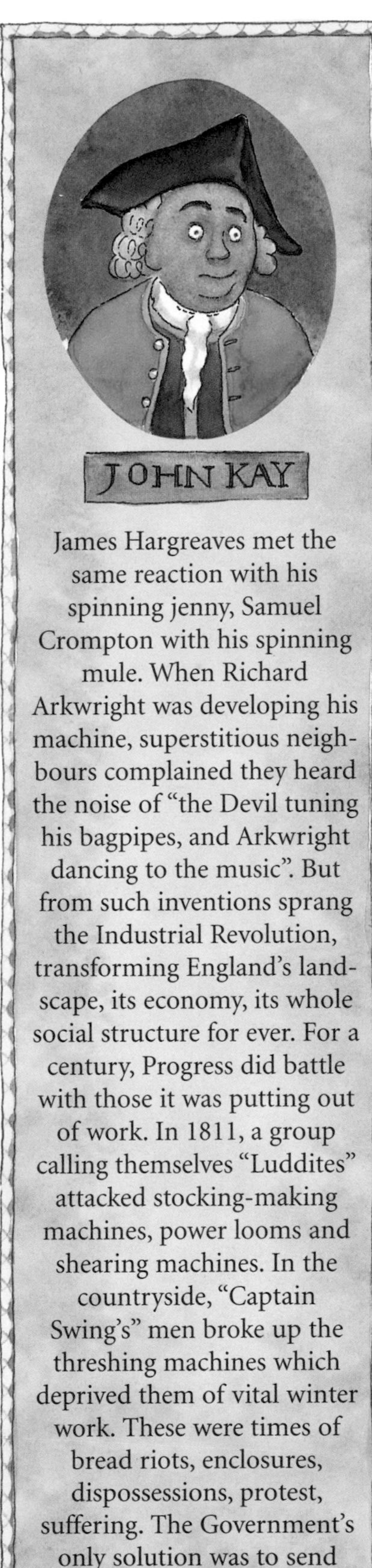

JOHN KAY

James Hargreaves met the same reaction with his spinning jenny, Samuel Crompton with his spinning mule. When Richard Arkwright was developing his machine, superstitious neighbours complained they heard the noise of "the Devil tuning his bagpipes, and Arkwright dancing to the music". But from such inventions sprang the Industrial Revolution, transforming England's landscape, its economy, its whole social structure for ever. For a century, Progress did battle with those it was putting out of work. In 1811, a group calling themselves "Luddites" attacked stocking-making machines, power looms and shearing machines. In the countryside, "Captain Swing's" men broke up the threshing machines which deprived them of vital winter work. These were times of bread riots, enclosures, dispossessions, protest, suffering. The Government's only solution was to send in the troops.

"Charlie Is My Darling"

1746

PRINCE CHARLES EDWARD, SON OF THE EXILED James Stuart III, landed at Eriskay determined to raise a rebellion and restore his father to his rightful position: King of England and Scotland. His Scottish supporters – Jacobites – came to greet him. But they watched appalled as the prince's troops came ashore. Where were the French armies that had been promised? How were they supposed to topple King George II from the throne with this pocket army? "You must go home, your Highness," they said.

"Home? I am come home!" declared the prince.

His youth, his energy won over the hard men of the glens. As the song runs:

They've left their bonnie Hieland hills,
Their wives and bairnies dear,
To draw a sword for Scotland's Lord,
  the young chevalier.
Oh! Charlie is my darling, the young chevalier!

At first they carried the day entirely, captured Edinburgh and took control of the borderlands. They had forced their way as far south as Derby before they fully grasped how incompetent their "Bonnie Prince Charlie" was. Did he really think he could take and hold London with an army of 5,000 men? They insisted he turn back. Pettish and sulking, Charles grudgingly agreed. In the meantime, the Duke of Cumberland was marching to intercept the rebels.

On 16 April 1746 he cut them off at Culloden Moor, and shot the heart out of the Jacobites. Afterwards he slaughtered their women and children too, winning himself the name "Butcher Cumberland". But the Culloden massacre lit such a fire of hatred that the Highlanders' love for their bonnie prince burned all the brighter. He was all they had left, and they guarded him like a treasure. King George offered £30,000 for the capture of the "Young Pretender", and yet no one informed on him. It was as if mists and heather had swallowed him up.

For five months, the fleeing Prince Charlie was passed from hiding place to hiding place, from caves to cellars, fed on the meagre supplies of his supporters. Told of the reward on his head, Charles grinned. "Then I offer £30 for the head of George II!"

The Kennedy brothers, wild and shaggy as Aberdeen bullocks, robbed a Hanoverian general of his baggage – all to provide the bonnie prince with a fresh suit of clothes.

When the redcoats swarmed in like red ants from all sides and not a rat could have crept away unnoticed, one of his bodyguards said, "Lend me your wig and cloak, sire. I will lead them off." Roderick MacKenzie went out into the open, showed himself and ran. He fetched after him horsemen, foot-soldiers, and such a hue and cry as the Highlands had rarely seen. They shot him down in Glen Moriston, and as he fell he shouted, "You have killed your prince!" The head was dispatched to London and put on public display – to show what became of ambitious usurpers. A one-time servant of Charles's went along – whether to grieve or simply to stare, no one knows. But in his astonishment he exclaimed aloud: 'That's no Charlie!" It was four days before the English troops discovered their mistake – and by that time Charlie himself was heading for the safety of the Hebrides.

No sooner had he put to sea than a storm hammered on the little boat and drove it sixty miles in ten pitch-black hours. Every moment, the men aboard thought to be hurled against rocks, shipwrecked on one of the islands invisible in the dark. But when dawn crawled in under the pall of black cloud, they spotted Benbecula, and were able to pull ashore. While the storm raged on, the prince took up "royal residence" in a doorless cow-house, with a rag of sailcloth for a blanket and nothing to eat but oatmeal and stolen beef.

From Benbecula, he set sail for Stornaway, but was driven ashore on Glass Island, where the people were hostile: he had to pretend to be a shipwrecked merchant. In Stornaway, one of the servants in the party got drunk and boasted wildly that he knew how the prince was going to get to France: that called for a change of plan. Putting in once more at Glass, the party was attacked and had to row on, without food or fresh water, for two days.

Spotted by an English man-of-war, the rowers bent their backs over the oars, rowing till the breath foamed through their gritted teeth. "I'll be sunk sooner than be taken," vowed the prince. Then the wind dropped, the warship was becalmed, and the oarsmen sculled out of sight of English telescopes. "It's clear," said Charles Edward, "I was not designed to die by weapon or water."

But when his friend Clanranald found him on the island of South Uist, the fugitive prince had been reduced to living in a hovel, on a diet of crabs, haggard by sickness and hunger, dressed in filthy rags. It was decided he must be got away to Skye.

So it was that the bonnie prince met Flora of the clan MacDonald, who lived by the Uist seashore. Her mother, Lady MacDonald, lived on Skye, which gave Flora the perfect excuse for making the voyage there.

When Flora entered the hut where the prince was hiding, she carried under her arm a bundle of clothes which she told him to put on: a flowery linen dress and a deep-hooded bonnet. Bonnie Charlie became "Betty Burke", and "a very old, muckle ill-shaken-up wife", by all accounts, striding out with his skirt in his fists, towards the rowing boat on the beach.

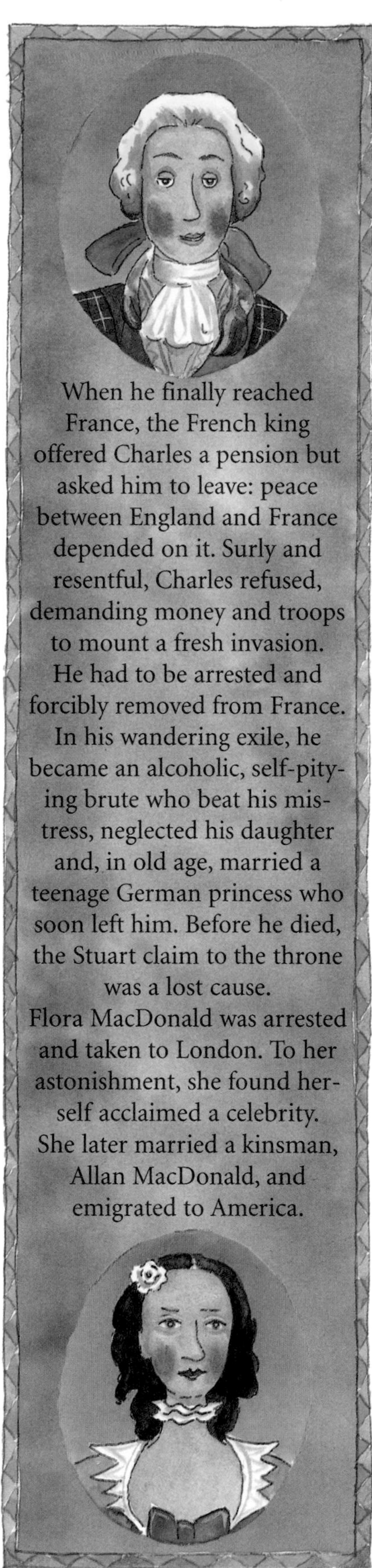

When he finally reached France, the French king offered Charles a pension but asked him to leave: peace between England and France depended on it. Surly and resentful, Charles refused, demanding money and troops to mount a fresh invasion. He had to be arrested and forcibly removed from France. In his wandering exile, he became an alcoholic, self-pitying brute who beat his mistress, neglected his daughter and, in old age, married a teenage German princess who soon left him. Before he died, the Stuart claim to the throne was a lost cause.

Flora MacDonald was arrested and taken to London. To her astonishment, she found herself acclaimed a celebrity. She later married a kinsman, Allan MacDonald, and emigrated to America.

As the little boat, carrying Flora, "Betty Burke" and three kinsmen, rolled ashore over the Skye surf, a detachment of militiamen came pelting down the beach to seize them. "Put out again! Pull away!" cried Neil MacDonald.

Flash. Flash. The flash of the muskets reached them before the noise. *Crack. Crack.* Musket balls dug tussocks of spray out of the water. "I beg you, Miss Flora, lie down in the bottom of the boat or you may be hit!" said the prince.

"I shall not, unless you do so yourself, sir," replied Flora.

"Me? I was not designed to die, either by . . ."

"Then I shall not, sir." They argued briefly, while the musket balls kicked splinters out of the boat's side. In the end, the prince had to agree to lie alongside her, while the oarsmen heaved away, and the waves rose up between guns and boat.

At long last they succeeded in landing Bonnie Prince Charlie on Skye – though truly it was no safer a place than any of the others; his life was still in hourly danger. He made a very poor woman, by all accounts. "Your enemies call you the 'Pretender'," joked one friend, "but you are the worst I ever saw!" "Betty" lifted her skirts too high when they forded one stream, and let her petticoats trail in the water at the next one. Passers-by stared at her, house-maids fled her. It was finally decided that "she" would be safer dressed as a man.

And so it was to a Scotsman, dressed in traditional tartan coat and waist-coat, kilt, wig and bonnet that Flora MacDonald said farewell. The militia were closing in; cordons were thrown across the countryside like nets to catch salmon. And yet the prince was still smiling when she parted from him, still confident that he would reach France and come back one day as king. It was that certainty which made his supporters believe in him when all hope seemed gone. But it was their selfless bravery which saved Charles's skin and wrapped him round in the myth of the "bold young chevalier".

"Give Us Back Our Eleven Days!"

1751

EVERYONE KNOWS THAT there are 365 days in a year. By 1752, nearly everyone knew why: because it takes 365 days for the earth to circle the sun once.

But astronomy, though it deals with such vastnesses as space and time, is an exact science. The cleverest of astronomers had already worked out that it took precisely 365 days 5 hours 48 minutes and 49 seconds – which is exact, but harder to remember. Also, calendars are incapable of dealing in hours and minutes and seconds.

If left uncorrected, century by century, a gap would develop between the seasonal year and the calendar – summer would fall in spring, winter in the autumn.

The Romans had found the solution centuries before – the leap year – and in 1582 the Pope had adjusted his calendar to match that of the Caesars. England, however, had not. In 1752 Parliament decided to accept the New Style Calendar. It almost solved the problem. Only eleven days were left – the accumulation of 1,500 years of sloppy time-keeping. The only tiny adjustment which still remained was to change 3 September to 14 September, and England and Europe could start again, level.

Say, "Time" to an astronomer, and he sees planets swinging through aeons of silent space.

Say "Time" to a mathematician and he sees a column of figures.

But say "Time" to ordinary, uneducated people who can neither read nor add up and have no interest in astronomy, and they see a collection of minutes with birth at one end and death at the other. The Bible speaks of three score years and ten allotted by God to Man. But precious few people lived to seventy in 1751, and death lurked in ambush round every corner. Suddenly it was announced that 3 September had become 14 September, and all they could see was that they were eleven days closer to their deaths.

Eleven sweet days had been sliced out of their lives; eleven days in which to earn money to feed their children, eleven days to share with their families before they died. It was as if they had gone to sleep and woken up eleven days later. They were convinced they had been robbed: the Great Time Robbery. No matter what the clever, educated people said – "All right for them; they live longer than us!" – the poor, unlettered, uninformed common people did not listen. Panic made them deaf. They poured on to the streets, rioting and yelling, "Give us back our eleven days! Give us back our eleven days!"

The Church might have soothed them. But churchmen (who tend to deplore change) dug in their heels and complained that the religious festivals were fixed by God and that Parliament could not slide them about like so many pieces on a chessboard. "We shall abide by the old ways!" they said, and clung doggedly and unhelpfully to their old calendars. Anything sooner than conform to a popish one. There was only one thing for the Government to do: wait for the outrage to burn itself out, for the protests to fizzle out, and for the eleven days to be forgotten.

Time, after all, is a great healer.

The Julian Calendar, adopted by Julius Caesar in 46 BC, was reformed in 1582 by Pope Gregory XIII: 5 October became 15 October. Italy, France, Spain and Portugal accepted this, but England and Russia (disinclined to do anything at the suggestion of a pope) did not. Two hundred years later, Europe and England were operating eleven days apart, and the 4th Earl of Chesterfield took it upon himself to put matters right. He published articles, then drew up a bill to put it through Parliament. Not only was 3 September to become 14 September, New Year's Day – formerly 25 March - was now to be 1 January. Chesterfield never foresaw what a furore he would cause.

You would expect the hundredth year of every century to be a leap year. But, to keep the New Style Calendar accurate, only one century in four follows this rule.

Slave in a Free Country

1763-1765

"SHIPPED BY THE grace of God in good order and well conditioned, 200 slaves marked and numbered . . . God send the good ship to her desired port safely. Amen."

So read the bill of lading on the day 200 (or 300 or 500) men, women and children were herded aboard a ship, branded with hot irons, manacled and kept in order with whips and boiling water. This was the slave trade, and until 200 years ago, it was thought of as any other trade. The Africans carried off by force from their homelands to work as slaves on the cotton and sugar plantations of America and the Caribbean were, in law, "goods and chattels" to be bought and sold like livestock. Such big profits came from the plantations and from the slave trade itself that few questioned the cruelty, the downright sin of enslaving fellow human beings.

Black faces were a common sight in London in the eighteenth century. West Indian merchants would bring with them their household servants. The London newspapers often carried advertisements for runaway slaves, offering a reward for their return. So it was not the novelty of seeing a Negro which stopped Granville Sharp in his tracks that day. It was the desperate state of the young man.

He had a bloody rag tied round his head and was feeling his way along the railings of Mincing Lane, knees bent, back rounded, jaw sagging with misery. The curly black hair above the bandage was crisply matted with blood.

"Who are you, sir? You need help. What has happened to you? I was on my way to visit my brother – he's a doctor. Won't you let me take you to him?"

The man's head rolled on his shoulders. He was close to unconsciousness. "Jonathan Strong, sir . . . my name. My master . . . my master . . ."

Granville's brother took one look and said, "He must be got to St Bartholomew's or he won't last."

On the way to the hospital, they listened, in incoherent snatches, to Strong's story. He was the slave of a Barbados lawyer called David Lisle who had returned to live in London. Lisle had, in a fit of rage, smashed his pistol down repeatedly over Strong's head. Then, finding he had as good as blinded the man, he had pushed him out of doors as being of no further use.

For days Jonathan Strong, his skull fractured, hung between life and death. It was four months before he was able to leave hospital. All this while, the Sharp brothers visited him, and afterwards found him a proper, paying job. He was very happy and undyingly grateful.

But two years later, Jonathan was walking down a London street when a shout made him turn. There, like a scene from his worst dream, stood Lisle, red-faced with fury, pointing his finger at Strong and shouting, "Stop that man! Escaped slave!" A brief scuffle, and Strong was seized; people turned aside to avoid the unpleasantness.

Not so Granville Sharp. When Strong got word to him, Sharp went in high dudgeon to the Lord Mayor's office, and took out a summons against Lisle for detaining Jonathan without a warrant.

It was not that Lisle wanted his slave back for his own use. Seeing his slave was fit to work again – his "damaged property" mended – Lisle promptly "sold" Strong to a Jamaican planter. He shook hands on the deal, at least, though the planter would not part with hard cash until his purchase was aboard ship.

That is why it was the captain of the ship who arrived at court on the day of the Lord Mayor's decision. He had come to collect his cargo.

"It seems to me," said the Lord Mayor querulously, "that the lad has not stolen anything, and is not guilty of any offence. He is therefore at liberty to go where he pleases."

Granville Sharp raised both fists in triumph and his face broke into a grin. But not Strong's. "What's the matter, Jonathan? You're free! Didn't you hear?"

Strong shook his head sadly. "If you think that, sir, you know little of my master."

And he was right. No sooner did he step outside into the street than the sea captain grabbed him by the arm: "You're coming with me, piccaninny."

"Sir! I charge you for an assault!" Sharp's cheeks were flushed and his white lace stock rose and fell as he struggled to master his anger. The captain's hand slid off Jonathan's arm. "I want no trouble, me," he muttered.

Hotly indignant, Sharp strode home, Jonathan following after him with a hasty skip and a jump. While he was in Sharp's company, he was safe; no one dared touch him. And that was almost as good a feeling as being a free man!

The lawyers all told Granville Sharp that, in law, Jonathan was not a man but a "chattel". They said there was no chance of winning any court case. Granville was outraged. Where was the justice in that? So he set about studying the law himself, to find if it were really true. And he published what he discovered:

"There is no law to justify . . . the servitude of any man in England."

Soon everyone was discussing it. At dinner tables up and down the land, families argued and took sides:

"I'll tell you what freedom means – the freedom of an Englishman to trade in slaves, without these meddling do-gooders interfering!"

"Oh, but tolerance and liberty, my dear! They've always been at the backbone of England's greatness! How can there be slaves *in England*? Surely, in England . . ."

Meanwhile, the wheels of law slowly turned. Lisle brought a lawsuit against Granville Sharp. Being a lawyer, he won, too. Triple damages were awarded against Granville. Law, it seemed, had decided that Jonathan Strong was *not* a free man. He was a slave. And that made him the property of Lisle to do with as he liked.

The judgement caused a stir. Granville Sharp was the grandson of a bishop, not to mention a true Good Samaritan. What he had done, he had done out of kindness and Christian charity. And did English law favour *Lisle*? Lisle the brute? Lisle the lawyer? Surely that could not be right?

When, soon after, an almost identical case arose (concerning an escaped slave, James Somersett, wrestled off the London streets and sold back into slavery), the case of Jonathan Strong had so changed public opinion that this time the judge was ready to create legal history.

"As soon as a Negro comes into England, he becomes free," he declared as he gave judgement. The escaped slave left the court a free man.

But it was a judgement made too late to save Jonathan Strong. He was "property" once more: a chattel to be shipped in chains, flogged, forced to work for nothing for the rest of his natural life. Every crusade leaves behind its casualties. Jonathan was not the first, nor the last. He was simply the one whose face haunted Granville's dreams after he saw his friend herded aboard ship for Jamaica and clapped in the hold with the rest of the cargo.

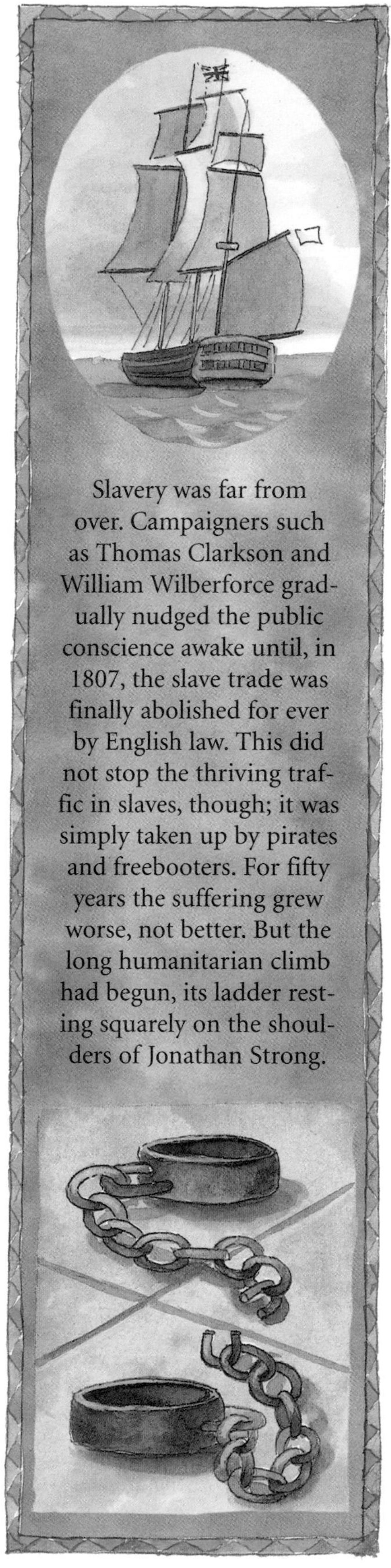

Slavery was far from over. Campaigners such as Thomas Clarkson and William Wilberforce gradually nudged the public conscience awake until, in 1807, the slave trade was finally abolished for ever by English law. This did not stop the thriving traffic in slaves, though; it was simply taken up by pirates and freebooters. For fifty years the suffering grew worse, not better. But the long humanitarian climb had begun, its ladder resting squarely on the shoulders of Jonathan Strong.

Mary's Bible

1804

There was a knock, and Mr Edwards went to the door. It was late for callers, and he was surprised to find a young girl on his doorstep. Her clothes were covered in grass and her hems were black. She looked exhausted. Mr Edwards thought she might be going to ask for money as she thrust a money-box at him.

"Mr Edwards, sir? My name is Mary Jones and I've come from Abergynolwyn. Your friend Mr Hughes sent me. I've been saving up, you see. Are there any left? He said they might all be gone!"

Mr Edwards looked up and down the street for signs of a cart. "You have come all the way from Abergynolwyn today? How did you get here?"

"I walked. I'm good at walking. I walk to school every day and home again."

"But it must be twenty-five miles, child! You must be worn out – famished! Come in, come in!"

As she ate supper, the girl explained in breathless, excitable Welsh, how she had come to buy a Bible with the pennies she had saved.

"Oh, but Mary, do you read English well enough to read the Bible?"

"Oh, not an *English* Bible," Mary said. "I've come to buy a Welsh one."

"Oh, but Mary! Did Mr Hughes not explain? The Bible in English you might just afford, but in Welsh? Welsh editions are fearfully costly."

"That's why it has taken me so long to save up," said Mary patiently. "I knitted socks to sell at market. I helped with the harvest. I did gardening and washing for the neighbours . . . The village helped, too, of course: they gave the last shilling. So it only took me six years."

Mr Edwards was astounded. He gazed at this small, solemn, brown-eyed girl. "And do you mean to say you have worked for six years and come all this way to Bala, just to have a Welsh Bible of your own?"

"It's all I have ever wanted," she said simply. "Ever since the village got a school and I learned to read . . . Do you think there *will* be one left?"

The supplies of Welsh Bibles were indeed strictly limited. They arrived a few at a time, at the house of a local minister, the Reverend Thomas Charles, and quickly sold out – to wealthy householders and clergymen and schools. There was just one left when Mary and Mr Edwards reached the minister's house. The two men watched Mary Jones run her fingers over the tooled binding, the marbled end pages, the maze of Welsh words, then fold it to her chest in blissful delight. A moment later she said, "I must be going. I've twenty-five miles to go by nightfall. It will be easier going back," she explained. "I don't have all that money to carry, and I can always stop along the way and read my Bible."

The Reverend Charles could not get it out of his mind – that young girl's heroic endeavour, her single-minded determination. It thrilled and delighted him . . . and at the same time it enraged him. No one should have to scrimp and save and work and wait six years then walk twenty-five miles to own a Bible in their own language!

At the next conference he went to in London, he stood up and told Mary's story.

"Inspiring!" said the people who heard it. "Marvellous! Charming!"

"Yes, but *wrong*," said the Reverend Charles. "A Bible should not be a luxury, whatever your language. It should be affordable to everyone, rich or poor, Welsh or English."

"No matter what language they speak!" cried a fervent voice from the back of the hall. "So let's do something about it! God has shown us our duty through this child!"

A clamour of boots hammered on the hall floor like a roll of divine thunder.

Out of that evening, the British and Foreign Bible Society was formed – a society which still exists today to make sure the Bible is affordable and available to no matter who, no matter where. And Mary Jones was the cause of it all. It was as if her determination and perseverance had been large enough to inspire a thousand others to do as she had done and to make the impossible happen.

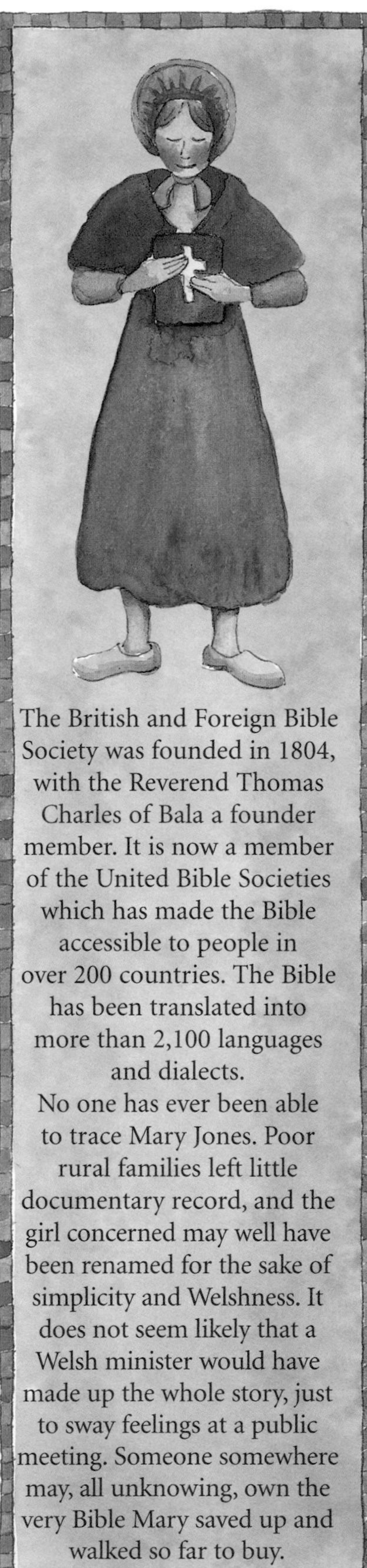

The British and Foreign Bible Society was founded in 1804, with the Reverend Thomas Charles of Bala a founder member. It is now a member of the United Bible Societies which has made the Bible accessible to people in over 200 countries. The Bible has been translated into more than 2,100 languages and dialects.

No one has ever been able to trace Mary Jones. Poor rural families left little documentary record, and the girl concerned may well have been renamed for the sake of simplicity and Welshness. It does not seem likely that a Welsh minister would have made up the whole story, just to sway feelings at a public meeting. Someone somewhere may, all unknowing, own the very Bible Mary saved up and walked so far to buy.

England Expects

1805

THE SNIPER AMONG THE CREW OF THE *REDOUBTABLE* WAS SENT aloft into the rigging as soon as the fleet took up battle formation. The French and Spanish ships of the combined fleet were a magnificent sight, stringing out into a huge crescent – the cupped hand which would seize England for Emperor Napoleon Bonaparte. Nothing stood in Napoleon's way but this last great sea battle. Trafalgar, it would be called, after the nearby Spanish headland.

Through his spyglass, the French sniper saw the flagship, *Victory*, and a tingling shiver ran through him. Nelson's ship! Heart of the English fleet. Within its soaring wooden walls rode the commander-in-chief on whom the English pinned all their hopes: the famous admiral who suffered seasickness when he put to sea!

Soon the British fleet would also be stringing out into a crescent opposite the combined fleet, and the two lines of ships would blast relentlessly away at each other with cannon fire until one side or other could take no more. The sniper breathed a prayer for his ship's safe deliverance.

But the British fleet did not string out. It came steadily on – two clusters of warships sailing head-on into the crescent. It was madness! Without turning broadside to the enemy, they could not fire their guns! With a roar like a dragon waking, the French and Spanish cannon opened fire. For twenty minutes they spat venom at the *Victory* and the huddle of ships beyond her, and yet the British fleet did not turn to fire a single shot in return! The signal flags with which Nelson had addressed his sailors – "England expects that every man will do his duty" – soon hung in smoke-soiled rags and tatters, the rigging in knotty festoons.

But at the end of that twenty minutes, the *Victory* was passing close by the stern of Villeneuve's flagship, the *Bucentaure*, gun doors open, cannon primed. When at last she fired such a broadside into the *Bucentaure*, 400 men fell instantly to the deck, dead or wounded.

Suddenly the English ships were rubbing sides with the French and Spanish ones, firing into them from such close range that great gaping holes were blasted in the wood walls, and buckled cannon rolled over into the sea. Villeneuve had never encountered these tactics, and by the time he realized that Nelson had rewritten the manual of sea-going warfare, it was too late to think up counter measures. The English ships grappled with the combined fleet, and English sailors swarmed over on to French and Spanish decks. The battle of Trafalgar was to begin with a surprise and end in hand-to-hand combat.

Up on his masthead perch, the French sniper watched in horror the rack of the combined fleet. He saw twelve good ships sunk or disabled, saw his own ship grappled and pulled close to the *Victory. Redoubtable* heeled and lurched over. The top of the mizzen mast was caught in the broken and flying rigging of the *Victory* and, for a while, the two ships clung to each other like wrestlers in a fight to the death.

And there he was on the quarter-deck: Nelson! It had to be him! His uniform did not give him away, for he was not wearing all the gold braid and epaulettes of dress uniform, but he was wearing the four medals of knighthood which his adoring country had awarded him. And it was on those medals that the sniper took aim.

Such a tiny man – small as Napoleon himself! Skinny, too. Only one arm, one eye and built like a sickly stray kitten. How had this man cast such a vast shadow over the destiny of his country? The sniper's hands shook with excitement, but he aimed true. He could at least make Horatio Nelson pay for thwarting Bonaparte. The flash of the musket blinded him for a moment, then the smoke cleared, and he saw Nelson on his knees – a frozen tableau of officers watching their commander fall. Nelson slumped over on to his side.

Someone shouted, "There he is!"

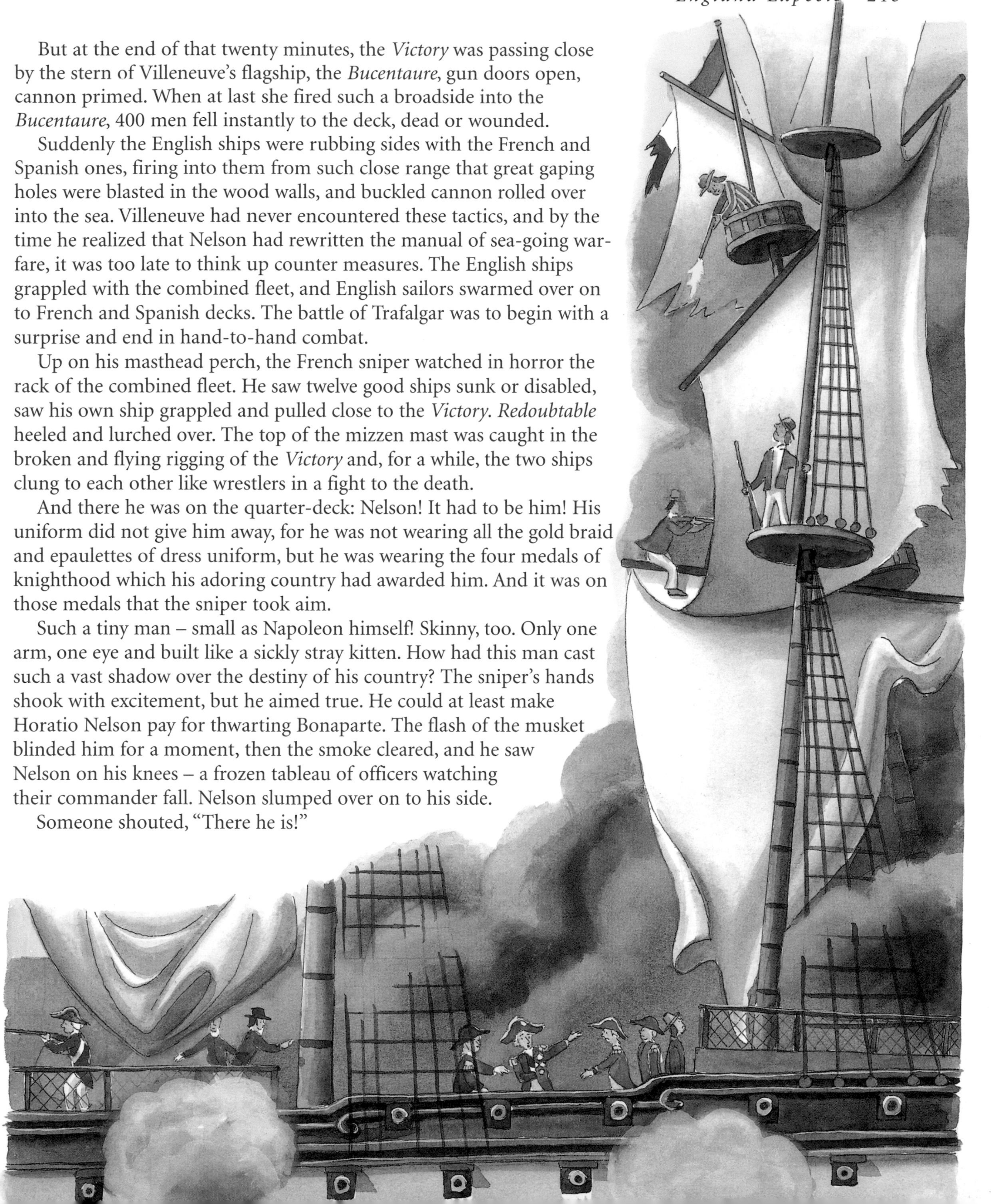

The Frenchman in the rigging of the *Redoubtable* put a hand to his chest in wonderment. Could he be feeling the little Englishman's pain! Was this the penance for taking a hero's life? To feel his death pangs? Then the sniper looked down and understood. He saw the English sharp-shooter, musket smoking. As he fell out of the rigging, he thought: "*Enfin. Je l'ai tué*." At least I killed him.

Nelson was carried gently below decks. Officers clamoured and crowded round, calling for the ship's surgeon, telling themselves that he was not badly hurt . . . But Horatio Nelson knew he was dying. Inside his head images of his past life were flooding in like the sea into a holed ship: the coldness of the surgeon's knife that day his arm was amputated; the glitter of flying stone fragments before his right eye was blinded. The polar bear loomed up again over him which, at sixteen, he had fought on the Arctic pack-ice. The parsonage where he was born. The face of Lady Hamilton, passion of his life. One kiss from her soft lips and the pain in his side would surely cease . . .

"Kiss me, Hardy," said Nelson, to the officer crouching beside him. They puzzled over it a long while after. Had he perhaps said, "Kismet – (Fate) – Hardy"? They scribbled them down, these last, strange words of a famous man. "Have them take care of Lady Hamilton. Without my protection, I fear . . ." Hardy soothed his commander with assurances, promises, a kiss of farewell. Word came that the battle was won; England had carried the day. "Thank God – I have done my duty," whispered Nelson.

Not far off, an explosion seemed to rupture the ocean: a French battleship burnt down to its store of gunpowder. Before the splinters of timber had finished rattling down on to the littered sea, Horatio Nelson was dead.

The other casualties were buried at sea, but Nelson was the hero of the hour; he must receive a funeral befitting a saviour of his country. So his little battered and maimed body was put into a barrel, steeped in brandy to preserve it, and guarded night and day by a sailor with a drawn sabre. HMS *Victory* limped home, as mangled by war as Nelson had been, slow to reach harbour and the waiting crowds.

As well as the grand officials, the knights and earls and statesmen who walked behind the flag-draped coffin to St Paul's Cathedral were forty-eight common sailors who had served under Nelson. Weeping openly, those forty-eight were allowed to tear fragments from the flag as keepsakes of their dead commander.

But Emma Hamilton, great love of Nelson's life, was shunned, abandoned to poverty and loneliness. It was as if the nation's tears had blinded them to her very existence.

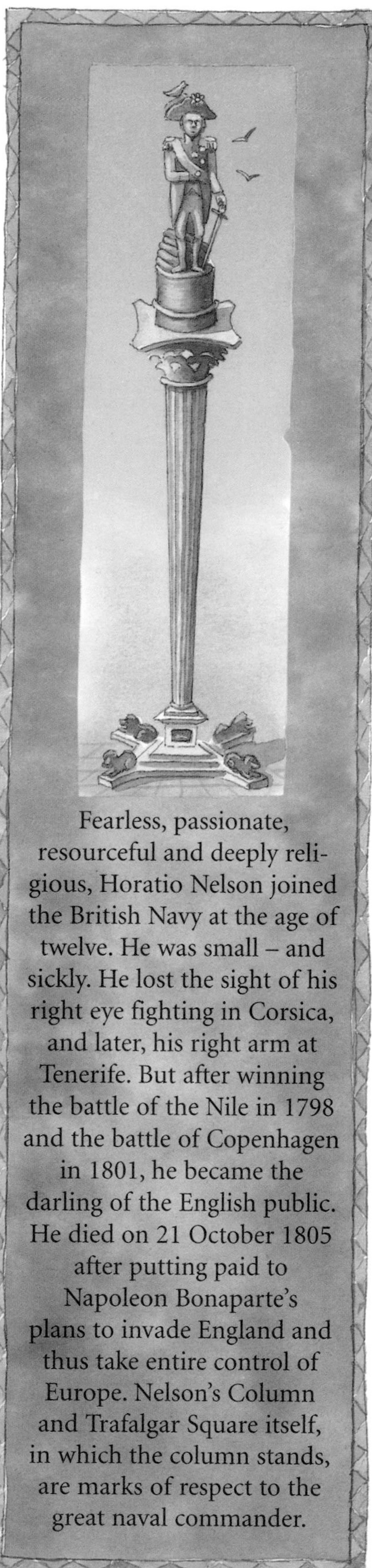

Fearless, passionate, resourceful and deeply religious, Horatio Nelson joined the British Navy at the age of twelve. He was small – and sickly. He lost the sight of his right eye fighting in Corsica, and later, his right arm at Tenerife. But after winning the battle of the Nile in 1798 and the battle of Copenhagen in 1801, he became the darling of the English public. He died on 21 October 1805 after putting paid to Napoleon Bonaparte's plans to invade England and thus take entire control of Europe. Nelson's Column and Trafalgar Square itself, in which the column stands, are marks of respect to the great naval commander.

The *Rocket* Speeds to Victory

1829

"NOW LADS, I VENTURE TO TELL YOU THAT I think you will live to see the day when railways will supersede almost all other methods of conveyance in this country, when mail coaches will go by railway and railroads will become the great highways for the King and all his subjects." In the heady excitement of the opening, George Stephenson's words swept his employees up on a tide of enthusiasm. They cheered and stamped their heavy boots. But could it really be true? Could railways really be the transport of the future? Here, at Stockton, they were busy assembling a 90-ton train the like of which had never been seen before: six freight wagons, a covered coach for VIPs, twenty-one coal wagons kitted out to carry 450 passengers, and six more full of coal! And *Locomotion* was supposed to pull it – an engine barely taller than a man, Stephenson's brainchild. In front rode a horseman holding a green flag – almost as if they were going into battle.

But as the train gathered speed, Stephenson had to shout for the flag-man to get out of the way. Other riders galloping alongside for the sport of racing the train were left far behind, as *Locomotion* accelerated to the fabulous speed of 15 miles an hour (24 kph)!

There was a hero's welcome waiting in Darlington – and 150 more passengers and a brass band wanting to join the return journey to Stockton.

The Stockton–Darlington line, though, was just a freight line – a means of shifting large quantities of coal very cheaply along a shuttle line. When it came to building the first passenger line, from Liverpool to Manchester, the investors employed George Stephenson as chief engineer, laying the tracks, but announced a competition to find the best locomotive for the route. The deadline was 6 October 1829, the prize £500.

This time George worked with his son Robert to develop his entry for the competition. They incorpo-

rated a tubular boiler, which allowed large quantities of water to be heated up at any one time. There were two other locomotives entered: Braithwaite and Ericsson's *Novelty,* and the *Sans Pareil* built by Hackworth. Between 6 and 14 October, there was a gala atmosphere at Rainhill, Liverpool, with huge crowds attending every day, bands playing and a great grandstand seating such dignitaries as the Duke of Wellington, then Prime Minister.

The referees looked over the *Sans Pareil* and declared it did not comply with the rules . . . but she would be allowed to compete anyway. The course was a stretch of track rather more than two kilometres in length, which had to be completed, there-and-back, ten times over. On the eighth trip the pump broke and the *Sans Pareil* puttered to a halt.

The crowd had taken a fancy to the *Novelty*: it was small and spry, with only the vestige of a chimney, and a jolly red flag flying. But with an alarming bang, the boiler blew after just two trips. "And they say these things will take the place of horses?" people snorted to one another.

Up and down, up and down, up and down went the *Rocket.* Tireless as a donkey giving rides on a beach, the *Rocket* lumbered to and fro. Pulling a load of 17 tons, she travelled the 30 miles stipulated – then she travelled them again to please the crowds. At one point she touched 30 mph (48 kph) – faster than any stagecoach could go. The crowd was a roaring sea of cheers, thousands of day trippers witnessing this dawn of a new age. The Duke of Wellington stood up in the bandstand and waved his hat as Stephenson's *Rocket* trundled by yet again, steam flaring from the crown-shaped tip of its sturdy flue.

One year later, a similar locomotive was coupled up to thirty-three carriages, all packed with notables: the Duke of Wellington, Sir Robert Peel, the Rt Hon William Huskisson MP for Liverpool . . . and steamed out of Liverpool to the music of an on-board band. Despite the flying smuts which blackened their faces and clothes, despite the noise, and the juddering of the hard seats, the passengers were cock-a-hoop. They were in at the beginning of something momentous. Here was history in the making!

At Parkside, the train wheezed to a halt to take on water. Some of the gentlemen passengers, including Mr Huskisson, got off to stretch their legs. They strolled down the track . . . ignorant of the fact that another string of carriages was moving down the adjacent track. As they saw the danger, the knot of men scattered, all jumping clear of the tracks, except for Mr Huskisson, who tried to re-board the train.

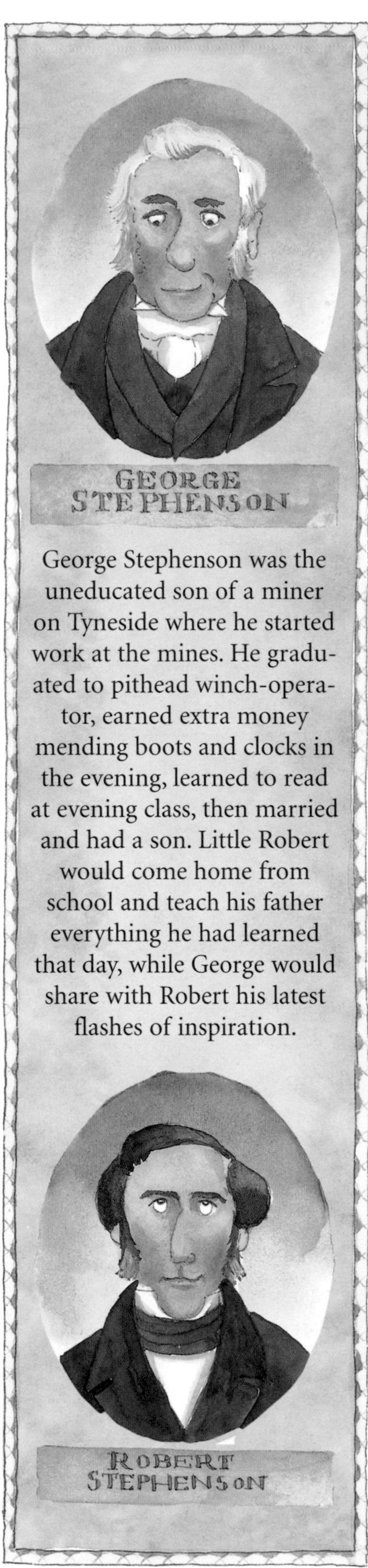

He got the carriage door open, but it swung back on him and barged him off his feet – knocked him on to the rails, in fact, where one of the great slicing, steel wheels rolled over him.

Suddenly there was no more music, no more singing, no more cheering. As the litter bearers carried the man away and the locomotive gathered speed, its steam cast a pall over thirty-three silent carriages. Women dabbing cinders from their eyes, dabbed away tears as well. It was no longer a day of triumphant celebration. William Huskisson had died of his injuries. The festivities planned in Manchester were cancelled. George put his arm around his son's shoulders. "There's no undoing what's done," he said. "No going back."

The Resurrection Men

1829

"ANOTHER ONE FOR THE GRAVEROBBERS, EH, William?" said Burke.

"Disgraceful trade. Fancy a man engaging in a Godless business like that, William," replied Hare with a snigger. "Sacrilege, I call it."

Many of the graves in the cemetery had recently been surrounded with great iron railings – as though the dead had been penned into their plots. But then, understandably, mourners did not want grave robbers digging up their nearest and dearest within hours of them being laid to rest. And there was a thriving market for bodies dug up on dark nights among the lowering yew trees. The medical profession needed its cadavers and would pay good money for one, without asking where it came from. The police were cracking down, patrolling cemeteries, making arrests, but even so, today's grave would have a grille of iron around it before nightfall.

The crunch, crunch of the constable's boots on the pavement behind them held no fear for Hare and Burke. Their conciences were clear. As far as they were concerned, the crack-down on grave-robbing could only serve to boost business; they were not in that line of work.

"Our meat is *fresher*, eh William?" whispered Hare, and lifted his hat to the constable.

Burke and Hare went home to their wives, and their wives agreed: there were easier ways to lay hands on supplies than wrestling iron bars in the graveyard and dodging watchful policemen. They all went out to an inn for supper, and struck up a friendship there with a young man.

"Won't you come home for a nightcap?" asked Mrs Hare. "William and I do so welcome company…"

Burke set down a sack in the ill-lit basement yard, and money changed hands. Their customer was bursting to tell them of a comical story he had just read in his newspaper. "Did you hear tell of the old woman who sneezed?" he snickered. "I read they opened the coffin – and up she sat and sneezed! Ha! ha! ha!"

"There's no fear you'll be troubled in that way," muttered Hare. "This one died of natural causes

Ever since medicine became a clinical science, there has been a need for cadavers or dead bodies. Students of medicine need to dissect bodies to understand the nature and workings of human anatomy. In nineteenth-century Edinburgh (as elsewhere) they were kept supplied by body-snatchers who stole newly-buried corpses from graveyards. In Edinburgh, Doddingston Village churchyard was frequently pillaged by these so-called "Resurrection Men". Fortifying the graves, and a police crackdown in the 1820s helped to stamp out the practice. But some body-snatchers simply resorted to a worse way of acquiring bodies. William Hare and William Burke may never even have bothered to rob graves. They were arrested in 1829 for murdering fifteen people for the sake of their cadavers. Their wives had helped them lure victims to their deaths. Hare offered to co-operate in return for supplying evidence which sent Burke to the gallows; in fact he was probably the worse villain of the two.

three days back." There was a brief glimmer of light as the sack was taken in at a basement door, then renewed darkness.

Next day, as the student doctors crowded about the scrubbed dissecting table of Edinburgh University, the corpse upon it was the finest yet. It showed no sign of decay. It had surely never lain underground, in the damp Edinburgh clay. In fact the young man lying dead on the table looked very much as he had looked in life, apart from a certain blueness in the face.

"Good God! I know him!" exclaimed one of the students, turning deathly white.

"Didn't you know he was dead? Didn't anyone tell you he died?" his colleagues asked, each wondering how he would feel if the body in front of him proved not to be a nameless stranger.

"And how would they? I was *drinking* with him last night!" spluttered the student.

"I fear our friends have overstepped the mark this time," remarked Dr Knox.

But he continued his lecture. For it was hardly *his* fault if Burke and Hare had graduated from grave-robbing to cold-blooded murder. And there was no point in wasting such an excellent cadaver.

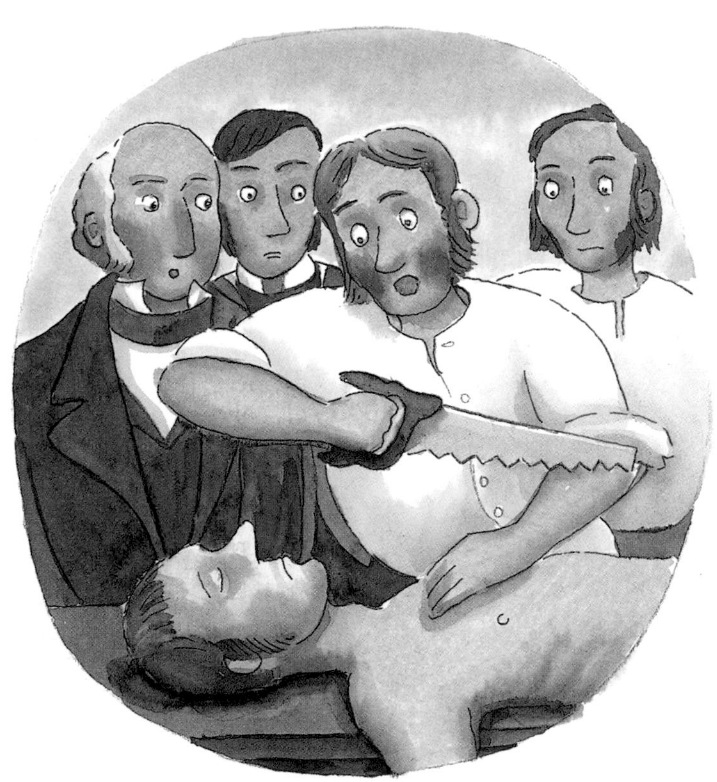

Victoria's Room

1837

"I CRIED MUCH," WROTE ALEXANDRINA VICTORIA in her diary that night. She was eleven years old, and she had just been told the secret her mother had been keeping from her: one day she would be queen.

Why did she cry? Perhaps she was afraid. Perhaps she could see ahead of her a life of unrelenting hard work, never free to do as she liked. Maybe she thought that the loneliness of her childhood would now go on for ever.

At least now she could make sense of all the studying her mother made her do, all the huffy unkindness of her English relations who looked upon her as a little German interloper, all the loneliness.

Once a week, a child was invited to play – a child chosen by her mother. Not the same child every week, so that they could become firm friends. Never anyone silly or mischievous who might make her laugh – just a succession of miscellaneous strangers, once a week. "I may call you Jane, but you must not call me Victoria," she would tell them, not knowing why, only knowing that life was governed by her mother's rules. She had her dolls – her host of elegant china-headed dolls. But somehow they were not the same as having a true friend.

For all she was a princess, no one showered her with toys or treats or sweets. No, it was bread and milk out of a little silver bowl for Victoria. She was not allowed to read stories: after all, what *use* were stories except for frivolous entertainment?

Lonely but never alone, Victoria could not even escape to the solitude of her own bedroom. Every night she had to bed down in the great hollow emptiness of her mother's bedroom, and every time she woke, it was to the sound of her mother's soft breathing. Sixteen, seventeen, eighteen, and still she was sharing a bedroom! How she longed for a room of her own.

Victoria woke one morning sensing that something momentous had happened. Her mother was whispering to her in German: to get up, to put on her wrapper; there was an important visitor to see her. Fuddled with sleep, her heart jumpy with odd foreboding, Alexandrina Victoria fumbled her feet into her satin slippers and made herself presentable.

As soon as she saw the Archbishop of Canterbury, po-faced, holding himself as he did at state occasions, she knew that someone had died. It was her Uncle William, he told her. The King of England was dead.

With a rustling flurry, like a theatre curtain falling, the ladies in the room sank down. For a moment Victoria thought they had fainted with shock, but no. They were curtseying to their new monarch – to her – to eighteen-year-old Queen Victoria.

A million thoughts and images tumbled through her head in those first few moments: the hot, distant countries she had never seen and over which she now held absolute sway. Those dark, frightful valleys she had visited with her mother, where coal dust had turned all the

After moving to Buckingham Palace, Victoria arranged for her mother's suite of apartments to be a long way from her own. By 1840, she was no longer lonely: she had married her cousin Albert – a suitable candidate found for her by her family, but a love-match as far as Victoria was concerned. They were to have nine children.
The English monarchy was in a bad state when Victoria came to the throne. A string of kings, mad, bad or just plain despised had brought royalty into disrepute. She changed all that. She ruled for longer than any other monarch in the history of England. Albert fired her with enthusiasm and energy for all kinds of projects, including the Great Exhibition of 1851. She was a devoted mother, had a will of steel and ruled at a time when the economy was, in any case, thriving. In 1876, she became Empress of India. The British people, the British Empire, adored their little Queen, and when Albert died and she retired into perpetual mourning, they resented her absence from public life. She died aged eighty-one and gave her name to an entire era.

people and houses and grass coal-black. All those huge cathedrals and little parish churches where every day from now on prayers would be offered up for "Victoria our Queen". The Houses of Parliament which smelled of leather and passed the laws to which she must now set her signature. The marriage which would now be arranged for her – how she hoped it could be to cousin Albert! She thought of the pageant of kings and queens which had already filed past into history, of the soldiers in red who would die for her in foreign wars. All these thoughts and more fell like an avalanche on Victoria, on this tiny, slender girl in her night clothes.

But her first command, as Queen of England, was for a room to be prepared: a room of her own.

"I will try to fulfil my duty towards my country and to do what is fit and right," she wrote that night. And when she closed her diary, the room around her listened in respectful silence. Though a thousand choices were closed to her, she felt a new sense of freedom. It was up to her now, how she lived the lonely life of a queen.

Her china-headed dolls sat quietly round, watching her, outnumbered now by millions of other loyal subjects.

Fire Down Below

1838

DR DIONYSIUS LARDNER SAID IT COULDN'T BE done. No steamship could carry enough fuel, he said, to voyage more than 2,000 miles, and America was 3,000 miles away; it was totally impractical to talk of sailing steamships between England and New York.

The shipping companies prayed he was wrong. To win the race across the Atlantic was everything. The rewards would be huge to whichever steamship company could first prove Dionysius Lardner mistaken!

Whichever ship was first across the Atlantic was certain to make headline news. Already the *Sirius* was preparing to set sail from Cork in Ireland – the furthermost westerly point. But a rival ship was out to beat her – and to beat her in style, sailing not from Ireland but from England, a day farther east.

On Saturday, 31 March, the SS *Great Western*, dream-child of Isambard Kingdom Brunel, set sail from Blackwall Docks in London. Down the Thames, round the south coast and she would be in Bristol, bound for New York. There were passengers in plenty ready to sail on her: after all, her designer was an acknowledged genius. Brunel had built bridges and viaducts, railways and tunnels. He had spanned gorges and linked cities . . . and now he had turned his attentions to the Atlantic.

But at the mouth of the Thames, disaster struck. The brand-new felt cladding the brand-new boilers caught fire, filling the engine room with dense, choking smoke. Captain Claxton ran the *Great Western* ashore on the mudflats and everyone tackled the fire.

Claxton himself went down into the noxious fumes and the heat. Overhead, flames were licking the underside of the decking. The boiler was singing with heat. The great pillars of steel, like the columns of a Greek temple, were ringing with a discordant music all their own. Claxton called for the fire-hose to be turned on and directed it at the fire which hissed steam, in addition to the smoke and fumes. Soon he was ankle-deep in water, and the fire reduced to sullen red embers glimmering in the corners of the boiler room like the eyes of a hundred rats.

All of a sudden, a weight like a sack of grain fell on him from above, knocking all the wind out of him. He cursed choicely and picked himself up. What had hit him? Who was dropping things on to him from the open hatchway? None too gently, he felt for the thing with his foot: it was soft and sodden. A man! And, lying face-down in dirty water, he was either dead already or about to drown! Instantly Claxton snatched hold of him. Then he cursed again. "Hoi! Up there! Fetch ropes! Hurry! It's Brunel! He's fallen!"

I.K. Brunel began his career working for his engineer father. He went on to become chief engineer of the Great Western Railway, designing lines, trains, sheds and stations, then set his sights on grander, interlinked networks of travel. After the *Great Western* came the *Great Britain*, at that time the biggest ship in the world, the first with an iron-hull, the first to be driven by a screw-propeller rather than paddle-wheels. Next came the monumental *Great Eastern*, four times larger, capable of carrying a year's exports to India in one trip. In no other age could Brunel have achieved what he did. The Victorian passion for tech-no-logy put him to work and, in return, he added hugely to Victorian prosperity. Bridges, railways, buildings, ships, tunnels, viaducts still exist today as monuments to his genius.

In climbing down to help Claxton, Brunel had rested his foot on a burned rung which gave way. If Claxton had not been standing underneath, he would have crashed on to metal from a dizzying height.

Claxton tied a rope under his friend's armpits, and somehow they manhandled Brunel up through the funnelling smoke and steam towards the blue square of the forehatch. Even laid out on deck, with a sail for a bed, he remained unable to speak. But until the fire was under control there was no time to care for him any more tenderly.

They set him ashore at Canvey Island, and sailed on without him. They were in Bristol within forty-eight hours. It astounded the crowds who had heard tell of the fire and quite thought the *Great Western* a burned-out hulk in the Thames estuary. Here she was, with nothing to show for the fire but a few scorchmarks.

They would not sail on her, though. Only seven passengers were ready to put their faith in the *Great Western*; the rest had been scared off by the fire. For those seven it was a memorable voyage. One wrote in his journal that New York harbour was crowded with welcoming boats, "Flags were flying, guns were firing, and cheering rose from the shore, the boats and all around loudly and gloriously . . . It was a moment of triumph."

Not that they had won the race: *Sirius* had arrived just hours before, despite departing earlier and farther west. But *her* coal had been all used up, and her crew had had to burn everything combustible on board – including passengers' luggage – just to make harbour. The *Great Western*, on the other hand, had used only three-quarters of her fuel. Dr Lardner had been proved wrong: steamships *could* link England and America.

Sixty-eight passengers made the return voyage to England, and for twenty years the SS *Great Western* plied the oceans of the world, a handsome tribute to her designer. When she was broken up in 1857, Isambard Kingdom Brunel was there to bid her farewell.

Saving Grace

1838

IT WAS FOUR IN THE MORNING WHEN GRACE PULLED ON HER CLOTHES AND climbed the stairs to the light. It was her turn to check the lighthouse lamp then sit up, so that her father could get to bed. All around her the storm raged: torrential rain and the everlasting thunder of the sea rolling against England's north-east coast, breaking against the Longstone Rock, throwing its spray as high as her bedroom just below the lamp. The noise of it drowned out even the click of the lighthouse engine as she sat in her room watching for first light when she must douse the light. Her window was cloudy with condensation from her wet stockings and petticoat. She and Father had got soaked through the previous afternoon, lashing down the coble-boat.

It was not until she went back up the steep steps to put out the light that she looked across towards Brownsman Island to glimpse her old home and saw not the abandoned buildings of Brownsman Island but the huge, dark looming prow of a ship.

"Father! Father! Father! A wreck! A wreck, Father!" she shouted, running backwards down the spiral stairs. "A ship is wrecked on Big Harcar!"

"Now God help us, and your brother not here!"

From five till seven they stood there in the lamp room, William Darling holding a telescope, Grace a pair of field glasses. The storm-clouds kept the scene almost as dark as night, and all they could make out was that the vessel was a steam paddle-ship – the *Forfarshire*, perhaps. And if it were the *Forfarshire*, William knew there were probably sixty people on board.

It was not until the eye of the storm passed over the reef that a shaft of light, like God's own sword-blade, lit Big Harcar and showed the huddle of people clinging to the rock itself.

"Can it be done, Father?" asked Grace.

"Maybe, if Brooks were here."

It was true, that if Grace's brother, Brooks, had been at home that night, instead of on the mainland, he would have gone with his father in the coble – gone to try to lift those people off before the sea did. "Then I must take Brooks's part!" said Grace.

Her mother was dead set against it. She had heard the bang of the maroons – the signal which summoned out the lifeboat – and she knew the coble needed three strong men to row it in rough weather.

But William Darling knew the lifeboat would never arrive in time. The sea's huge swell heaved up like a great grey tongue to lap at the survivors. He must mount a rescue mission or stand and watch those people washed away, one by one.

Instead of a tender goodbye, Grace got nothing but reproach from her mother, who said she would hold Grace to blame if William drowned. Grabbing up a shawl, a blanket and a bonnet, and slipping off her flannel petticoat to save it getting soaked, Grace helped her father unlash the rowing boat. Spray covered her like thick, white sheets. The oars rattled like bones in their rowlocks. But Grace rowed. Sometimes the water tried to wrench the oar out of her hand, at others she found herself scooping at empty air, but she went on rowing. She rowed alongside her father, her shoulder against his, as though through a tunnel of sea. She rowed until her hands were full of blisters. All she could think of were those other cold, white hands clinging and clawing, slipping and losing their grip on the treacherous rocks. Big Harcar was no more than a perch for puffins, a basking place for seals; its rocks disappeared with every breaking wave.

They could not row there direct, but had to let the wind drive the little boat south, into the lee of the reef and then row in from there. And *if* there was someone there, among the survivors on the rock – some strong, uninjured man not yet perished with cold or mad with fright – they might just be able to make the rescue and get back to the lighthouse. If not, there was no chance. Grace and her father would join the casualties lost in the sinking of the steamer.

Back in the lighthouse, Mrs Darling watched for a sight of them. Despite a lifelong horror of heights, she dragged herself up one flight of stairs after another, hoping each one would raise her high enough to see over the towering waves. But the little coble had utterly disappeared, as if the sea had swallowed it whole. Fainting with horror, it was not until she came round that she glimpsed it – pitching like a shuttlecock over the mountainous swell.

There were nine on the rocks, including one woman, clasping her two dead children, not realizing the cold had stolen them from her. And there *was* a seaman still calm, still strong enough to pull on an oar. For a few horrific minutes, William Darling leapt across to the rock, and Grace was left trying to hold the boat steady, all alone, with oars set so far apart that her arms were at full stretch just to grip them.

Five people were taken off. The other four had to wait for the coble to make a return trip. Two of the men agreed to go with William on that second voyage. So while Mrs Darling and Grace wrapped the survivors in blankets and plied them with black tea, the lighthouse keeper went out again into the storm, which was working itself into a frenzy. Grace and her mother hardly expected to see him again. But finally, finally, he and the other six staggered in, dumb with weariness, numb with cold, their faces caked into masks by the sea's salt.

Like the pillar of stillness at the centre of a tornado, the Longstone Lighthouse cocooned those twelve people until the sea slackened, the clouds cleared and the rain ceased to fall. While they waited, William Darling wrote up his report on the wreck, mentioning only in passing that nine lives had been "saved by the Darlings". Little did he know what a storm of praise, congratulation, publicity and admiration would break over their heads when the rescue was reported. When people read in their papers of the lighthouse keeper and his brave daughter, Grace's adventure had only just begun.

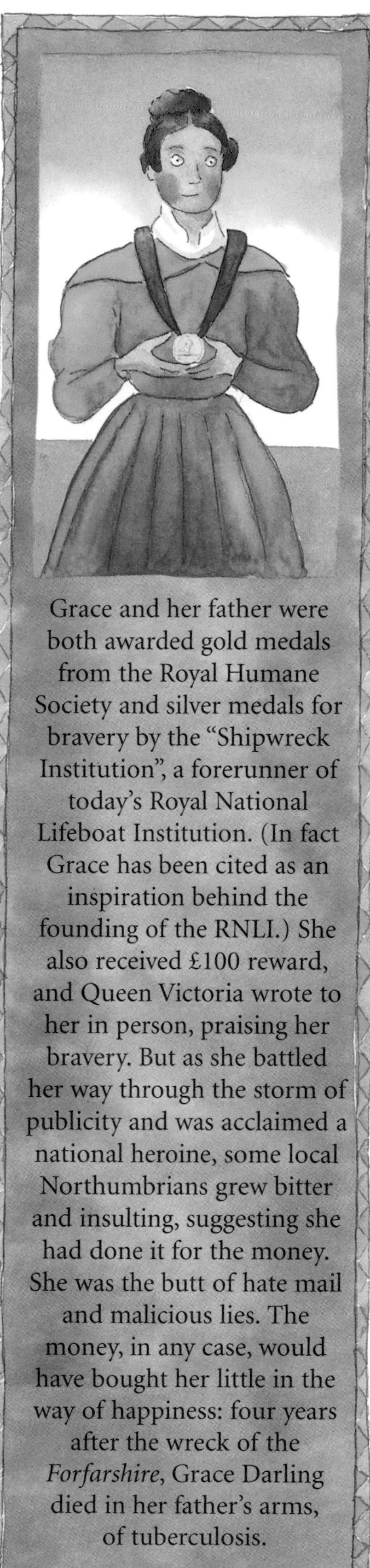

Grace and her father were both awarded gold medals from the Royal Humane Society and silver medals for bravery by the "Shipwreck Institution", a forerunner of today's Royal National Lifeboat Institution. (In fact Grace has been cited as an inspiration behind the founding of the RNLI.) She also received £100 reward, and Queen Victoria wrote to her in person, praising her bravery. But as she battled her way through the storm of publicity and was acclaimed a national heroine, some local Northumbrians grew bitter and insulting, suggesting she had done it for the money. She was the butt of hate mail and malicious lies. The money, in any case, would have bought her little in the way of happiness: four years after the wreck of the *Forfarshire*, Grace Darling died in her father's arms, of tuberculosis.

Rebecca and Her Daughters

1840s

"And they blessed Rebekah and said unto her, Let thy seed possess the gate of those which hate them." That was the verse which began it. That was where the Bible fell open, those were the words which sprang off the page. Just when every Welsh heart was brooding bitterly about having to pay tolls to the Government – just to be allowed to pass along a road! – there was the Good Book speaking out on the matter. And the Welsh have always taken their Bible seriously.

Dafyd, the Turnpike, keeper of the toll-gate on the London road, woke to the sound of horns and whistles and gunfire, and tumbled out of bed. Along the road came a crowd of people led by five or six women – at least they were *dressed* like women. They wore bonnets and dresses and aprons, though to judge by the size of their boots, they were six feet tall and shaved once a week. The people in the procession behind them were locals – poor hill-farmers, dyers and tradesmen. Dafyd knew it, though it was hard to make out particular faces in the dark.

"Now I don't want no trouble," said Dafyd, trying to sound commanding (though that is difficult for a man in his nightshirt). "Why don't you all go off home now?"

The biggest of the "women" simply turned to the crowd and said, in a ringing Welsh bass, "My children, this gate has no business here, has it?"

The crowd roared, "No, Mother, it has not!"

"Then what is to be done with it, children?"

"Mother, it must be levelled to the ground!"

Then the axes came out. Rebecca and her Daughters were destroying yet another toll-gate, hacking the bars from their cross-trees, the hinges from their posts.

Dafyd ran a few steps forwards. After all, he was paid to man the gate; he ought to defend it. But the Daughters restrained him with huge, calloused hands. "We mean you no harm, man. Best just pack up your things."

Knowing that already half the toll-gates in Carmarthen were down, Dafyd hurried indoors and began to carry his few possessions – bed and chair, breadbin and toolbag – out of doors. Then the toll-booth too was destroyed – set alight with Dafyd's own lantern.

The horns and whistles blew, the guns sent Dafyd's cat haring into the wood, then "Rebecca and her Daughters" were gone. The local people disbanded silently and the darkness swallowed them up.

Within the hour, a detachment of special constables came trotting along the road to where Dafyd sat in his fireside chair on the grass verge of the road. "You're too late, as usual," he said. "Far too late."

In Carmarthen that June, thousands of protesters carrying placards, scythes and pitchforks marched into the town and began pulling down the workhouse. Beds were tumbled out of windows; pots and pans rained on to the cobbles. To poor, working people, the workhouse represented everything wrong with society: a prison for the poor, where the only crime of the inmates was to be penniless. That's why they tore it down. For long enough the rich landowners and businessmen had grown fat on the toil and tolls of the poor. Now that was all about to change.

The magistrates went out to remonstrate with the mob, reading them the Riot Act: "You are hereby charged to disperse peaceably . . ."

The mob washed over them like the sea over sandcastles.

Then the dragoons arrived from Cardiff – a sixty-mile gallop from barracks. Two of their horses dropped dead as they entered the city, but for the first time the rioters were obliged to break off from their vandalism and run.

The dragoons used the flat of their swords, not the sharp edges. After all, they were Welshmen themselves, from poor Welsh homes, and knew injustice when they saw it. They scattered the mob and took a hundred prisoners, but they did it gently, almost sympathetically.

Before long, Rebecca and her Daughters regrouped stronger and more determined. There was no *one* Rebecca, you see. No *one* ringleader. The men in bonnets and aprons began to meet in secret and to list their demands, instructing the magistrates, the landowners, the Church to dismantle their toll-gates or to expect a bullet through the window or a fire in their stables.

Righteous anger had given way to thuggery and terrorism. One night, an old woman on the Glamorgan-Carmarthen border was shot dead in cold blood, just for manning a toll-gate. The law had become so weak that the inquest jury declared she had died from a "suffusion of blood . . . cause unknown". The coroner did not even dare condemn the crime of murder.

But when the toll-gate in Gower Street, in the heart of London, was filed off its hinges overnight the Government felt the Welsh problem had come too near to home. It stirred itself like a sleeping dog. The movement was destroyed, hacked apart as ruthlessly as any toll-gate or turnpike booth. It imprisoned the ringleaders or sent them to a life of hard labour in Australia.

But while, with one hand, the authorities meted out prison sentences and transportations, with the other hand it wrote legislation for the abolition of toll-gates from the nation's public roads. So the sound of those horns and whistles and pistols, the swish of petticoats and the tramp of worn boots *had* been heard, even from the other end of the long London Road.

The early years of Queen Victoria's reign were marked by huge social unrest. Poverty and hardship caused by an economic depression gave rise, in 1838, to the Chartist Movement, which agitated for every man to have the vote and for reform of Parliament. The Charter petition was signed by so many that when rolled along the lanes to London, it was the size of a cartwheel. Parliament ignored it. A "Chartist" rebellion at Newport, Wales, in 1839 was put down with great ferocity. This is the setting into which Rebecca and her Daughters were born. The many anonymous Rebeccas would have been Chartists to a man.

Father of Nobody's Children

1869

AT SIX O'CLOCK THE CHILDREN SAID A PRAYER THEN clattered towards the door. Some were more eager than others: it was cold outside. One boy dawdled at his desk, wiping his slate, and dropping his chalk. "Run off home, boy," said the teacher.

"Please, sir. Let me stop."

"Nonsense. It's time to go. Your mother will wonder what is keeping you."

"I ain't got no mother." The lad scuffed a bare foot on the plank floor.

"Where do you live, then?"

"Don't live nowhere."

The teacher sighed. After ten hours teaching he was weary and wanting his supper. He did not know the boy by sight – every day new pupils found their way to the charity school; he hoped this was not going to be some hard-luck story. Barnardo knew home life was hard – downright miserable – for most of the children attending his ragged school. But he had never set much store by melodramatic tales of children living rough on the streets, parentless and homeless. That was just romantic exaggeration. Surely. "Where did you sleep last night?" he asked.

"Down Whitechapel, sir, along o' the Haymarket, in one of them carts as is filled with 'ay. Then I met a chap as telled me to come up 'ere to school and you'd maybe let me lie near the fire all night. I won't do no harm, sir, if you let me stop."

A coldness blew through Barnardo which had nothing to do with the bitter weather. "Is it possible?" he asked himself. Then he asked Jim Jarvis: "Are there other boys who do that – sleep where they can – out in the open?"

"Oh yes, sir, lots. Heaps on em! More'n I could count!"

Barnardo took Jim Jarvis home and gave him hot coffee. He was a perky lad, witty and cheerful – except for his eyes where some drowning-depth of sorrow contradicted the saucy grin. Over supper Jim told his life story. From the age of five he had been on his own, fending for himself, an orphan. He got work with a man called "Swearing Dick" on the barges who beat him regularly, and threatened to set his dog on Jim if he tried to run away. A job on a market stall was no better. It was the police he feared most, because they would either kick him or arrest him and send him to the workhouse.

At about midnight, Barnardo set off with Jim Jarvis to see the boy's "lay", as he called it. Jim led the way to Petticoat Lane, to an old-clothes market, where he scrambled up on to the iron roof of a shed. Reaching down a stick, he helped Barnardo up too. Alongside was a hayloft and, though it was padlocked shut, some of the hay had trickled out through the slats. Eleven boys had grubbed together these wisps and were lying stretched out on them now, on the tilt of the roof, feet in the guttering. They lay close-huddled for warmth, like hamsters in a nest. No blanket over them, no clothes capable of keeping out the cold. Their sleeping faces were white and thin as skulls.

"The foxes have their holes, the birds their nests, but the Son of Man has nowhere to lay his head."

Thomas Barnardo had thought God was calling him to go to China, to be a missionary. For years he had cherished the idea – only really filling time in London, until his posting came through. Now, all of a sudden, he realized: God had not been whispering "China" in his ear. God had been bellowing in his face: "Help these children. Save these children. They have no one but you. They are nobody's children but yours and Mine!"

Barnardo could not bear it. To wake the boys would have been like fetching the dead from their graves. They would clamour at him for food, turn those hollow, reproachful eyes on him. The horror of their loveless, hopeless lives gripped him as he climbed down, legs trembling. Jim Jarvis watched him, bird-like, head cocked on one side, but the doctor could say nothing, do nothing but walk away, striding out faster and faster, until he was almost running.

Thomas J. Barnardo founded a home for homeless boys and soon afterwards another for girls. He was tireless in his efforts, not only to help the children but to enlighten the comfortable middle classes who genuinely did not know what was happening in the streets of their Victorian cities. He tackled all the social evils, turning drinking halls into evangelical tea-halls, turning drunkards and criminals into evangelists. He taught and preached, raised money, wrote articles and addressed public meetings. He told the story of Jim Jarvis many times, embroidering it considerably over the years but always to good effect.

A complex man, Barnardo gave himself the title "doctor" though he never qualified as one. He was criticized for "staging" the photographs he sold to raise funds: before-and-after photographs of his forlorn street children. Hugely slandered, hugely admired, he drove himself repeatedly into a state of nervous collapse. But his homes multiplied, his message got through. Barnardo Homes became an institution of British life for which thousands and thousands of children, right up to the present day, have had cause to be thankful.

The Last Train Ride

1879

EVERYONE WAS IN A HURRY TO GET HOME – Scotsmen returning to Scotland for the holidays, families who had been south for Christmas, workers anxious to get back to the warmth of a fireside and a good supper . . . Though Christmas was over, the New Year was still to come.

It was a filthy night, but the lights of Dundee burned all the brighter for that. And crossing over the Tay would be part of the fun. The new bridge was still a wonder to those contemplating a trip over it – a stone and metal monument to progress and prosperity.

By seven in the evening, the wind was howling, hurling itself against the signal boxes as if it would swallow them whole; unfurling dense, silver banners of rain across the starless sky. With each new gust, the carriages juddered and the luggage jumped about in the luggage van. Children with their noses pressed to the steamy windows would recoil against their mothers, then be drawn back to cloud the windows even more with their excited breathing. The noisy rhythm of the wheels on the track – "nearly-there-nearly-there-nearly-there" – was all but drowned out by the storm.

Then, all of a sudden, the countryside of lashing trees and huddled buildings gave way to rainy darkness: the train was crossing the Firth of Tay (though the river far below was not even visible through the rain). The locomotive gave a baleful whistle which the wind tore in shreds.

Two signalmen stood discussing the safety of their signal box – whether it might blow down, whether the storm would blow itself out by morning or racket on into Hogmanay. The London–Dundee train went by them wrapped in its cloak of sooty steam, slowing down for the bridge. Out over the Tay it thundered, a snake of lights, a wisp of white steam. Then a plume of sparks rose up – golden rain amid the silver. There was a tremendous flash.

Too far off for sound to carry. But as the signalmen watched, the snake of lighted carriages disappeared abruptly from sight.

Passengers on board, tumbled together by sudden braking, felt nothing now – nothing but an absence of sound. Oddly, for a second or two, the rain outside the windows rained upwards, because they were falling so fast. No time for anything more than a joining of hands, then the Tay was boiling over the wreckage and the storm was hooting.

Running down to the foreshore, the two signalmen shouted out at every tight-closed front door they passed: "*The bridge! The bridge! The train!*" But when they reached the mudflats (where the waves were breaking big as the open sea) there was nothing to do but stare into blackness. With a triumphant flourish, the storm uncovered the moon, briefly casting a ghastly, ghostly pallor over the river. The whole centre section of the Tay Bridge was gone, like a smile with its teeth smashed away. The train must have driven out on to thin air, then plunged into the deep, icy water of the Tay.

Next day, divers were needed to find the sunken train, rolled and scoured by the river's current. Of the seventy-nine people aboard, not one lived to see in the New Year of 1880.

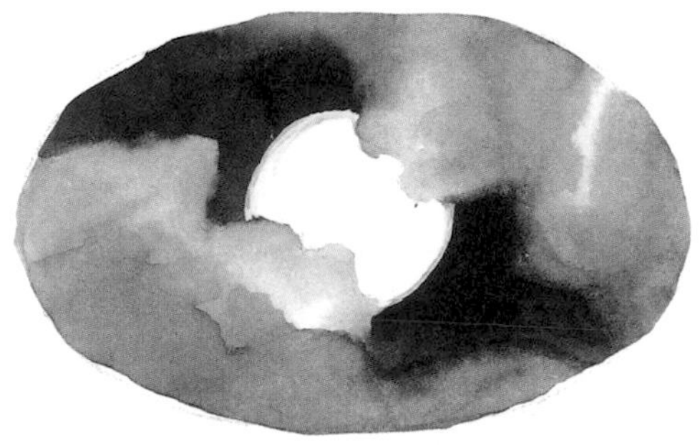

The bridge, 3¼ kilometres (nearly 2 miles) long, had only been open for nineteen months when on 28 December 1879 half a dozen of its central spans collapsed into the river. 1880 claimed the eightieth victim of the disaster. Architect Sir Thomas Bouch (who had designed the bridge with insufficient strength to withstand even low winds) died, vilified and reproached for his incompetence. A second, unfinished bridge of his had been found to be as dangerous as the first. Fortunately or unfortunately, the disaster was immortalized by the so-called poet William McGonagall in a work of such awfulness that it is performed today as a comic turn. He followed it up with an ode to the beautiful *new* Tay Railway Bridge, which was completed in 1890.

Dr Crippen on the Waves

1910

NOT FOR THE FIRST TIME, Captain Henry Kendall wiped the glass of the bridge-house and peered at the couple on the deck below: Mr Robinson and son. In his many years at sea, Kendall had developed an eye for oddities among his passengers, and there was something distinctly odd about Mr Robinson and son.

Why, for instance, did they stay so muffled up in this fine July weather? And why, when they thought no one was looking, were they *holding hands*?

Before setting sail, he had read newspaper descriptions of a couple wanted for murder. Old newspapers were probably still lying around the ship detailing the sensational crime. As far as he remembered, a dentist's wife had been done to death, her body cut up and hidden under the floorboards. Her husband, mysteriously gone missing with a lady friend called Ethel, was number one suspect. Captain Kendall's thoughts returned time and time again to the description of the man called Crippen.

And yet this ship had set sail from Antwerp in Belgium, not from Britain. Could Crippen have escaped to Belgium before the body of his wife was found? Could this be him now, trying to reach Canada and a new life with his accomplice? Was "Master Robinson" the reason Hawley Crippen had murdered his lawful wedded wife?

Captain Kendall left the bridge and strolled down to the sundeck. Casually he struck up conversation with Mr Robinson and son, though the two seemed in no mood to talk. Robinson's lids were slightly closed and there were pad marks on the bridge of his nose, though he had not worn glasses since boarding.

Dr Crippen had worn glasses.

Robinson's top lip was paler than the rest of his face. He had recently shaved off a moustache.

And Dr Crippen had worn a moustache.

The son wore a trilby hat several sizes too big, and an awkward, hesitant smile. His hands were very small and pale, and his coat too broad for his shoulders.

Kendall was certain. But what to do about it? The SS *Montrose* was outside British waters now, and, when it docked in Canada, Crippen would be on foreign soil. He might get clean away.

At least he might have got clean away, had he taken passage on a less modern ship.

Kendall hurried along to his brand-new radio room and told his brand-new radio operator, "Here's a job for you. Radio London and tell them we have Dr Hawley Crippen and his lady friend Ethel aboard."

When Chief Inspector Walter Dew received the telegraph from Captain Kendall, he left at once for the docks. He took passage aboard the SS *Laurentic*, a faster ship than the *Montrose*. In a matter of days, he could overhaul Kendall's ship and be in Canada ahead of Crippen. But the arrest must be made aboard the British ship, and that meant boarding her before she docked. Nothing must be left to chance.

"Mr Robinson!" said Captain Kendall, and the little man gave a visible start. His top lip was no longer white, thanks to the sea air, but his expression was still nervy and anxious. "Soon be there now," said Kendall, bluff and jovial. "I have just taken aboard the local pilot to see us safely into the mouth of the St Lawrence River. I wondered, would you and your son care to meet him?"

Mr Robinson and his son exchanged glances. He smiled weakly. "Delighted, I'm sure." The shores of Canada were within sight. A new life was so close that Hawley and Ethel could almost smell it. Where was the harm in accepting the captain's invitation? They could not very well refuse.

As they entered the captain's cabin, a man stood up. He was not their idea of a shipping pilot: a tall man in a bowler hat and overcoat.

"Hawley Harvey Crippen . . . Ethel Le Neve – I arrest you for the murder of Belle Crippen on or before 9 July 1910."

The little man trembled violently from head to foot; the woman beside him clutched the sleeve of his coat. "Thank God it's over," said Crippen. "The suspense has been too great. I couldn't stand it any longer." And meek as a lamb, he allowed Chief Inspector Dew to handcuff him and lead him away.

US-born Dr Hawley Crippen was the first criminal to be captured through the invention of ship-to-shore radio. He disappeared from his home in Camden Town on 9 July, shortly before police discovered his wife's dismembered body under the floorboards. The mild-mannered dentist had escaped from England with his lover, Ethel Le Neve, and reached Belgium undetected. But on 20 July, they boarded the SS *Montrose* bound for Quebec. The arrest took place on 31 July. He was promptly returned to London and charged at Bow Street court one month later. He was hanged on 23 November the same year.

The First and Last Voyage of the *Titanic*

1912

BEN GUGGENHEIM SLIPPED HIS ARMS INTO THE silk-lined sleeves of his evening jacket and turned to his cabin mirror to fasten his tie. "What say we take a turn around the deck and listen to the band?" he said to his secretary.

Outside, on deck, it was a beautiful, frosty, starlit night – only a chilly breath of a breeze and a calm, smooth sea. The ship was ablaze with lights. The band played a lively little dance number from its huge repertoire. An altogether perfect evening . . . were it not for the screaming.

All round, people were praying and running, sobbing and swearing, hugging or struggling to climb up high. Steerage passengers were still streaming up from the lower decks, and the ship groaned in agony as its back prepared to break.

"Unsinkable" they had said in the advertisements: "the ship that cannot sink". The newspapers had made much of her size and safety, her luxury and collision-proof double hull. Pride of the White Star Line, the *Titanic* was the last word in elegance and technology. People had flocked to buy tickets for her first voyage – the rich and glamorous, quite at home beneath the chandeliers of her immense ballroom, poor Irish emigrants who could only afford the smallest, cheapest cabins on their trip to a new life in America. The ship was a little world in miniature: rich on top, poor on the bottom, but all heading in the same direction. And she was so *big* – the length of London's Shaftesbury Avenue, and just as brightly lit!

The iceberg, by contrast, moved like a dirty brown slab, hidden for the most part underwater. It had broken away from the polar pack ice to float aimlessly south across the shipping lanes. And it too was titanic.

The look-out Fred Fleet saw it at the last moment and shouted a warning, clanged the alarm bell three times. The ship seemed only to graze against the great ice hulk, then sail by, a rattle of ice skittering across the decks. "That was a close shave," said Fleet to himself.

But there was a ninety-metre gash below the waterline, a gash which had pierced both layers of the double hull and buckled the whole structure. Icy water was already pouring in. The "unsinkable" *Titanic* had two hours to live.

The bow and wheel-house were already underwater, but the stern was still afloat and reasonably level. One of the huge funnels disintegrated and toppled into the water amid the swimmers and rafts and life-boats.

There had not been enough lifeboats – not enough for even half the people aboard. A strange oversight. Perhaps on an unsinkable ship, lifeboats had not seemed important. Some boats had capsized on launching. As a result, the lifeboats, floating now within the glow of the ship's lights, were crammed with precious cargoes of silks, satins, furs and diamonds. Women and children first. That is the rule at sea.

Of course some men had been too panic-stricken to care about the etiquette of the sea. Some had tried to disguise themselves as women. Some had jumped into the water and been pulled aboard. And there were the sailors who had had to get the boats away. But for the most part, true gentlemen had stayed behind: Jack Phillips the wireless operator, for instance, tapping away at his Morse key over and over and over again: "Come at once. We have struck an iceberg. It's CQD, old man. Position 41° 40'N, 50° 14'W. Come at once. We have struck –" Gentlemen.

Like the ones in the water who had found the rafts too crowded to take another soul, and swum away again, with a cry of "Good luck – God bless you!" Gentlemen.

Like the engineers still labouring to provide power, so that all the lights in the ship could blaze during the evacuation, be seen by rescue ships, raise the spirits of those caught up in the death of the *Titanic.* True gentlemen.

Like the musicians playing even now a jaunty little tune, while the deck beneath them tilted more and more steeply. True gentlemen.

There were wives, too, who chose to stay behind with their husbands.

And men like Ben and Victor, who seeing how some must live and some must die, had thrown off their life-jackets and turned away from the lifeboats. "Tell my wife I played the game out straight to the end," Ben had called to those in the boat. "No women shall be left aboard this ship because Ben Guggenheim is a coward."

The band struck up "Abide with me." The lights were flickering now in some of the portholes. It was two in the morning of 15 April, and the ship was going down. The entire front half disappeared. The stern section stood on end, then, like a still photograph, hesitated for a full five minutes before slipping out of sight.

Built to carry 2,435 passengers and crew, the *Titanic* was equipped with enough lifeboats to save just 1,178 people. Of the 2,200 souls who left Southampton on 10 April 1912, bound for New York, only 705 lived. The distress signal was picked up. Help did come, but not until the *Titanic* was 4 kilometres down on the bottom of the Atlantic. The disaster gave rise to new safety regulations, but never again has a ship claimed to be "unsinkable". The *Titanic* had restored people's humility in the face of the pitiless sea.

CQD – "Come Quick, Danger" – were the Morse letters used before the introduction of SOS as the international distress signal.

"Just Going Outside"

1912

THERE WAS NOTHING TO BE GAINED BY SUCH A JOURNEY, except honour and adventure. And yet honour is everything to such men. They wished for the honour of being first to set foot at the South Pole.

So the worst thing that could happen to them, it seemed at the outset, was that the Norwegians would get there first. The competition was so fierce between Captain Scott's team and Roald Amundsen's that the desperate cold, the grit-sharp flying snow, the blinding brightness of the polar plains did not seem the real enemies at all. Scott and Wilson, Evans, Bowers and Oates left their last depot with nine days' supplies, expecting that two long marches would make them the first men in history to visit the South Pole. The excitement lent them an energy they could never otherwise have mustered.

Then they saw it – a black speck in the distance, something which did not belong in the white, untrodden snow of virgin territory. When they got closer, their worst fears were confirmed: it was a flag. There were sledge tracks, too, and paw prints. The desolate Antarctic, last unconquered territory on the planet, was no longer theirs, no longer the prize they had expected after months of agonizing effort. Amundsen was ahead of them.

In a way, it would have been less terrible to turn back then and there, not to have to march on, dragging the cripplingly heavy sledge, eating up more of their dwindling provisions. Then they would not have had to stand at the South Pole and taste the bitterness of defeat. Their achievement was immense, and yet they accounted it "a horrible day" that 17 January when they stood at the bottom of the world amid the footprints of another expedition. The Norwegians had beaten them by just thirty-five days. "All the daydreams must go," wrote Scott in his diary, "it will be a wearisome return."

And so it was. The calm weather which had made it possible to trek so far from help or shelter began to break up. A change of wind blew snow through the fabric of their clothes and filled up their mittens. The weather was deteriorating unexpectedly early, the temperature dropping unimaginably low, the wind stiffening. The cold was unspeakable – unspeakable chiefly because these men were English officers and gentlemen; to have complained or inconvenienced their friends would have been dishonourable. And honour was everything.

Then Edgar Evans died.

Laurence Oates got frostbite in his foot. It had been troubling him even at the Pole; ten weeks later, he could go no further. He knew that he too was going to die, but took comfort from the thought that his regiment might be proud of him. On the night of 6 March, he bedded down, fervently hoping to die in his sleep. Once again luck was against him. He woke to the knowledge that his failure to die promptly would delay his friends – perhaps even prevent them reaching safety themselves. As undemonstrative as ever, he crawled out of his sleeping-bag and got painfully to his feet. A blizzard was blaring outside: a white madness.

"I am just going outside and may be some time," he said.

The others sat up. "No!"

"We can still make it, old boy!"

"You said yourself . . ."

But the tent flap dropped back into place, and Oates was gone: no grand scene, no heroic declamation – "just going outside".

"We knew that poor Oates was walking to his death," wrote Scott, ". . . it was the act of a brave man and an English gentleman."

His self-sacrifice would be wasted if the others did not push on, try to reach the depot. Twenty miles to go. But they knew inwardly, beneath their endlessly cheerful banter, that they would probably not make it. They were down to their last primus-filling of oil and next to no food: a smear of cocoa and lump of pemmican. Scott succumbed to frostbite, but there was such a short way left to go – only fifteen and a half miles! He knew he would lose his foot, but would he lose his life too? Eleven miles.

Wilson and Bowers were planning to go ahead to the depot, for more fuel. But the blizzard shut down, as if the flapping tent of frozen sky had fallen on them. Discussing how they should best finish their doomed expedition, they resolved to go out and meet death face-to-face, to walk, with or without baggage, until they dropped in their tracks. But the blizzard thwarted them. The blizzard had picked up the outside world and shaken it out of existence. Besides, a tent and sledge might be found, whereas three men, falling separately, along an unmarked path would soon be obliterated by the snow, never to be found. So they settled themselves as comfortably as they could and waited. It would not be a long wait.

On 20 March, they had enough tea for two more cups, enough food for two meagre days. On the twenty-ninth the blizzard was still raging, and Scott wrote the last words in his diary: "For God's sake, look after our people."

The snow did all it could to bury the tent, but its flue and a bamboo upright on the sledge still showed above the drifts when a search party found Scott's last camp, eight months later. The three had come to within eleven – about sixteen kilometres – miles of safety.

They lay in their sleeping-bags, letters and diaries intact. Even the worst luck, the worst weather, the worst wilderness in the world could not succeed in erasing the indelible mark left by such courageous men.

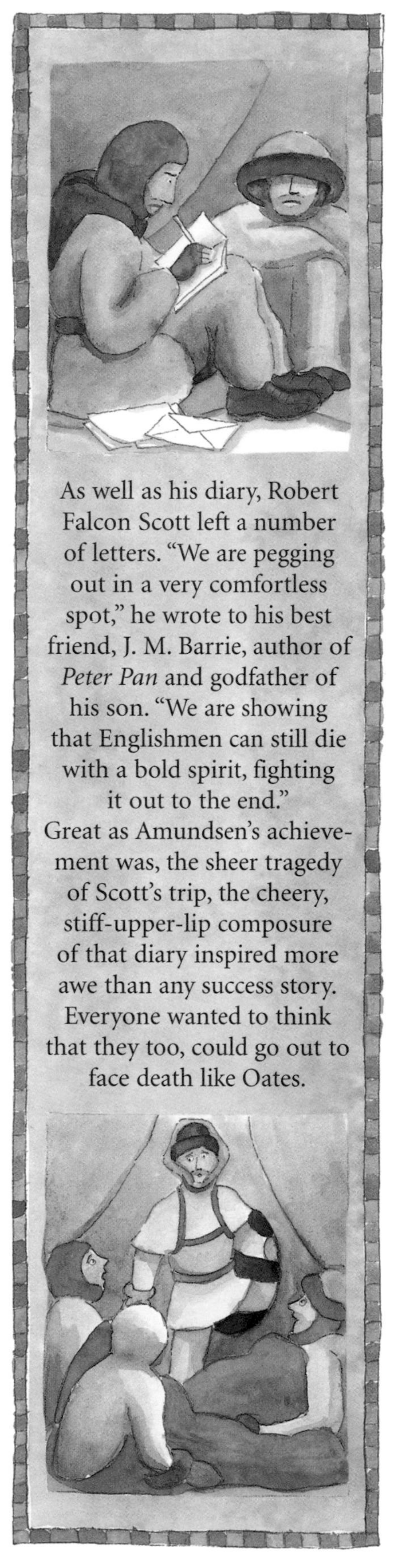

As well as his diary, Robert Falcon Scott left a number of letters. "We are pegging out in a very comfortless spot," he wrote to his best friend, J. M. Barrie, author of *Peter Pan* and godfather of his son. "We are showing that Englishmen can still die with a bold spirit, fighting it out to the end." Great as Amundsen's achievement was, the sheer tragedy of Scott's trip, the cheery, stiff-upper-lip composure of that diary inspired more awe than any success story. Everyone wanted to think that they too, could go out to face death like Oates.

Votes for Women!

1913

ABOARD THE TRAIN THERE WAS A HOLIDAY atmosphere. Everyone was travelling to the same destination: Epsom Downs. It was Derby Day, and people who never thought of going to the horse-races flocked to Epsom for the grandest race of the year. Families with picnic baskets and six sticky children, clerks and factory workers, young couples smiling shyly at each other, brash men in loud sports coats. No one paid much attention to the young woman sitting in a corner of the carriage, her handkerchief held to her mouth.

"Now, George, I don't want you gambling your money away."

"Just a flutter, dear. Just a flutter."

"Perhaps just a shilling on the King's horse. It's only patriotic to bet on His Majesty's horse . . ."

The young woman's teeth tore a small hole in the corner of her handkerchief. Emily Davison stepped down from the train, and the cheerful crowd swept her along. The green of Epsom Downs was submerged beneath the colourful holiday clothes of the race-goers. The amplified voices of stewards speaking through megaphones sounded like dogs barking. Bookmakers stood on boxes shouting the betting odds they were offering. Bookies' runners gesticulated like lunatics, using their secret sign language. Emily too, had a secret. Someone had daubed "Votes for Women" on the fence. Her fingers brushed the words as the crowd carried her along.

She did not place any bets. She did not sip tea at the cafeteria or look over the horses in the saddling enclosure for a likely winner. Not until the big event – the Derby Sweepstake itself – was about to begin did she worm her way through the crowds to a place by the white rails of the race course. From there she would have a perfect view of the runners thundering down the straight. The crowd gave a single excited cry of "They're off!" and the 1913 Derby had begun.

The King's horse did not take the lead. It was halfway down the field as the runners entered the straight. The crowd to either side of Emily leaned forwards, shouting for the horse they had backed. Perhaps they thought Emily was doing the same.

"Votes for Women!" Her voice came out small and piping. How fast they moved. She had not realized how fast a galloping horse moved. Slipping under the rail, she felt the ground tremble under her feet.

Someone made a grab to pull her back, but she ducked forwards – a small, pale figure in hat and gloves, purse hanging from her wrist. The front-runners tried to avoid her, but the ones behind had no time. She flung herself under the hooves of the King's horse – it was done in a flash – and many in the crowd saw the muddle of hooves and clothes and thought a jockey had come unseated. Then a strange, delayed gasp of revulsion went up, half drowned by the shouts of the spectators down by the winning post, still cheering their horses on.

". . . sheer suicide . . ."

". . . madwoman!"

". . . what possessed her . . ."

". . . anything to draw attention to themselves . . . Is she dead?"

". . . these suffragettes."

The voices reached Emily as if down the dark shaft of a well. The stewards and first-aiders who came to her side were sharp-voiced with disgust. She had spoiled the day for so many people.

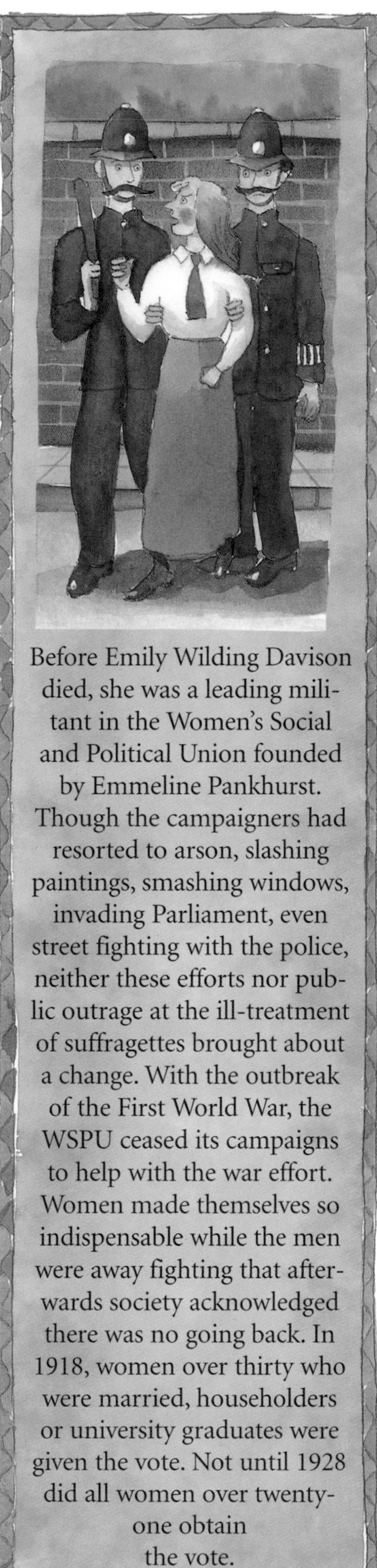

Before Emily Wilding Davison died, she was a leading militant in the Women's Social and Political Union founded by Emmeline Pankhurst. Though the campaigners had resorted to arson, slashing paintings, smashing windows, invading Parliament, even street fighting with the police, neither these efforts nor public outrage at the ill-treatment of suffragettes brought about a change. With the outbreak of the First World War, the WSPU ceased its campaigns to help with the war effort. Women made themselves so indispensable while the men were away fighting that afterwards society acknowledged there was no going back. In 1918, women over thirty who were married, householders or university graduates were given the vote. Not until 1928 did all women over twenty-one obtain the vote.

No Man's Land

1914

It was Christmas Day, but nothing to show for it being Christmas. There was no snow, no laughter, no celebration. Nothing to celebrate. The guns had fallen silent, but before long they would be pounding again, shaking the mortar out of the sky, shaking the rats out of their holes, making the dead tremble out on no-man's-land. Rags of torn clothing hung on the barbed wire out there, like bunting, but they hung there every day, gradually losing their colour. It was not Christmas which had put the bunting there. It was the war.

"It will be all over by Christmas," they had said at the beginning. But they had not said *which* Christmas or whether, when it finally ended, there would be anyone left alive to see it.

"Stille Nacht, heilige Nacht
Alles schlaft, einsam wacht . . ."

The soldiers sitting slumped in their swampy trenches, remembering past Christmases, thought at first that the carol was in their imaginations. Then they realized that the singing was real, that it was drifting over from the German trenches on the other side of no-man's-land. The enemy were remembering Christmas, too.

Of course they were. Christmas is universal. And what were they – those German infantrymen over there – but young men far from home, wishing they were somewhere else this vile, wartime Christmas Day in France. Only weeks before, the British Tommies might have believed all that propaganda about Germans murdering babies and burning churches. But they knew better now. The enemy they knew as "Jerry" was just as frightened, just as homesick. He, too, had a wife back somewhere – children maybe – sitting through Christmas Day clutching his mud-spattered letters home and remembering . . .

"Silent night, holy night
All is calm, all is bright . . ."

The Welsh Fusiliers over in the next trench were joining in now. Forever singing, those Taffies. Some of them were singing in Welsh, others in English. Same carol, just different words. Same meaning. Same Christmas.

Suddenly *everyone* burst out singing.

Then a German called out: something about schnapps: something about sharing a drink. He rose up into view, and the singing petered to a halt. Would he be shot down by a sniper? What sniper? How can you shoot a man when you've just been singing along with him? Other heads rose above the muddy parapets, dirty, fatigued faces looking at one another across the grassless, treeless, lifeless no-man's-land which separated the German trenches from the English ones.

Something round and brown dropped out of the slab-grey sky, and all the heads ducked. Hands flew up to shield vulnerable eyes and ears. Was it a shell? A mortar? The brown globe bounced two or three times, then rolled to a standstill. It was a football.

A football in no-man's-land? Was it English or Welsh or German? It was neutral. No-man's-land is neutral. It belongs to nobody, except perhaps the dead who die out there, hanging on the barbed wire.

First one, then five, then a dozen men scrambled out of their trenches, each one exhorting the men behind to follow. A few hung back – suspicious of an ambush. But enough jogged out on to the barren wasteland, greatcoats dangling stiffly down to their ankles, cigarette smoke curling from the cupped palms of their hands. Enough for a game of football.

Jerry and Tommy exchanged cigarettes, swigs of liquor. Someone marked out goal-mouths with bundled up coats. There were shouts and cheers, and little puffs of smoky breath as the players panted in the cold air. For half an hour or more that game lasted.

Then somewhere far off – far up the line – artillery started up: a gentle *whoomp, whoomp*, like a heartbeat. The smokers dragged deep on their cigarettes and threw them down. The players shook hands, gathered up their greatcoats, pointed to the faint red glare in the distant sky. The sound of gunfire came closer.

Without anyone giving a direct command, the men returned to their respective trenches. They did not hurry. Machine-gunners checked their ammunition. Riflemen eased the springs of their carbines. The Welsh were the last to stop singing.

Nothing had changed. The end of the war had come no closer. There would be no spontaneous laying down of arms in defiance of the commanding officers, no mutinous refusal to fight any more. But something had happened, out there in no-man's-land; something every man there would remember until he died – whether he died next morning out on the wire or lived to see other, peacetime Christmas Days.

The mortars began to thud, crazing the slab-grey sky, making the muddy earth trickle in slurries down into the trenches. Cowering soldiers hunched their shoulders against it and buttoned up their greatcoats. Out on no-man's-land the football lay forgotten, like a Christmas hazelnut after a splendid meal.

The sculptor-artist Henri Gaudier-Brzeska, as well as several other eye-witnesses, wrote of the Christmas Day football match in his letters home. He was killed, aged twenty-four, in 1915, fighting in a war which, between 1914 and 1918, would see nine million die.

Derailing the Country

1926

TIME WAS, IT WAS EVERY BOY'S DREAM TO DRIVE A railway engine, and one engine in particular: the *Flying Scotsman*. Bob Sheddon, however, saw it as his patriotic duty – to keep the railways running. The strikers had vowed to bring the country to a standstill, but Bob was determined to drive the *Flying Scotsman* from Edinburgh to London on Monday, 10 May.

The view from her twelve carriages that day was of quiet streets, smokeless factory chimneys, silent stockyards. It was like Sunday in the mid-week. The country was holding its breath, waiting to see whether the Government or the trade unions would be the first to back down in their argument over the miners' dispute.

Bob's volunteer fireman was a student from Edinburgh University, Robert Aitken. Some of his friends were working at the docks or driving lorries, helping to defeat the strike. Not that his friends would ever do that kind of work once they had their degrees. Indeed, they might never dirty their hands again with machine oil or crates of fish, but it was a lark – or else their patriotic duty: every volunteer had his own motives for trying to break the General Strike. Some thought the striking miners and transport workers and dockers and factory hands were bloody-minded Communists trying to bring down the Government and sow the seeds of anarchy. Some thought that the suffering caused to ordinary people – if London, say, ran out of food – was simply not justified. For some it was just a game: to break the strike.

The *Flying Scotsman* rattled along, trailing steam-clouds of glory. "What speed did you say she could do?" said Robert.

"Sixty mile an hour," said Bob. "Not through Dam Dyke, naturally."

The huge, sleek engine sighed steam as she slowed to a mere six miles an hour for the level crossing near Cramlington. That was when they saw it – a gap in the rails ahead.

Robert hung half out of the cab, peering through the steam. "Piece of rail – gone!" he gasped. "We'll never stop in time!"

Bob slammed on the brakes. The gigantic metal wheels spun on the tracks, and sparks flew. But a steam engine needs time to slow down and stop, even from six mph. She trundled on, wheels skidding, the carriages jolted by the sharp braking. On and on she rolled, until in ponderous slow motion one wheel found no rail under it, and she slumped over sideways. The *Flying Scotsman* jumped the tracks and ploughed into a disused signal box at the side of the line. The first carriage jack-knifed. The guard's van was thrown on to its side. All along the length of the train passengers slithered to the floor. There was a smell of burning and cries of "Fire!"

Police and firemen and ambulances were quick to arrive. So, too, were crowds of onlookers . . . only they did not rush forward to offer help or comfort. They held off at a distance, flapping their caps and grinning. As passengers staggered away, dishevelled and shaken, some in tears, some dazed and expressionless, the crowd began to jeer and whistle. Strikers from nearby Cramlington. Perhaps they were only jeering the driver and volunteer fireman. Or perhaps they deemed the passengers strike-breakers, too, for trying to travel despite the strike.

Sabotage, the police said, carrying away two iron bars and a sledge hammer from near the scene of the crash. Still, no serious harm was done. Only one person was injured. The boilers of the *Flying Scotsman* were doused and she was not much damaged. Copies of the *British Gazette* blew about on the lines and were turned back to pulp by the rain. Tomorrow's edition would say how the *Flying Scotsman* had been derailed by strikers.

But there would be other train crashes to report as well. That same Monday, at Bishop's Stortford, a goods train ran into a passenger train and one man was killed. Between Berwick and Edinburgh three people died in a collision.

Were they casualties of the strike or of the strike breakers? It depends on your point of view. Either way, they were just as dead.

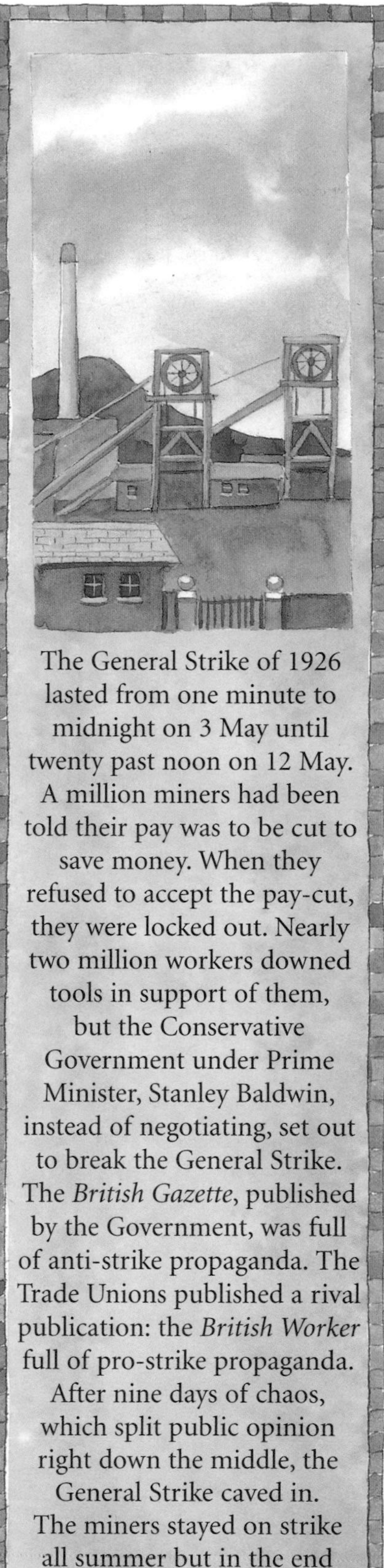

The General Strike of 1926 lasted from one minute to midnight on 3 May until twenty past noon on 12 May. A million miners had been told their pay was to be cut to save money. When they refused to accept the pay-cut, they were locked out. Nearly two million workers downed tools in support of them, but the Conservative Government under Prime Minister, Stanley Baldwin, instead of negotiating, set out to break the General Strike. The *British Gazette*, published by the Government, was full of anti-strike propaganda. The Trade Unions published a rival publication: the *British Worker* full of pro-strike propaganda. After nine days of chaos, which split public opinion right down the middle, the General Strike caved in. The miners stayed on strike all summer but in the end poverty defeated them.

Memories of a Jarrow Marcher

1936

WHEN THE BIG CRANES CAME DOWN, I FINALLY grasped the truth. The shipyard was gone, closed, finished, and every man who worked there was out of work for good. Including me.

Grandpa refused to believe it. He kept going down there, oiling things, keeping things serviceable for when it opened up again. Me, I knew better. I was out grubbing up coal dust for fuel. It was risky: I could have been caught and fined, but I couldn't have Mam and the bairns shivering. The lad next door stayed in bed a lot – just to keep warm. You can't feel hungry if you're asleep.

The streets were always ringing empty. Me, I went walking. All the way to Newcastle and back was nothing. We were always good walkers, we Jarrow lads, and it passed the time.

We couldn't move away to seek work. Dad had spent his savings buying the house, but he couldn't have sold it for a ten-shilling note. Who'd want to live in Jarrow where three men in four were out of work?

Mothers didn't eat; they gave what food there was to their menfolk and bairns. This is the twentieth century I'm talking about, and women and babies were so weak with hunger that they died of the least little thing. My sisters Jean and Annie got out. They went south and got work in London as waitresses. Some days, I thought I'd never see them again.

A year went by and nobody at Westminster even troubled to come and see what the shipyard closure had done to us.

Then up gets Joe Symonds – I'll never forget it. "I am prepared to march 7,000 men to London and demand justice!" says Joe. "The working-class people of this town must rise in strength and demand that something be done!"

Well, everyone liked the idea; we all wanted to go. There *could* have been 7,000. But the organizers said thousands would be hard to feed and shelter, so they settled on 200. We drew lots in our house. I won. But our Jack gave me his waterproof, Dad gave me his suit, our Tom gave me his cap. Mam gave me a kiss. So in a way we all went on the Jarrow Crusade.

Red Ellen led us – our MP, Ellen Wilkinson. They called her Red Ellen because of her hair, not because she were a Communist. This had nothing to do with politics, see? This was about starvation.

We didn't want charity; we wanted work. We wanted people down south to know what we were suffering up in Jarrow. So we would walk all the way to London and present a petition to Parliament, and along the way we could tell people how we came to be in such a plight.

It put heart into us, just to be *doing* something for a change. We were going to call it the Jarrow Hunger March, but then one of the marshals said "Crusade" would be nicer. So Jarrow Crusade it was. We carried a banner with those two words, ahead of 200 men all in their Sunday best, and the Mayor of Jarrow and Red Ellen – not forgetting Paddy the dog, of course. He was our mascot. He trotted along with us, chipper as you like, all those miles to London.

We walked for fifty minutes, rested for ten, and kept going ten hours a day. Every town we reached, we rushed to the post office to collect letters from our families. That helped with the homesickness. After a while we were all best-muckers – friends to the end! We looked out for each other. Tynesiders might be rough, tough men, but they can be tender as lassies when there's a need.

Jarrow, Chester le Street, Darlington, Ripon, Harrogate, Leeds, Wakefield, Sheffield, Chesterfield, Nottingham . . . Everywhere we stopped, people welcomed us. That "Crusade" idea caught their imagination. Also, we didn't make political speeches. We just told how it was: how many were out of work, how many babies died before their first birthday. People who, up till then, had been calling us a bunch of bolshevik trouble-makers, found themselves cheering Miss Ellen and writing letters to the papers saying, "Something must be done!"

Leicester, Northampton, Bedford, St Albans . . . And folk were so *good* to us! They laid on hot dinners, campsites, sandwiches. A cinema manager let us in free to see a moving picture. A theatre owner sent the artistes round by taxi to give us a show. The Leicester Co-op workers stopped up all night mending our boots. Medical students turned out all along the way to cure our ills, and never charged a penny piece. And we got fit and we got fed and we

were treated decent – which is more than we had been back home. We missed our wives and bairns, of course we did, and the walking was hard on the feet, but it was a fine time – a grand time.

Then we reached London.

The police were suspicious of us, but they couldn't stand in our way. We weren't the Peasants' Revolt. We were a bunch of men all spruced up, carrying a message from 11,572 people to their elected government. And any Englishman has a perfect right to petition his government about an injustice.

We had a rally in Hyde Park. That was the best day for me: holiday crowds and music. Someone called my name – and there was Jean and Annie! – along with hundreds of other Jarrow-born lassies and lads who'd gone after the work in London. A few tears flowed, I can tell you!

Then there was that meeting in Farringdon. That put the cap on things. Maybe Sir John thought he was helping; maybe he fancied the cheers. But up stands Sir John Jarvis, MP, and says he's opening a new tube works at Jarrow. The journalists grabbed the news and ran.

Next day the papers were full of it: "Jarrow To Have New Works", it said. So that was all right, wasn't it? The happy ending everyone wanted. The great British public breathed a sigh of relief – and put us clean out of mind.

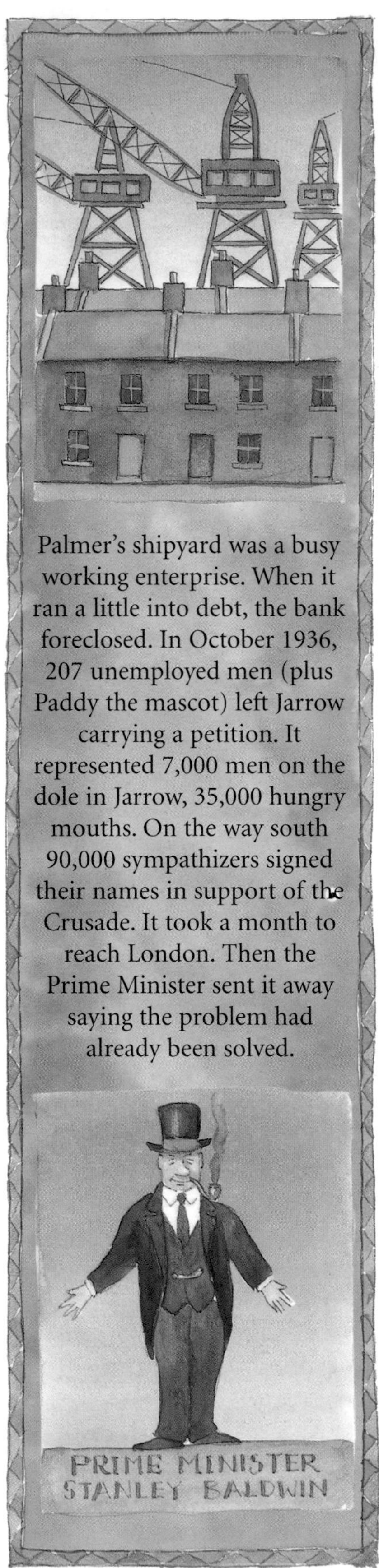

Palmer's shipyard was a busy working enterprise. When it ran a little into debt, the bank foreclosed. In October 1936, 207 unemployed men (plus Paddy the mascot) left Jarrow carrying a petition. It represented 7,000 men on the dole in Jarrow, 35,000 hungry mouths. On the way south 90,000 sympathizers signed their names in support of the Crusade. It took a month to reach London. Then the Prime Minister sent it away saying the problem had already been solved.

Next day we were offered a jolly trip on the Thames. We didn't know it was a trick to get us out of the way. When we got back, the petition was already handed in. The politicians had said, "Yes, but look: the Navy will be ordering new ships soon, from some place or other, and Sir John is opening these tube works . . . What more is there to say?"

Billy Thompson – our Mayor – was grand. He showed them his chain-of-office – a chain of little gold hawsers and anchors to represent the thousand ships built in Jarrow. "If you're not going to help us, this means nothing," he said, and dropped it – *clunk* – on the table. Grand gesture. Then we all shuffled off.

Do I sound ungrateful to the great Sir John Jarvis, MP? Well, Sir John's tube works, if they ever opened, would employ 150 men: 150 out of 7,000. And just by talking about it, he had lost us everything. So we took out the ten-shilling notes we had saved for the train fare, smoothed them flat, and bought our tickets home.

Of course, when the orders for new Navy ships came along, they did not go to Jarrow. Palmer's shipyard had been sold off, hadn't it? All its machinery sold for scrap to the Belgians. The Belgians put in a bid and got the work. Well, they had the machinery, didn't they?

It did no good at all, the Jarrow Crusade. It was a grand effort – got the whole country stirred up – but it did no good. When we got home, the cranes were still gone. The streets of Jarrow were always ringing empty. It was a ghost town. A dead town. Red Ellen said it had been murdered.

The Brave Little Boats of Dunkirk

1940

We knew things were going badly when the command came to retreat. Tanks were breaking through our lines, we were passing whole convoys of lorries on fire, and there was shellfire all around. We knew things had gone wrong altogether when they told us to destroy all our kit. But I could barely believe it when I realized that the whole British Expeditionary Force was on the retreat across France.

Each man was supposed to keep one blanket and a full pack: everything else had to be destroyed to keep it out of German hands. Wireless sets lay about with their valves smashed and their insides hanging out. Gun-sights had to be broken and the breeches of the big guns blocked with concrete or rocks. I remember Harry and I had nicked a case of wine along the way. We had to smash even that. It drained away into the ground like blood. All the time, droves of miserable, muddy men were streaming by on foot.

The Germans had us pretty much surrounded on three sides. Then it rained again. It rained hard.

Trouble was, the vehicles abandoned by one platoon blocked the roads for the rest of us trying to get west to the coast. It was chaos – mud and confusion. Finally, about twenty-five miles from Dunkirk, the road ahead was clogged solid and we had to pick our way on foot, single-file. Down every road came these single-file streams of men, all converging on Dunkirk like rivers giving into the sea. The beaches, when we got there, were a mass of men. I never saw a crowd like it. My stomach turned to water at the sight. We were sitting ducks! The German army was closing in on us and the German air force could fly over to bomb and machine-gun us whenever they liked. Soon we would all either be dead or taken prisoner. I remember saying to Harry, "This is the end of the war for us, mate."

There were a handful of destroyers off shore, sent to take off as many as possible of us. But there were just so many to be taken off! Already the destroyers were being dive-bombed and sunk.

Harry and I took shelter in the cellar of a house near the beach, waiting for our turn to go aboard the rescue ships. How can I describe it? It was the biggest queue in the world: men waiting to go home, to stay alive. The queue moved forward twenty metres each hour. But it was quite well organized. Food was being shared out and there were pickets on duty to make sure no one jumped the queue.

Oddly, the Germans did not come when we expected. Our air force had lots of planes in the air, trying to protect us from the bombing and machine-gunning. Harry and I broke into a shop and took some deckchairs and food and drink; then we sat and got rather woozy, I have to admit, trying not to think about our chances. Surely, Hitler had won. It's not a wide stretch of water, the English Channel, but it's quite wide enough. You can't walk home across it. So what escape did we have, realistically?

I was out there three days. Others were there eight or nine. We were like mice trapped in the corner of a room, just waiting for the cat's paw to drop. Still the Germans did not arrive. It was uncanny, inexplicable. Harry said, "Maybe they don't like sand in their boots." Day and night, day and night. The beaches stank of death, noxious smoke, sewage, blood, iodine and wet wool.

Then, do you know what? Other boats started to appear off-shore – not naval ships but private boats – ferries, yachts, tugs, barges, launches. It was like a regatta! Practically every English boat capable of crossing the Channel seemed to have come to help pick up men! All day they kept coming. All day and all night.

Soldiers were wading out into the water to climb aboard: some, more organized, were waiting their turn at the harbour. They waited for the signal, then ran zig-zagging at full tilt along the harbour wall to some grey navy ship or millionaire's sleek motor yacht.

When that low-flying bomber came over, the vibration of its engine made my teeth chatter. It dropped a bomb ten metres away and I was drenched in sand. Harry was killed outright. That's when my nerve broke. I ran into the water, heading out for a motor-boat put-putting towards the beach.

It was the kind of boat you might take for a trip round the bay. A big sea would have swamped it. And here it was, my one tiny chance to get away. Up to my waist. Up to my shoulders. Trying to keep my feet. The water was cold: it climbed inside my clothes, layer by heavy layer. A helmet floated past. I think I trod on a man's kitbag.

There was an old man aboard the motor-boat. He left the helm and came to pull me aboard – me and six or seven others. We were so eager to climb in, and so clumsy, that we nearly overturned him. As he leaned towards me, his face was grey and drawn with fright, cold, uncertainty. I suppose mine was much the same, though, and I was less than half his age.

The beach was a seething mass of men and noise: shouting, explosions. But out on the water, I don't believe we spoke one word all the while the boat was picking its way through the other craft and out to sea. Then the Frenchman beside me started repeating over and over and over again: "*Merci. Merci, merci, merci.*"

Sometimes the old man acknowledged another boat-owner with a nod or a brief wave: sailing people all know each other. There were bankers and factory hands and doctors and teachers and fishermen, sea scouts and taxi-drivers; boys too young for the army and old men who had fought in the last war. There were fireboats and fishing smacks and lifeboats. A lovely old paddle-steamer chugged and splattered past us, like something from an older, sweeter world. Some vessels had been across the Channel several times already, and picked up soldiers and taken them home, then come back for more. The risks were horrific, what with German planes overhead and the shelling. I saw a pleasure boat blown out of the water, a yacht turned over. I saw a destroyer burning on the horizon under a pall of smoke. This was no trip around the bay. I cowered down in the bottom of the boat, my head up against a slopping petrol can. It's not a wide stretch of water, the Channel, but it's wide enough to die in.

The old man told us how he had been listening to the wireless when the call had gone out: "The Admiralty has made an order to all owners of pleasure crafts, fishing boats, or freighters between thirty and one hundred feet in length to report to the Admiralty at Dover."

This was his fourth trip.

I never saw a sight so stirring as the white cliffs of Dover parting the sky from the sea, and the winking of the harbour lights. There was hot food waiting, and first-aid for the wounded as well as blankets and smiles. As I climbed the steps up the harbour wall, I realized that I did not even know the name of the man who had rescued me. I turned to ask, but he was already pushing off again, putting out to sea, heading for the Dunkirk beaches to snatch up a few more lives.

That was four years ago – May 1940. Now I'm going back, too. It is 6 June, and we are all set for the big one – the Allied Invasion of Europe. Back then, the papers called it the miracle of Dunkirk – a victory! That was no victory. As Winston Churchill said, "You don't win wars by evacuations." No, Dunkirk was a hellish, humiliating defeat for us. Now the same men are going back over there to take Europe from the Nazis. You want to see what victory looks like? Watch us.

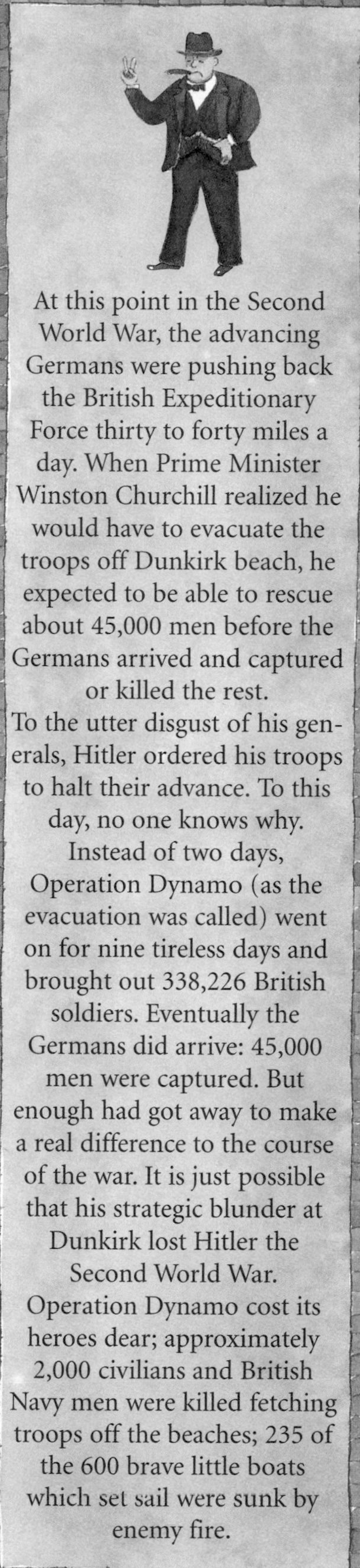

At this point in the Second World War, the advancing Germans were pushing back the British Expeditionary Force thirty to forty miles a day. When Prime Minister Winston Churchill realized he would have to evacuate the troops off Dunkirk beach, he expected to be able to rescue about 45,000 men before the Germans arrived and captured or killed the rest.

To the utter disgust of his generals, Hitler ordered his troops to halt their advance. To this day, no one knows why.

Instead of two days, Operation Dynamo (as the evacuation was called) went on for nine tireless days and brought out 338,226 British soldiers. Eventually the Germans did arrive: 45,000 men were captured. But enough had got away to make a real difference to the course of the war. It is just possible that his strategic blunder at Dunkirk lost Hitler the Second World War.

Operation Dynamo cost its heroes dear; approximately 2,000 civilians and British Navy men were killed fetching troops off the beaches; 235 of the 600 brave little boats which set sail were sunk by enemy fire.

Improving on History

(50,000 BC, 1907, 1953)

AN EXPECTANT hush fell over the lecture hall as Charles Dawson rose to speak. The newspapers had hinted at what he would say, and no one in the world of archaeology wanted to miss it. He peered down at them from the lectern – a man known for his painstaking archaeology, for his thoroughness and attention to detail. He spoke of a gentle afternoon walk in the Sussex countryside. Not the stuff of headlines, surely?

"Two workmen were digging gravel . . . I asked if they had found bones or other fossils there . . . urged them to preserve anything they might find . . . One of the men handed to me a small portion of an unusually thick human parietal bone . . . Some years later, in the autumn of 1911, I picked up another and larger piece . . ."

Science called the find "Dawson's Dawn Man" of Piltdown – *Eoanthropus dawsoni* – a creature neither ape nor man but part-way between the two. Here was the living proof (fossilized proof, anyway) which archaeology had been longing for. Darwin's theory of evolution had been proved, and by a find in the English Sussex countryside!

Nearly one hundred years before, Charles Darwin had put forward the theory that mankind did not spring into existence perfectly formed, out of clay, by the finger of God, but had developed over millions of years, by random accident, from ape into man. Darwin had stirred up a hornet's nest; there were many people, even in 1912, who rejected Darwinianism as a wicked heresy against God. But now Dawson had found the *proof* – an example of a Dawn Man, part ape, part man. Piltdown Man was the missing link in a chain of conclusive evidence: mankind truly was descended from the apes.

The top of the Piltdown skull was shaped like early man's, the jaw like that of an ape. Immediately opinion was split between those who said jaw and skull had washed by chance into the same gravel bed, and those who accepted that jaw and skull belonged together. For a couple of years the controversy raged . . . until Dawson produced a *second* Piltdown skull, and there was no further talk of him having made a mistake. In fact he was the hero of the hour. He had found the missing link!

But shortly, the cataclysm of the First World War pushed Dawson's discovery out of everyone's mind. What did it matter how mankind had originated: the question was, did mankind have a future?

Charles Dawson, briefly feted and famous, fell ill in 1915 and by the following year himself lay buried in the English countryside. Now it was up to his friend and colleague, Arthur Smith Woodward, to defend Piltdown Man from doubting Thomases, to field the questions of palaeontologists wanting to research further. His life's work, whether he chose it or not, became Piltdown Man.

Time passed. In China, Java and Africa other ape-men were found: Darwin's theories were proved time and again. Oddly, though, these new finds had jaws like early man and crania like apes. Well, perhaps primates had evolved by two *different* routes into modern man: one jaw-first, one cranium-first.

Then carbon-dating – a method of testing bone – was developed which could prove, past doubt, whether Dawson's jaw and cranium were of the same age and therefore parts of the same skull. The test was made. To everyone's astonishment, all the bone proved much *younger* than expected.

Those who had always had their doubts began to mutter "hoax". Science steeled itself to study the two Piltdown skulls for signs of forgery. Once they started looking, the signs were easy to find.

The teeth had been filed down with a metal implement. The bones had been stained artificially to a similar colour. The jaw came from an orang-utan; the cranium was no older than the thirteenth century.

In 1953, the myth of Piltdown Man was exploded as a fake, an invention, a hoax. All those papers, all those debates and learned articles and digs had been for nothing.

But why? Why would anyone embark on such a hoax? To discredit a hated rival? As a student prank which got out of hand? Was it a plot by fundamentalist Christians wishing to discredit the whole theory of evolution? Or did someone want so *much* for the proof to be there that he felt driven to plant it himself? Did someone crave the glory of finding it – want his name associated with the most important find in the history of history? Could he not wait for the proof to surface of its own accord? Was it impatience with the slow unravelling of history?

History knit itself up over millions of years; it only unravels at its own measured pace. It will not be hurried, not for the glory of any one historian or to satisfy the curiosity of those most thirsty to know.

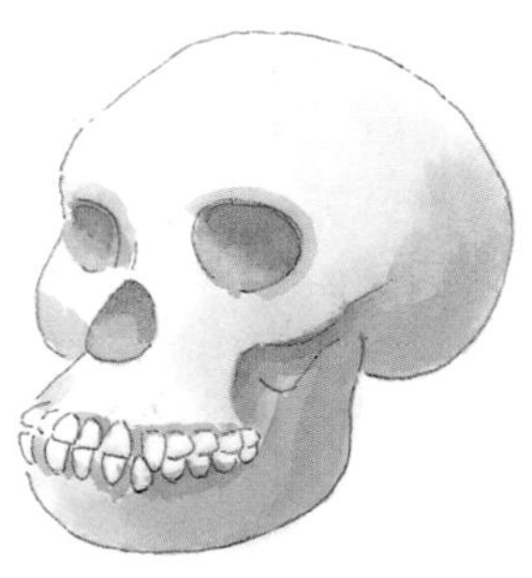

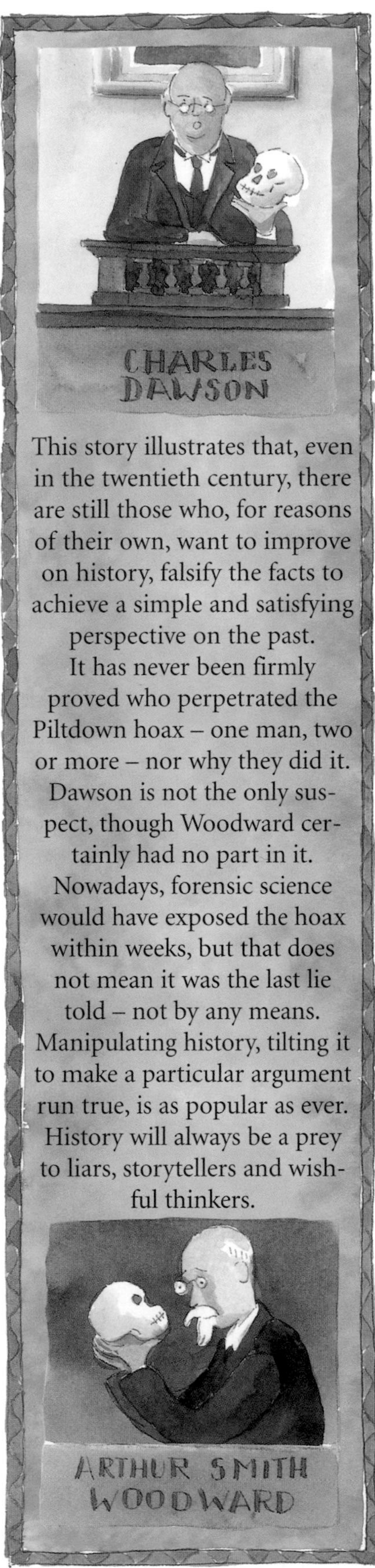

This story illustrates that, even in the twentieth century, there are still those who, for reasons of their own, want to improve on history, falsify the facts to achieve a simple and satisfying perspective on the past.

It has never been firmly proved who perpetrated the Piltdown hoax – one man, two or more – nor why they did it. Dawson is not the only suspect, though Woodward certainly had no part in it.

Nowadays, forensic science would have exposed the hoax within weeks, but that does not mean it was the last lie told – not by any means. Manipulating history, tilting it to make a particular argument run true, is as popular as ever. History will always be a prey to liars, storytellers and wishful thinkers.

Breaking the Time Barrier

1954

Roger Bannister sharpened his running spikes on a grindstone in the hospital laboratory. The weather was all wrong for running. This would not be the day when he ran his fastest race. But he went on sharpening his spikes . . . just in case the weather changed.

He was a medical student. His final exams were coming up. Soon the gruelling duties of being a young hospital doctor would leave no time for sport. So this might be his last summer's running. It would have been good to prove himself – to perform the impossible.

Bannister sighed and laid the spikes aside. What difference would sharp spikes make, when there was a gale blowing?

At the running track in Oxford, the wind tugged violently at the flag on the church roof. Bannister tried on his new, super-light running shoes, but his mind was pretty much made up: too windy for a record-attempt. At 5.15 p.m. it rained.

Watching the competitors limber up, the crowd was restless, keyed up. They had come there to see Bannister break the record for the mile. This was where he had run his first races as an Oxford student, so they were willing him on. They wanted him to perform the impossible tonight, in Oxford, in front of their very eyes.

If only they understood what they were asking! Only once would Bannister be able to pour all his nervous energy, his physical strength, his terror into making this run. If he tried and failed, it would not be in him to try again.

The flag on the church was wavering, the wind gusting more gently now. Bannister made his decision. He would try to run the mile in less than four minutes: a feat which had never been done, in the whole history of running.

The runners lined up. Perfect silence. *Bang!* . . . *Bang!* Two pistol cracks. A false start. A surge of fury went through Bannister.

The runners lined up again. This time there was no mistake. His friend Chris Brasher took the lead, setting the pace. "Faster!" hissed Bannister in his ear, but Brasher would not speed up, knowing that if Bannister sprinted too soon, his stamina would not last the mile. "Relax!" called a friend from the crowd.

The Oxford crowd was willing him on. Even the wind held its breath. But Bannister was barely aware of his surroundings. At the half-mile mark he knew he was in with a chance. His legs seemed to be working independently; the ground had no hold on them. His mind was detached. In a kind of trance he took over the lead, put in his final burst of speed.

The winning tape seemed to recede with every step. He must not slow, must not falter. His lungs had to go on feeding his blood; his heart had to go on pumping the oxygen round. This was his one chance in life to do a thing supremely well. If he failed, the world would turn a cold shoulder against him. The winning line taunted him . . .

He snapped the tape with his chest, snapped that invisible barrier everyone had said could not be broken. He had broken the four-minute mile.

It was then he realized – while pain wrung his muscles, and his lungs raged for air – while he collapsed into semi-consciousness – why he had been driving himself for eight years, why he had expended so much effort on achieving this moment. Suddenly he was free of the need to prove anything, free of the need to test himself, free of wanting something so very much. He was utterly, perfectly happy. Even though the crowd saw someone in a state of desperate, agonizing exhaustion, Roger Bannister was happier than he had ever been in his life. The tannoy announced: "Results of the one mile. In first place, Bannister with the time of three minutes . . ." The crowd's cheering drowned out the rest. Split seconds did not matter. For the first time a man had run one mile in less than four minutes.

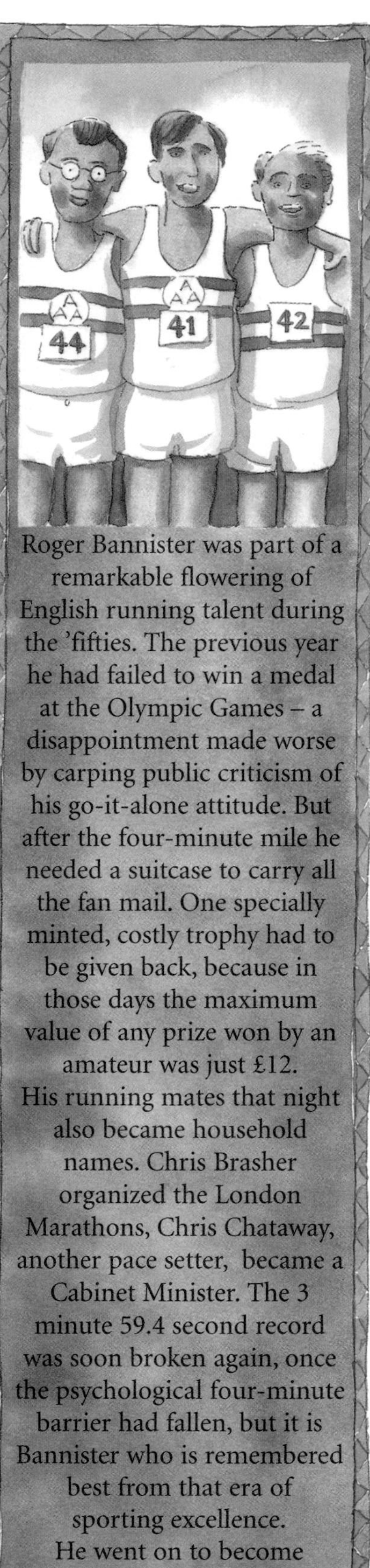

Roger Bannister was part of a remarkable flowering of English running talent during the 'fifties. The previous year he had failed to win a medal at the Olympic Games – a disappointment made worse by carping public criticism of his go-it-alone attitude. But after the four-minute mile he needed a suitcase to carry all the fan mail. One specially minted, costly trophy had to be given back, because in those days the maximum value of any prize won by an amateur was just £12.

His running mates that night also became household names. Chris Brasher organized the London Marathons, Chris Chataway, another pace setter, became a Cabinet Minister. The 3 minute 59.4 second record was soon broken again, once the psychological four-minute barrier had fallen, but it is Bannister who is remembered best from that era of sporting excellence.

He went on to become a neurologist.

Teaching the World to Sing

1984

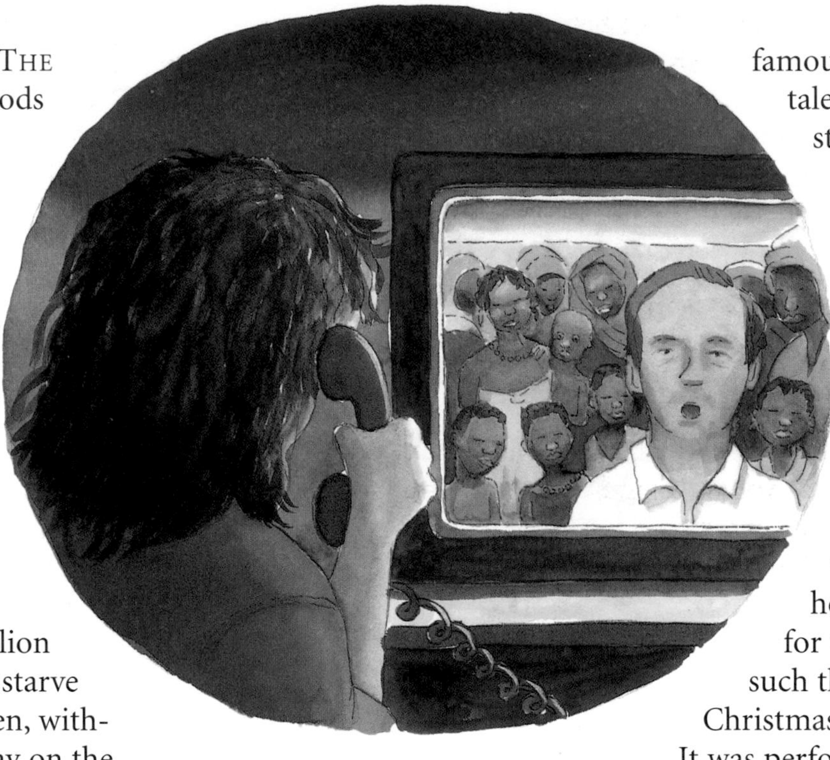

It was October. The first Christmas goods were appearing in the shops. Soon everybody would be out there again, spending too much money.

Bob Geldof sat in his London flat watching the television news. It was not Christmassy, the news. Famine and war. In Ethiopia and the Sudan several million people were about to starve to death. On the screen, withered, skeletal babies lay on the ground, fly-blown, grotesque, too weak to cry. Their mothers, old women in their twenties, looked at the camera expressionless; they had long since despaired of anyone helping them. They simply sat and watched their children die.

Viewers everywhere reached for their cheque books, knowing anything they could do would be too little too late: a futile gesture. Geldof reached for the telephone instead. He booked himself a flight to Ethiopia, and went there to see for himself. All the way there, all the way back, all the time he walked among the stench of death, he thought what everyone else was thinking: something ought to be done.

The difference was, Geldof did it.

When he got home, he called up his friends – his famous, glamorous, glitzy, talented, show-business, star-rated friends. He did not ask them for money. He asked them for their time. "There's this number I want to record," he said.

They called the group, "Band Aid". The song was titled, "Do they know it's Christmas?" It was in honour of those people for whom there can be no such thing as a happy Christmas.

It was performed by a larger number of famous recording artists than had ever gathered on one stage before. And the public loved it. It sold more copies than any other recording that year. And every penny of the £10 million profit went to Africa for famine relief.

What is more, it was fun to do! It was like one great party, where everybody arrives in party mood. Even Geldof had not foreseen how much fun it would be or how much money it would raise. He had to form a trust just to handle the proceeds. Somehow he had tapped into the conscience of the entire Western world.

But the world's poor swallowed it down like one drop of rain falling on a desert. So how could he say Band Aid was over, draw a line under it, call it a day?

Out of Band Aid grew Live Aid. One year later Geldof organized a sixteen-hour concert to be played live and screened all over the world. No one said no to Bob. People gave, free-of-charge, satellite time, studio time, technical support, transport, secretarial services . . . In a matter of weeks the idea took shape: not one, but two concerts – one in Wembley Stadium, London, the other in JFK Stadium, Philadelphia. Phil Collins sat down at a piano and sang in Wembley. Then he got on a plane and flew to Philadelphia, walked on to the stage in the JFK and sang the same song. The watching millions could not believe their eyes.

The truth was, the world had shrunk to such an extent that the people of a hundred nations were sitting together on one couch to watch TV and join in the singing. Forty per cent of the world's population were invited to that party, were asked by their favourite pop idols, heroes and statesmen to give money and to save lives.

It did not just "happen", of course. Celebrities did not simply roll out of bed and decide to go along. For ten weeks, hundreds of technicians, lawyers, politicians, secretaries, singers worked non-stop to make it happen. Not all of them were rock fans. ("I didn't even know who Geldof was," said the American producer of Live Aid. "My son did, but I didn't.") But the goodwill was there, because people knew it was going to work. It had the energy of youth behind it. And no one said no to Bob.

Well, perhaps there was one. During the concert, a light aircraft would persist in cruising over the JFK stadium towing advertising banners. The pilot refused to go away. So Bob Geldof asked Ronald Reagan, President of the United States, to telephone the airfield. He did. Within minutes, the light aeroplane was gone.

It was fun to do and it was fun to watch. It was the biggest party the world had ever known. And every pound, dollar and rouble, every shekel, lira and krona of the £48 million raised was going to put food in the mouths of starving children.

"Where do I go and what do I do?" asked superstar Dionne Warwick stepping out of a taxi. Everyone wants to help, if only someone is there to tell them how.

Out of Live Aid and Band Aid came Sport Aid – another £21 million – raised by running ten-kilometre races in nearly 300 cities throughout the world. These were phenomenal fund-raising efforts, galvanizing all the great names of the moment – far too many to list. They did not put an end to world poverty, but they did save thousands of lives. It was possible to invest in communities for the future, as well as saving them from destruction. They also made a whole generation confront the problem of world hunger, its root causes, and how much the developed world can do to ease it.

Set in a Silver Sea

1993

IT WAS AS THOUGH THE *BRAER*'S HEART FAILED HER in the face of the storm. Her engines fell silent and left only the miscellaneous clanking of a big metal ship adrift in a mountainous sea. For six hours she drifted, while those aboard and those on shore struggled to stave off disaster. Could a tug be got out to her? Could a tow line be attached? Could the engines be restarted?

But every minute, the sea was shouldering the *Braer* inexorably towards land, shoving and bullying her into the shallows. With a noise of rending metal, it ran her aground on the rocks of Garths Ness, stoving in her watertight sides. She bled black blood.

Oil, in thick clots, haemorrhaged out of her. Every wave carried some of the *Braer*'s cargo ashore and daubed it on the rocks, on the weeds, on the sand. Hour by hour, the *Braer* broke up.

Though the sea was rough, a black ring of calm lay around the stranded ship like an evil spell. The coastline, wild, beautiful and little visited till now, withered. The oil crawled in at the noses of seals and the gills of fish, larded the sea birds which landed on the flattened, oily waves, scalded all the fronded sea-plants, fish eggs and shrimps. Crustaceans let go their grip on the oily rocks and rattled away like black pennies on to the sea bed.

Disaster. An ecological tragedy. Those who went to the coast after the stranding of the tanker waded through an oily slick which pulsed with small animals in the last throes of death. They bewailed the devastation – done in a day, but never, surely, to be undone. At best, Garths Ness would take decades to recover: no wildlife, no livelihood for the fishermen, no delight to the senses – just the stench of oil and dead things.

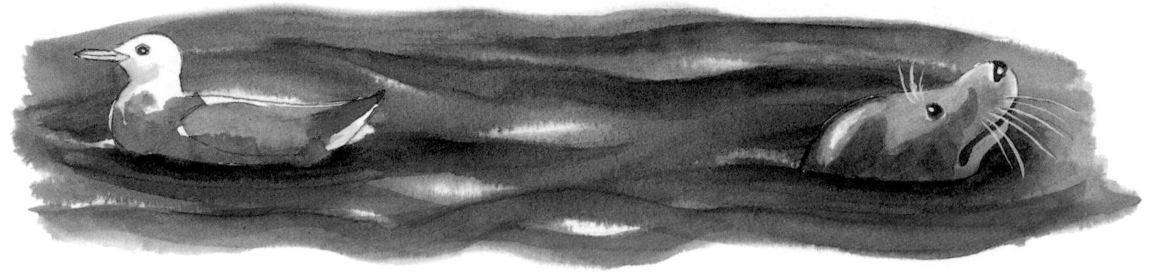

Five years later, an independent survey team went looking for the long-term effects of the *Braer* oil-spill. With more and more oil tankers plying the world's seas, such accidents are bound to happen increasingly often. So it is essential to know what other stretches of cliffs, inlets, bird colonies and fishing communities can look forward to. The worst had to be looked in the face.

The survey found . . . nothing.

Not a trace of oil remained. The sea's surf had scoured clean each pebble and shell. Its tides had dragged the black slime deep into its digestion, and its tide rips had shredded the slick into infinitesimal smallness. Fish shoals had come back. Birds had nested on the cliffs. A profusion of shellfish were busy muscling each other off the shining rocks.

The oil, prehistoric product of a million acres of primaeval forest, had become once again harmless vegetable matter – harmless as dead leaves in autumn crumbling into mulch.

The sea had proved so full of life, that though it had drunk poison, it had failed to die.

The *Braer* oil tanker was stranded at Garths Ness in the Shetlands on 5 January 1993. Science fully expected the oil-spill to do lasting damage, but all the gloomy predictions were proved wrong by the phenomenon of the self-cleansing sea. The story told here does not mean that the sea can digest any amount of pollution. (Every metre of the Atlantic sea lanes between England and America is now polluted, and inshore fishing has been seriously affected.) What it does prove is that nature has powers of regeneration which surpass our wildest imaginings.

And if you want still more stories . . .

The following titles are all works of fiction, set in the past, which you might well enjoy.
All books are in paperback unless otherwise stated.

All periods

Cooling, Wendy (ed)
Centuries of Stories
HarperCollins 0001857150

Lively, Penelope
The Driftway
Mammoth 0749707925

Sheppard-Jones, Elizabeth
Stories of Wales
Jones Publishing 1871083354

Myths and legends of the British Isles

McCaughrean, Geraldine
King Arthur and the Knights of the Round Table
Macdonald Young Books hbk 0750015276

Morpurgo, Michael
Robin of Sherwood
Pavilion hbk 185793718X

Nye, Robert
Beowulf
Orion 1857710760

Pre-history, Romans, Saxons & Vikings

Joy, Margaret
The Torc and the Ring
Faber 0571179444

King, Clive
Stig of the Dump
Puffin 0140364501

Price, Susan
The Saga of Aslak
A & C Black 0713646705

Sutcliff, Rosemary
The Eagle of the Ninth
Puffin 0140308903
OUP 0192717650

The Normans and the Middle Ages

Branford, Henrietta
Fire, Bed and Bone
Walker 0744554845

Chaucer, Geoffrey
The Canterbury Tales
(retold by Geraldine McCaughrean)
Puffin 0140380531

McCaughrean, Geraldine
A Little Lower than the Angels
OUP 0192717804

Sutcliff, Rosemary
The Witches' Brat
Red Fox 0099750805

Tomlinson, Teresa
The Forest Wife
Red Fox 0099264315

Tudors

Deary, Terry
The Knight of Stars and Storms
DOLPHIN 1858815177
(and other titles in the *Tudor Terror* series)

Doherty, Berlie
Children of Winter
MAMMOTH 0749718455

Graham, Harriet
A Boy and his Bear
SCHOLASTIC 0590133659

Hunter, Mollie
The Ghosts of Glencoe
CANONGATE 0862414679

Lively, Penelope
The Ghost of Thomas Kempe
MAMMOTH 0749707917

Morpurgo, Michael
My Friend Walter
MAMMOTH 0749712163

Walsh, Jill Paton
A Parcel of Patterns
PUFFIN 0140362592

Georgians and Victorians

Burgess, Melvin
The Copper Treasure
A & C BLACK hbk 0713649399

Doherty, Berlie
Street Child
HARPERCOLLINS 0006740200

Garfield, Leon
The Apprentices
MAMMOTH 0749715588

Hunter, Mollie
A Pistol in Greenyards
CANONGATE 0862411750

Pearce, Philippa
Tom's Midnight Garden
PUFFIN 0140364544

Pullman, Philip
Spring-heeled Jack
YEARLING 0440862299

Wilson, Jacqueline
The Lottie Project
YEARLING 044086366X

Twentieth Century

Gibbons, Alan
Street of Tall People
DOLPHIN 1858811937

Leeson, Robert
Harry and Bella, Jammy and Me
MAMMOTH 0749715766

Magorian, Michelle
Goodnight Mr Tom
PUFFIN 0141301449

Peyton, K.M.
Flambards
OUP 0192717839

Westall, Robert
Christmas Spirit
MAMMOTH 0749723971

Westall, Robert
The Machine Gunners
MACMILLAN 033033428X

Index